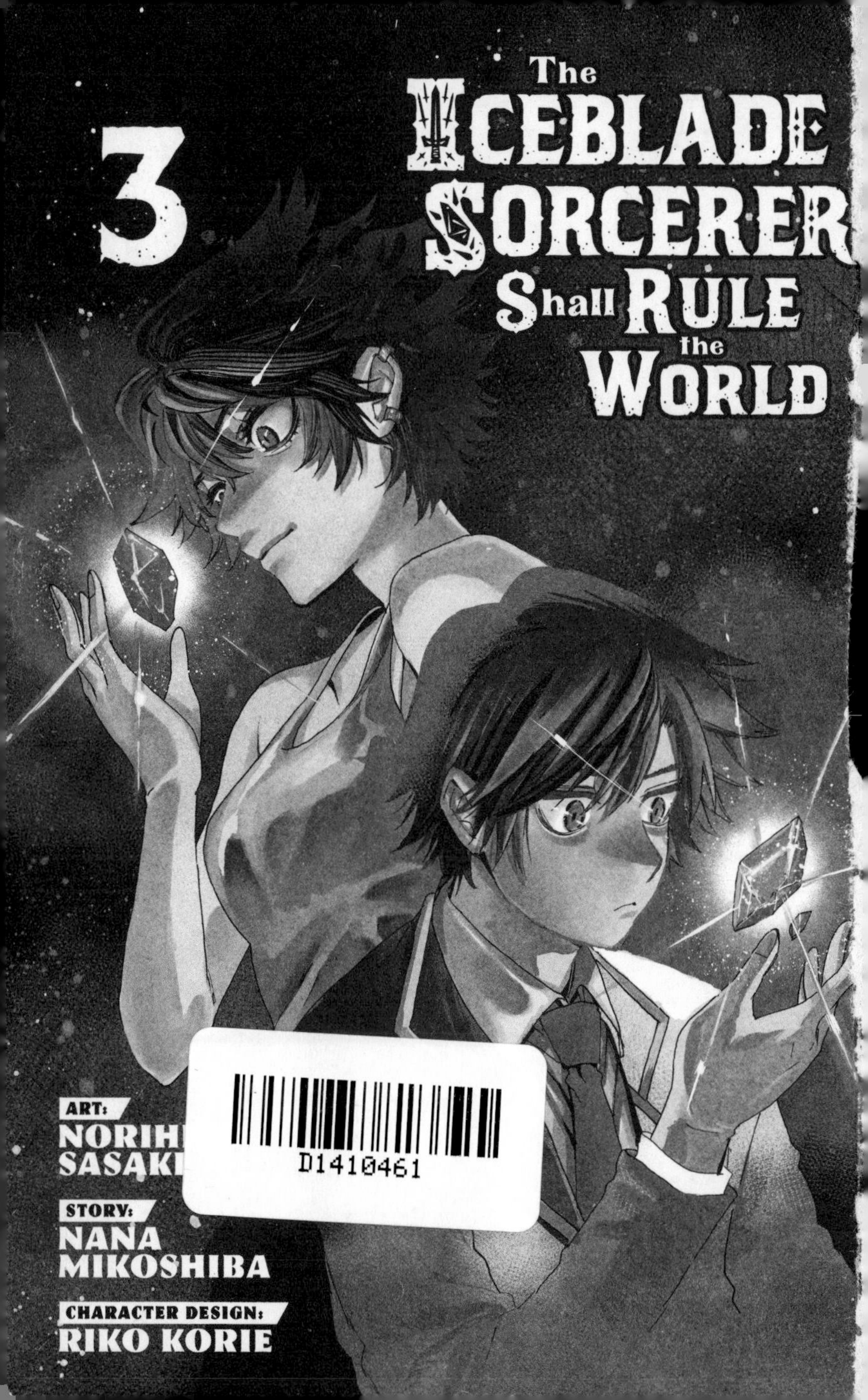
3
The ICEBLADE SORCERER Shall RULE the WORLD
ART:
NORIH
SASAK
STORY:
NANA
MIKOSHIBA
CHARACTER DESIGN:
RIKO KORIE

CONTENTS

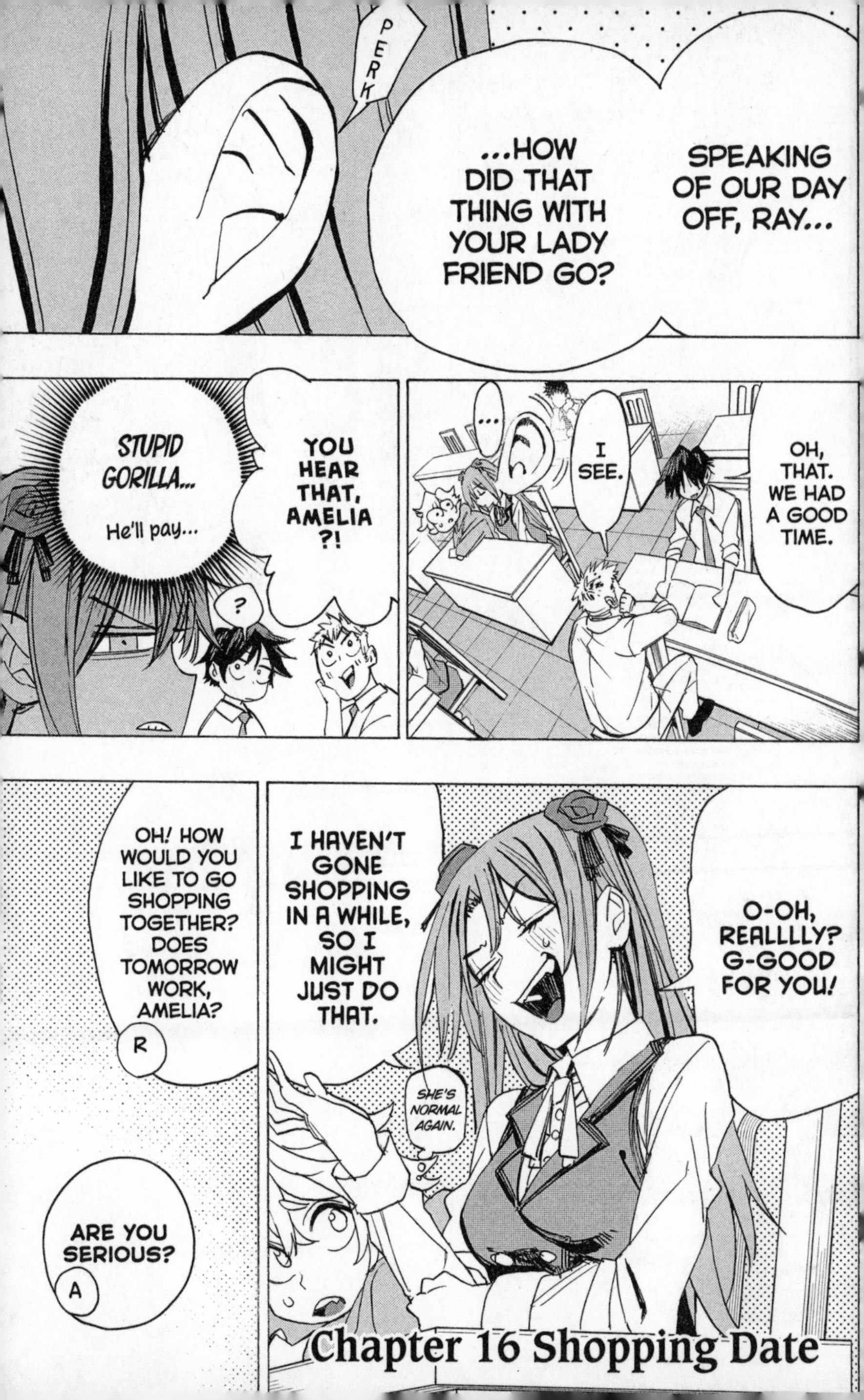
SPEAKING OF OUR DAY OFF, RAY...
...HOW DID THAT THING WITH YOUR LADY FRIEND GO?
PERK
OH, THAT. WE HAD A GOOD TIME.
I SEE.
...
YOU HEAR THAT, AMELIA?!
?
STUPID GORILLA...
He'll pay...
O-OH, REALLLLY? G-GOOD FOR YOU!
I HAVEN'T GONE SHOPPING IN A WHILE, SO I MIGHT JUST DO THAT.
SHE'S NORMAL AGAIN.
OH! HOW WOULD YOU LIKE TO GO SHOPPING TOGETHER? DOES TOMORROW WORK, AMELIA?
R
ARE YOU SERIOUS?
A

Chapter 16 Shopping Date

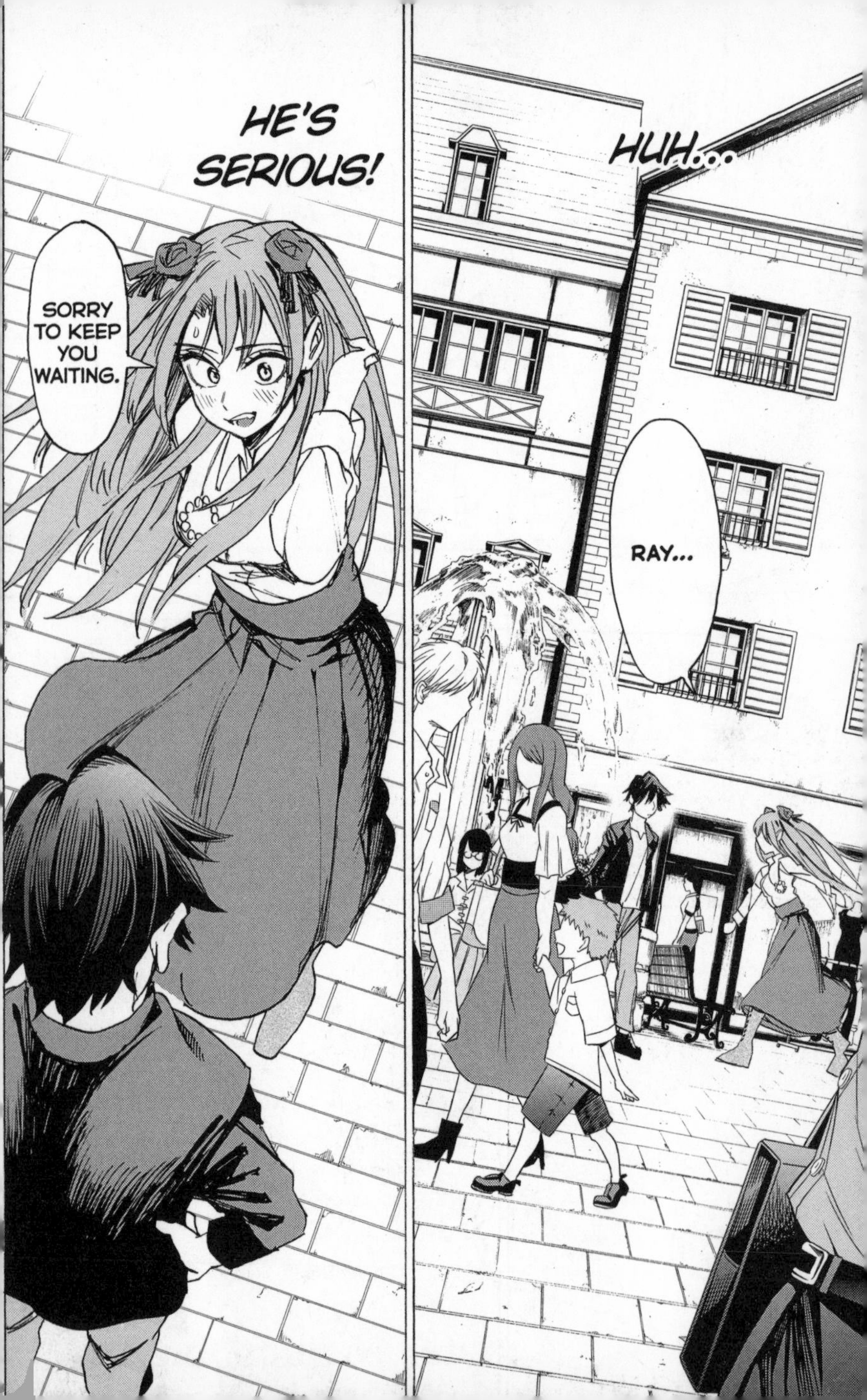
HUH...
RAY...
HE'S SERIOUS!
SORRY TO KEEP YOU WAITING.

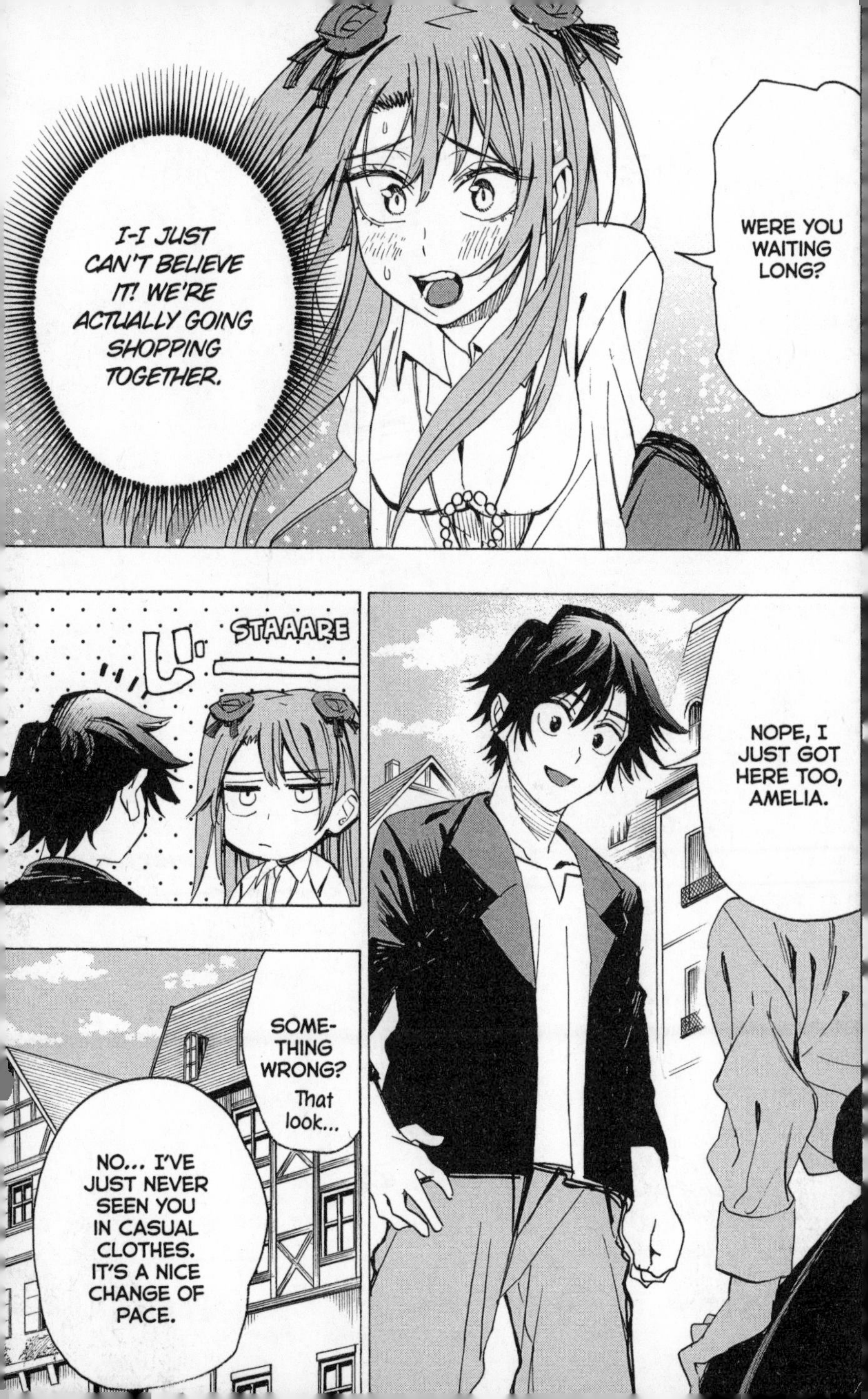
WERE YOU WAITING LONG?
I-I JUST CAN'T BELIEVE IT! WE'RE ACTUALLY GOING SHOPPING TOGETHER.
NOPE, I JUST GOT HERE TOO, AMELIA.
STAAARE
SOME-THING WRONG? That look...
NO... I'VE JUST NEVER SEEN YOU IN CASUAL CLOTHES. IT'S A NICE CHANGE OF PACE.

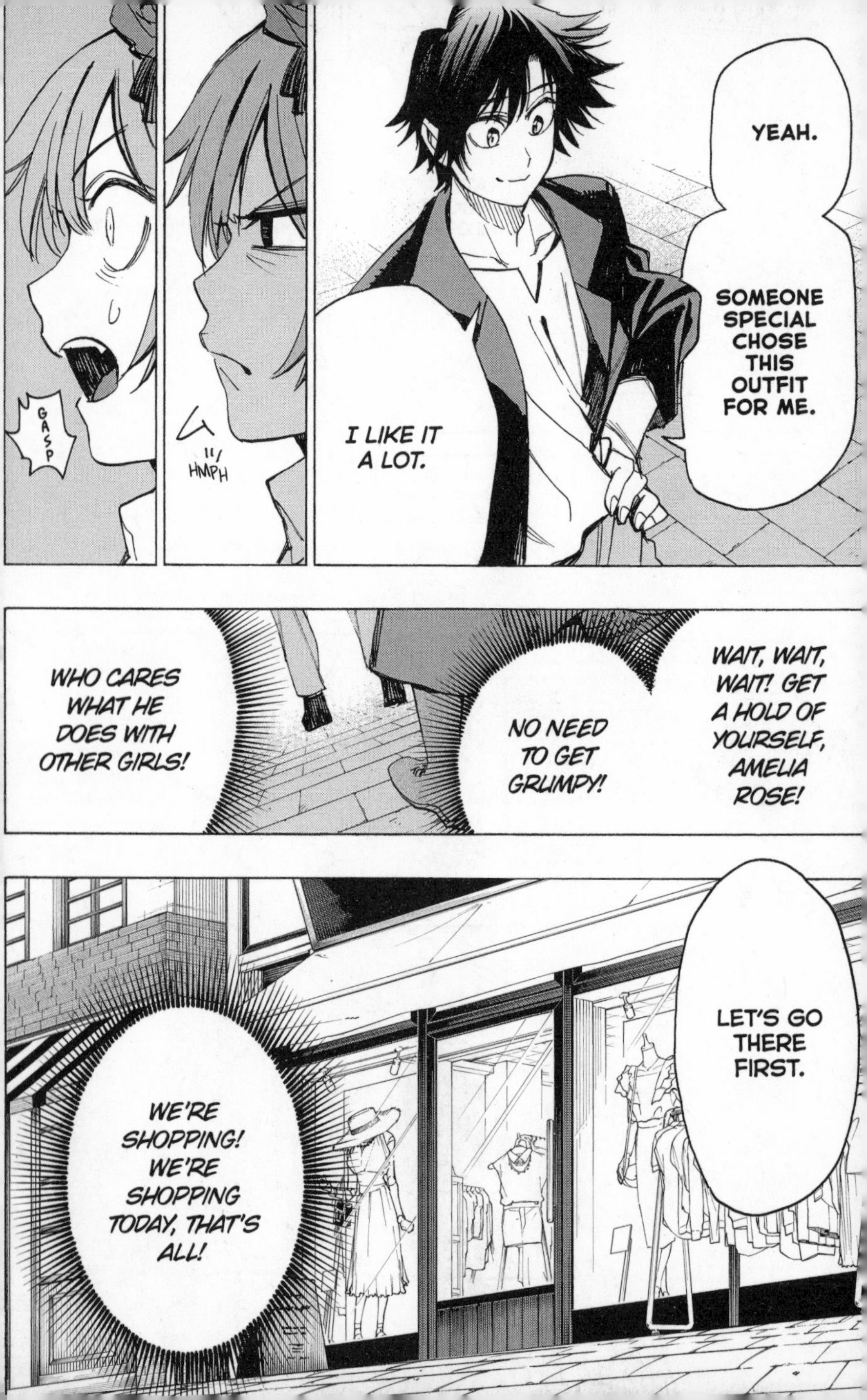
YEAH.
SOMEONE SPECIAL CHOSE THIS OUTFIT FOR ME.
I LIKE IT A LOT.
HMPH
GASP
WAIT, WAIT, WAIT! GET A HOLD OF YOURSELF, AMELIA ROSE!
NO NEED TO GET GRUMPY!
WHO CARES WHAT HE DOES WITH OTHER GIRLS!
LET'S GO THERE FIRST.
WE'RE SHOPPING! WE'RE SHOPPING TODAY, THAT'S ALL!

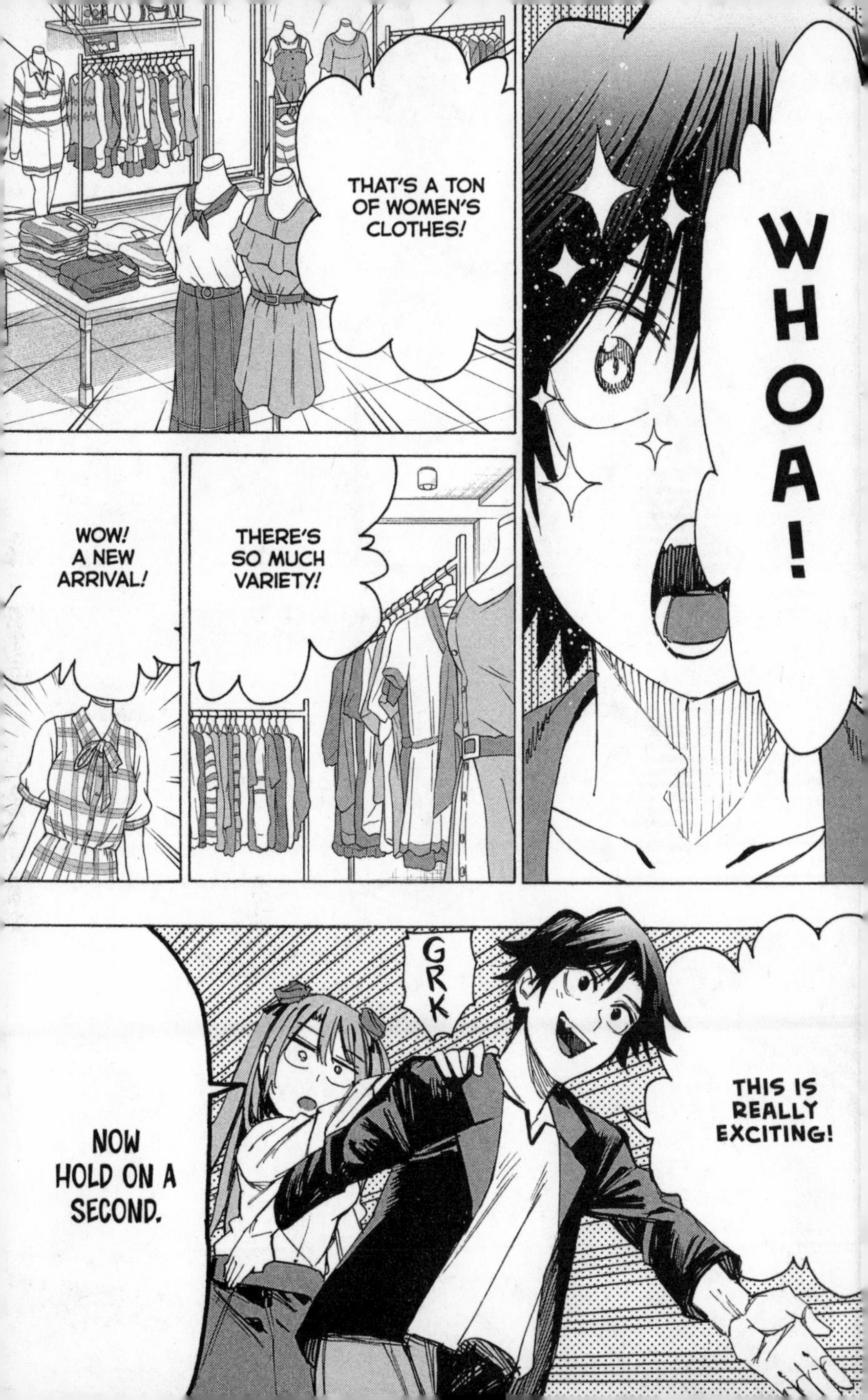
WHOA!
THAT'S A TON OF WOMEN'S CLOTHES!
THERE'S SO MUCH VARIETY!
WOW! A NEW ARRIVAL!
THIS IS REALLY EXCITING!
GRK
NOW HOLD ON A SECOND.

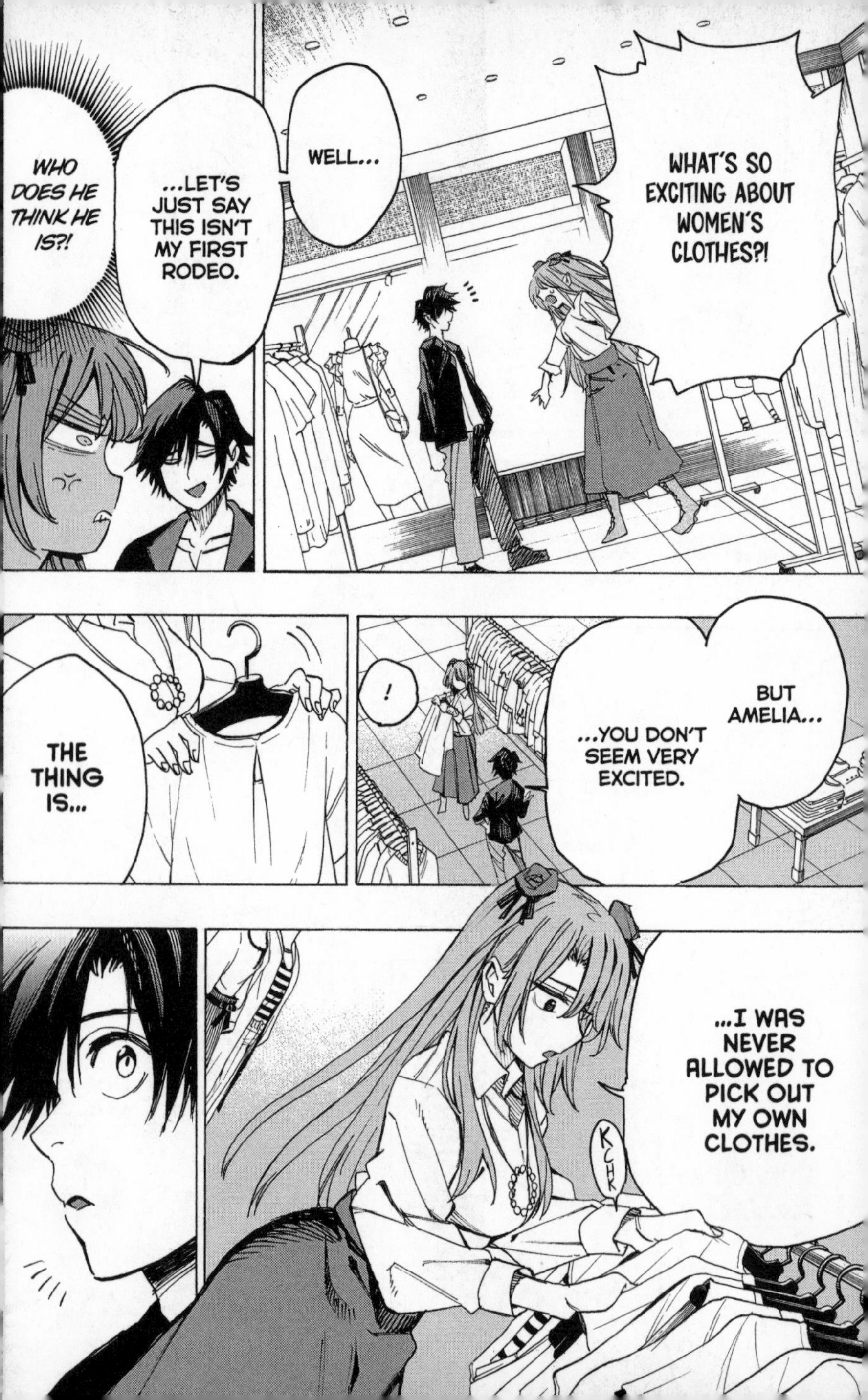
WHAT'S SO EXCITING ABOUT WOMEN'S CLOTHES?!
WELL...
...LET'S JUST SAY THIS ISN'T MY FIRST RODEO.
WHO DOES HE THINK HE IS?!
BUT AMELIA...
...YOU DON'T SEEM VERY EXCITED.
!
THE THING IS...
...I WAS NEVER ALLOWED TO PICK OUT MY OWN CLOTHES.
KCHK

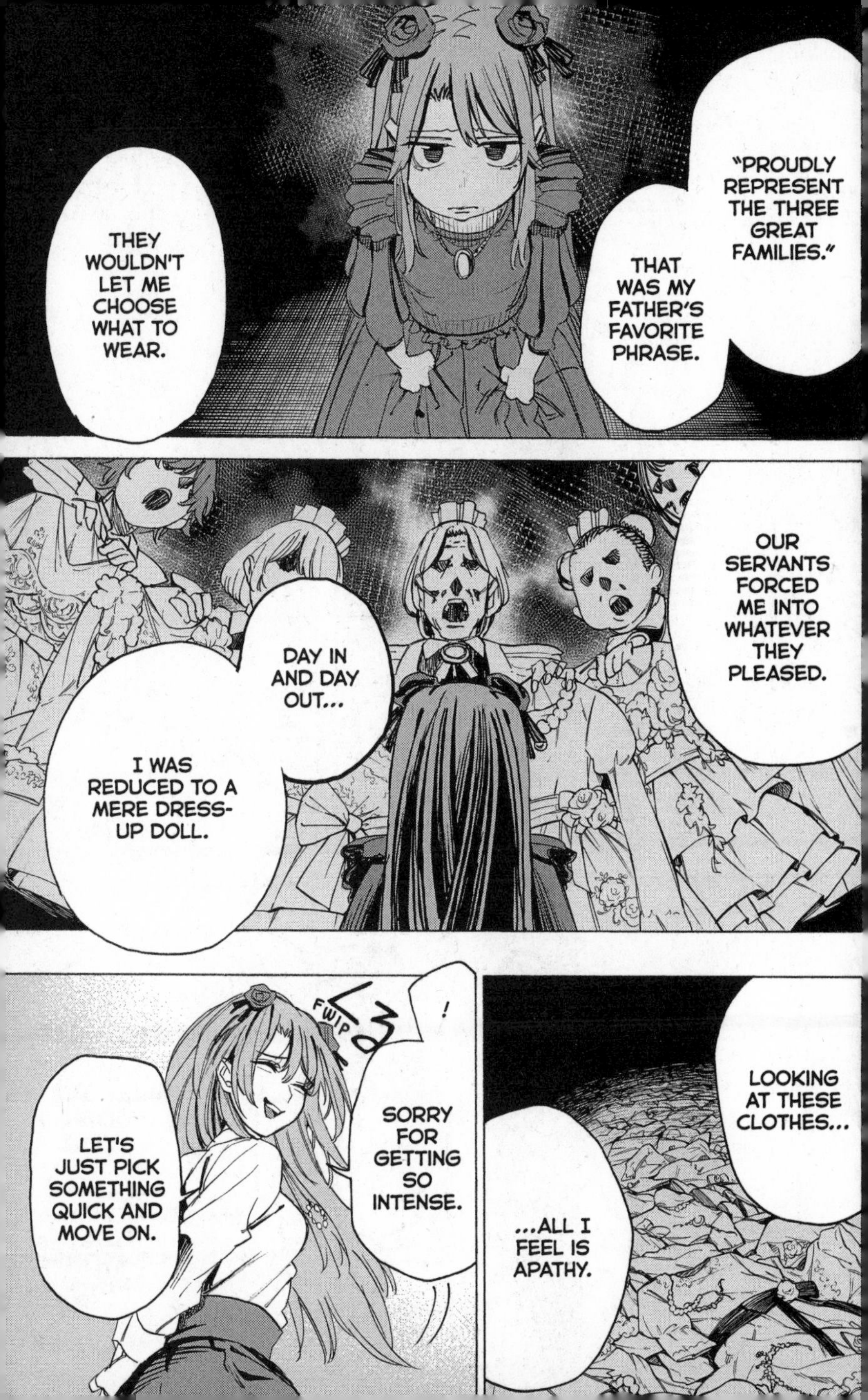
"PROUDLY REPRESENT THE THREE GREAT FAMILIES."
THAT WAS MY FATHER'S FAVORITE PHRASE.
THEY WOULDN'T LET ME CHOOSE WHAT TO WEAR.
OUR SERVANTS FORCED ME INTO WHATEVER THEY PLEASED.
DAY IN AND DAY OUT...
I WAS REDUCED TO A MERE DRESS-UP DOLL.
LOOKING AT THESE CLOTHES...
...ALL I FEEL IS APATHY.
!
FWIP
SORRY FOR GETTING SO INTENSE.
LET'S JUST PICK SOMETHING QUICK AND MOVE ON.

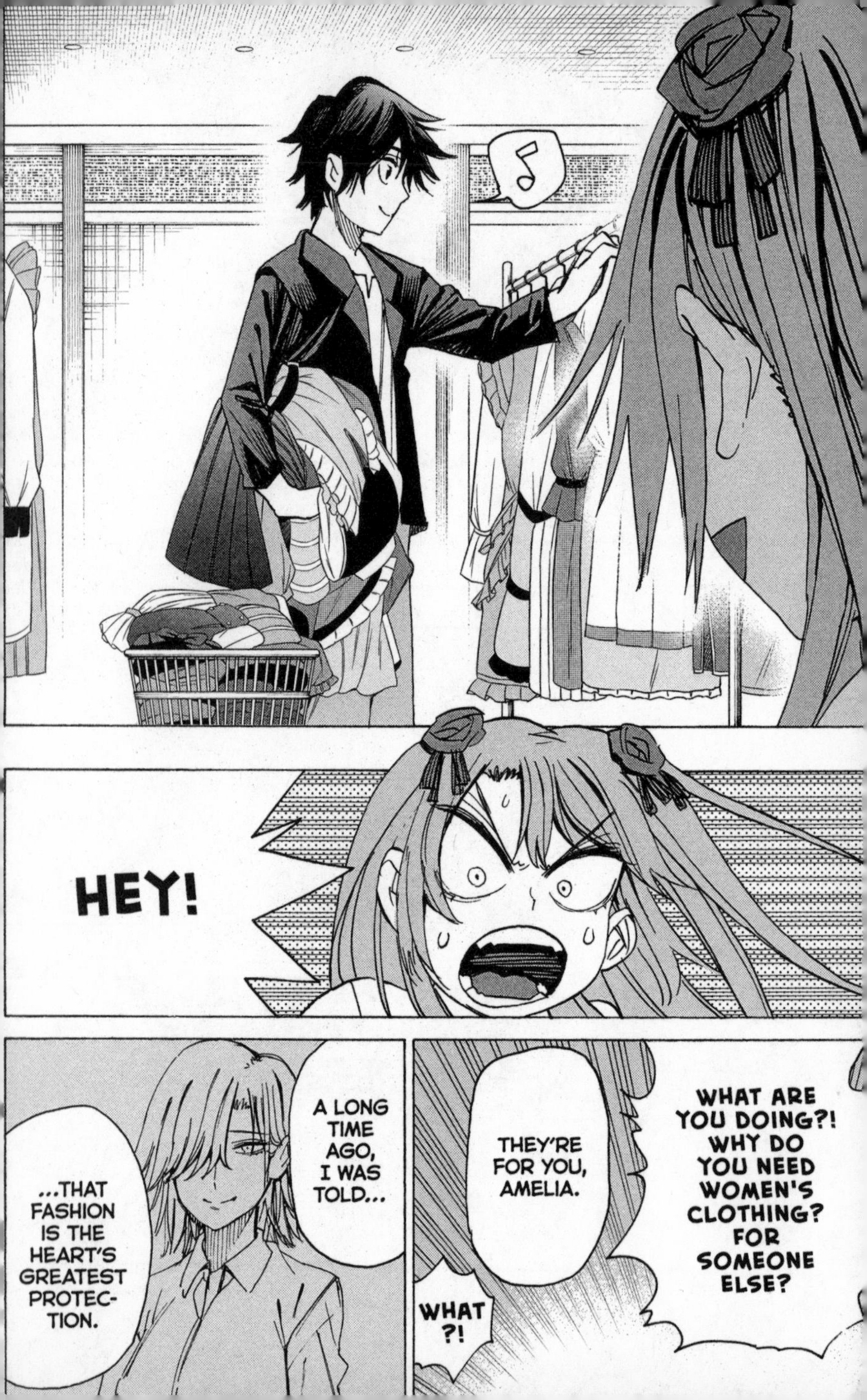
HEY!
WHAT ARE YOU DOING?! WHY DO YOU NEED WOMEN'S CLOTHING? FOR SOMEONE ELSE?
THEY'RE FOR YOU, AMELIA.
WHAT?!
A LONG TIME AGO, I WAS TOLD...
...THAT FASHION IS THE HEART'S GREATEST PROTECTION.

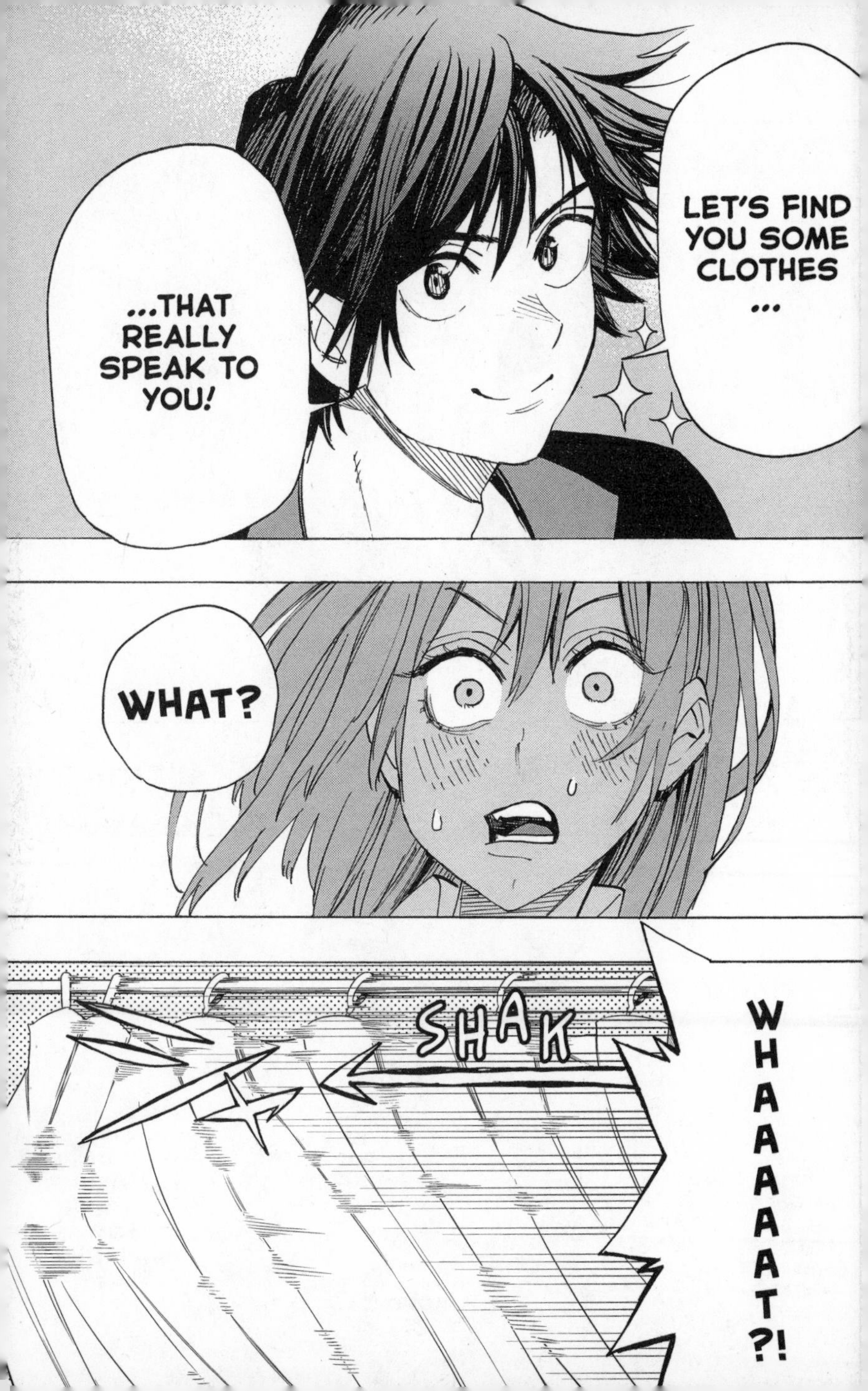
LET'S FIND YOU SOME CLOTHES ...
...THAT REALLY SPEAK TO YOU!
WHAT?
WHAAAAAT?!
SHAK

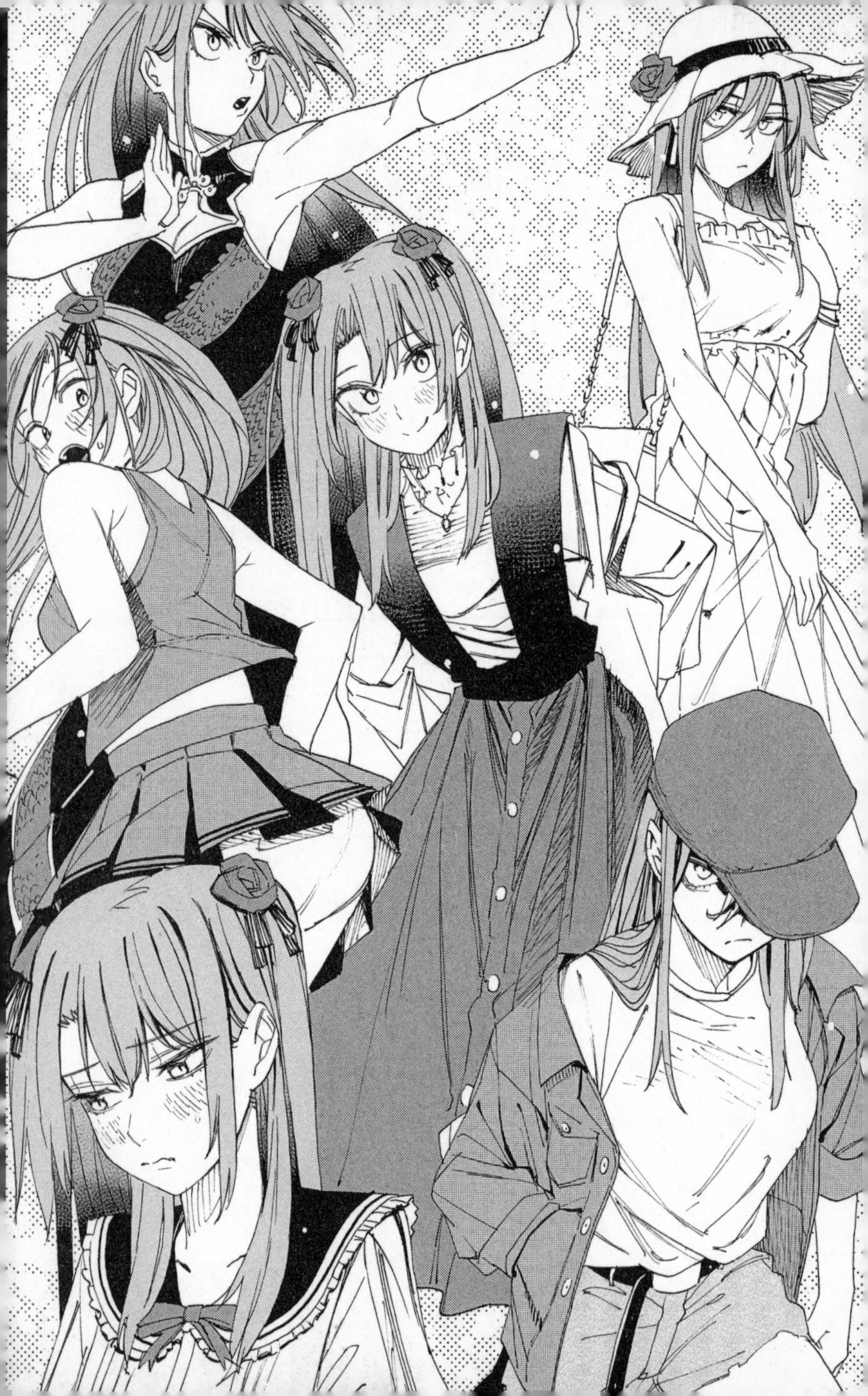

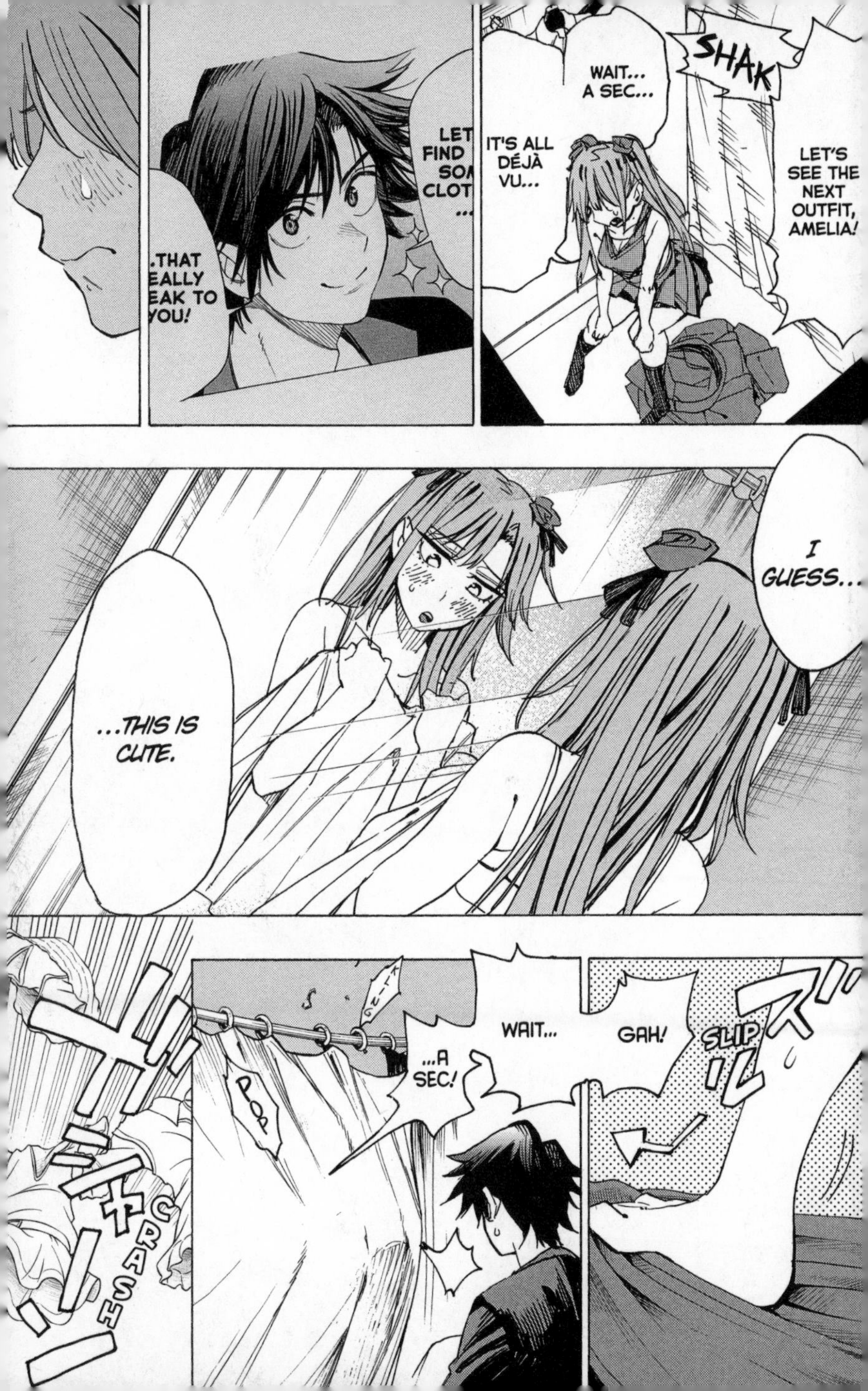
SHAK
LET'S SEE THE NEXT OUTFIT, AMELIA!
WAIT... A SEC...
IT'S ALL DÉJÀ VU...
LET FIND SOM CLOT ...
.THAT EALLY EAK TO YOU!
I GUESS...
...THIS IS CUTE.
SLIP
GAH!
WAIT...
...A SEC!
POP
CRASH

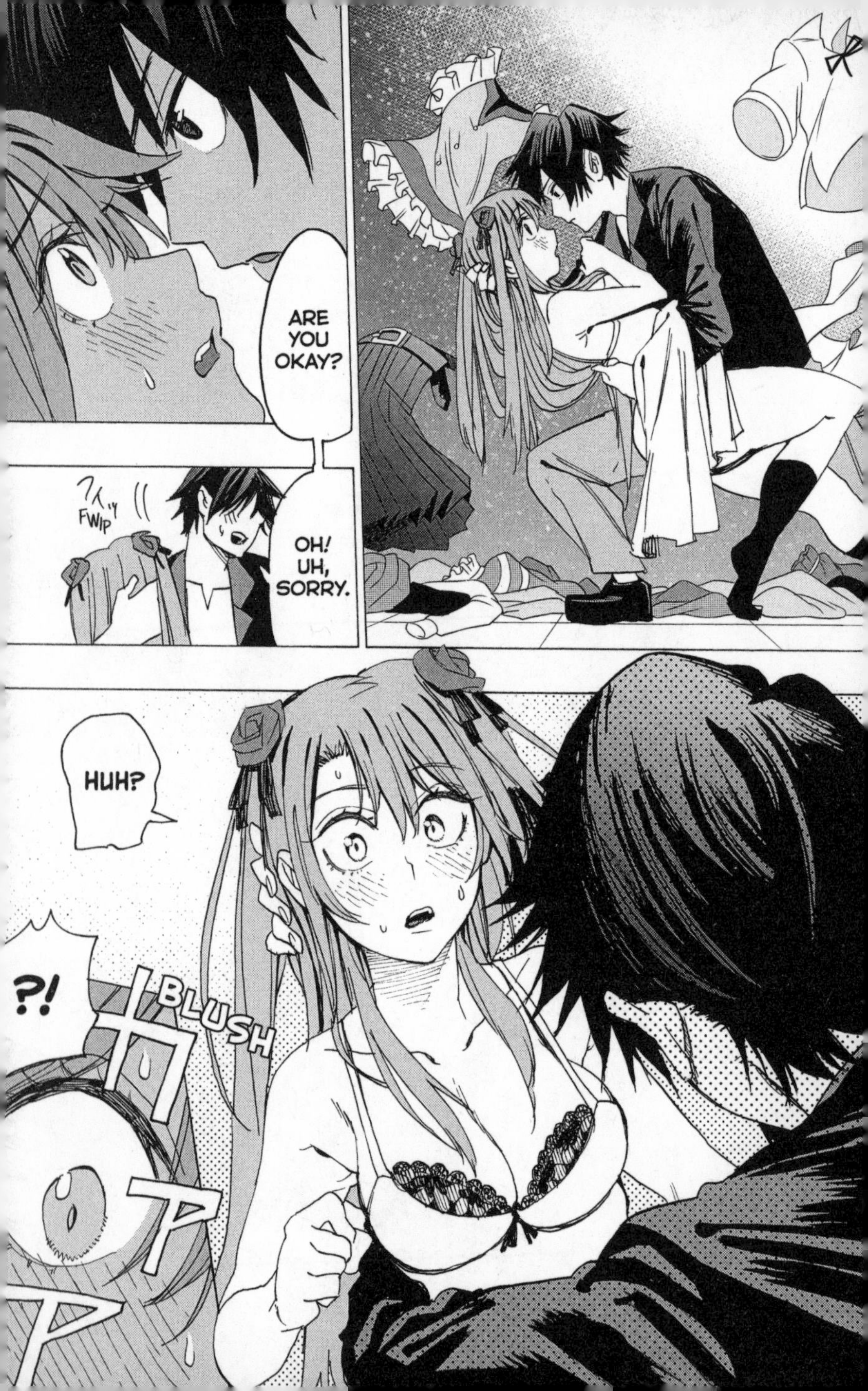
ARE YOU OKAY?
OH! UH, SORRY.
FWIP
HUH?
BLUSH
?!

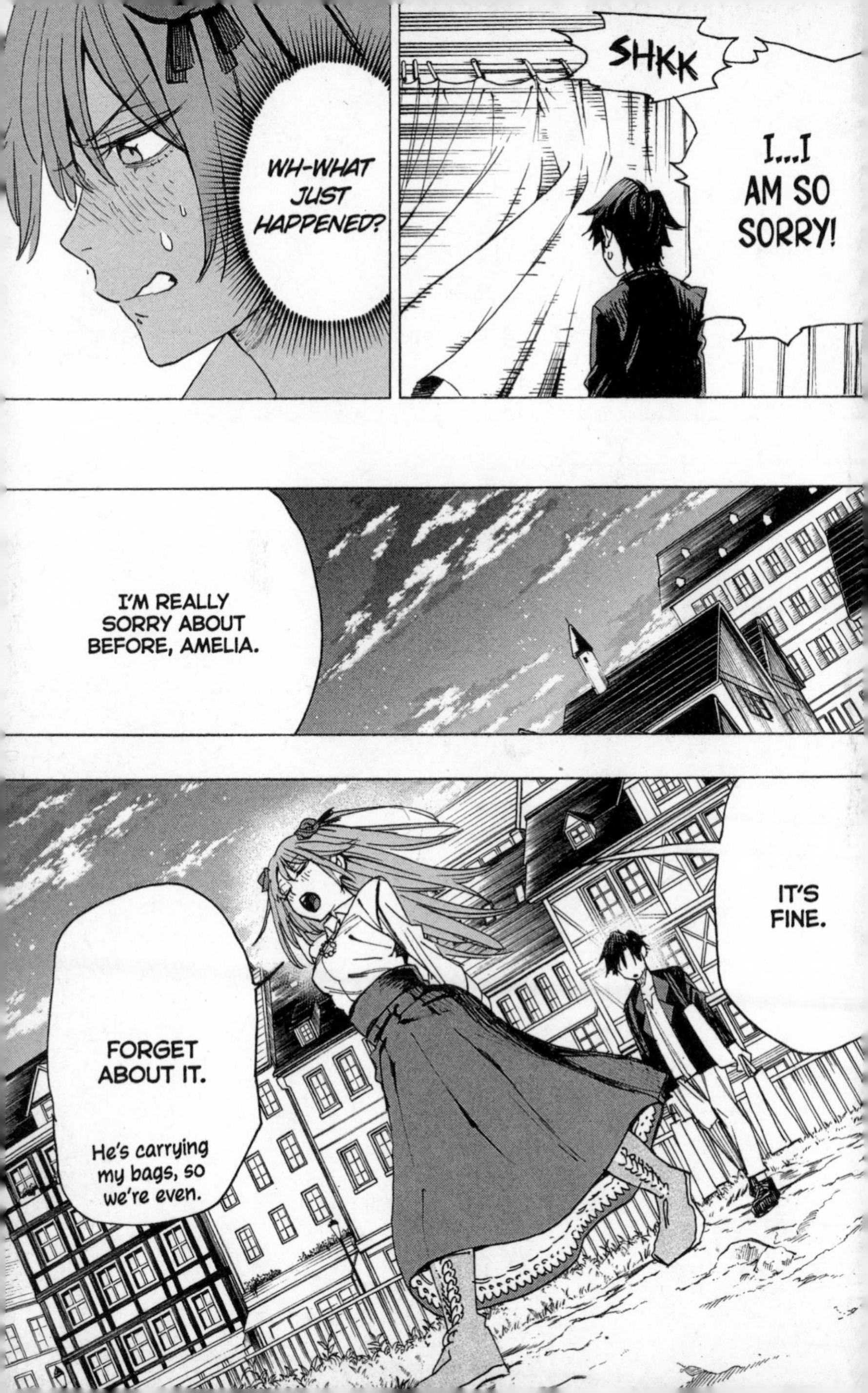
SHKK
I...I AM SO SORRY!
WH-WHAT JUST HAPPENED?
I'M REALLY SORRY ABOUT BEFORE, AMELIA.
IT'S FINE.
FORGET ABOUT IT.
He's carrying my bags, so we're even.

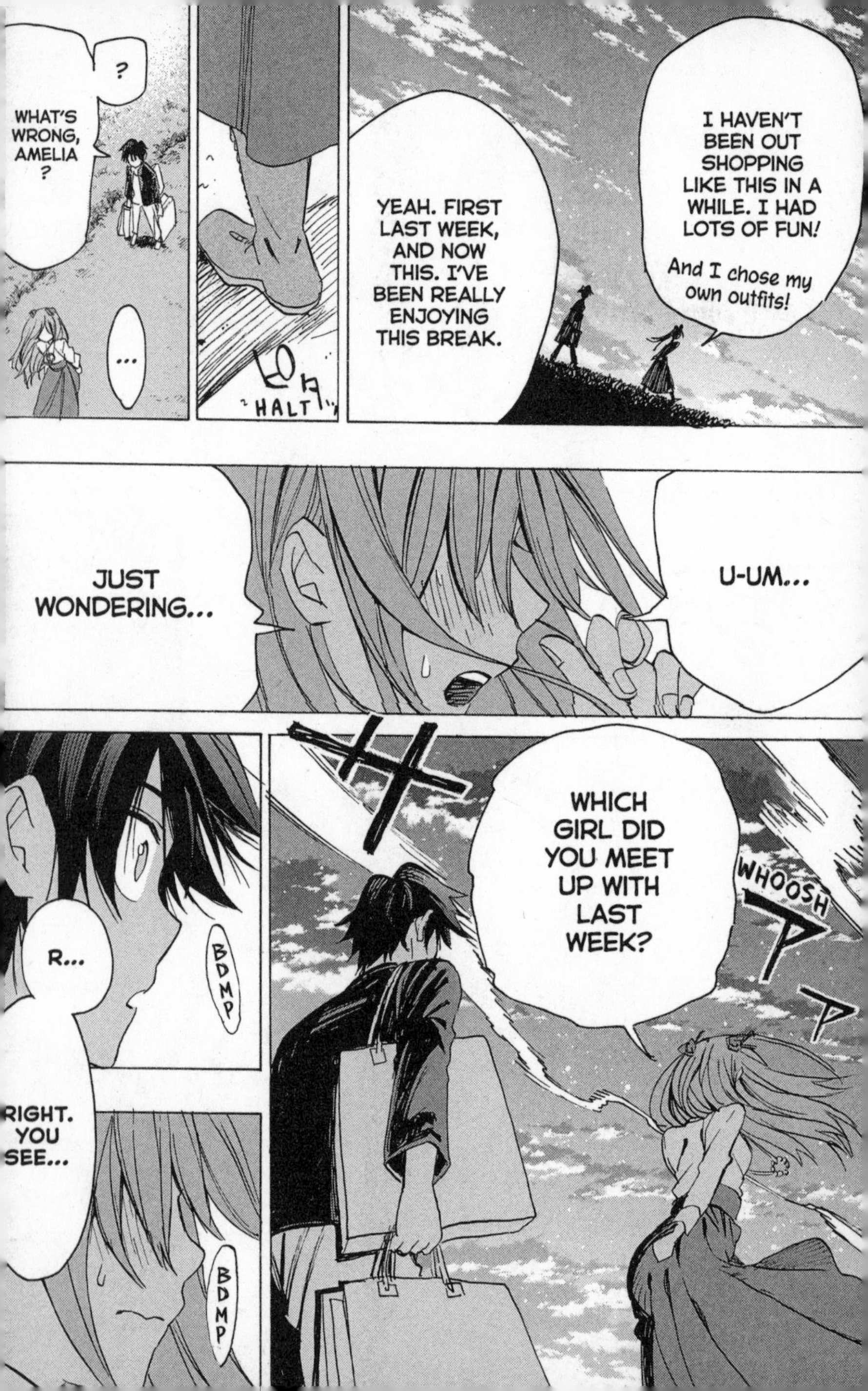

I HAVEN'T BEEN OUT SHOPPING LIKE THIS IN A WHILE. I HAD LOTS OF FUN!
And I chose my own outfits!
YEAH. FIRST LAST WEEK, AND NOW THIS. I'VE BEEN REALLY ENJOYING THIS BREAK.
HALT
?
WHAT'S WRONG, AMELIA?
...
U-UM...
JUST WONDERING...
WHICH GIRL DID YOU MEET UP WITH LAST WEEK?
WHOOSH
BDMP
R...
RIGHT. YOU SEE...
BDMP

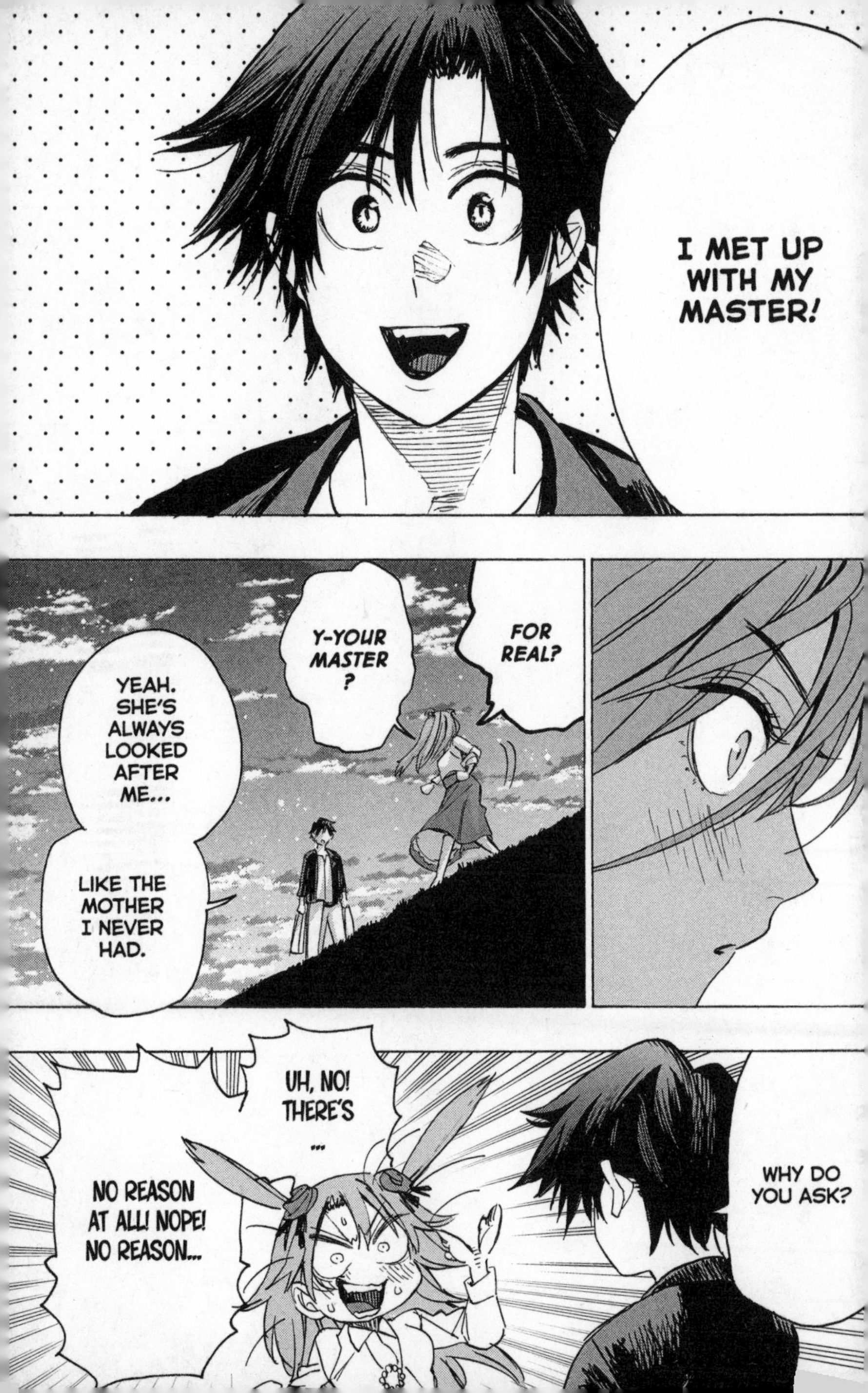
I MET UP WITH MY MASTER!
FOR REAL?
Y-YOUR MASTER?
YEAH. SHE'S ALWAYS LOOKED AFTER ME...
LIKE THE MOTHER I NEVER HAD.
WHY DO YOU ASK?
UH, NO! THERE'S ...
NO REASON AT ALL! NOPE! NO REASON...

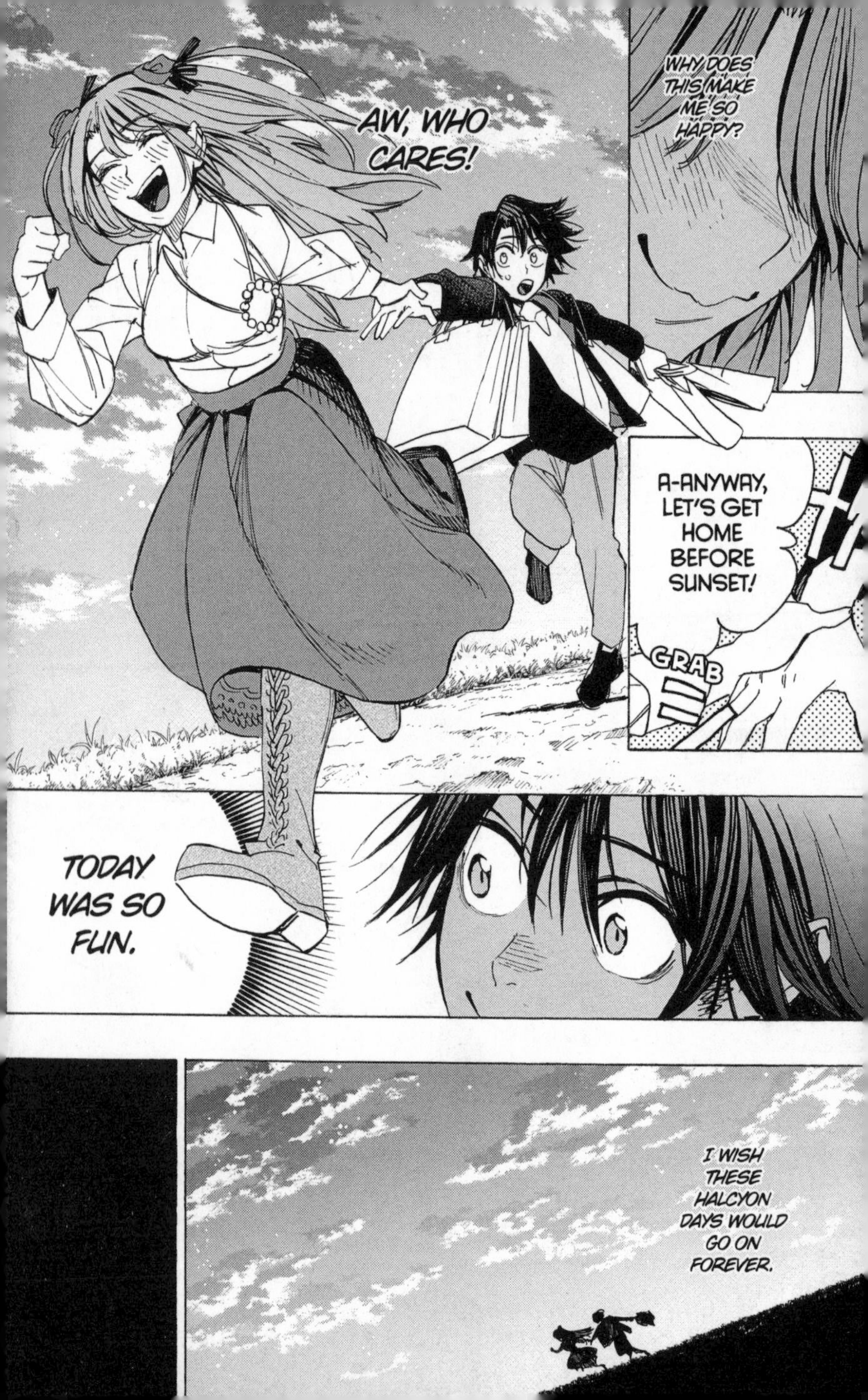
WHY DOES THIS MAKE ME SO HAPPY?
A-ANYWAY, LET'S GET HOME BEFORE SUNSET!
GRAB
AW, WHO CARES!
TODAY WAS SO FUN.
I WISH THESE HALCYON DAYS WOULD GO ON FOREVER.

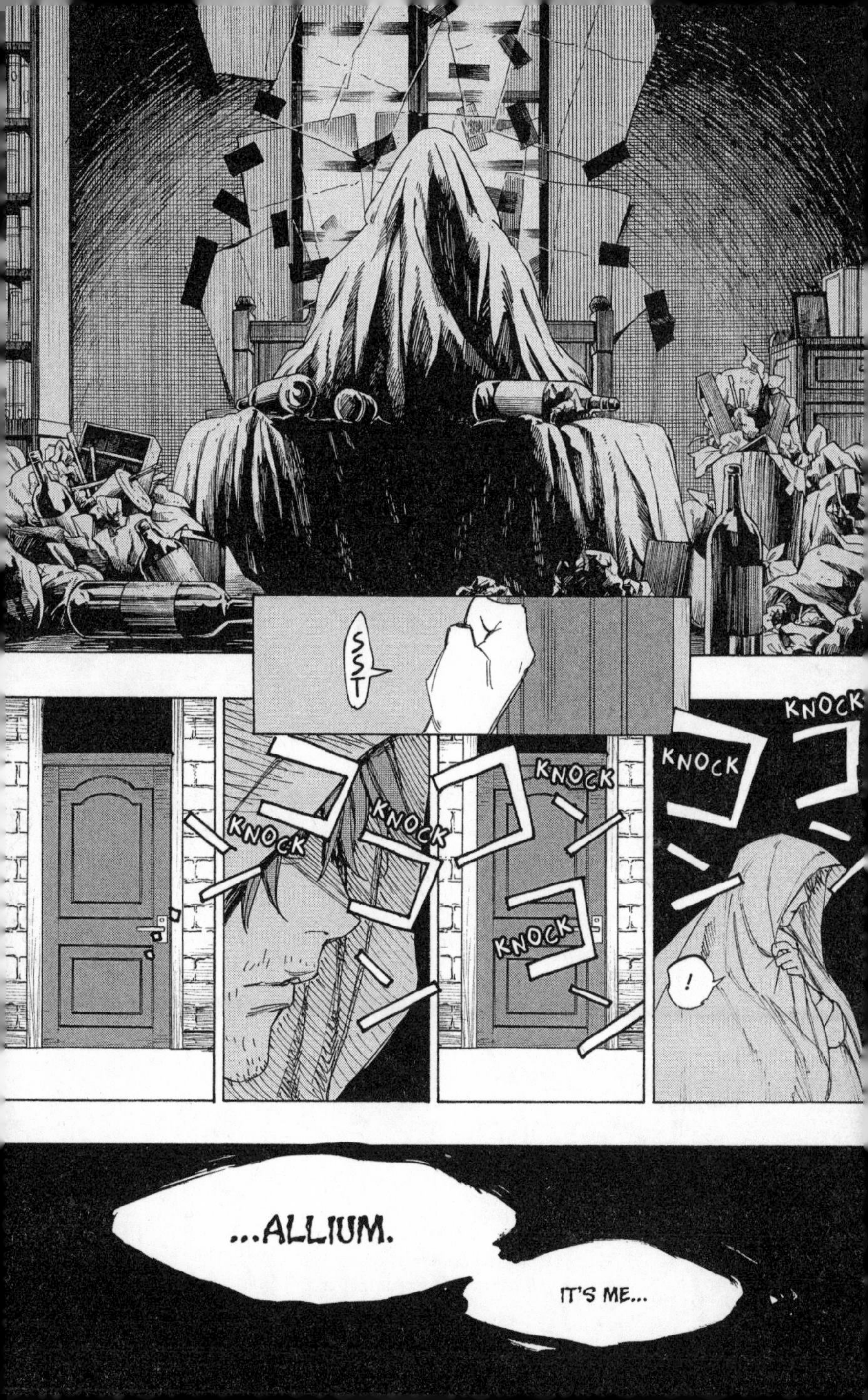
SSST
KNOCK
KNOCK
!
KNOCK
KNOCK
KNOCK
KNOCK
...ALLIUM.
IT'S ME...

THAT VOICE.

BUT WHY?

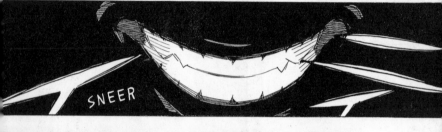

SNEER

KNOCK

KNOCK

ALLIUM.

OPEN UP.

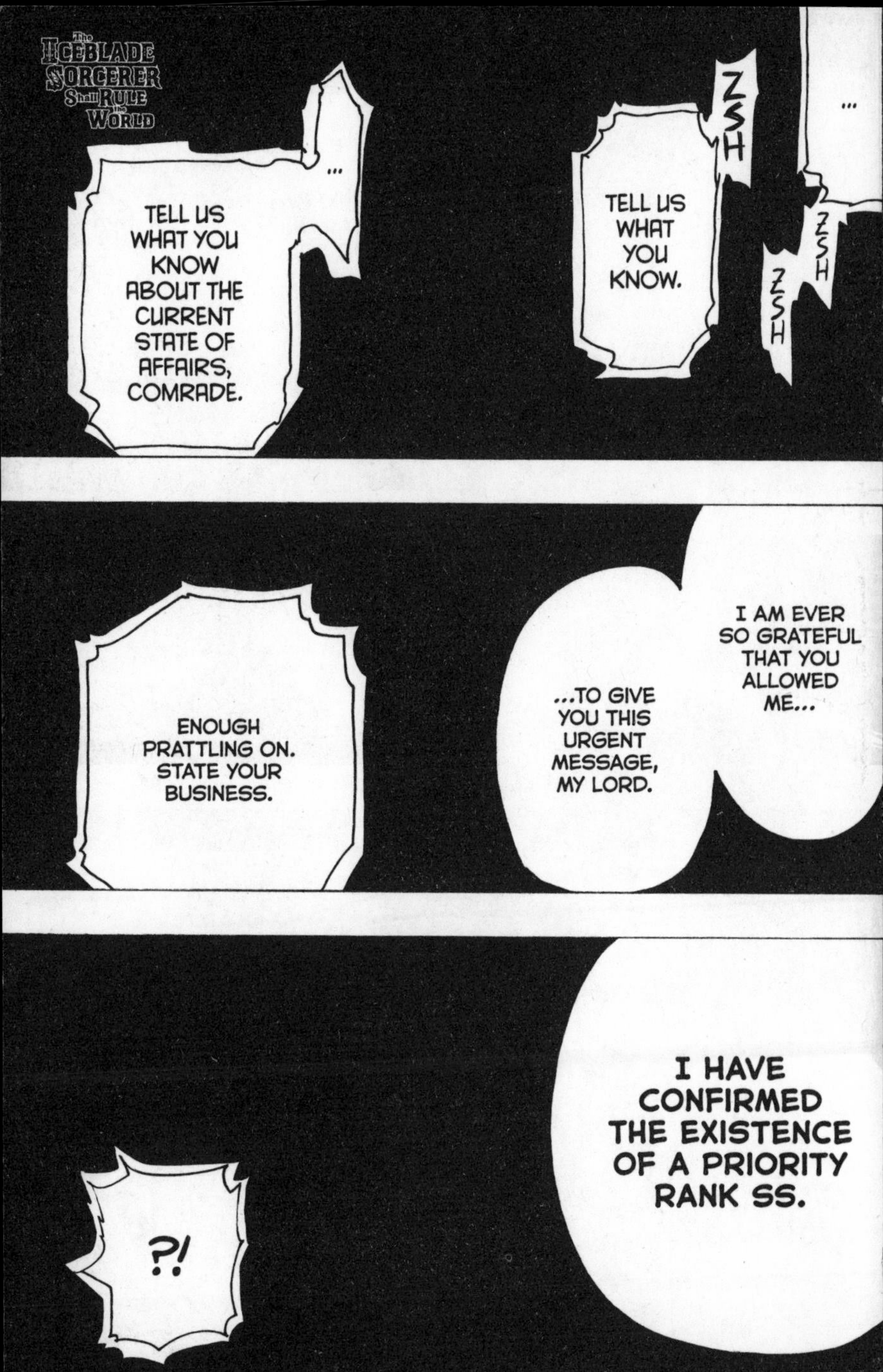
The ICEBLADE SORCERER Shall RULE the WORLD
...
ZSH
ZSH
ZSH
TELL US WHAT YOU KNOW.
...
TELL US WHAT YOU KNOW ABOUT THE CURRENT STATE OF AFFAIRS, COMRADE.
I AM EVER SO GRATEFUL THAT YOU ALLOWED ME...
...TO GIVE YOU THIS URGENT MESSAGE, MY LORD.
ENOUGH PRATTLING ON. STATE YOUR BUSINESS.
I HAVE CONFIRMED THE EXISTENCE OF A PRIORITY RANK SS.
?!

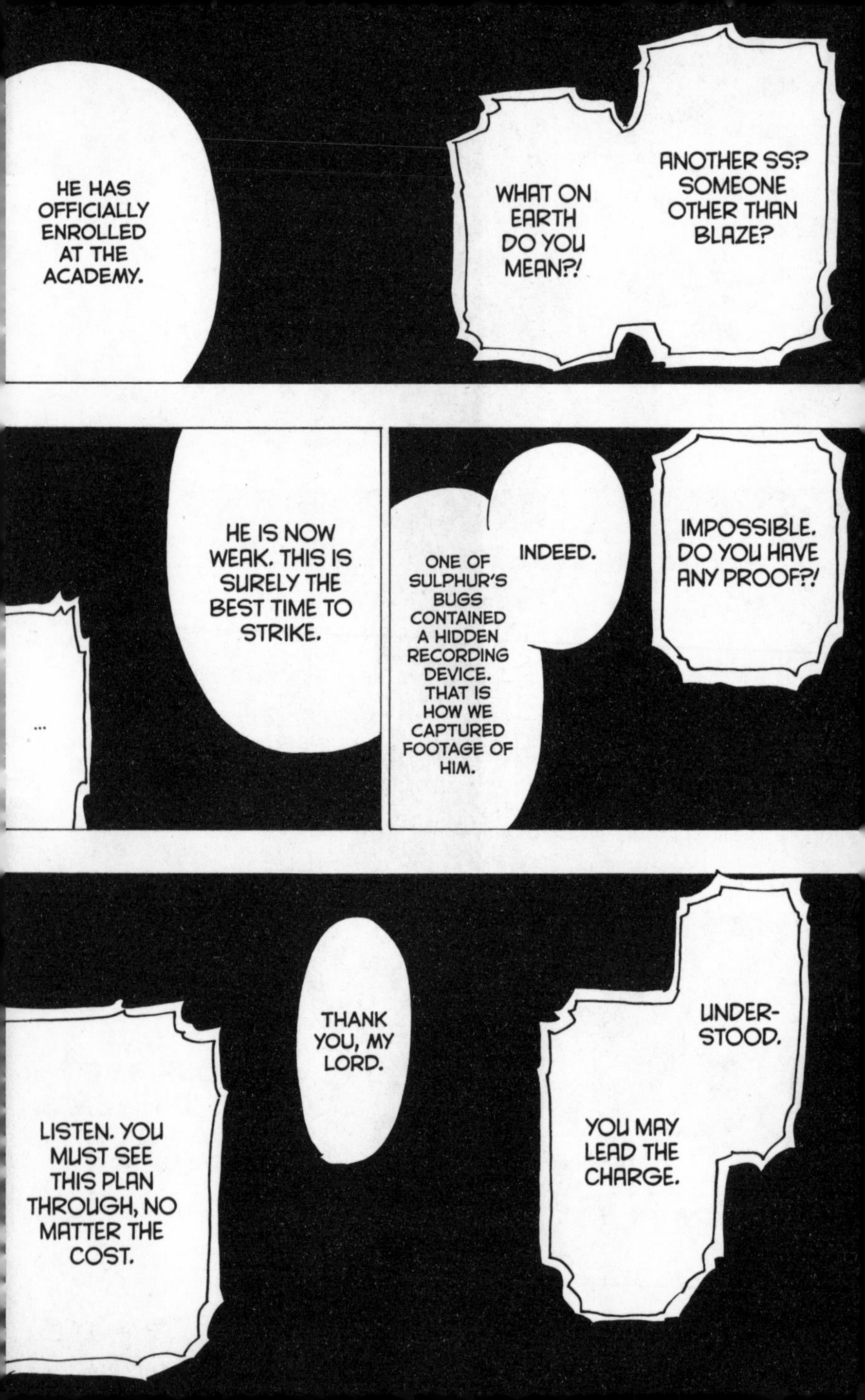

ANOTHER SS? SOMEONE OTHER THAN BLAZE?
WHAT ON EARTH DO YOU MEAN?!
HE HAS OFFICIALLY ENROLLED AT THE ACADEMY.
IMPOSSIBLE. DO YOU HAVE ANY PROOF?!
INDEED.
ONE OF SULPHUR'S BUGS CONTAINED A HIDDEN RECORDING DEVICE. THAT IS HOW WE CAPTURED FOOTAGE OF HIM.
HE IS NOW WEAK. THIS IS SURELY THE BEST TIME TO STRIKE.
...
UNDER-STOOD.
YOU MAY LEAD THE CHARGE.
THANK YOU, MY LORD.
LISTEN. YOU MUST SEE THIS PLAN THROUGH, NO MATTER THE COST.

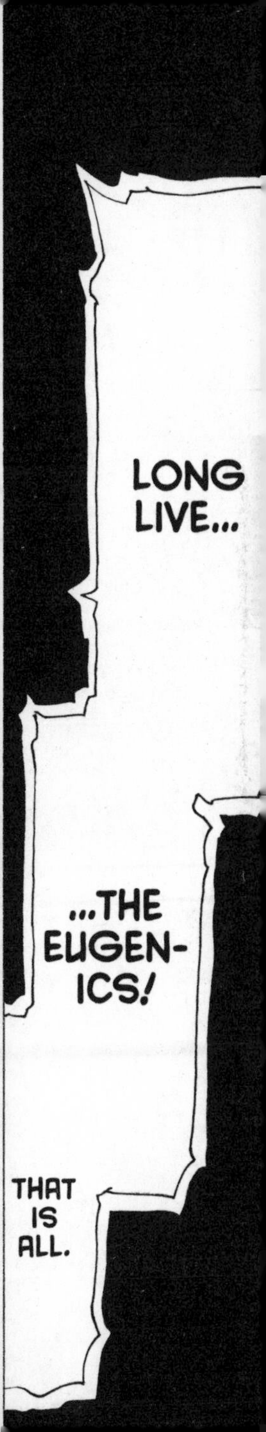
LONG LIVE...
...THE EUGEN-ICS!
THAT IS ALL.

Chapter 17
Warning

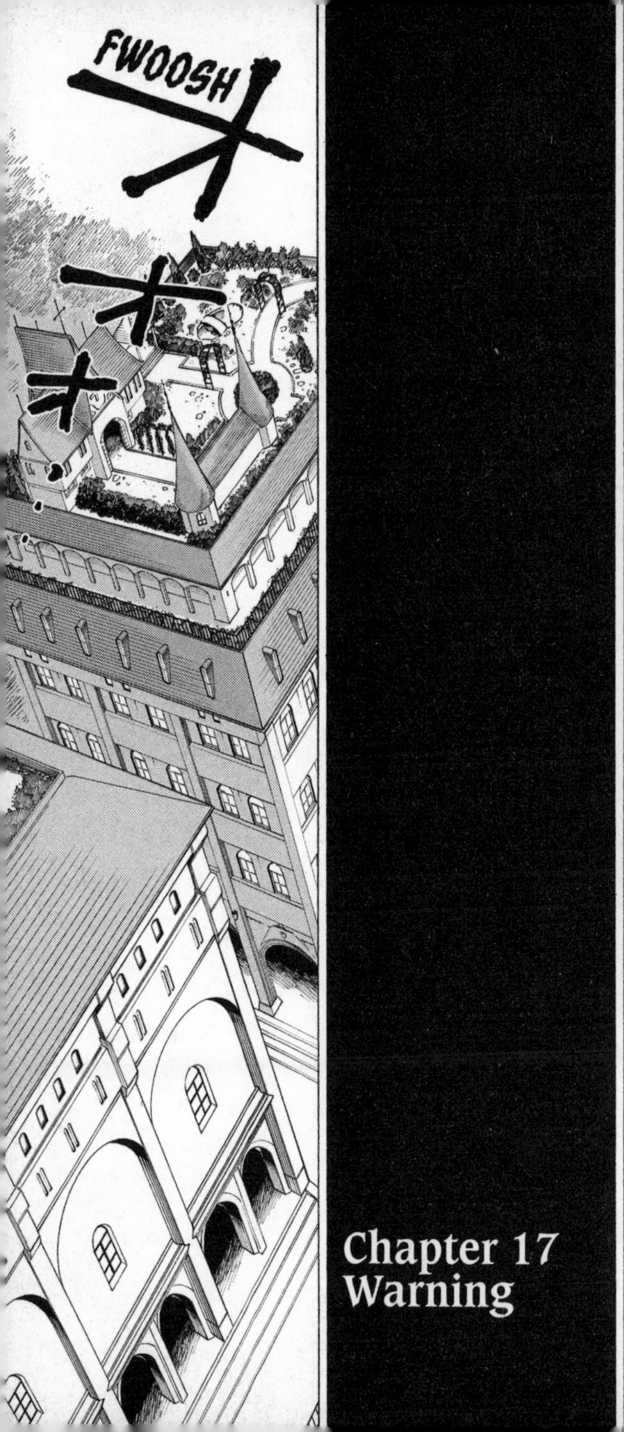
FWOOSH

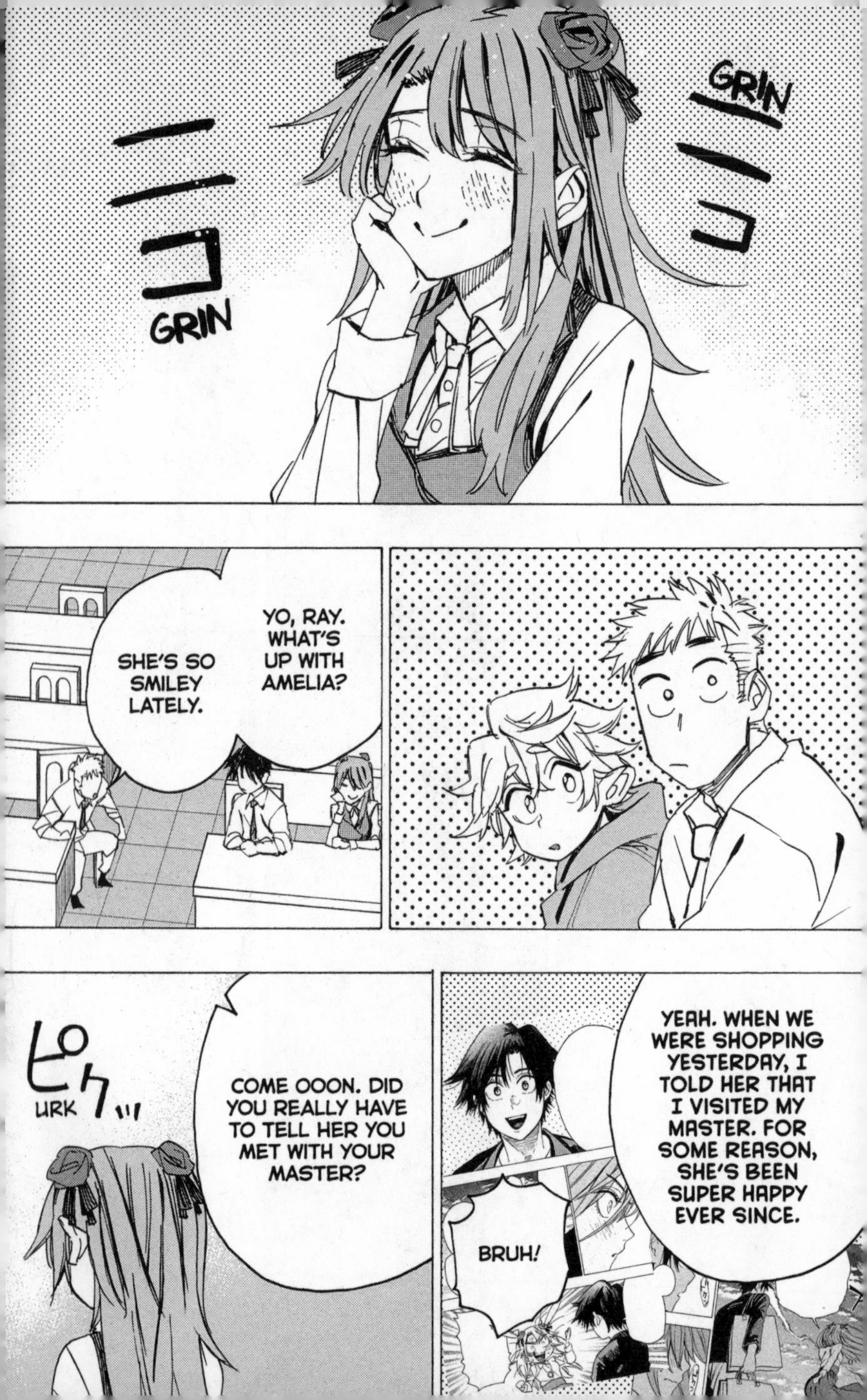

ニコ
GRIN
ニコ
GRIN
YO, RAY. WHAT'S UP WITH AMELIA?
SHE'S SO SMILEY LATELY.
YEAH. WHEN WE WERE SHOPPING YESTERDAY, I TOLD HER THAT I VISITED MY MASTER. FOR SOME REASON, SHE'S BEEN SUPER HAPPY EVER SINCE.
BRUH!
COME OOON. DID YOU REALLY HAVE TO TELL HER YOU MET WITH YOUR MASTER?
ピク
URK

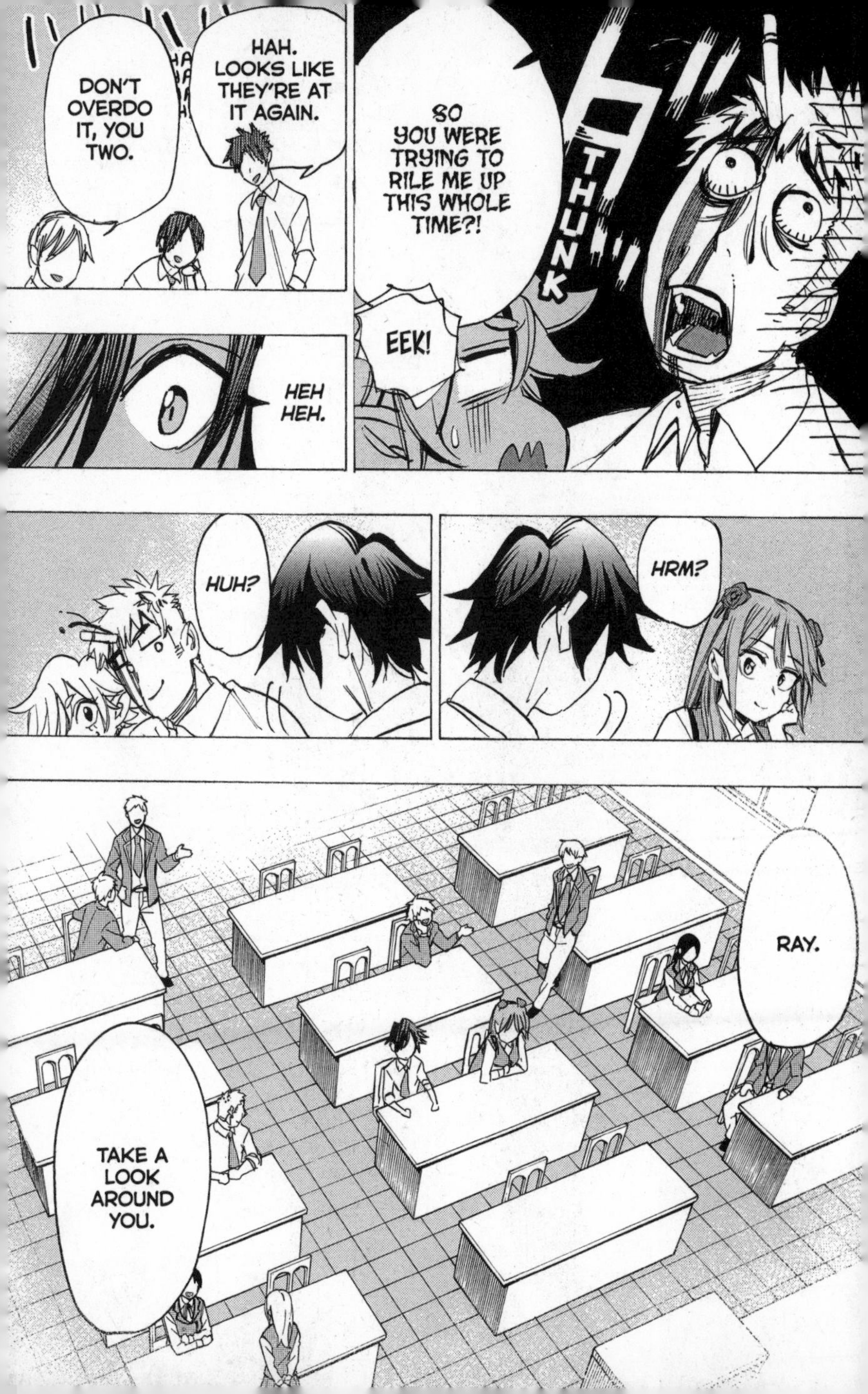
SO YOU WERE TRYING TO RILE ME UP THIS WHOLE TIME?!
THUNK
EEK!
HAH. LOOKS LIKE THEY'RE AT IT AGAIN.
DON'T OVERDO IT, YOU TWO.
HEH HEH.
HRM?
HUH?
RAY.
TAKE A LOOK AROUND YOU.

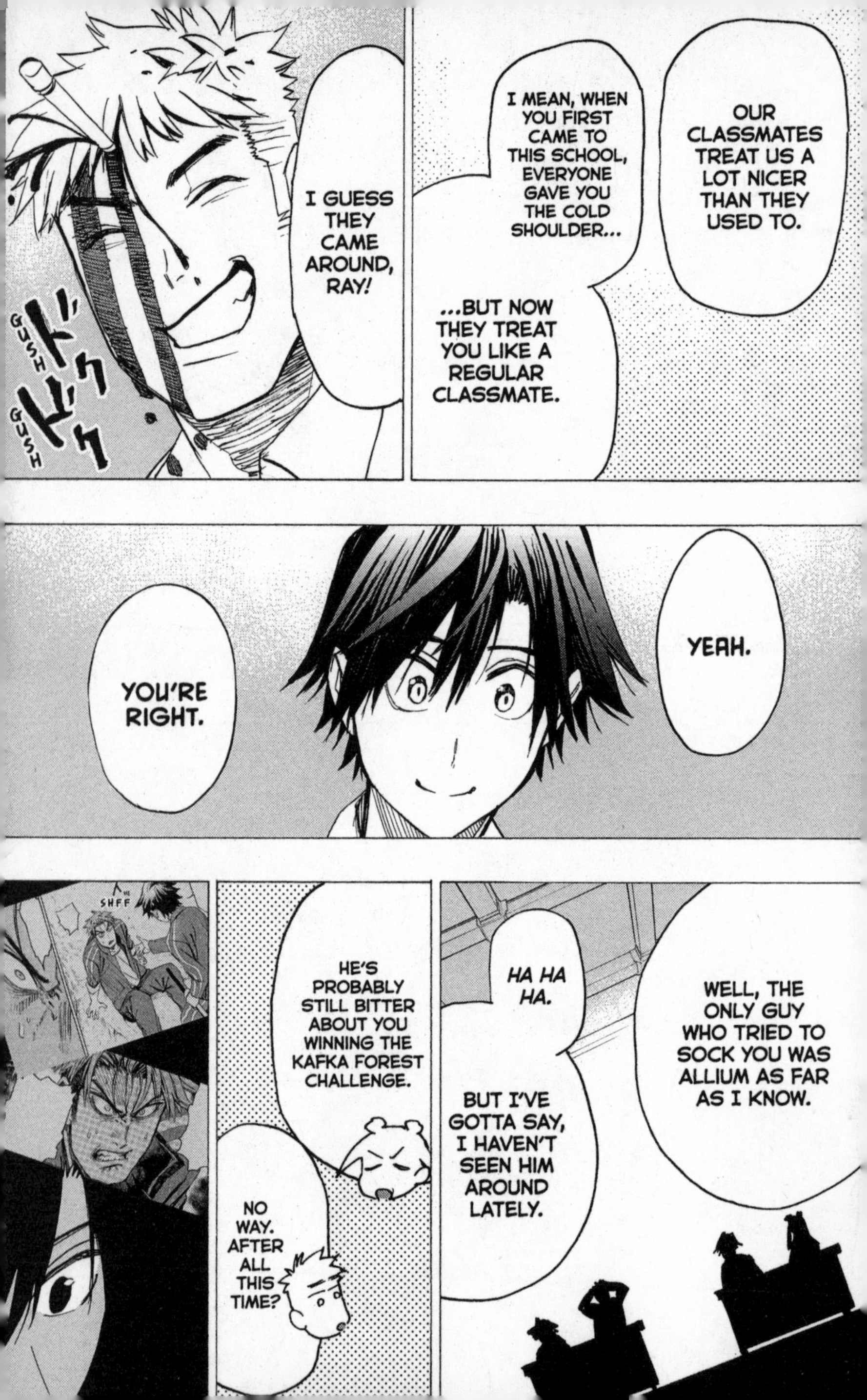
OUR CLASSMATES TREAT US A LOT NICER THAN THEY USED TO.
I MEAN, WHEN YOU FIRST CAME TO THIS SCHOOL, EVERYONE GAVE YOU THE COLD SHOULDER...
...BUT NOW THEY TREAT YOU LIKE A REGULAR CLASSMATE.
I GUESS THEY CAME AROUND, RAY!
GUSH GUSH
YEAH.
YOU'RE RIGHT.
WELL, THE ONLY GUY WHO TRIED TO SOCK YOU WAS ALLIUM AS FAR AS I KNOW.
HA HA HA.
BUT I'VE GOTTA SAY, I HAVEN'T SEEN HIM AROUND LATELY.
HE'S PROBABLY STILL BITTER ABOUT YOU WINNING THE KAFKA FOREST CHALLENGE.
NO WAY. AFTER ALL THIS TIME?
SHFF

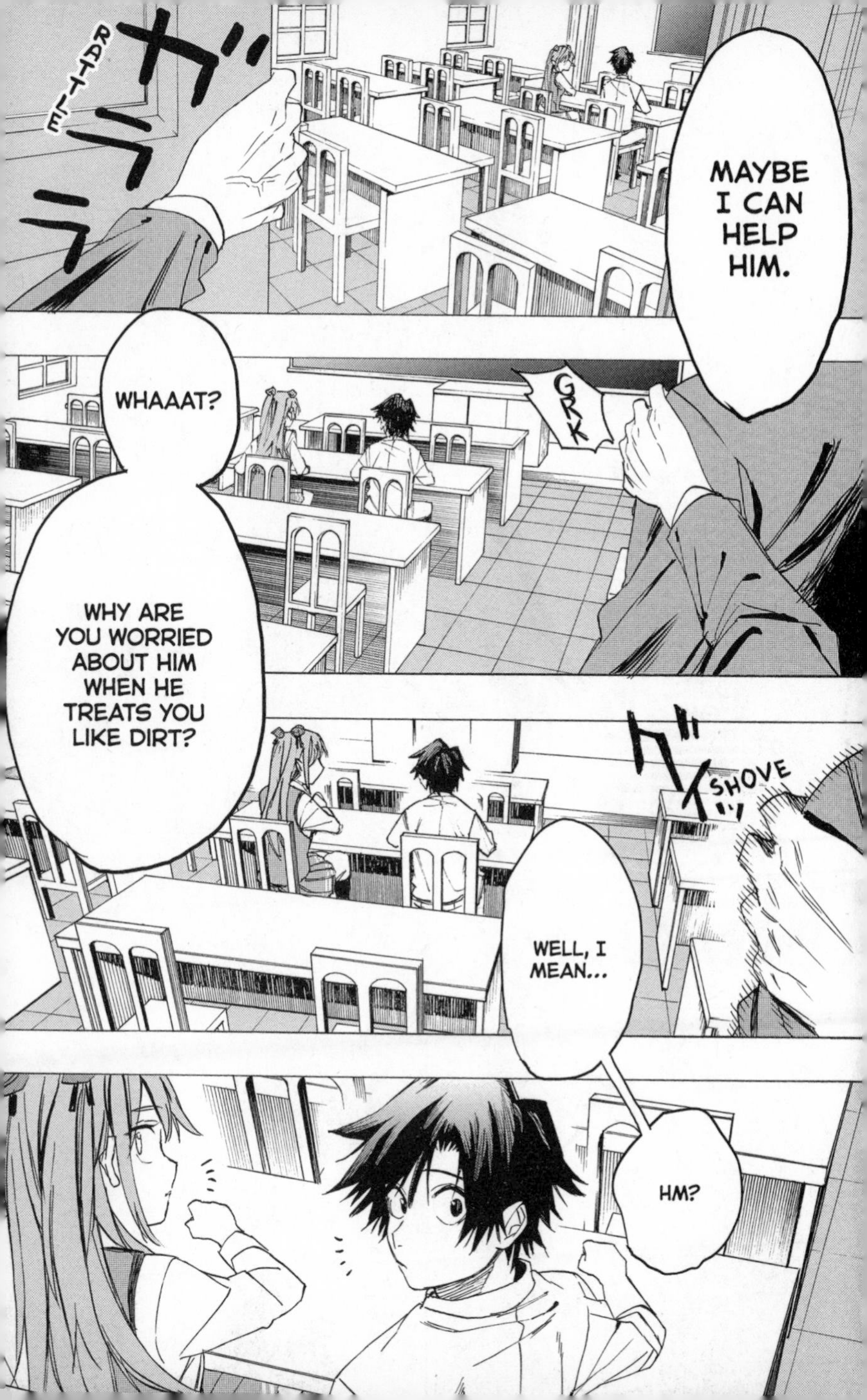
MAYBE I CAN HELP HIM.
RATTLE
GRK
WHAAAT?
WHY ARE YOU WORRIED ABOUT HIM WHEN HE TREATS YOU LIKE DIRT?
SHOVE
WELL, I MEAN...
HM?

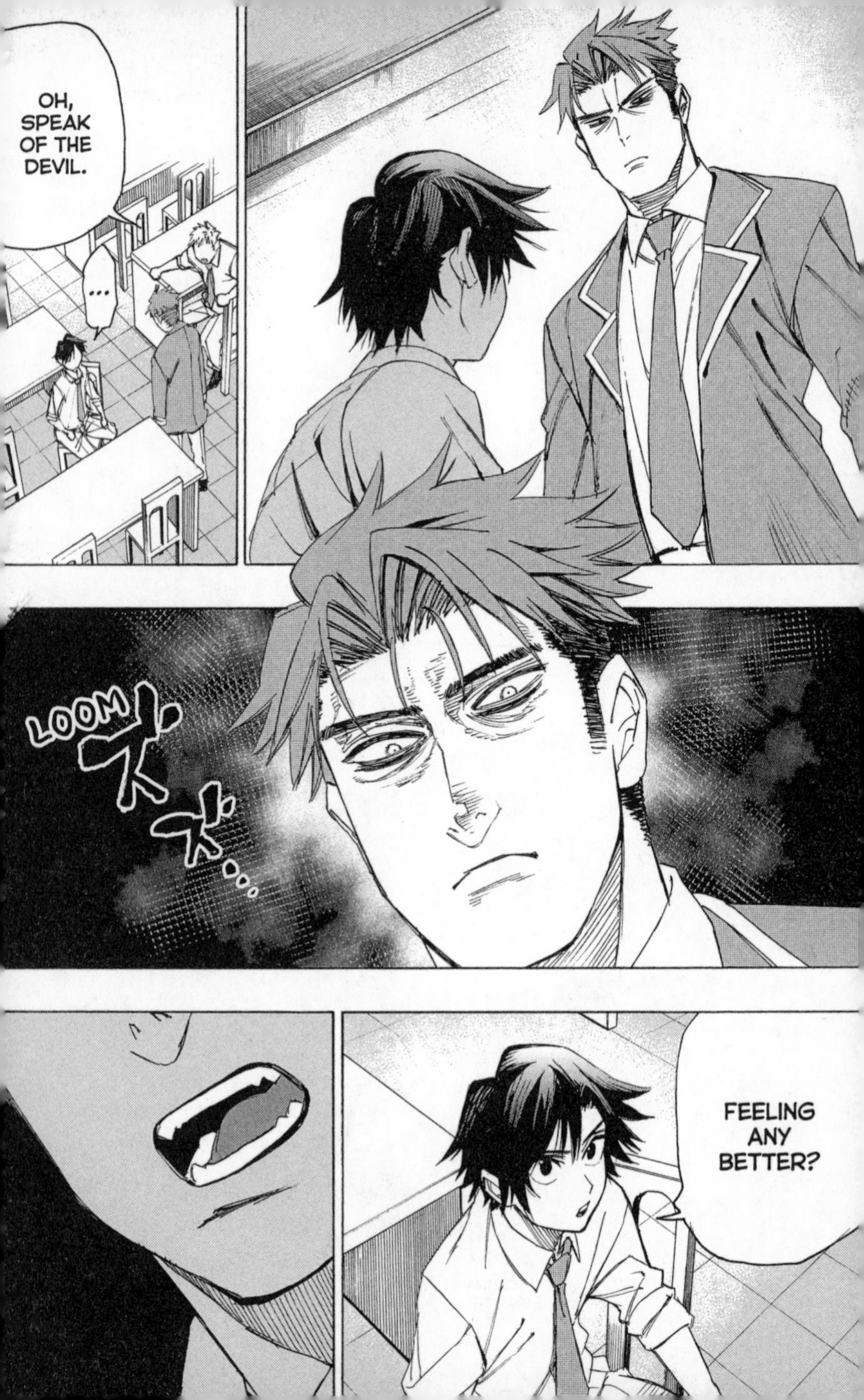
OH, SPEAK OF THE DEVIL.
...
LOOM
ズズ...
FEELING ANY BETTER?

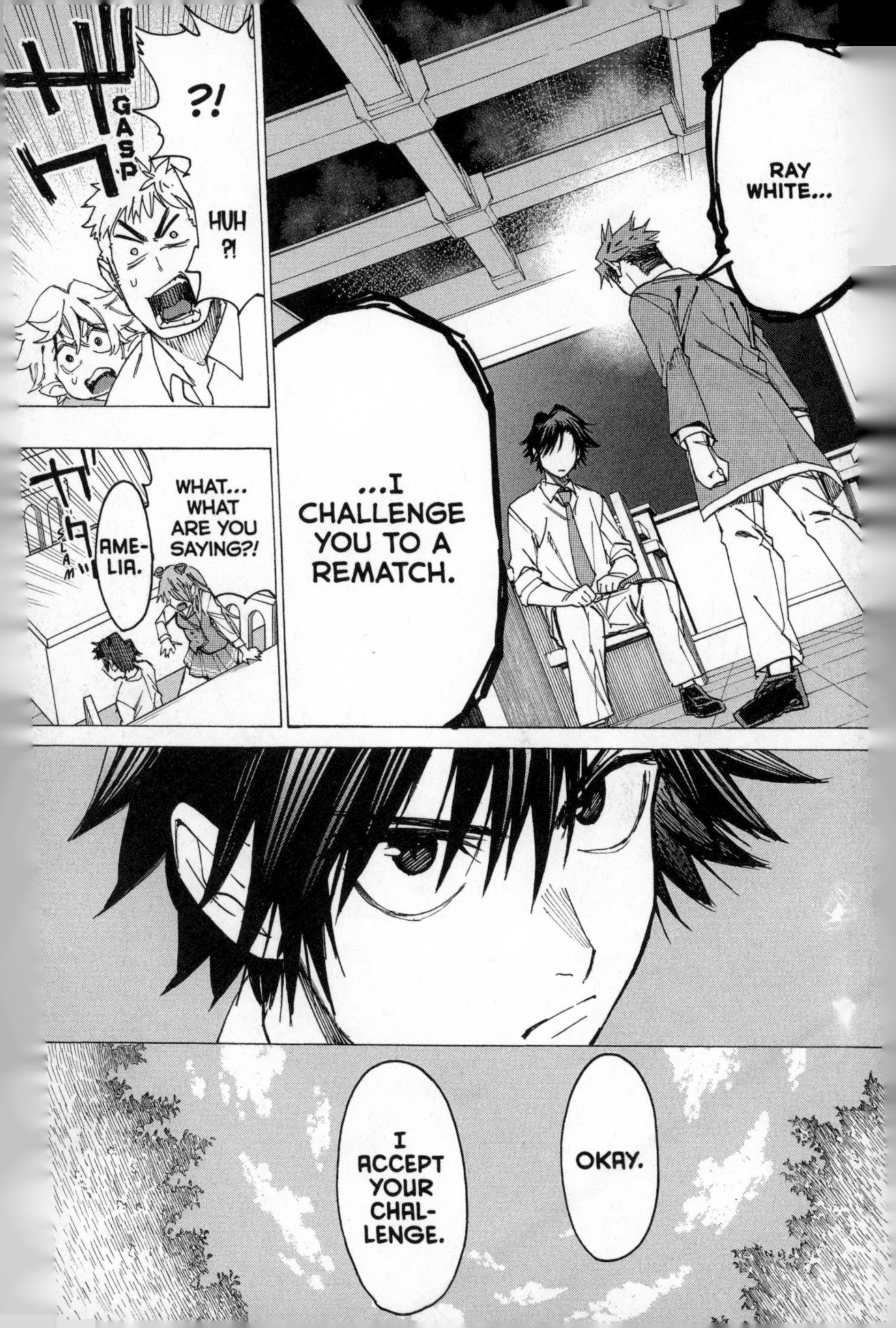
RAY WHITE...
...I CHALLENGE YOU TO A REMATCH.
?!
GASP
HUH ?!
WHAT... WHAT ARE YOU SAYING?!
AME-LIA.
SLAM
OKAY.
I ACCEPT YOUR CHAL-LENGE.

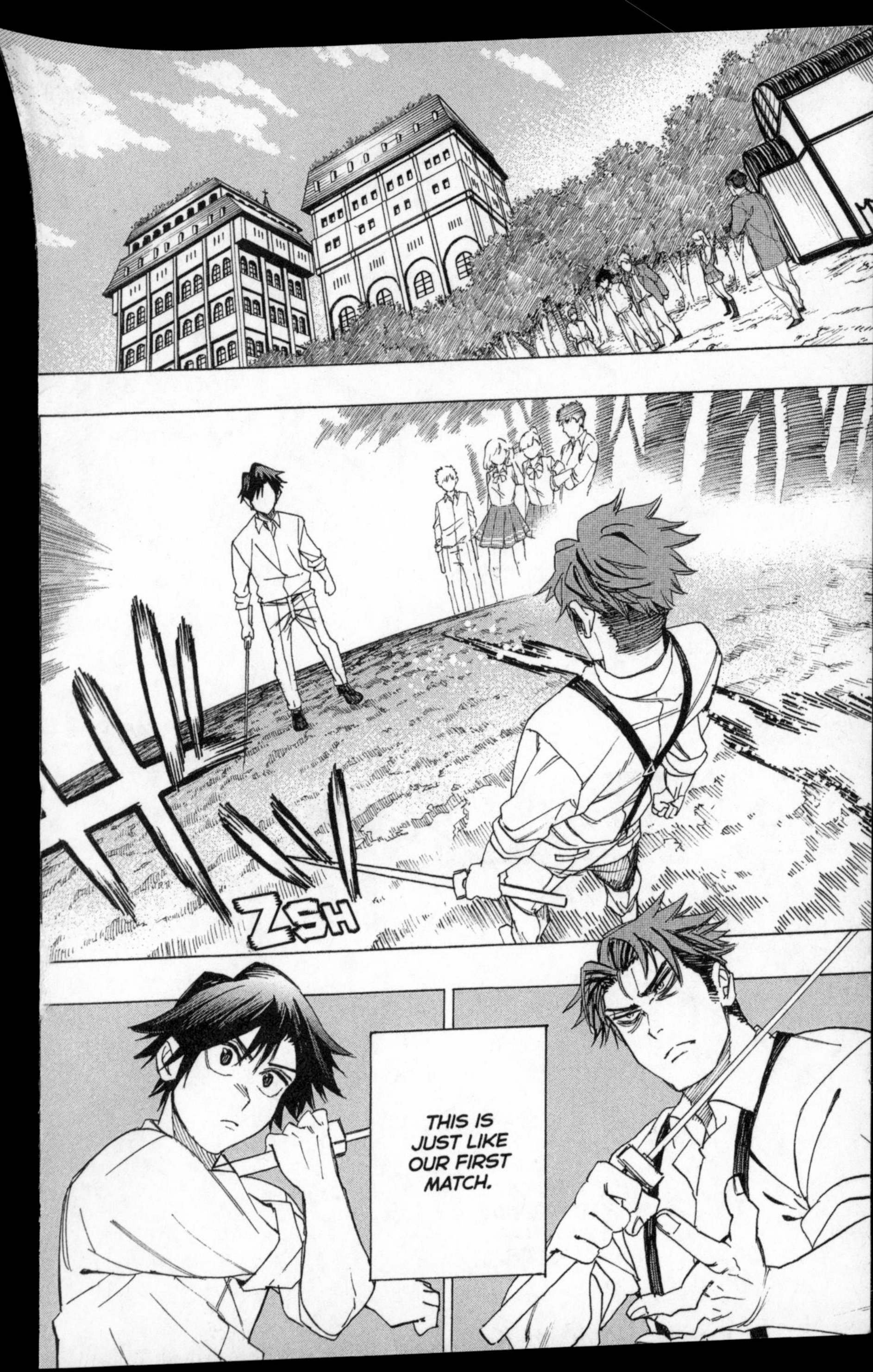
ZSH
THIS IS JUST LIKE OUR FIRST MATCH.

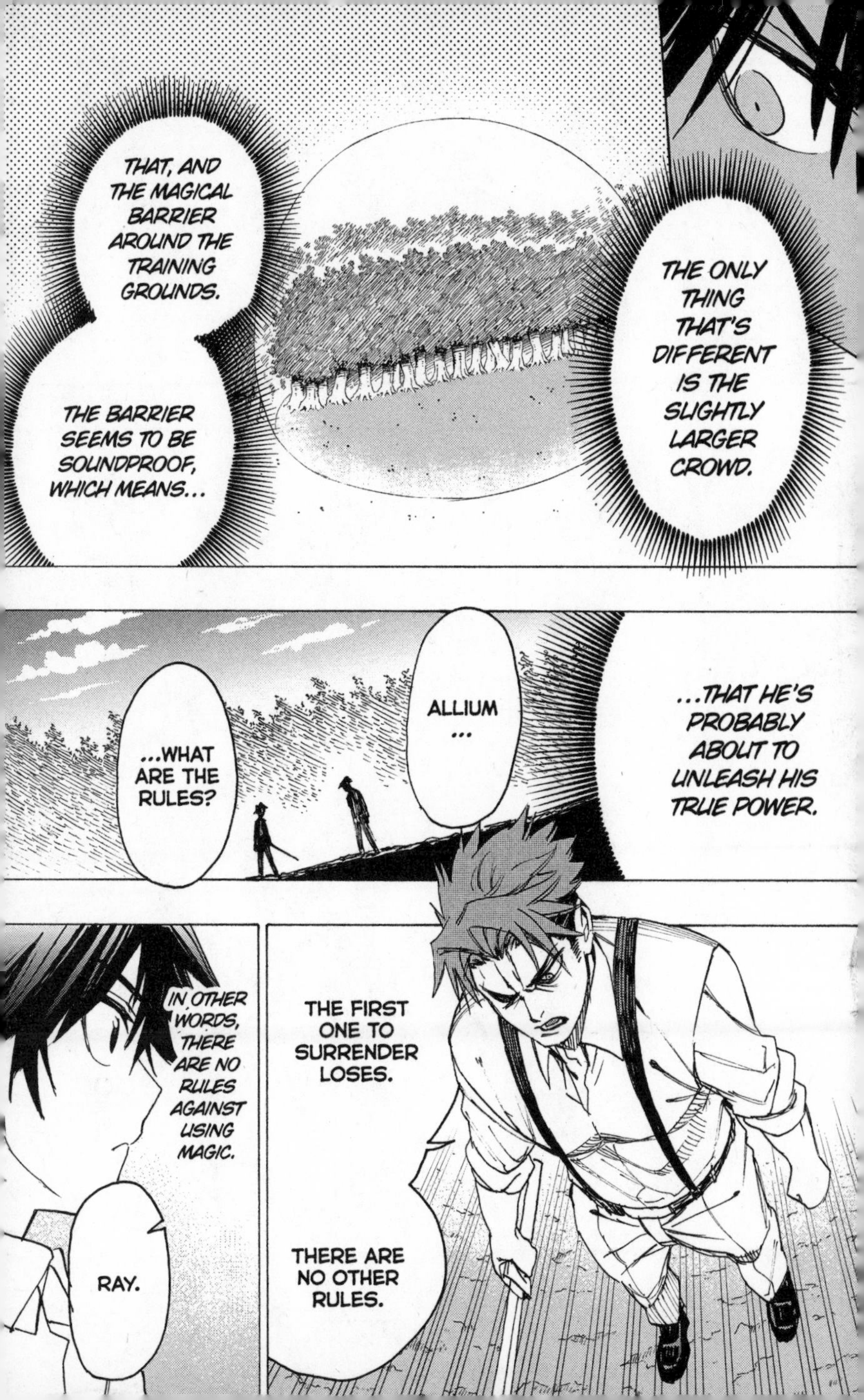
THE ONLY THING THAT'S DIFFERENT IS THE SLIGHTLY LARGER CROWD.
THAT, AND THE MAGICAL BARRIER AROUND THE TRAINING GROUNDS.
THE BARRIER SEEMS TO BE SOUNDPROOF, WHICH MEANS...
...THAT HE'S PROBABLY ABOUT TO UNLEASH HIS TRUE POWER.
ALLIUM...
...WHAT ARE THE RULES?
THE FIRST ONE TO SURRENDER LOSES.
THERE ARE NO OTHER RULES.
IN OTHER WORDS, THERE ARE NO RULES AGAINST USING MAGIC.
RAY.

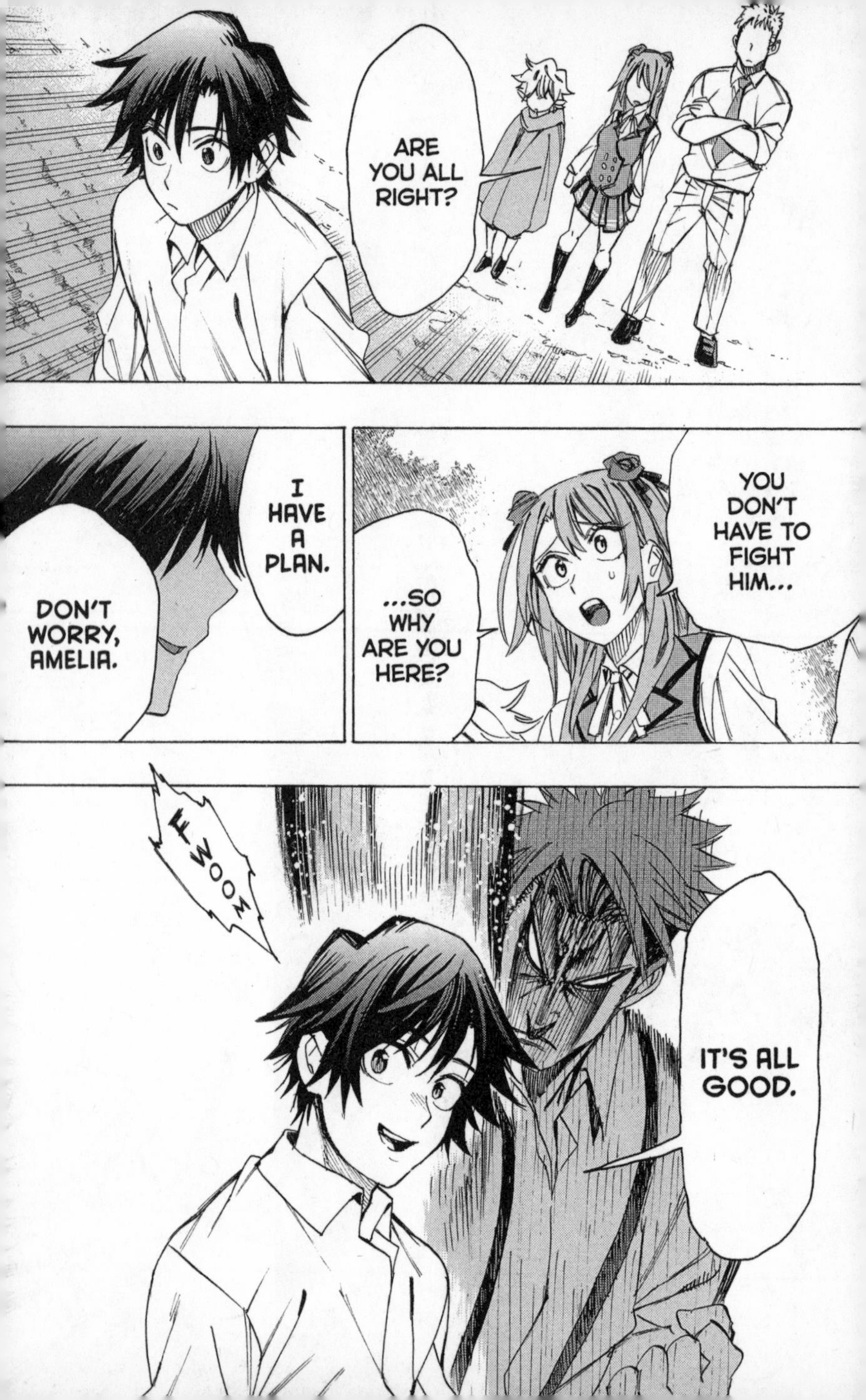
ARE YOU ALL RIGHT?
YOU DON'T HAVE TO FIGHT HIM...
...SO WHY ARE YOU HERE?
I HAVE A PLAN.
DON'T WORRY, AMELIA.
FWOOM
IT'S ALL GOOD.

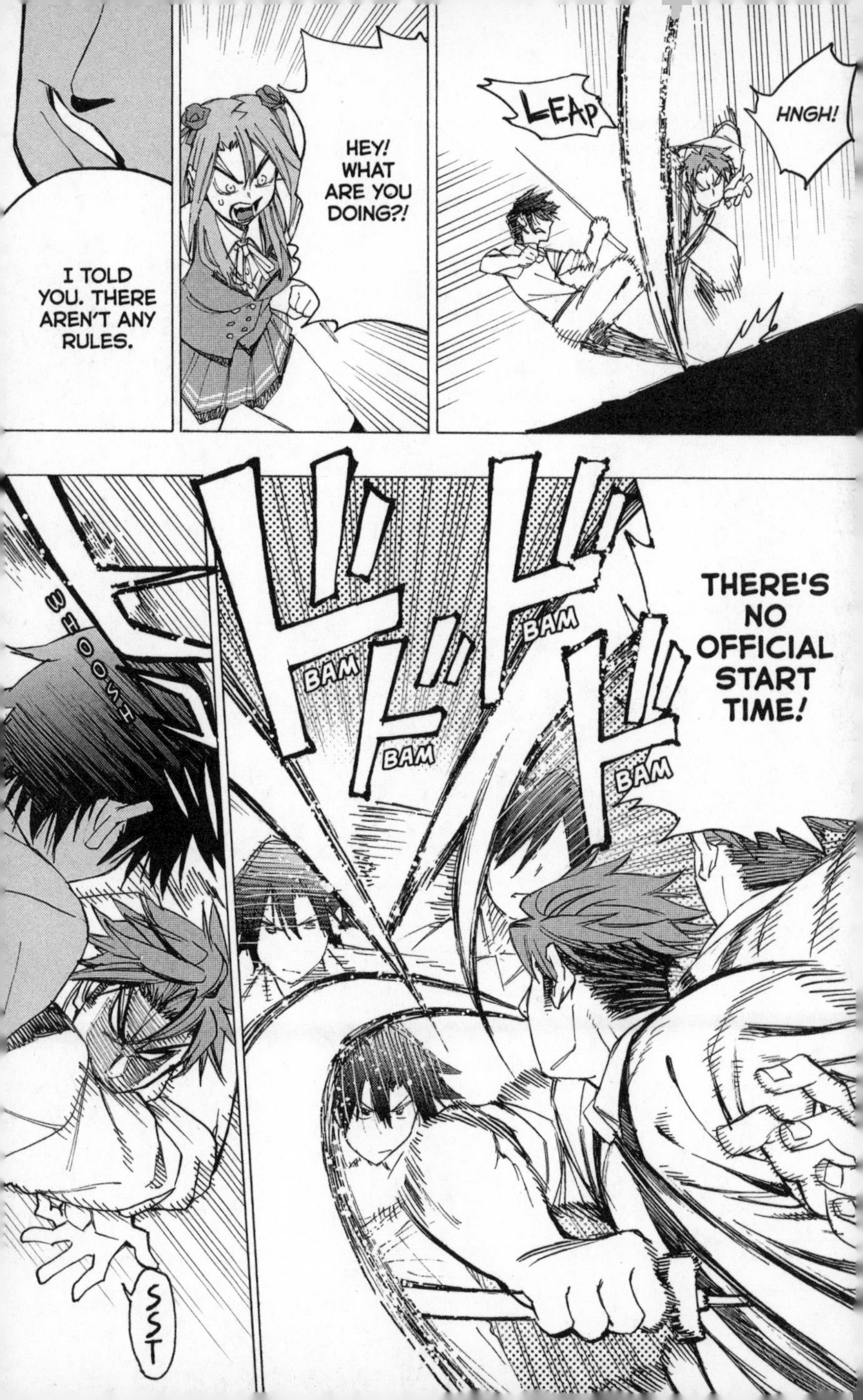
HNGH!
LEAP
HEY! WHAT ARE YOU DOING?!
I TOLD YOU. THERE AREN'T ANY RULES.
THERE'S NO OFFICIAL START TIME!
BAM
BAM
BAM
BAM
WHOOOSH
SSST

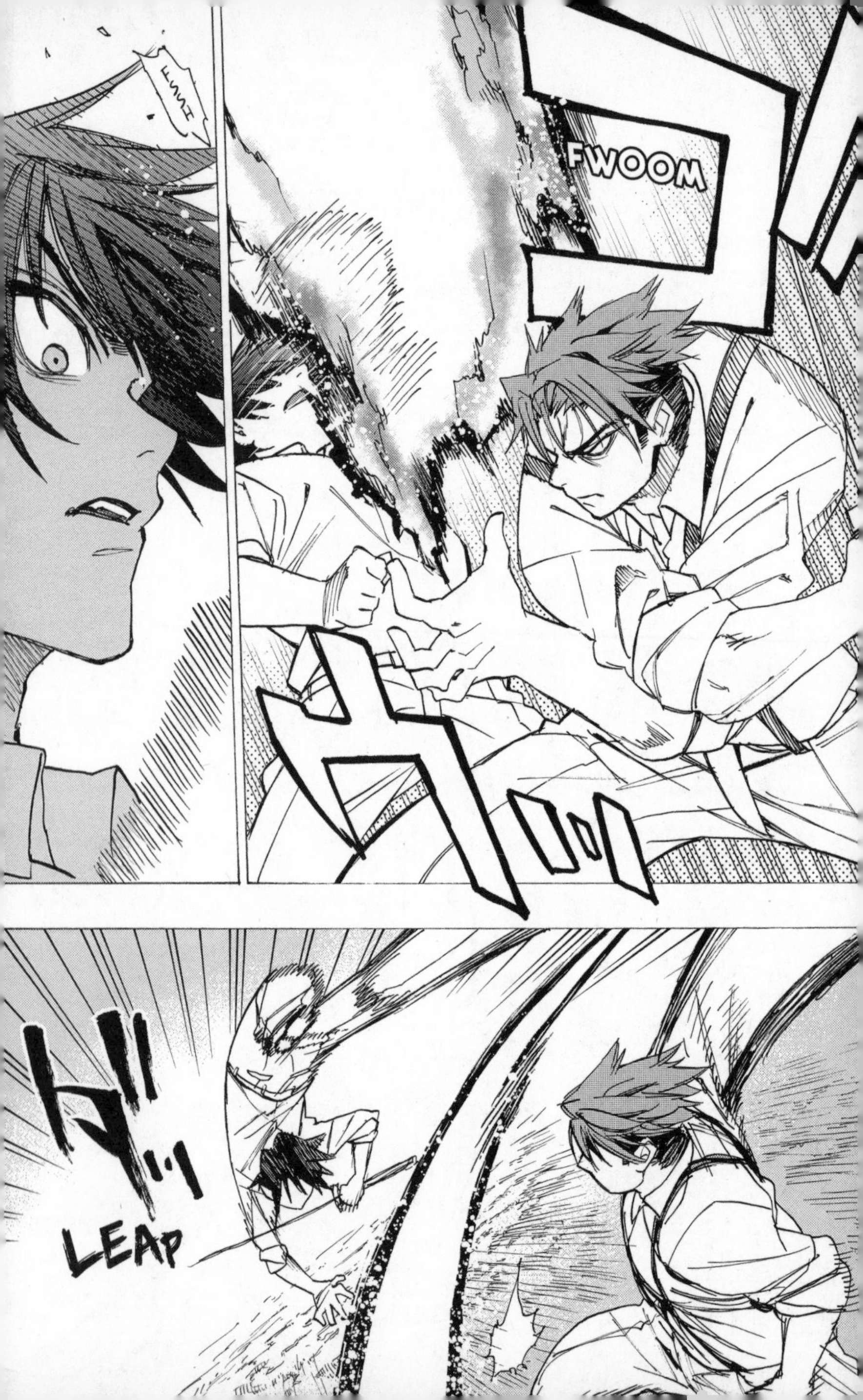
FWOOM
FSSSH
LEAP

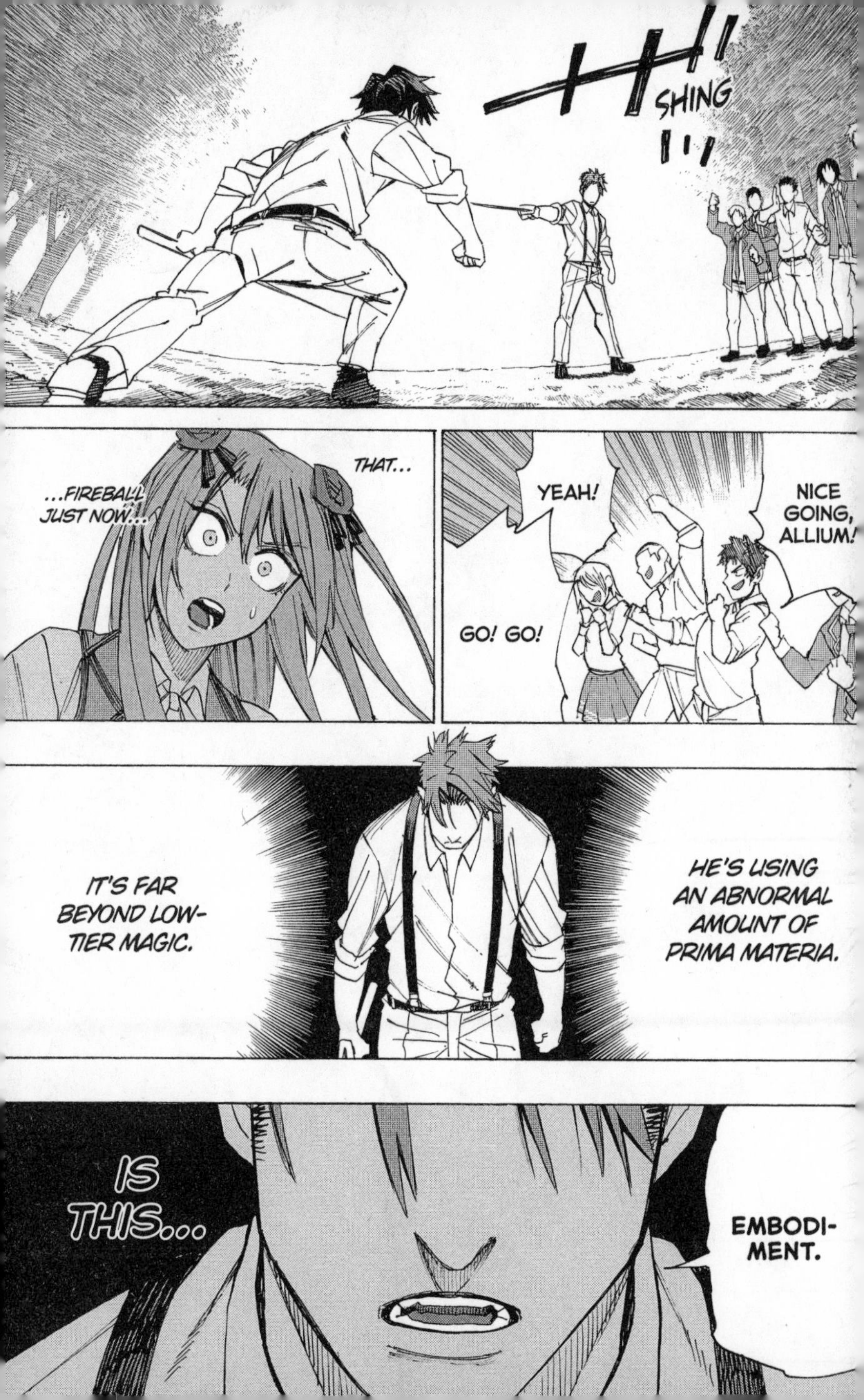
SHING
NICE GOING, ALLIUM!
YEAH!
GO! GO!
THAT...
...FIREBALL JUST NOW...
HE'S USING AN ABNORMAL AMOUNT OF PRIMA MATERIA.
IT'S FAR BEYOND LOW-TIER MAGIC.
IS THIS...
EMBODI-MENT.

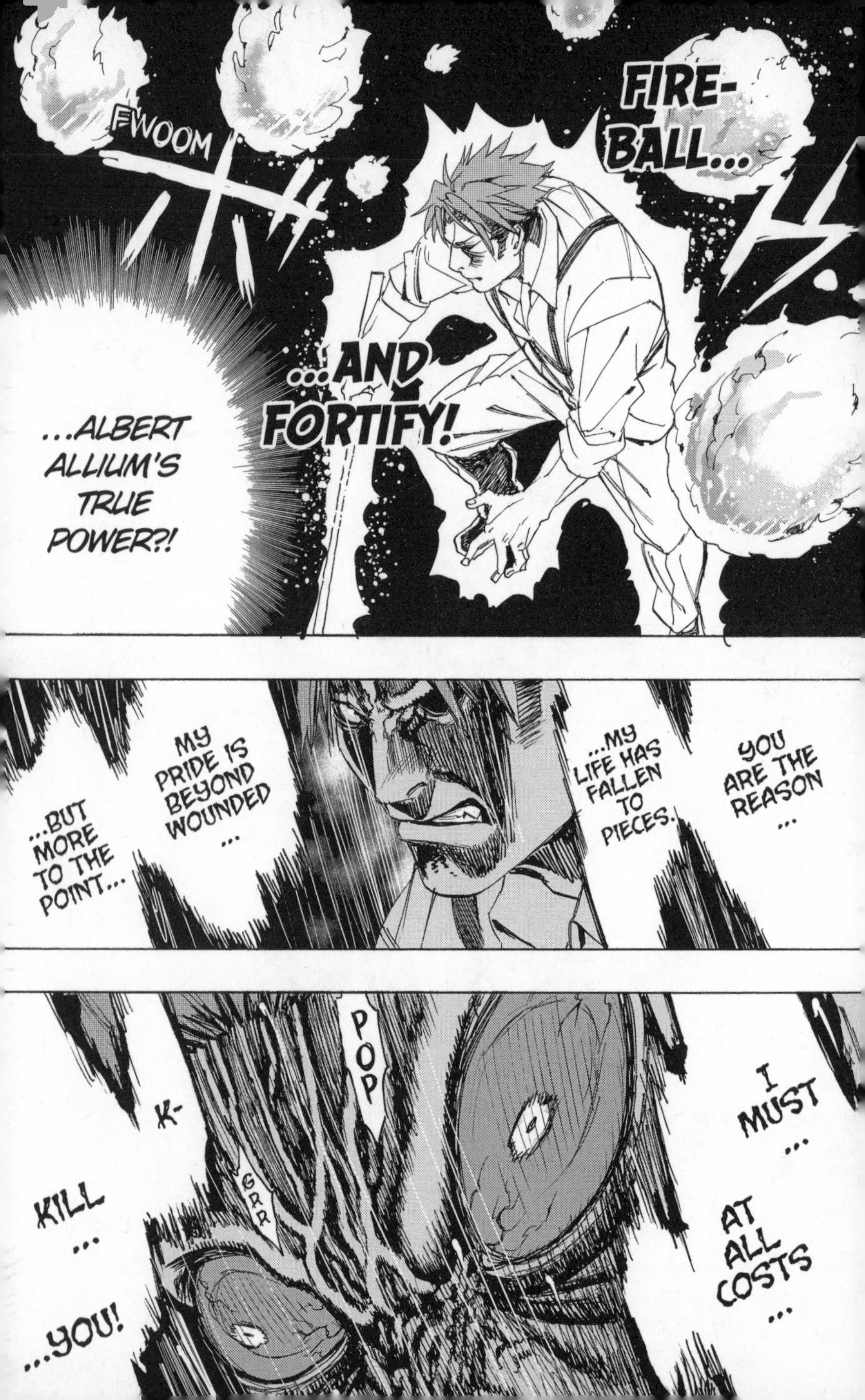
FIRE-BALL...
...AND FORTIFY!
FWOOM
...ALBERT ALLIUM'S TRUE POWER?!
YOU ARE THE REASON ...
...MY LIFE HAS FALLEN TO PIECES.
MY PRIDE IS BEYOND WOUNDED ...
...BUT MORE TO THE POINT...
I MUST ...
AT ALL COSTS ...
POP
GRR
K-
KILL ...
...YOU!

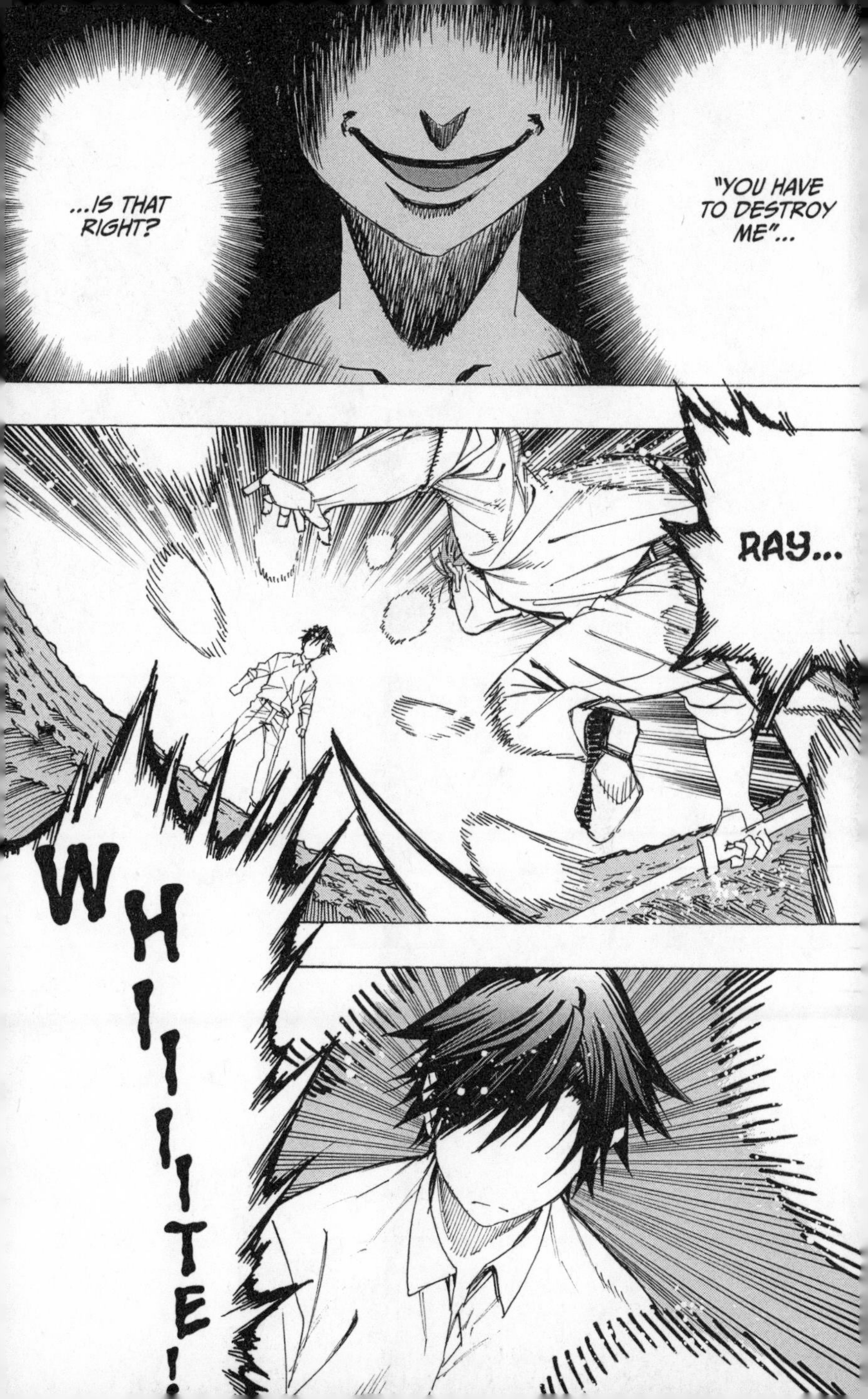
"YOU HAVE TO DESTROY ME"...
...IS THAT RIGHT?
RAY...
WHIIIITE!

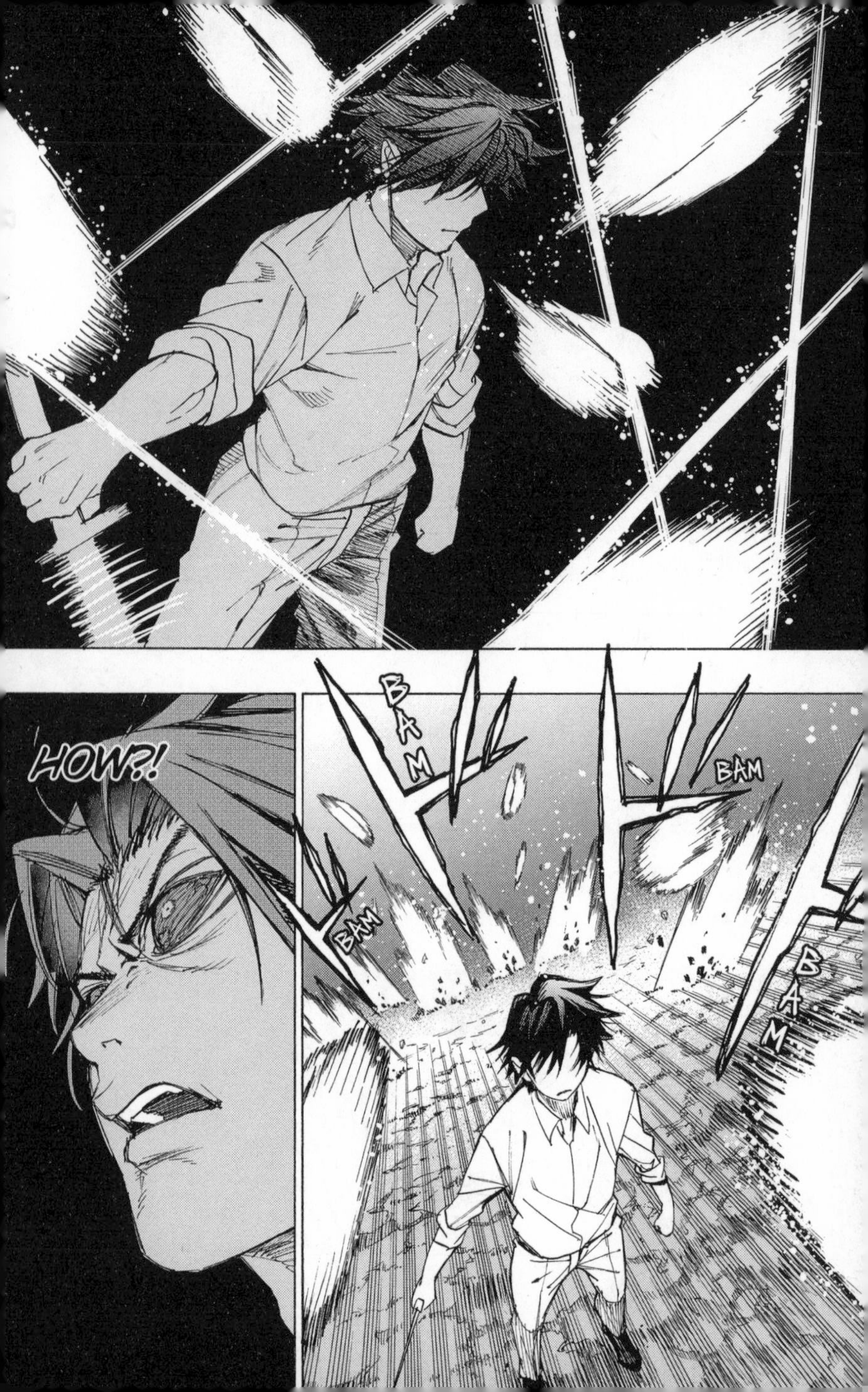
BAM
BAM
BAM
BAM
HOW?!

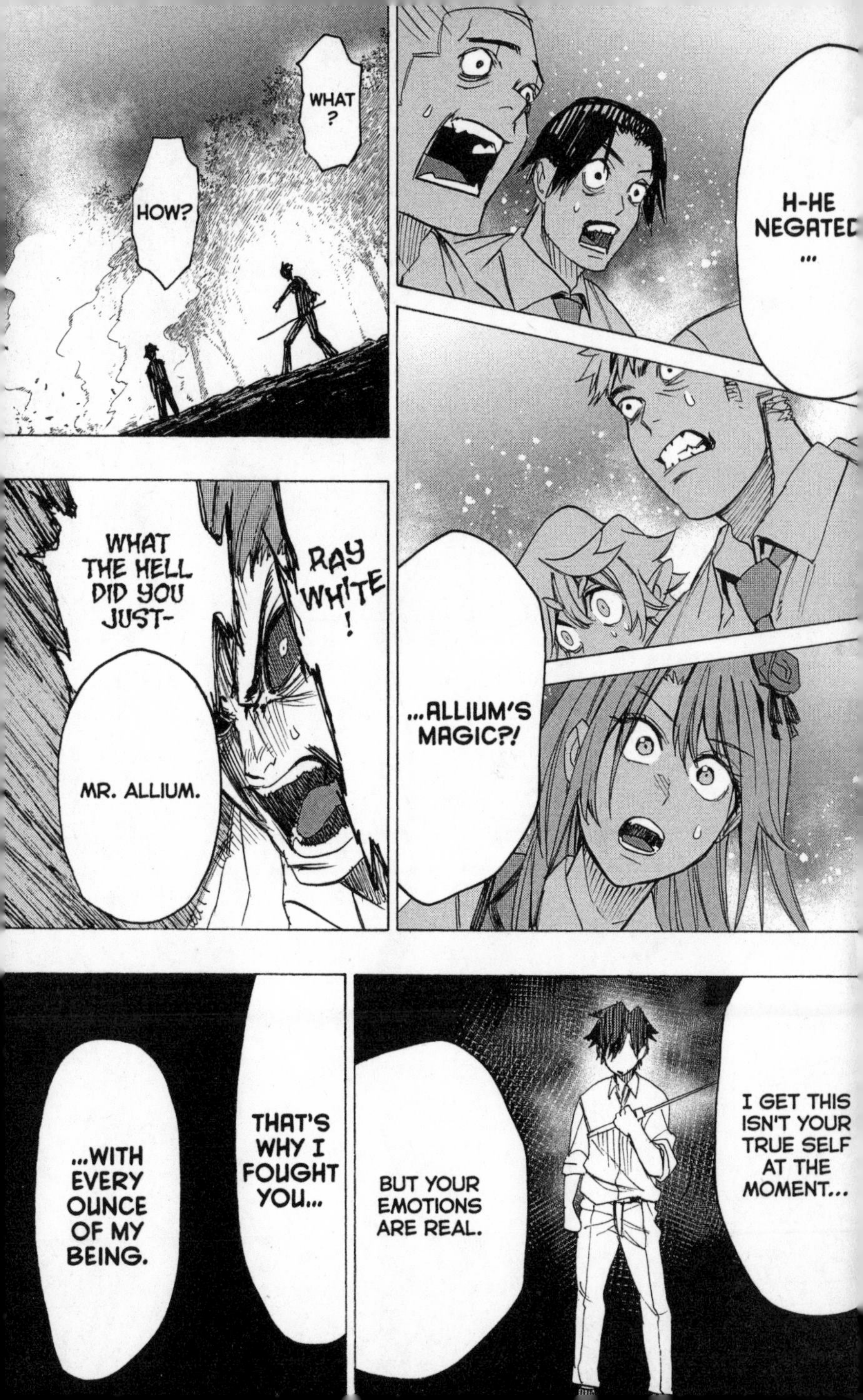
H-HE NEGATED ...
...ALLIUM'S MAGIC?!
WHAT ?
HOW?
RAY WHITE !
WHAT THE HELL DID YOU JUST-
MR. ALLIUM.
I GET THIS ISN'T YOUR TRUE SELF AT THE MOMENT...
BUT YOUR EMOTIONS ARE REAL.
THAT'S WHY I FOUGHT YOU...
...WITH EVERY OUNCE OF MY BEING.

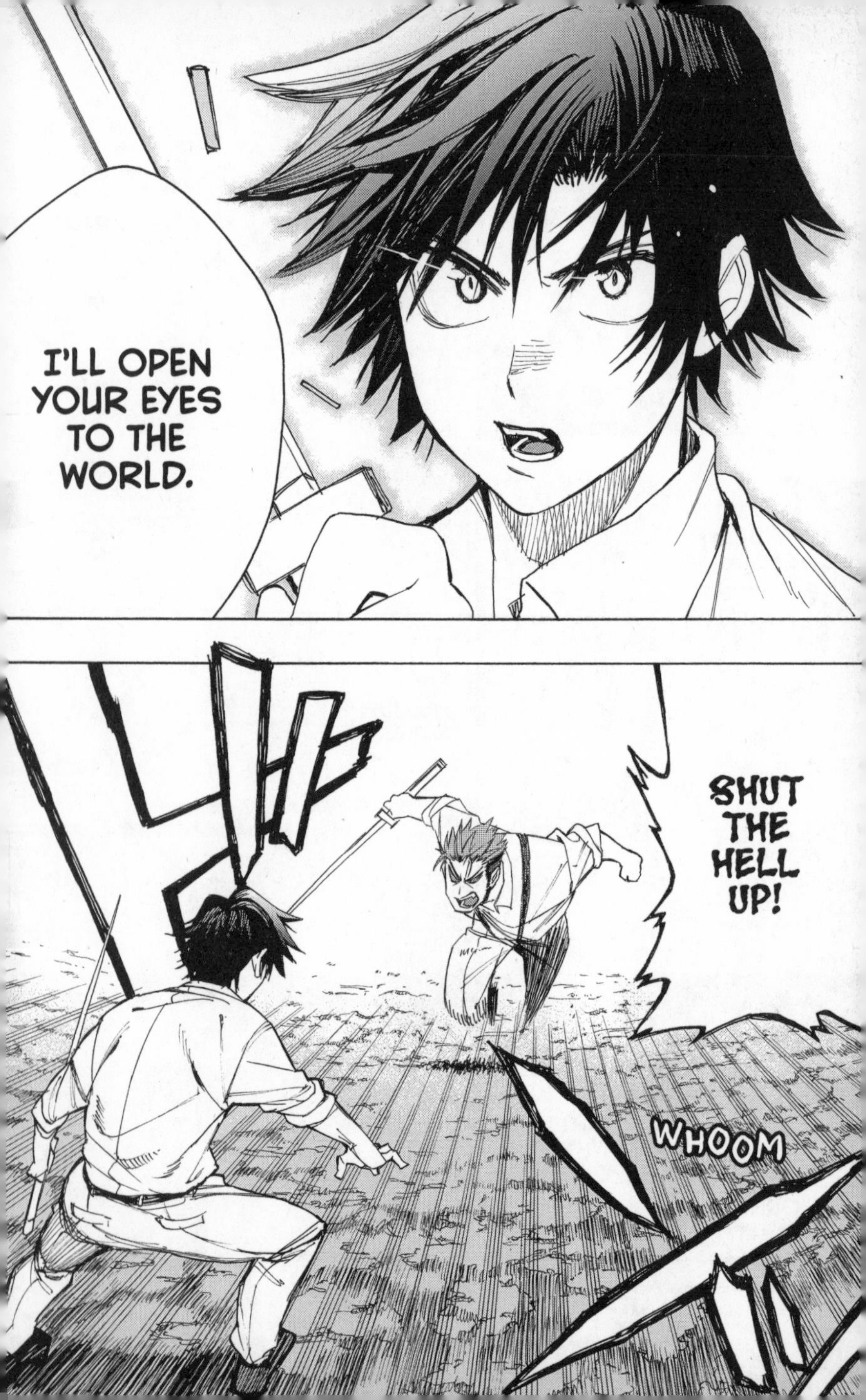
I'LL OPEN YOUR EYES TO THE WORLD.
SHUT THE HELL UP!
WHOOM

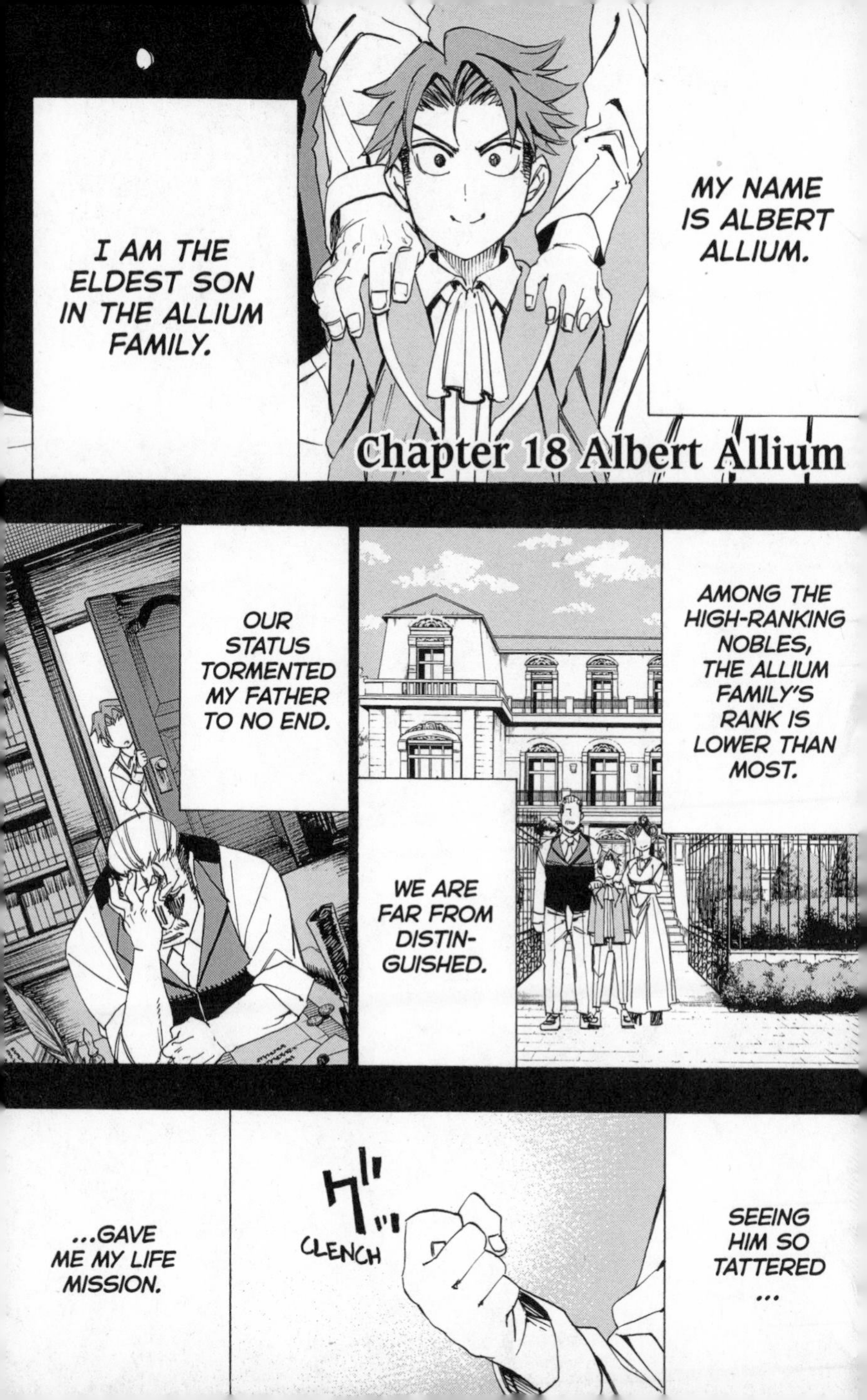
MY NAME IS ALBERT ALLIUM.
I AM THE ELDEST SON IN THE ALLIUM FAMILY.
Chapter 18 Albert Allium
AMONG THE HIGH-RANKING NOBLES, THE ALLIUM FAMILY'S RANK IS LOWER THAN MOST.
WE ARE FAR FROM DISTIN-GUISHED.
OUR STATUS TORMENTED MY FATHER TO NO END.
SEEING HIM SO TATTERED ...
CLENCH
...GAVE ME MY LIFE MISSION.

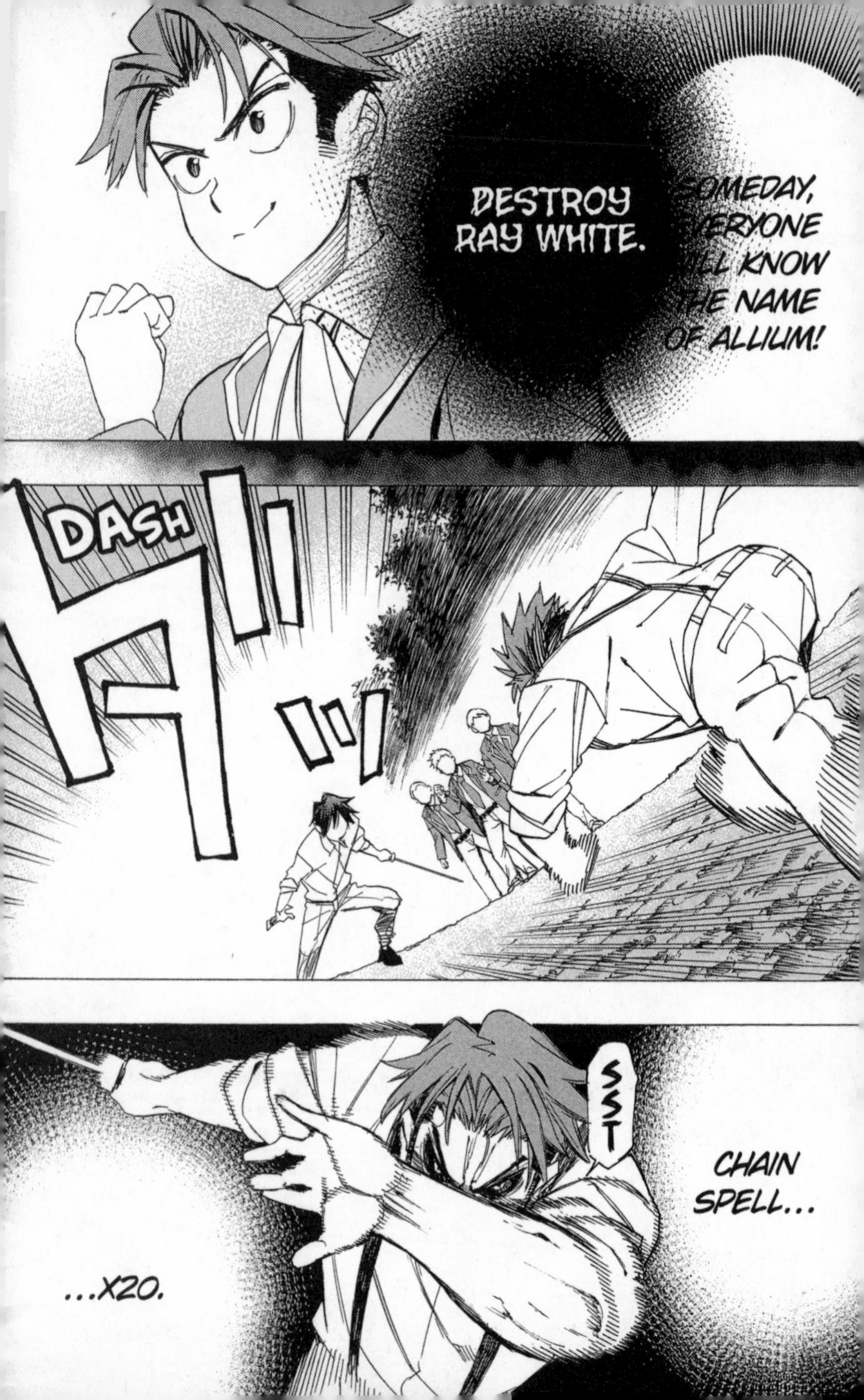
SOMEDAY, VERYONE LL KNOW THE NAME OF ALLIUM!
DESTROY RAY WHITE.
DASH
SST
CHAIN SPELL...
...X20.

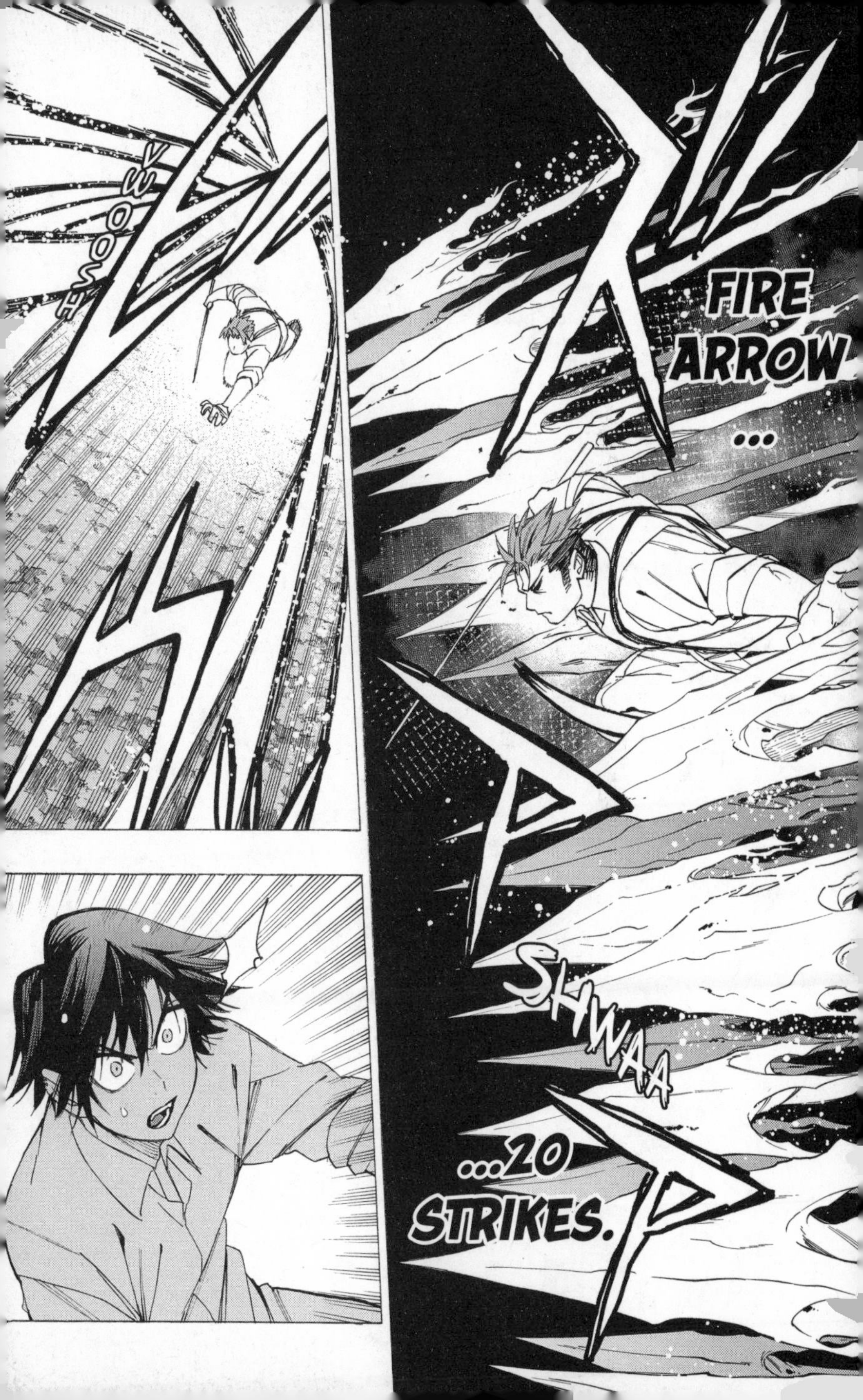
FIRE ARROW ...
SHWAA
...20 STRIKES.
VWOOSH

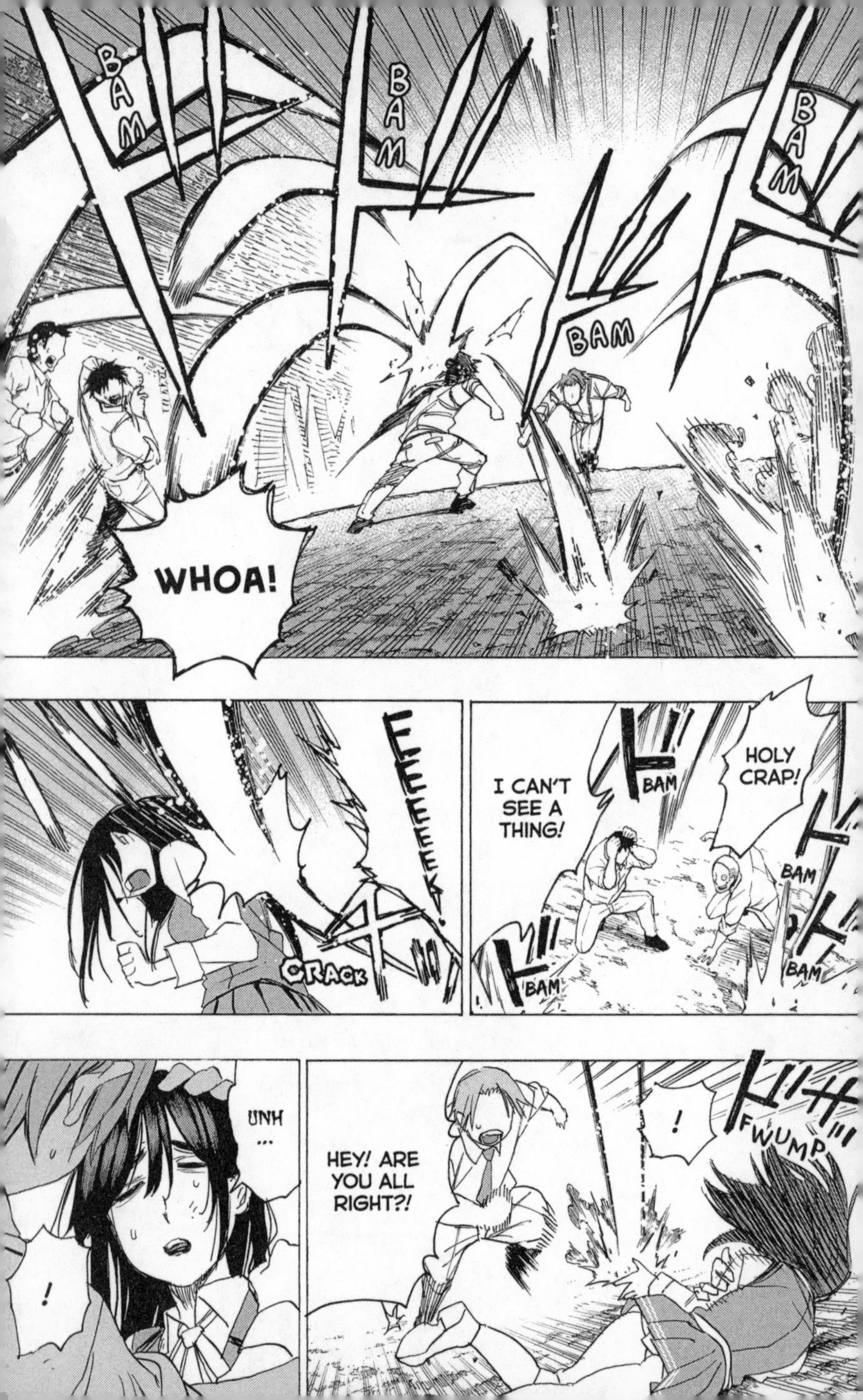
BAM
BAM
BAM
BAM
WHOA!
HOLY CRAP!
BAM
I CAN'T SEE A THING!
BAM
BAM
BAM
EEEEEEEK!
CRACK
FWUMP
!
HEY! ARE YOU ALL RIGHT?!
UNH ...
!

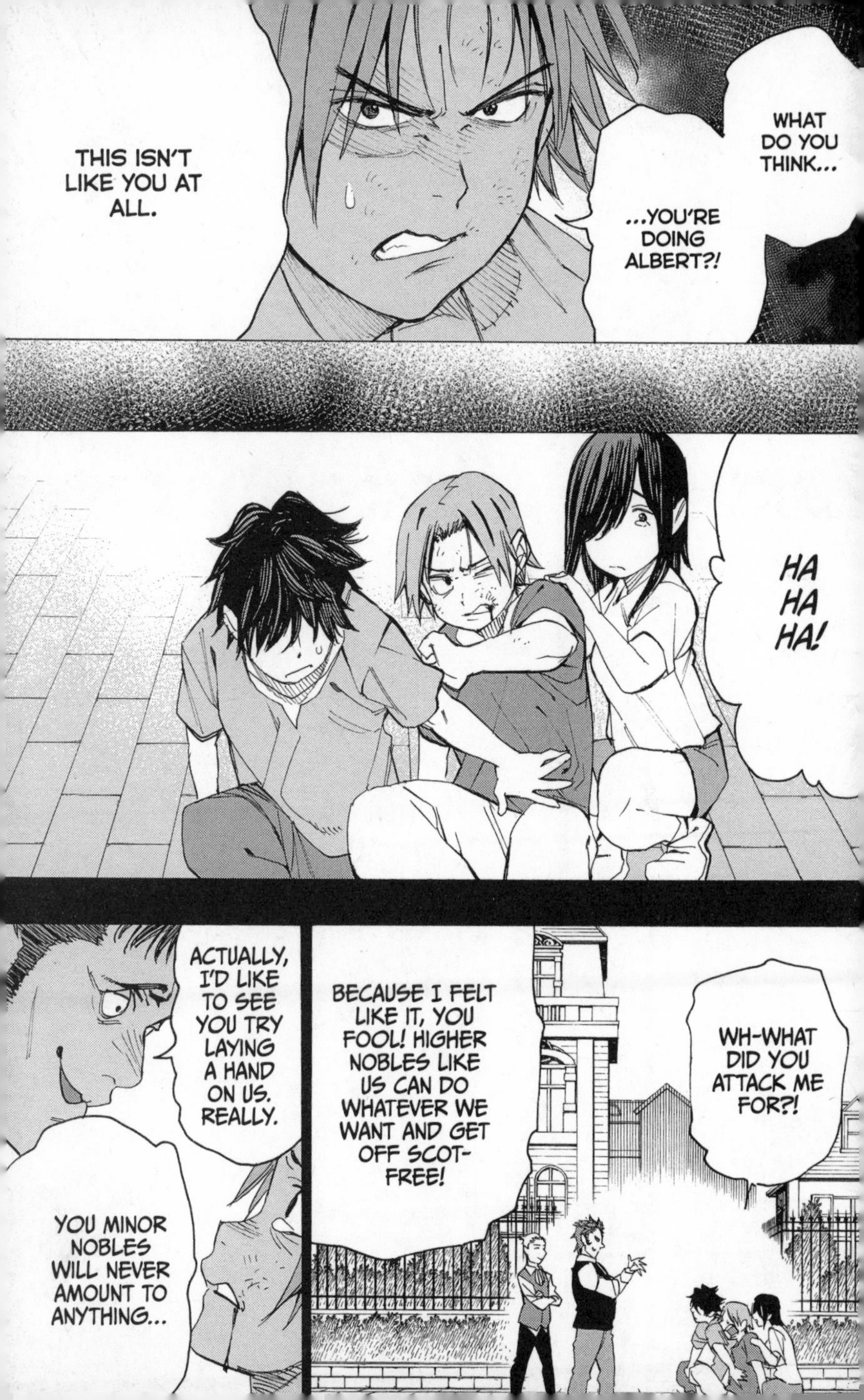
WHAT DO YOU THINK...
...YOU'RE DOING ALBERT?!
THIS ISN'T LIKE YOU AT ALL.
HA HA HA!
WH-WHAT DID YOU ATTACK ME FOR?!
BECAUSE I FELT LIKE IT, YOU FOOL! HIGHER NOBLES LIKE US CAN DO WHATEVER WE WANT AND GET OFF SCOT-FREE!
ACTUALLY, I'D LIKE TO SEE YOU TRY LAYING A HAND ON US. REALLY.
YOU MINOR NOBLES WILL NEVER AMOUNT TO ANYTHING...

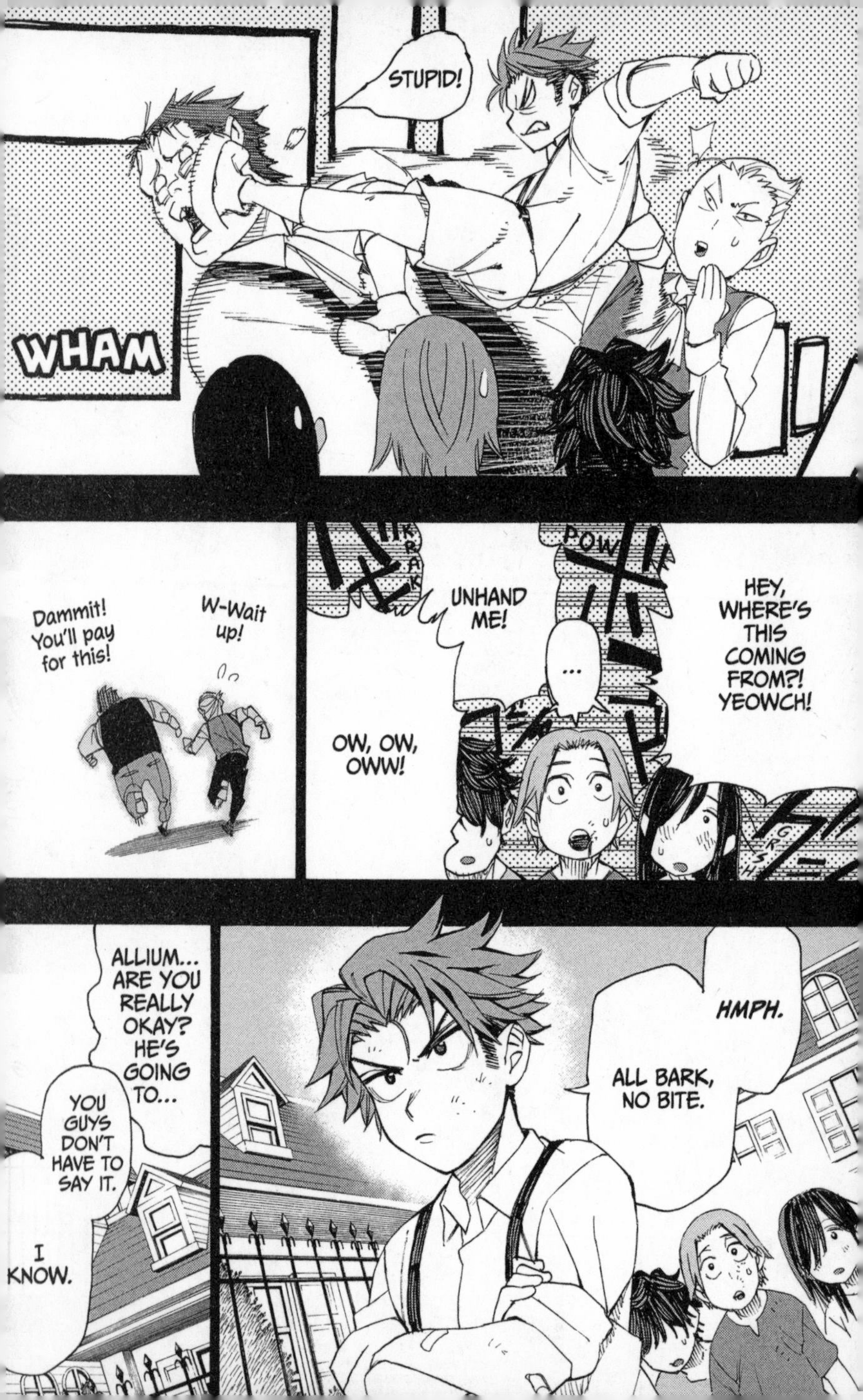
STUPID!
WHAM
POW
HEY, WHERE'S THIS COMING FROM?! YEOWCH!
KRAK
UNHAND ME!
...
OW, OW, OWW!
GRSH
W-Wait up!
Dammit! You'll pay for this!
HMPH.
ALL BARK, NO BITE.
ALLIUM... ARE YOU REALLY OKAY? HE'S GOING TO...
YOU GUYS DON'T HAVE TO SAY IT.
I KNOW.

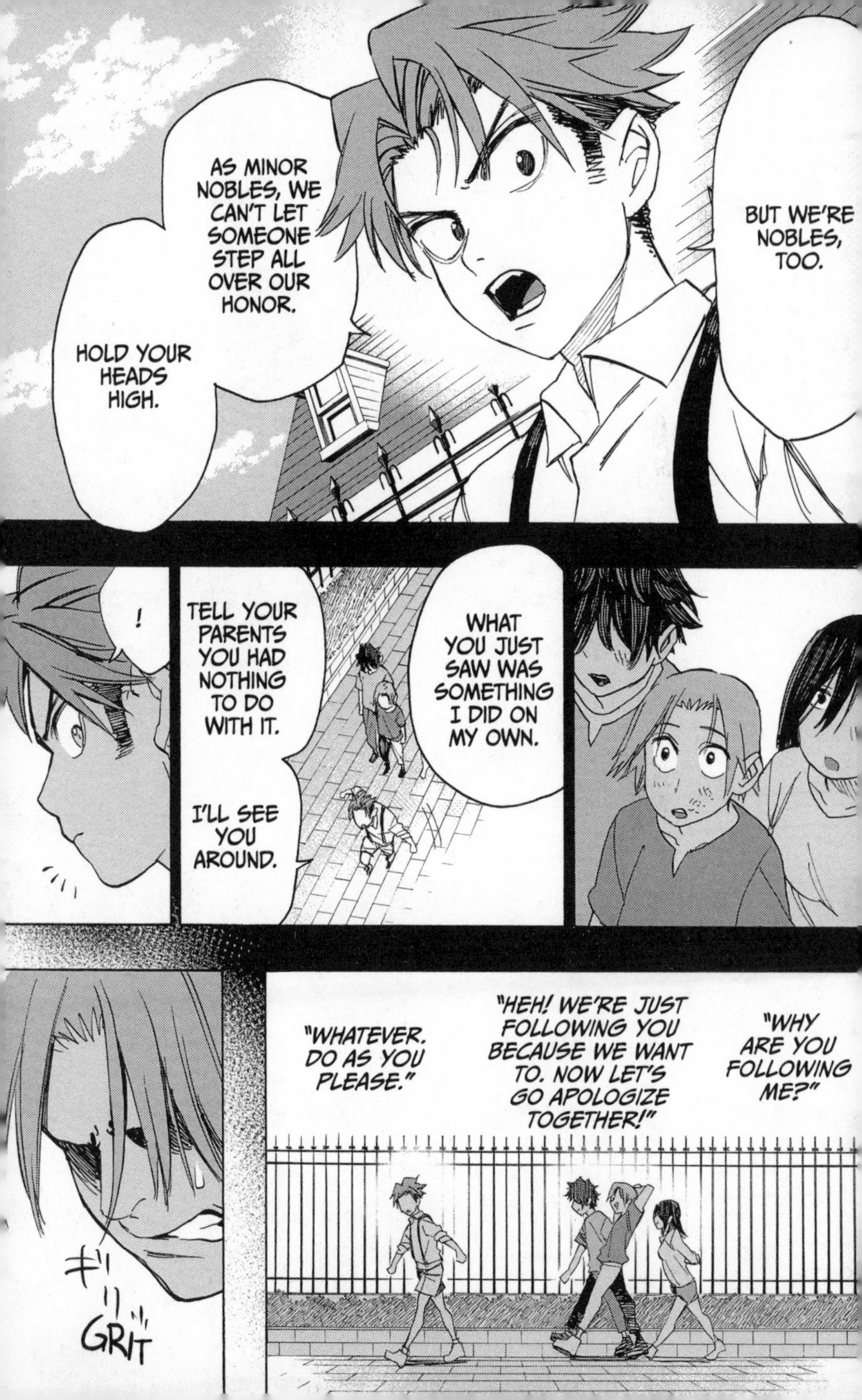
BUT WE'RE NOBLES, TOO.
AS MINOR NOBLES, WE CAN'T LET SOMEONE STEP ALL OVER OUR HONOR.
HOLD YOUR HEADS HIGH.
WHAT YOU JUST SAW WAS SOMETHING I DID ON MY OWN.
TELL YOUR PARENTS YOU HAD NOTHING TO DO WITH IT.
I'LL SEE YOU AROUND.
!
"WHY ARE YOU FOLLOWING ME?"
"HEH! WE'RE JUST FOLLOWING YOU BECAUSE WE WANT TO. NOW LET'S GO APOLOGIZE TOGETHER!"
"WHATEVER. DO AS YOU PLEASE."
ギリ
GRIT

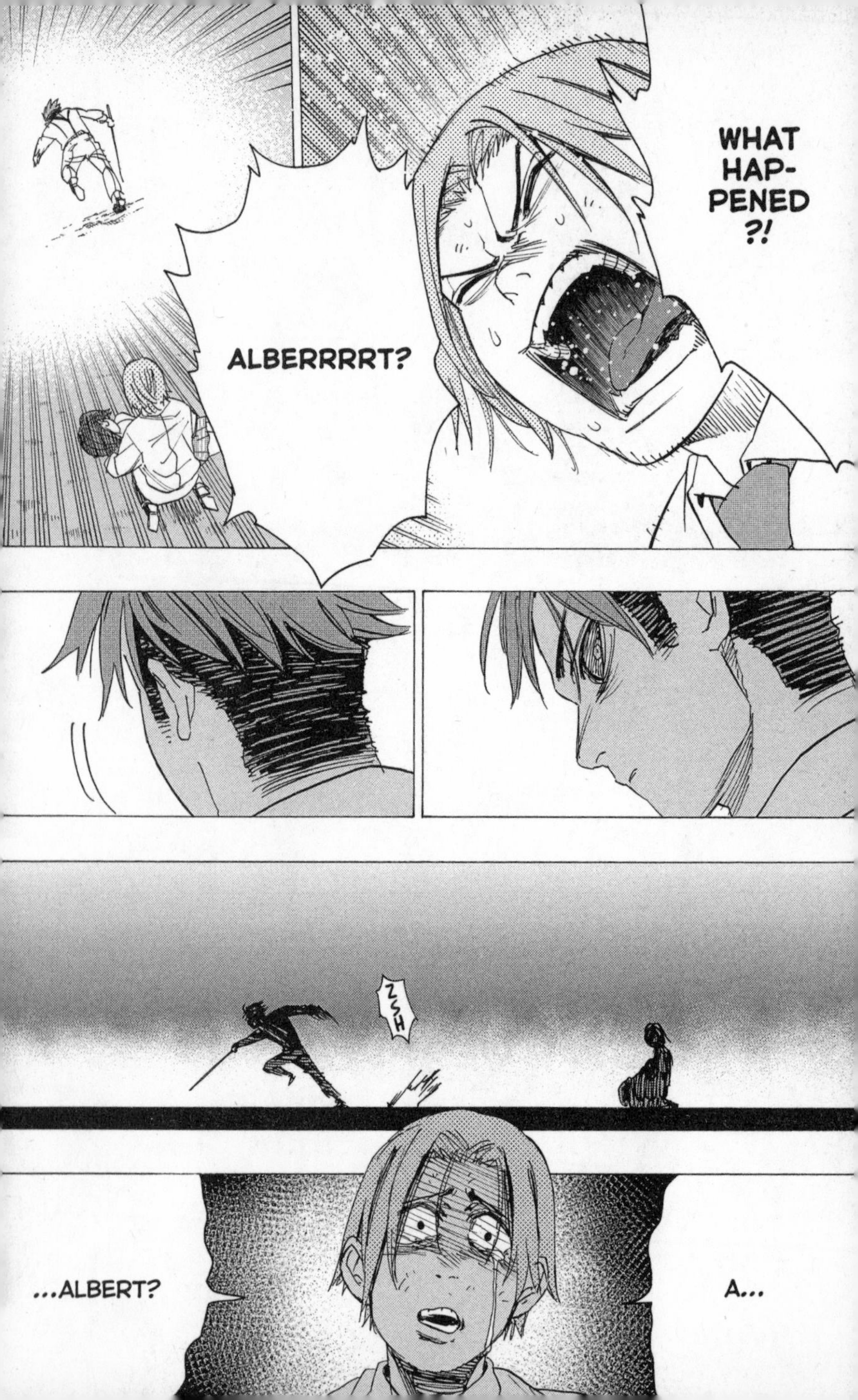
WHAT HAP-PENED?!
ALBERRRRT?
ZSH
A...
...ALBERT?

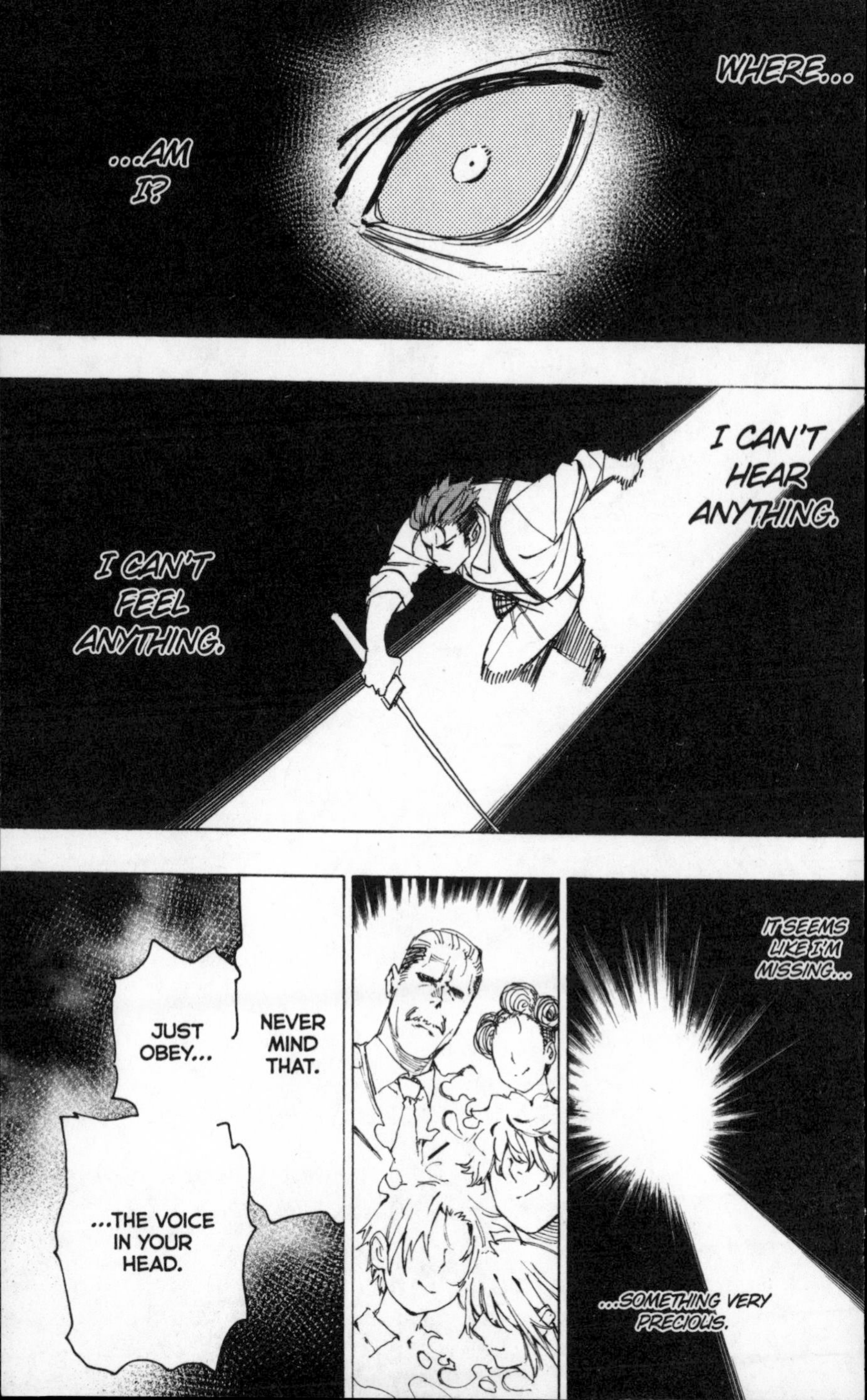
WHERE...
...AM I?
I CAN'T HEAR ANYTHING.
I CAN'T FEEL ANYTHING.
IT SEEMS LIKE I'M MISSING...
...SOMETHING VERY PRECIOUS.
NEVER MIND THAT.
JUST OBEY...
...THE VOICE IN YOUR HEAD.

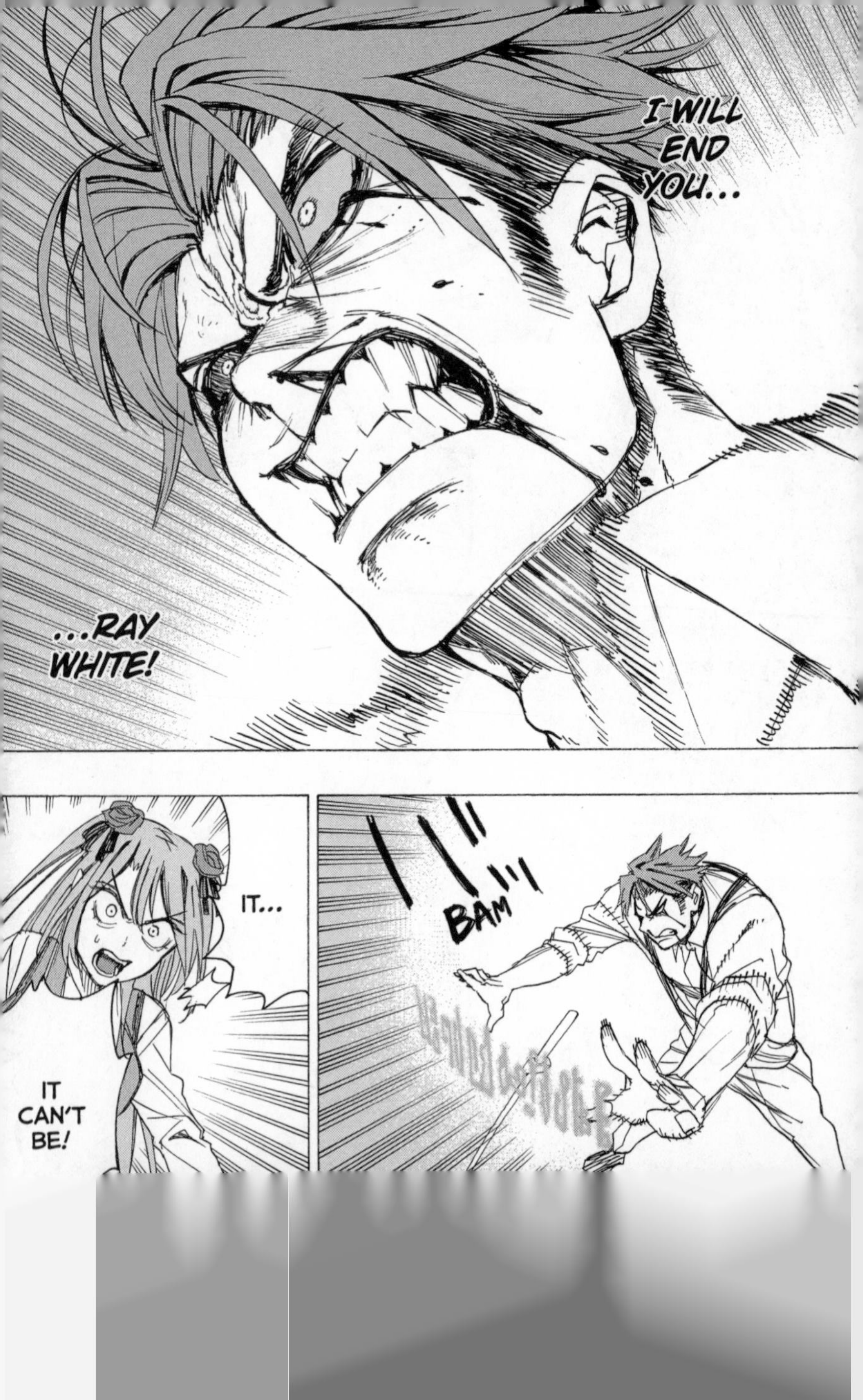
I WILL END YOU...
...RAY WHITE!
BAM
IT...
IT CAN'T BE!

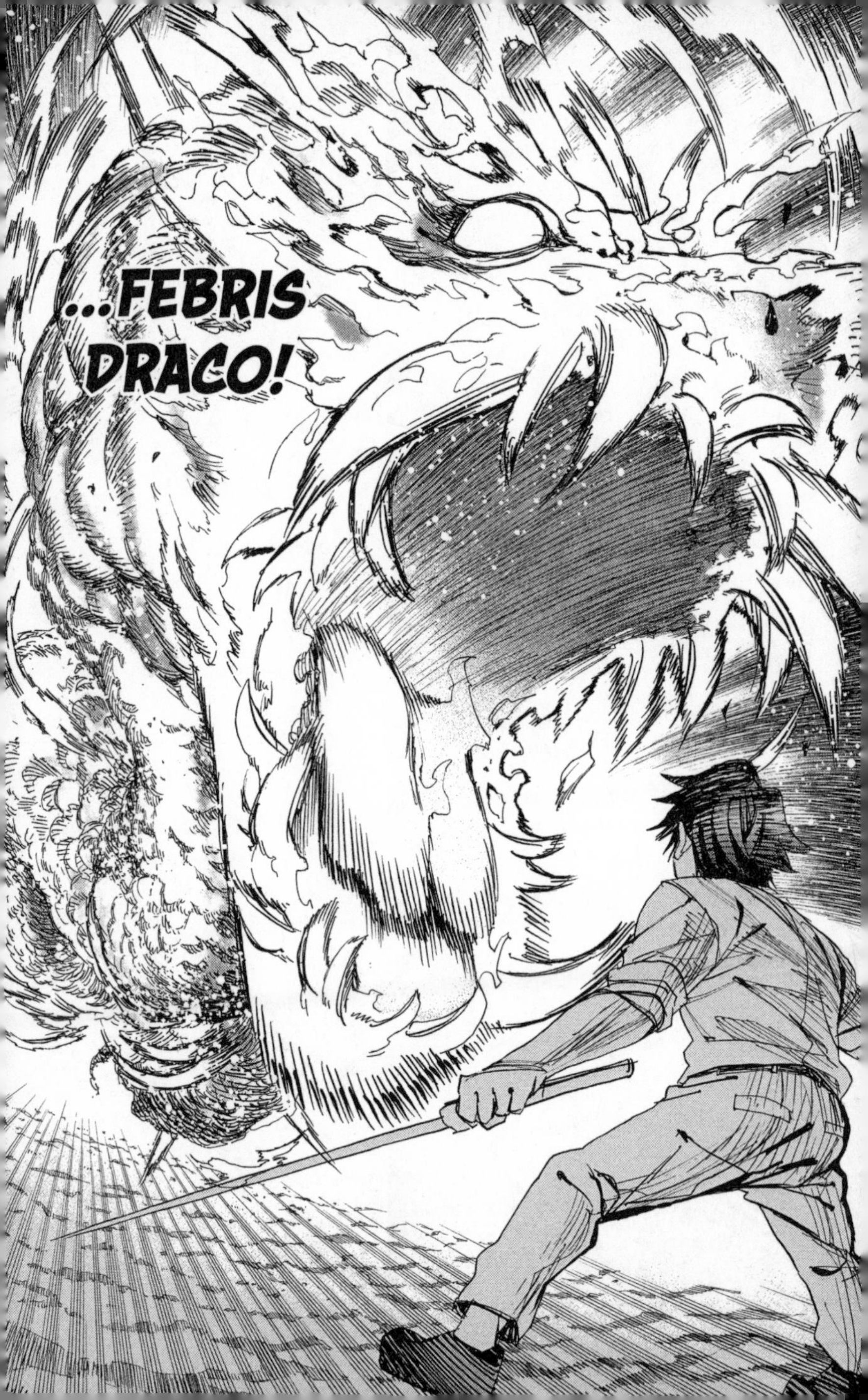
...FEBRIS DRACO!

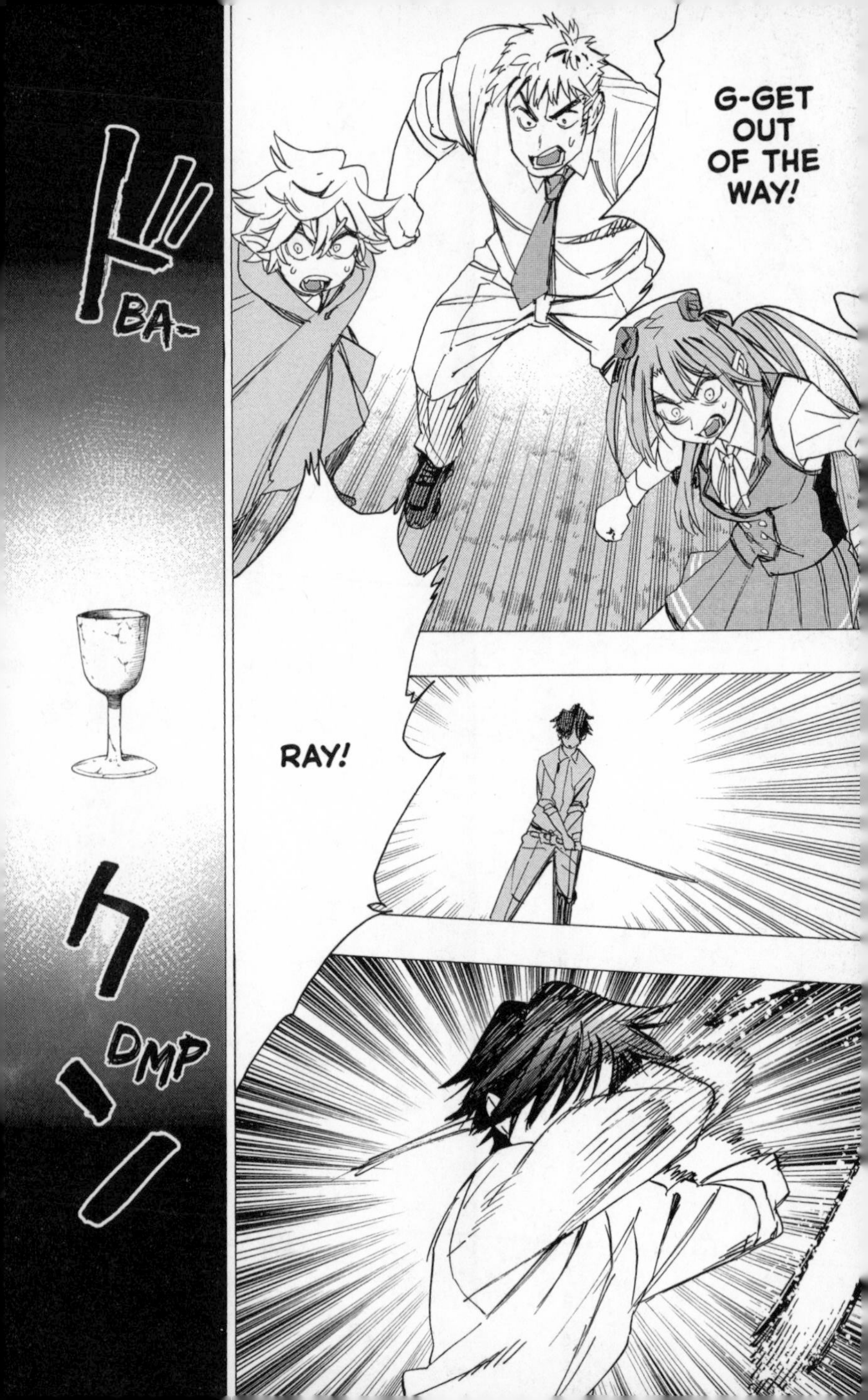
G-GET OUT OF THE WAY!
RAY!
BA-
DMP

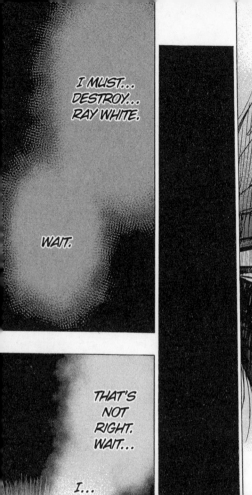

I MUST...
DESTROY...
RAY WHITE.

WAIT.

THAT'S
NOT
RIGHT.
WAIT...

I...

I'M...

FSH

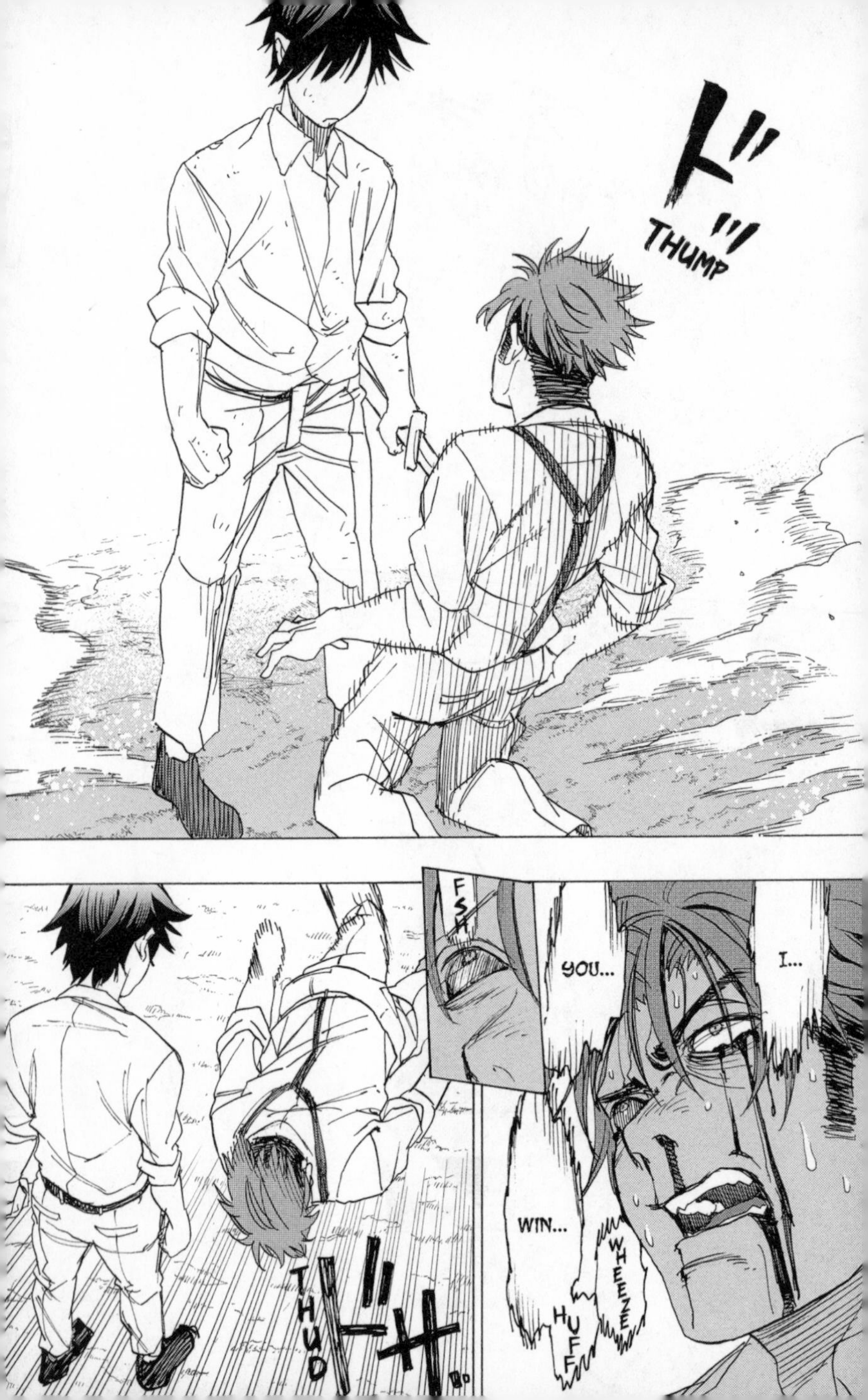
ド
THUMP
I...
YOU...
WIN...
WHEEZE
HUFF
FSH
THUD

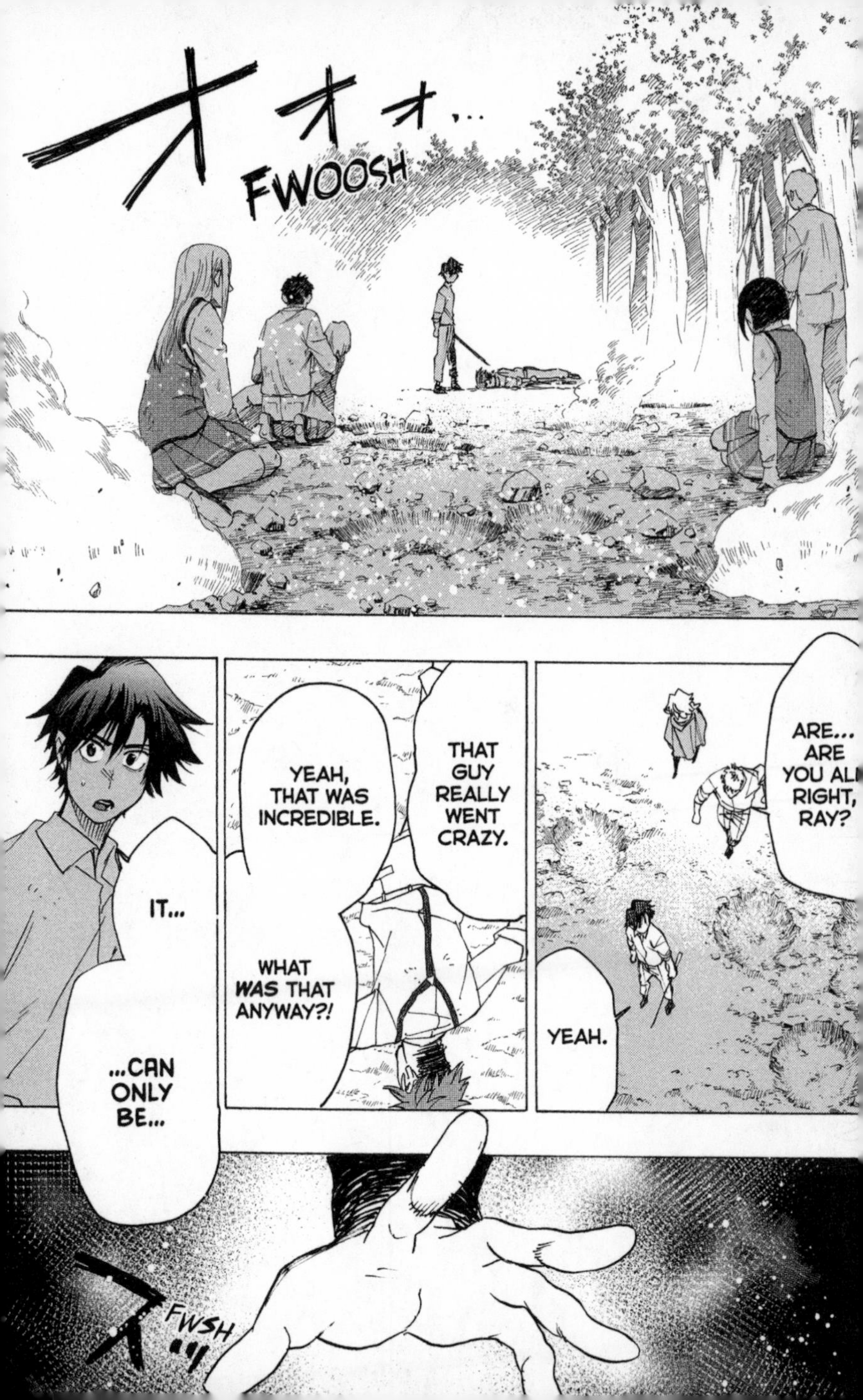
オォォ...
FWOOSH
ARE... ARE YOU ALL RIGHT, RAY?
YEAH.
THAT GUY REALLY WENT CRAZY.
YEAH, THAT WAS INCREDIBLE.
WHAT WAS THAT ANYWAY?!
IT...
...CAN ONLY BE...
FWSH

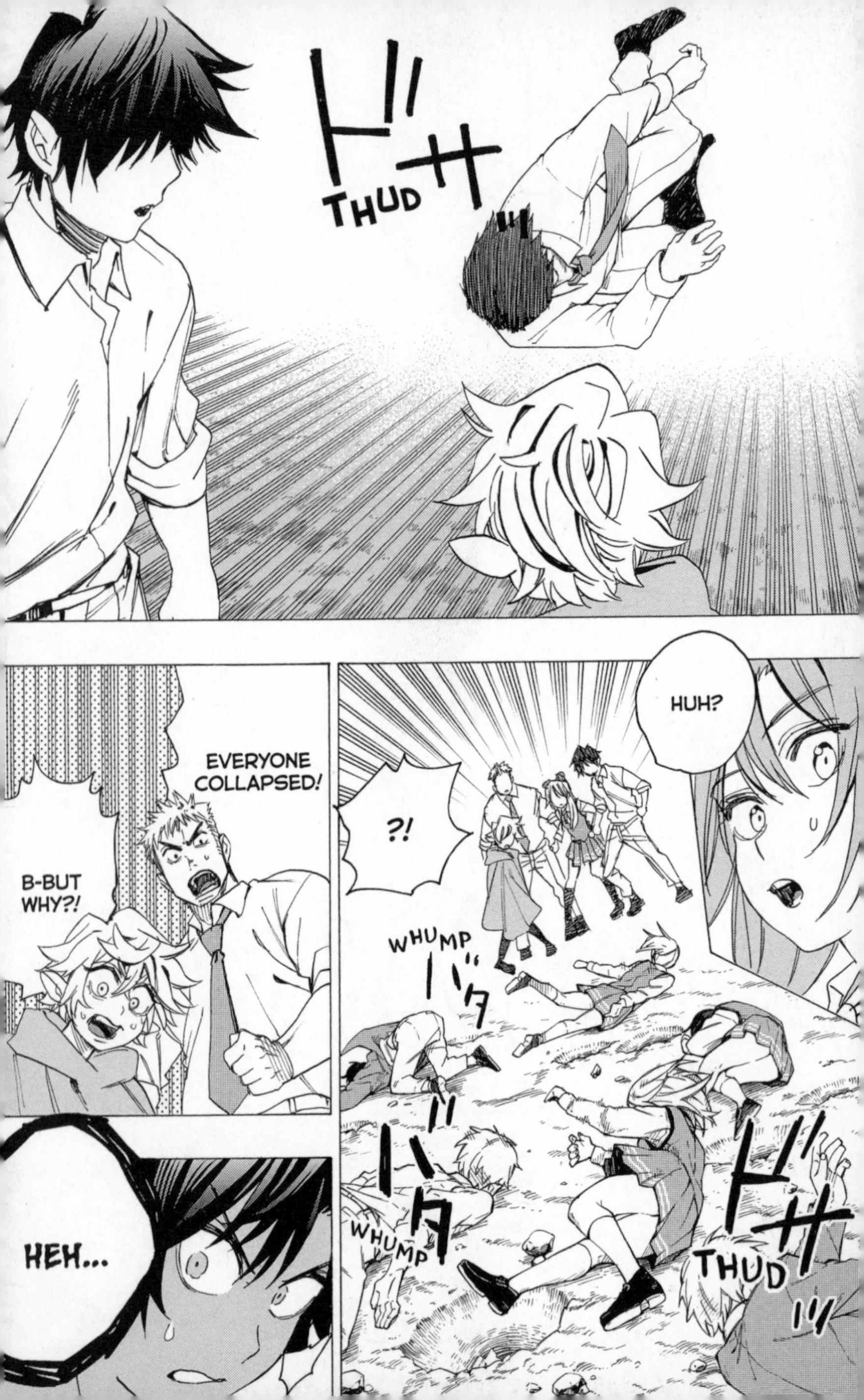
THUD
HUH?
?!
WHUMP
THUD
WHUMP
EVERYONE COLLAPSED!
B-BUT WHY?!
HEH...

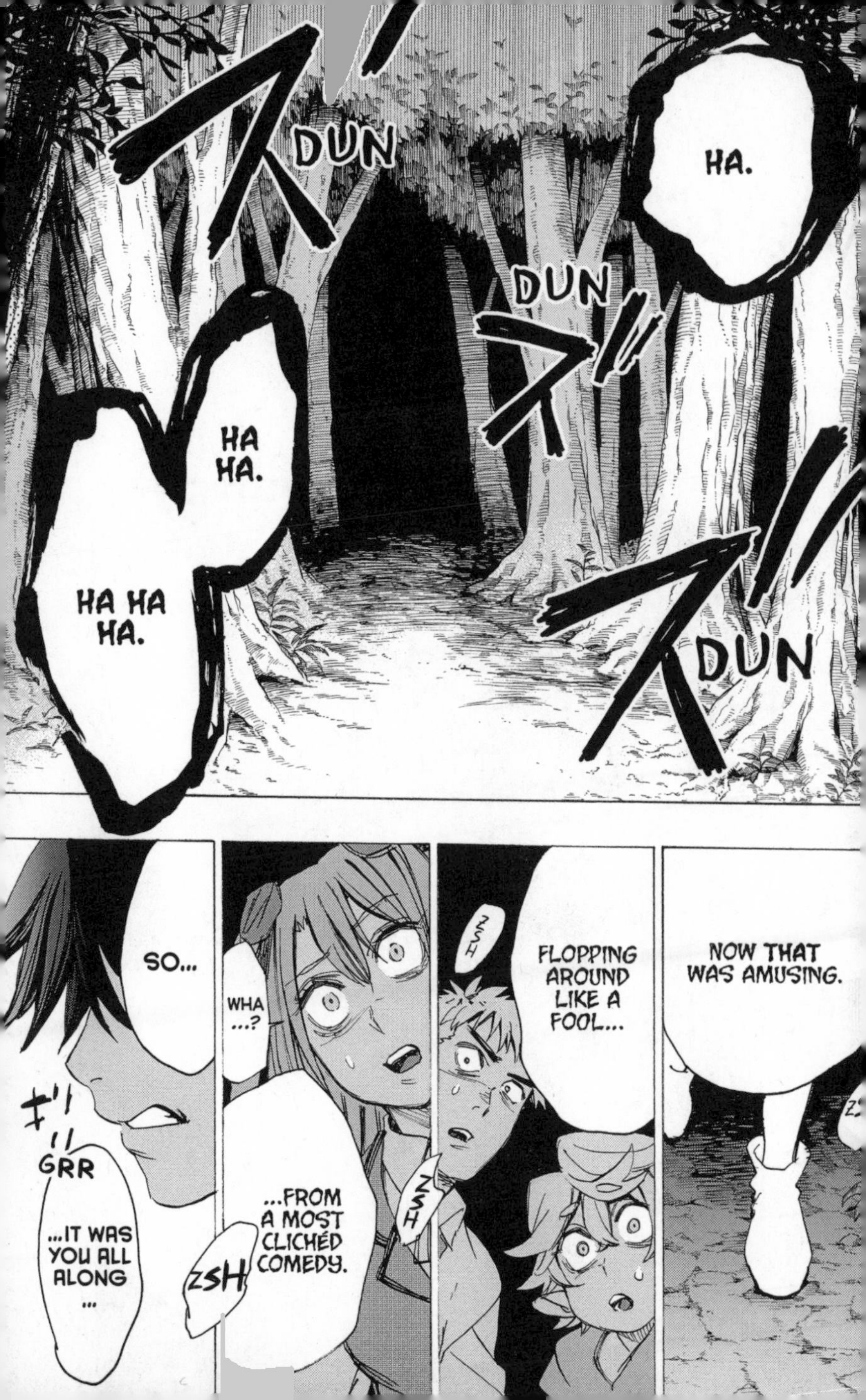
HA.
DUN
DUN
HA HA.
HA HA HA.
DUN
NOW THAT WAS AMUSING.
ZSH
FLOPPING AROUND LIKE A FOOL...
ZSH
WHA ...?
...FROM A MOST CLICHÉD COMEDY.
ZSH
SO...
GRR
...IT WAS YOU ALL ALONG ...

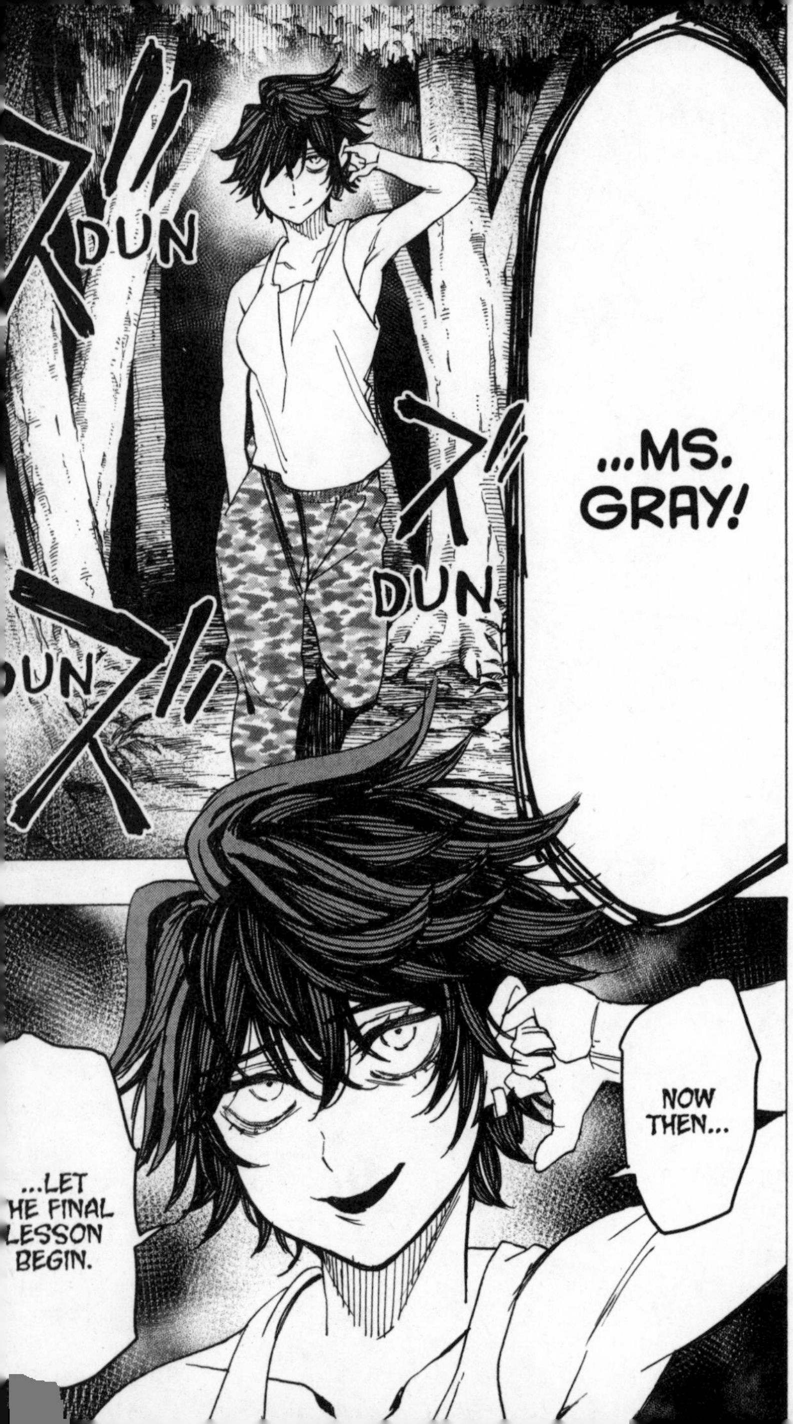
...MS. GRAY!
DUN
DUN
DUN
NOW THEN...
...LET HE FINAL LESSON BEGIN.

Chapter 19 The Mastermind

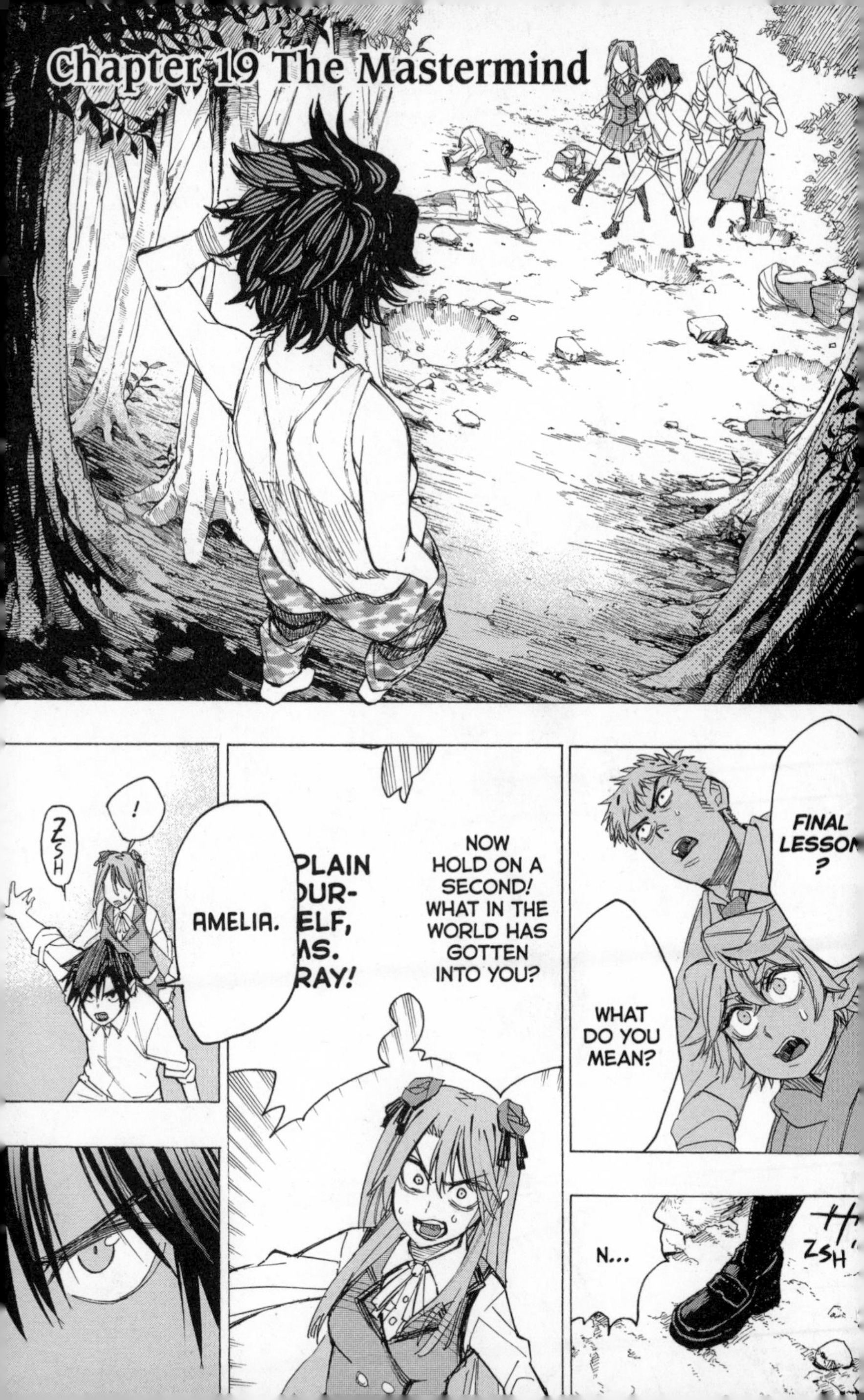
FINAL LESSON?
WHAT DO YOU MEAN?
N...
ZSH
NOW HOLD ON A SECOND! WHAT IN THE WORLD HAS GOTTEN INTO YOU?
PLAIN OUR- ELF, MS. RAY!
AMELIA.
!
ZSH

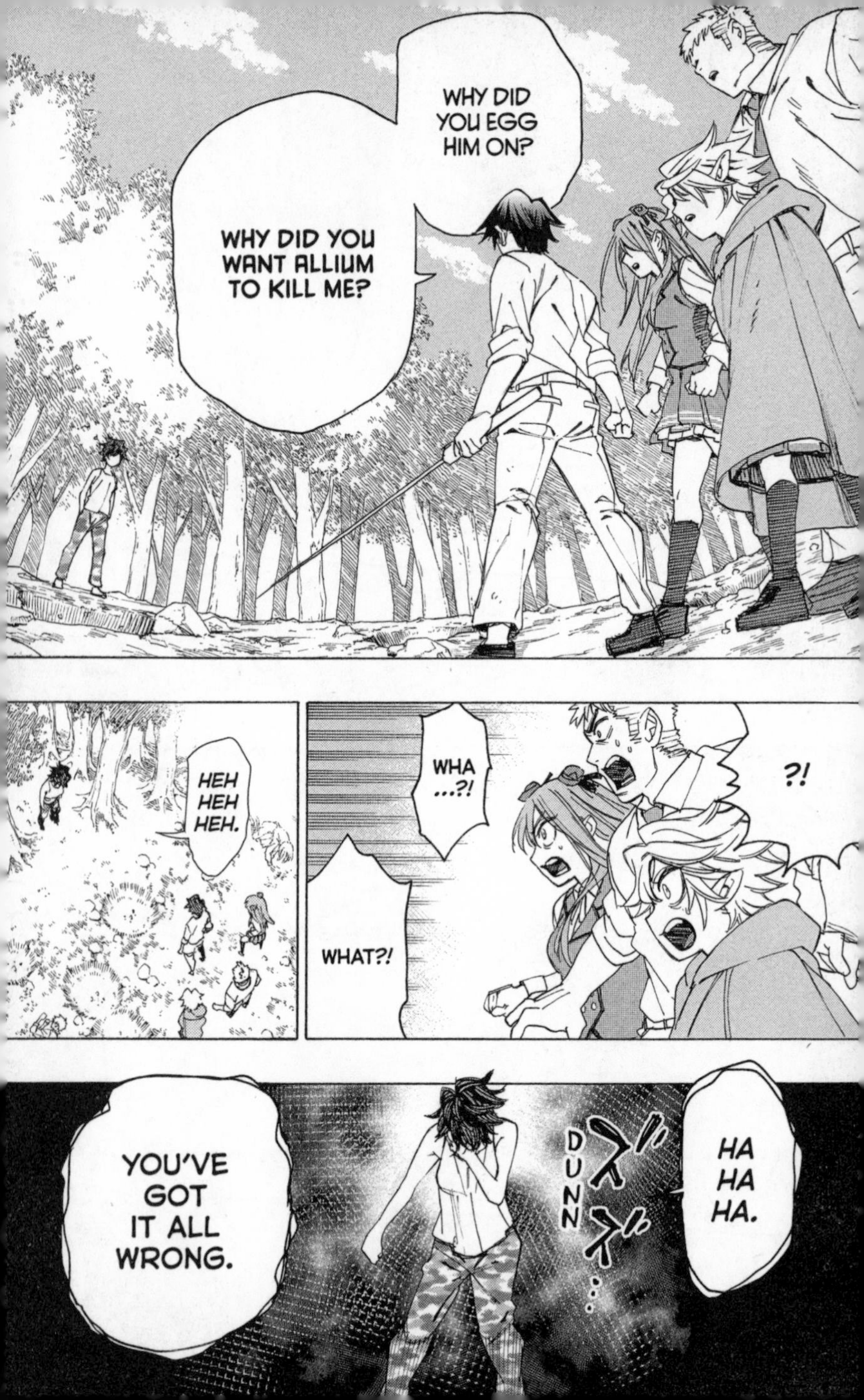
WHY DID YOU EGG HIM ON?
WHY DID YOU WANT ALLIUM TO KILL ME?
?!
WHA ...?!
WHAT?!
HEH HEH HEH.
HA HA HA.
DUNN
YOU'VE GOT IT ALL WRONG.

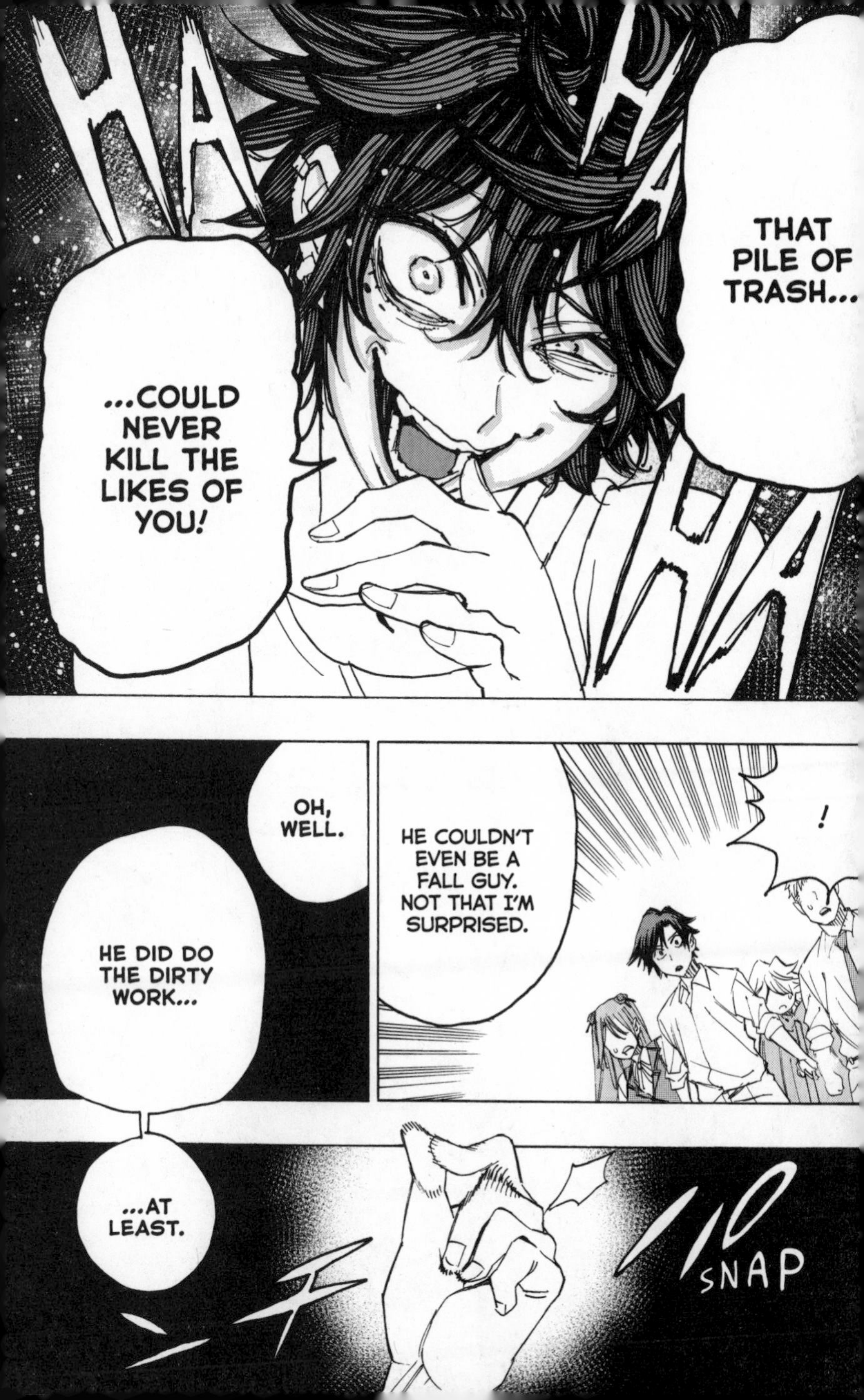

HA HA
THAT PILE OF TRASH...
HA
...COULD NEVER KILL THE LIKES OF YOU!
HAHA
!
HE COULDN'T EVEN BE A FALL GUY. NOT THAT I'M SURPRISED.
OH, WELL.
HE DID DO THE DIRTY WORK...
...AT LEAST.
SNAP

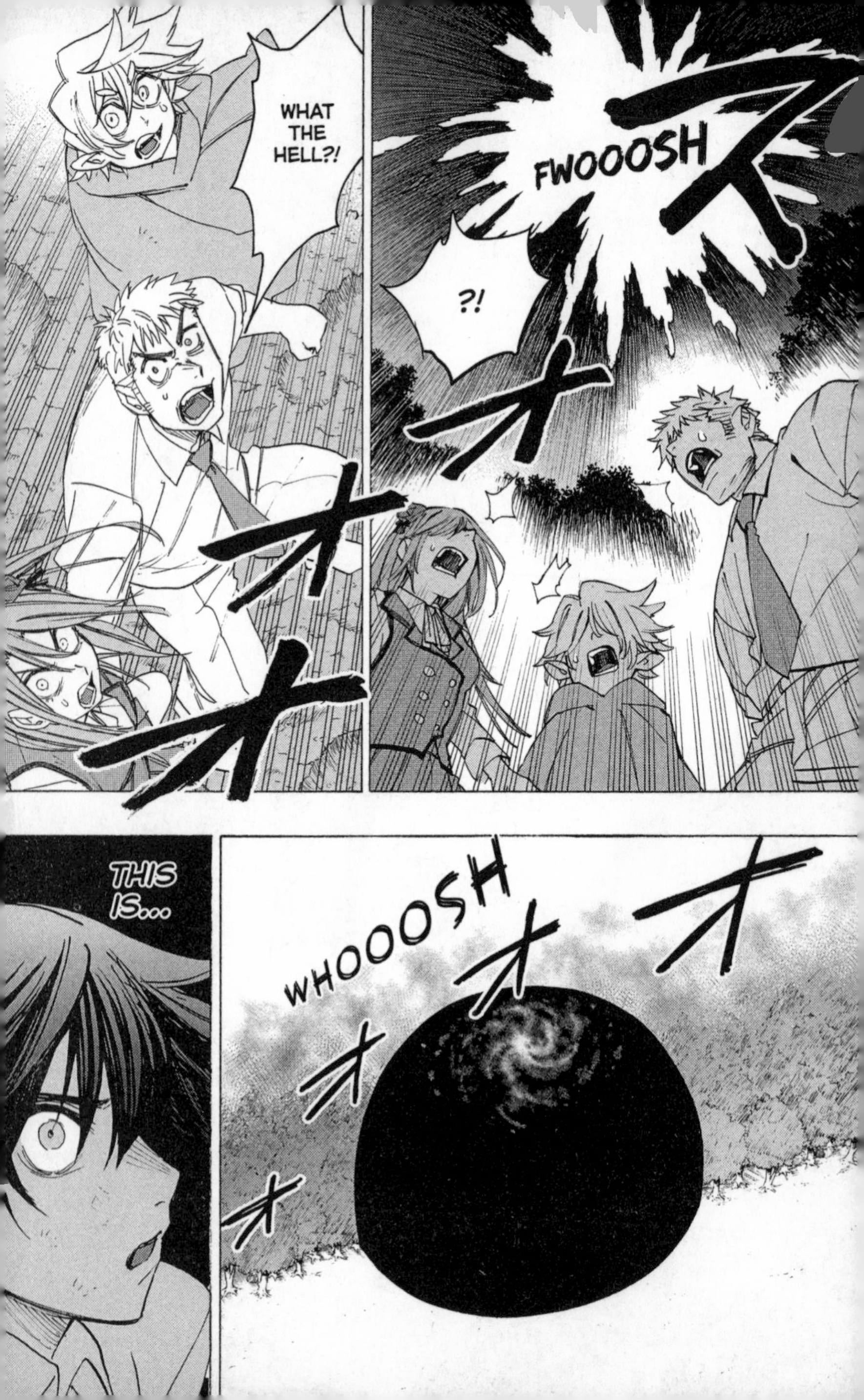
FWOOOSH
?!
WHAT THE HELL?!
WHOOOSH
THIS IS...

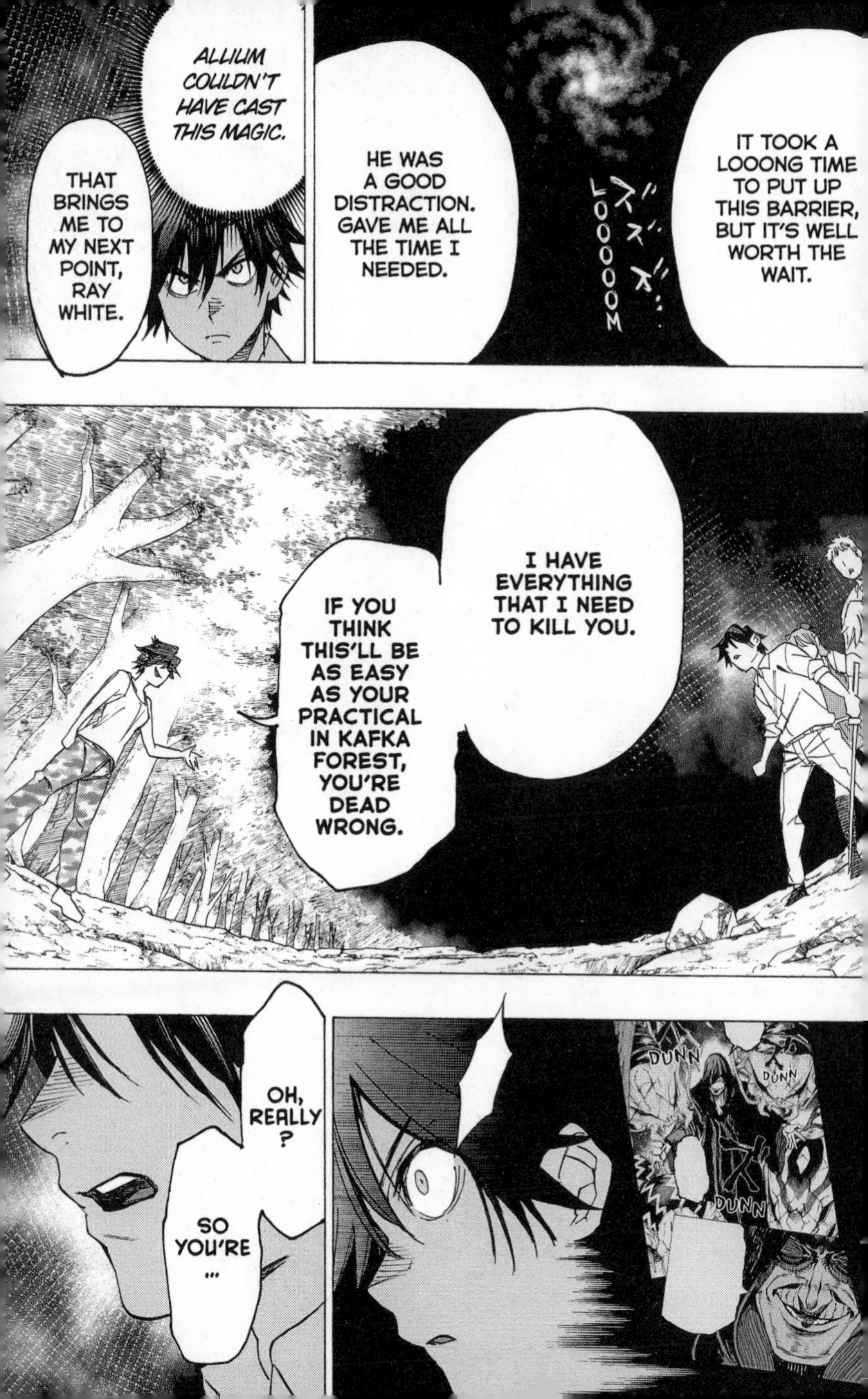
IT TOOK A LOOONG TIME TO PUT UP THIS BARRIER, BUT IT'S WELL WORTH THE WAIT.
LOOOOOM
HE WAS A GOOD DISTRACTION. GAVE ME ALL THE TIME I NEEDED.
ALLIUM COULDN'T HAVE CAST THIS MAGIC.
THAT BRINGS ME TO MY NEXT POINT, RAY WHITE.
I HAVE EVERYTHING THAT I NEED TO KILL YOU.
IF YOU THINK THIS'LL BE AS EASY AS YOUR PRACTICAL IN KAFKA FOREST, YOU'RE DEAD WRONG.
DUNN
DUNN
DUNN
OH, REALLY?
SO YOU'RE ...

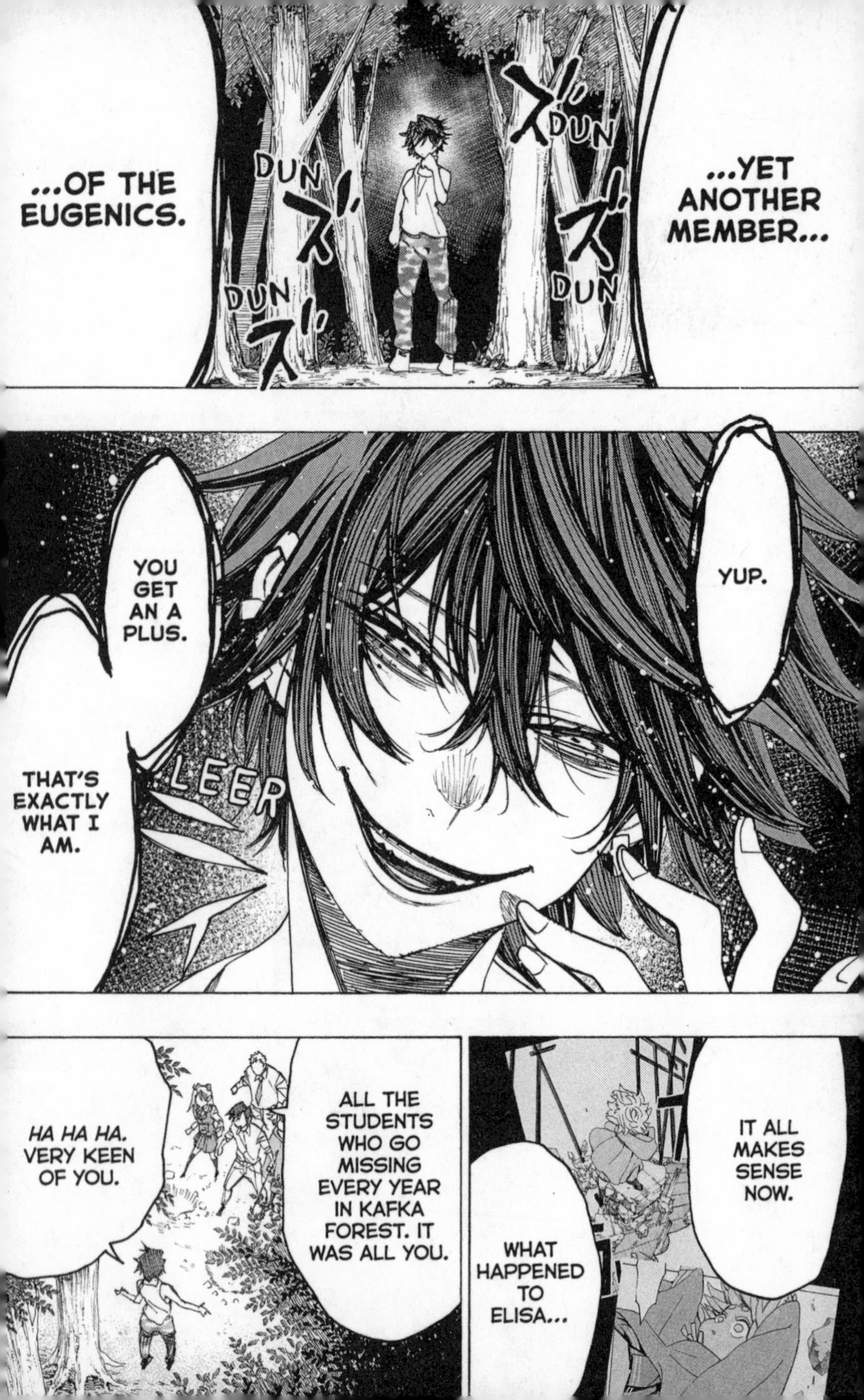
DUN
...YET ANOTHER MEMBER...
DUN
DUN
DUN
...OF THE EUGENICS.
YUP.
YOU GET AN A PLUS.
LEER
THAT'S EXACTLY WHAT I AM.
IT ALL MAKES SENSE NOW.
WHAT HAPPENED TO ELISA...
ALL THE STUDENTS WHO GO MISSING EVERY YEAR IN KAFKA FOREST. IT WAS ALL YOU.
HA HA HA. VERY KEEN OF YOU.

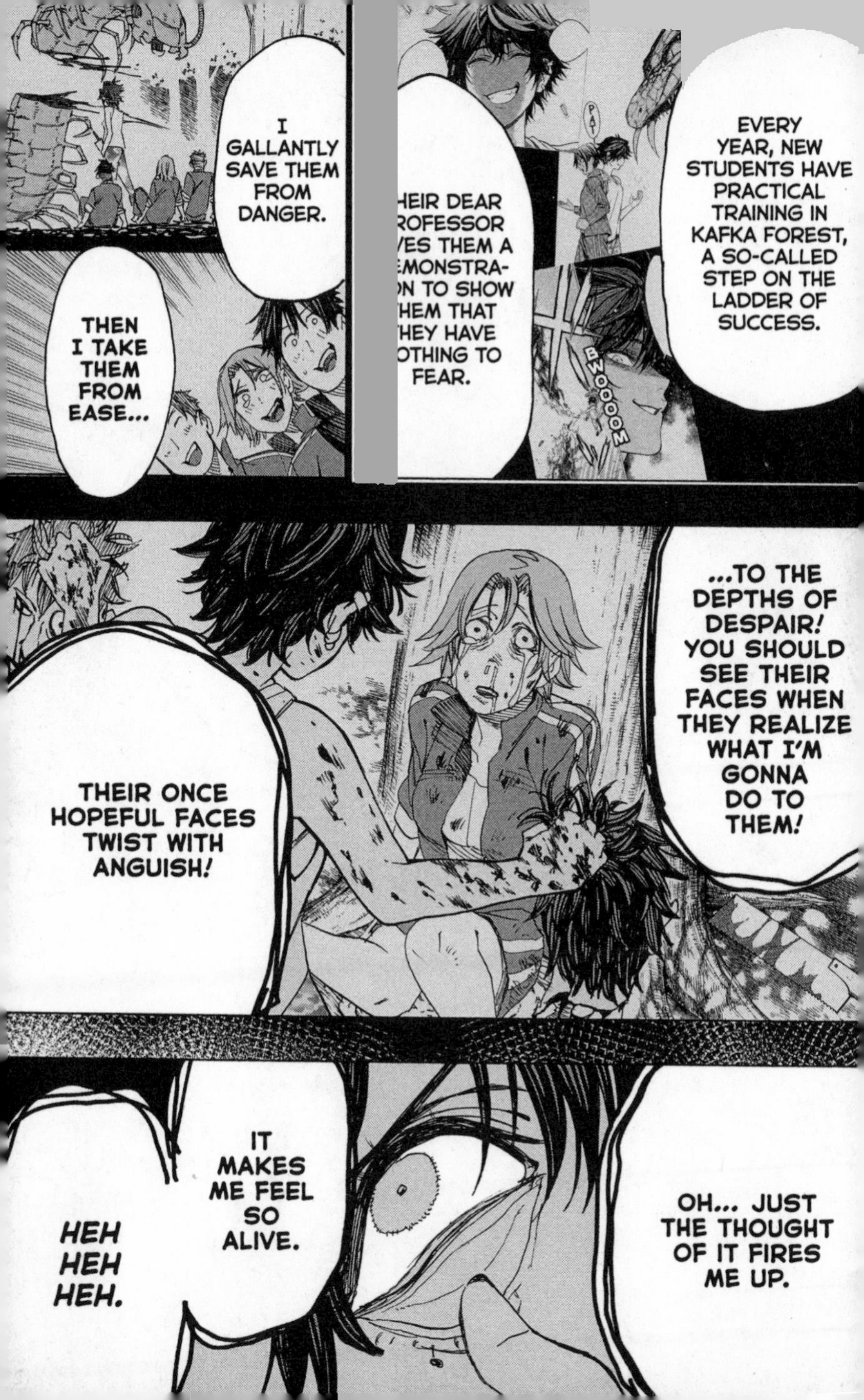
EVERY YEAR, NEW STUDENTS HAVE PRACTICAL TRAINING IN KAFKA FOREST, A SO-CALLED STEP ON THE LADDER OF SUCCESS.
PAT
HEIR DEAR ROFESSOR VES THEM A EMONSTRA- ON TO SHOW HEM THAT HEY HAVE OTHING TO FEAR.
BWOOOOM
I GALLANTLY SAVE THEM FROM DANGER.
THEN I TAKE THEM FROM EASE...
...TO THE DEPTHS OF DESPAIR! YOU SHOULD SEE THEIR FACES WHEN THEY REALIZE WHAT I'M GONNA DO TO THEM!
THEIR ONCE HOPEFUL FACES TWIST WITH ANGUISH!
OH... JUST THE THOUGHT OF IT FIRES ME UP.
IT MAKES ME FEEL SO ALIVE.
HEH HEH HEH.

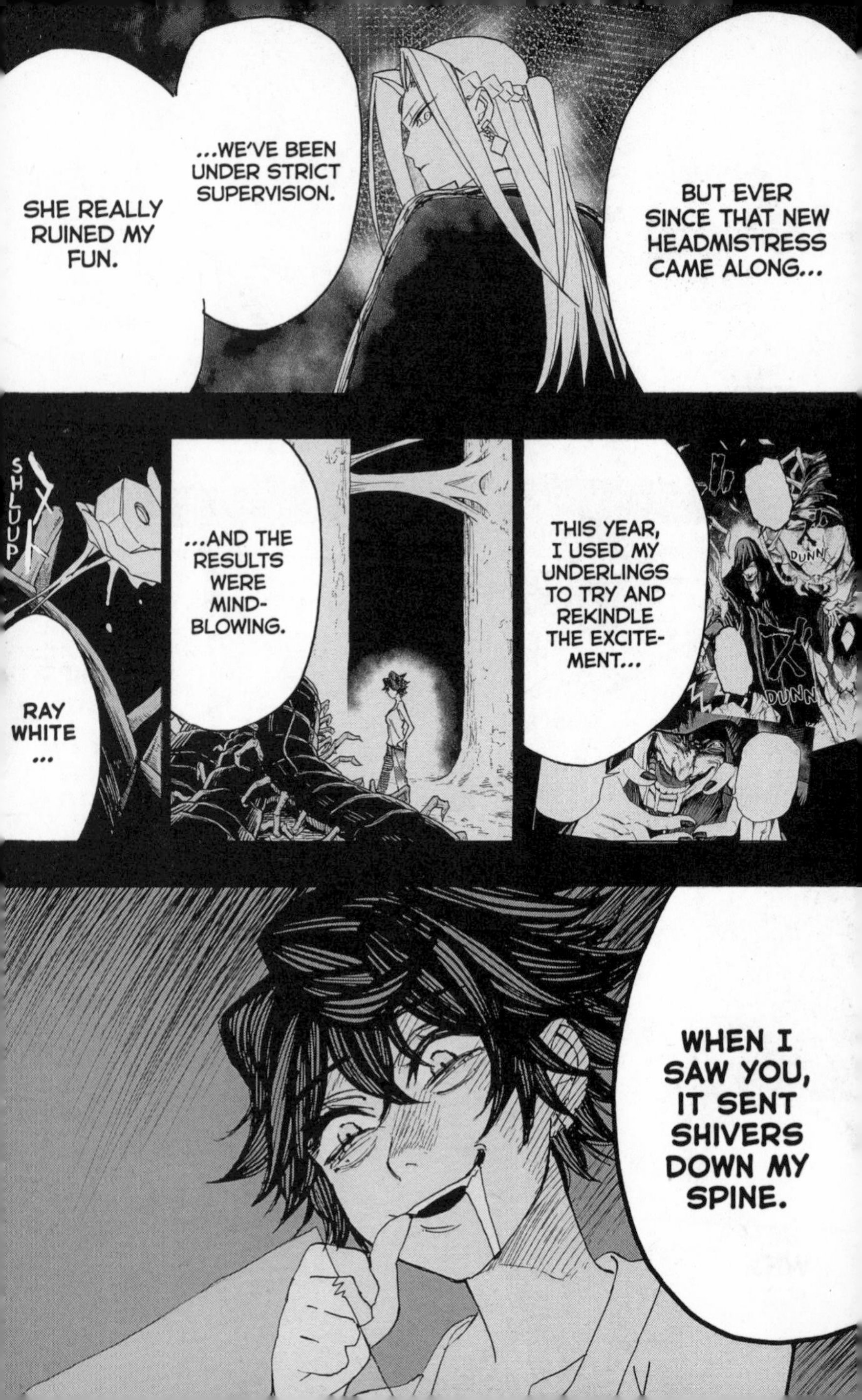
BUT EVER SINCE THAT NEW HEADMISTRESS CAME ALONG...
...WE'VE BEEN UNDER STRICT SUPERVISION.
SHE REALLY RUINED MY FUN.
THIS YEAR, I USED MY UNDERLINGS TO TRY AND REKINDLE THE EXCITE-MENT...
DUNN
DUNN
...AND THE RESULTS WERE MIND-BLOWING.
SHLUUP
RAY WHITE ...
WHEN I SAW YOU, IT SENT SHIVERS DOWN MY SPINE.

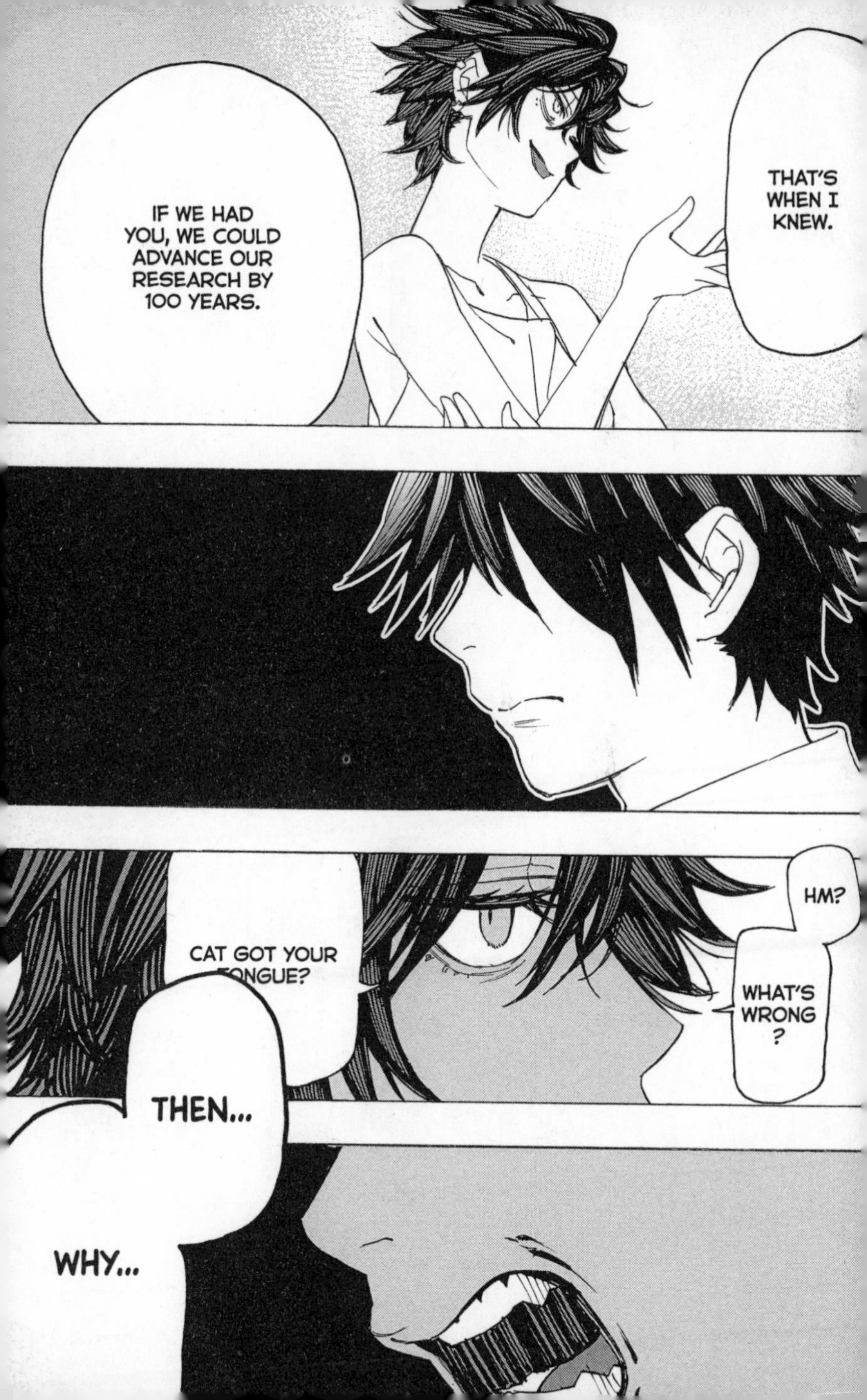
THAT'S WHEN I KNEW.
IF WE HAD YOU, WE COULD ADVANCE OUR RESEARCH BY 100 YEARS.
HM?
WHAT'S WRONG?
CAT GOT YOUR TONGUE?
THEN...
WHY...

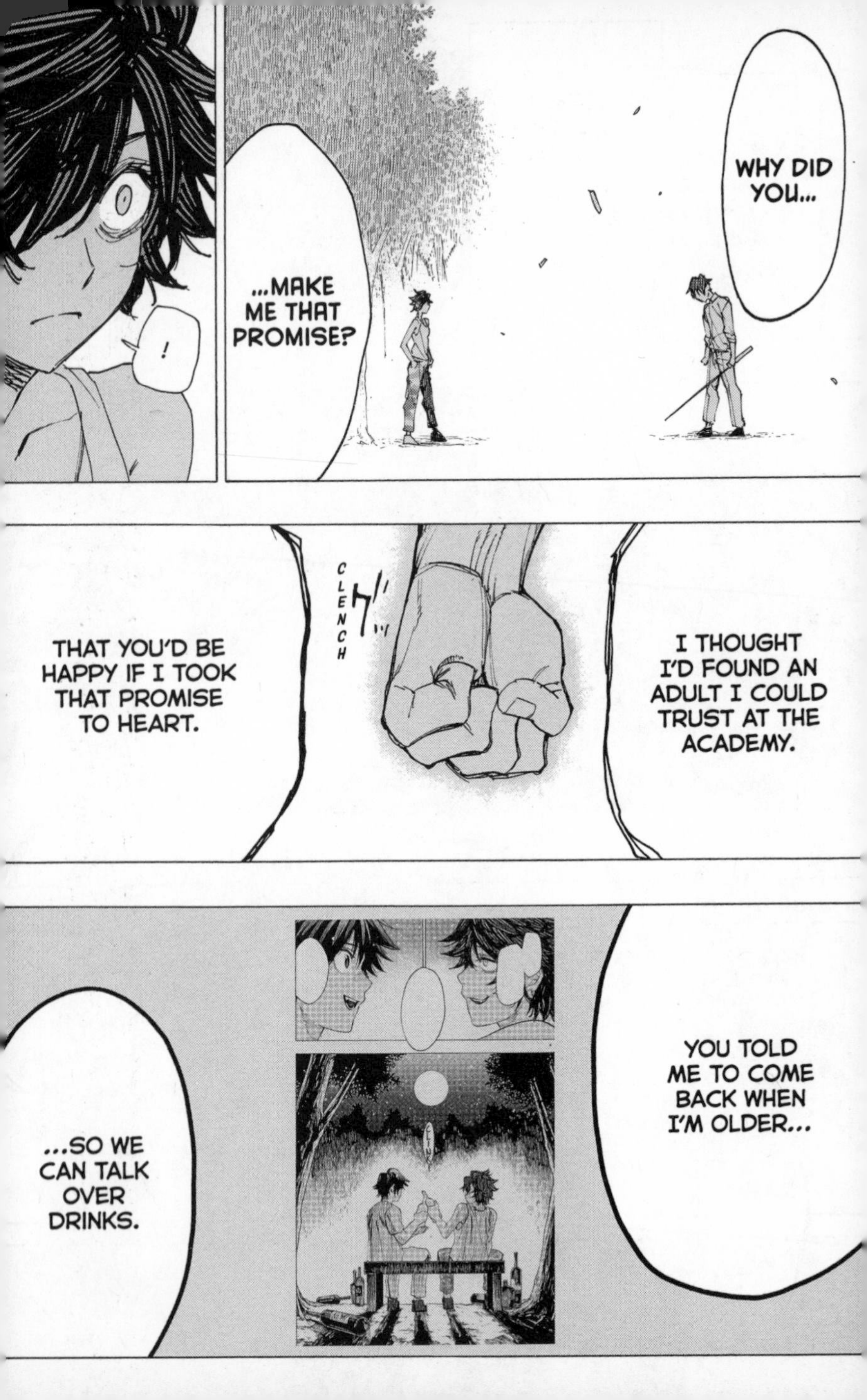
WHY DID YOU...
...MAKE ME THAT PROMISE?
!
I THOUGHT I'D FOUND AN ADULT I COULD TRUST AT THE ACADEMY.
CLENCH
THAT YOU'D BE HAPPY IF I TOOK THAT PROMISE TO HEART.
YOU TOLD ME TO COME BACK WHEN I'M OLDER...
...SO WE CAN TALK OVER DRINKS.

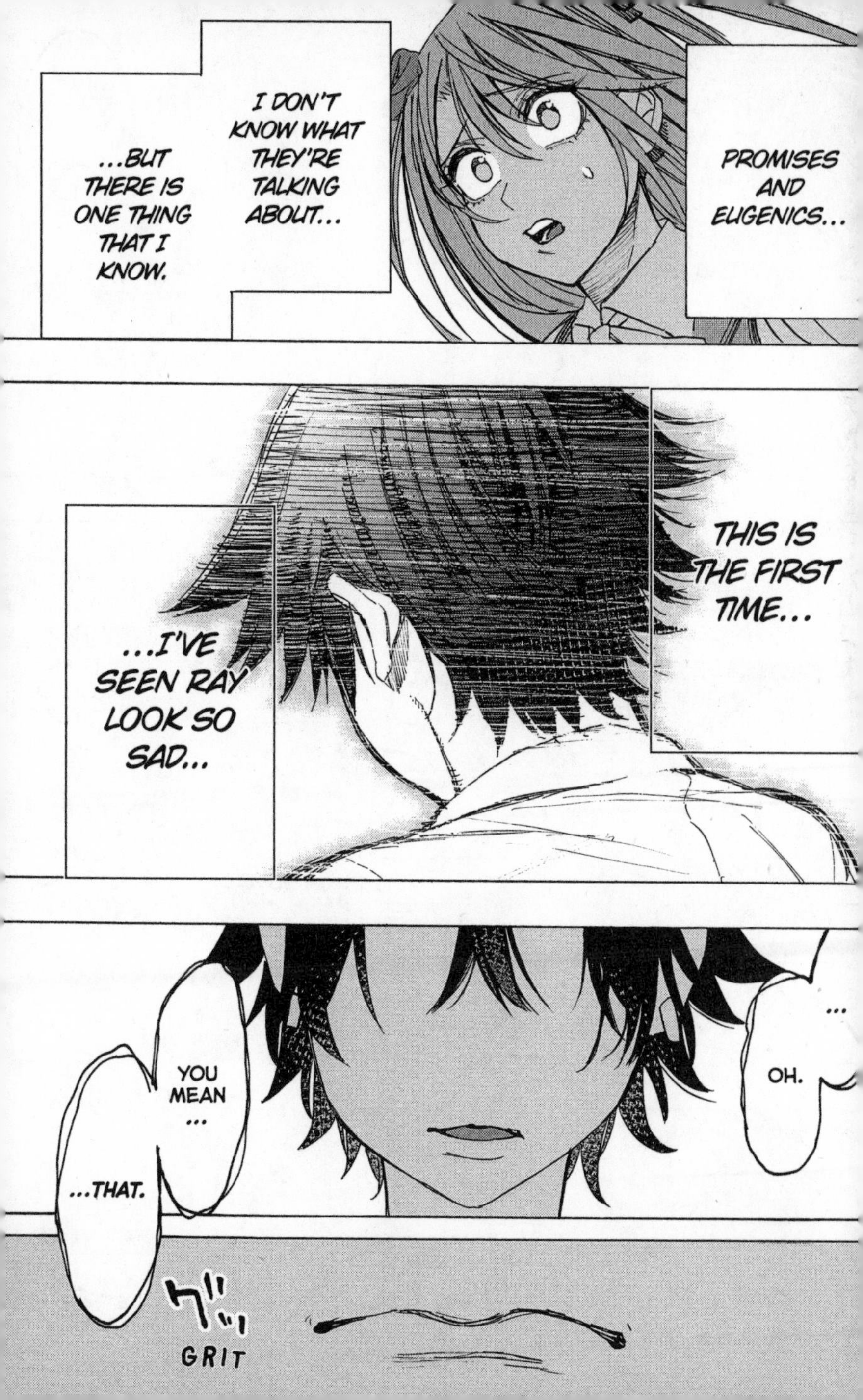
PROMISES AND EUGENICS...
I DON'T KNOW WHAT THEY'RE TALKING ABOUT...
...BUT THERE IS ONE THING THAT I KNOW.
THIS IS THE FIRST TIME...
...I'VE SEEN RAY LOOK SO SAD...
... OH.
YOU MEAN ... ...THAT.
ギッ
GRIT

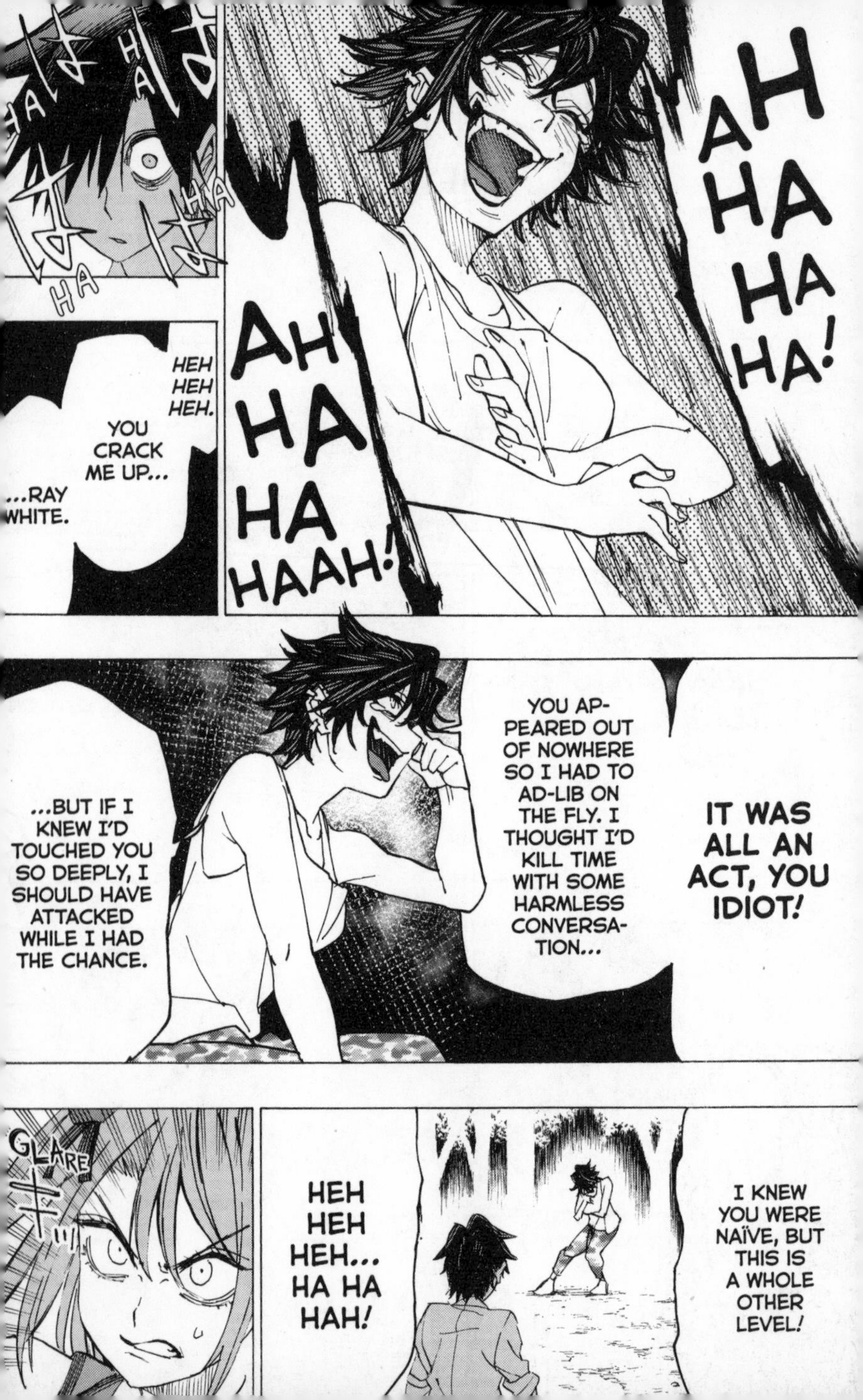
AH A HA HA HA!
AH HA HA HAAH!
HA HA HA HA
HEH HEH HEH.
YOU CRACK ME UP...
...RAY WHITE.
IT WAS ALL AN ACT, YOU IDIOT!
YOU APPEARED OUT OF NOWHERE SO I HAD TO AD-LIB ON THE FLY. I THOUGHT I'D KILL TIME WITH SOME HARMLESS CONVERSATION...
...BUT IF I KNEW I'D TOUCHED YOU SO DEEPLY, I SHOULD HAVE ATTACKED WHILE I HAD THE CHANCE.
I KNEW YOU WERE NAÏVE, BUT THIS IS A WHOLE OTHER LEVEL!
HEH HEH HEH... HA HA HAH!
GLARE

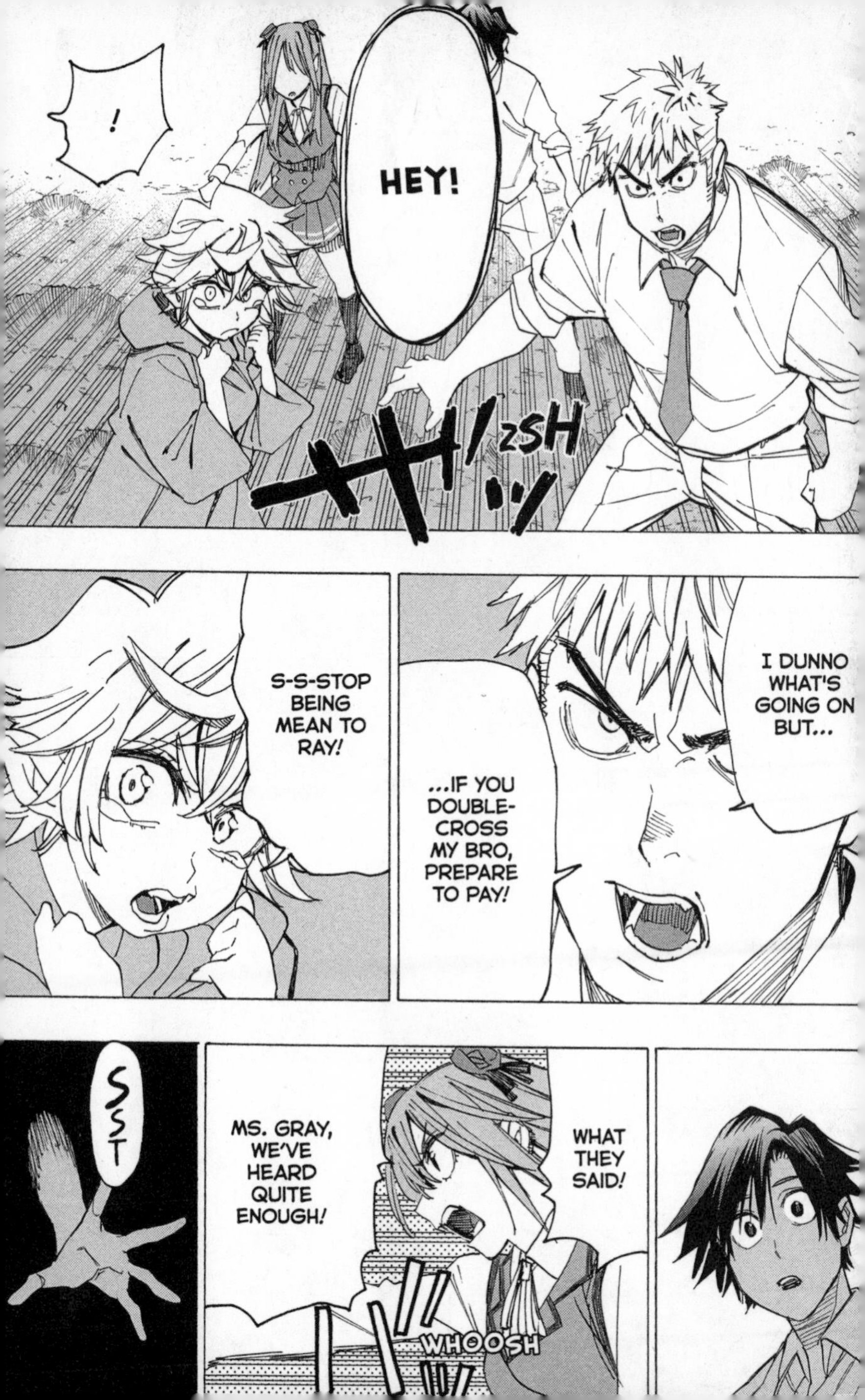
HEY!
!
ZSH
I DUNNO WHAT'S GOING ON BUT...
...IF YOU DOUBLE-CROSS MY BRO, PREPARE TO PAY!
S-S-STOP BEING MEAN TO RAY!
WHAT THEY SAID!
MS. GRAY, WE'VE HEARD QUITE ENOUGH!
WHOOSH
SST

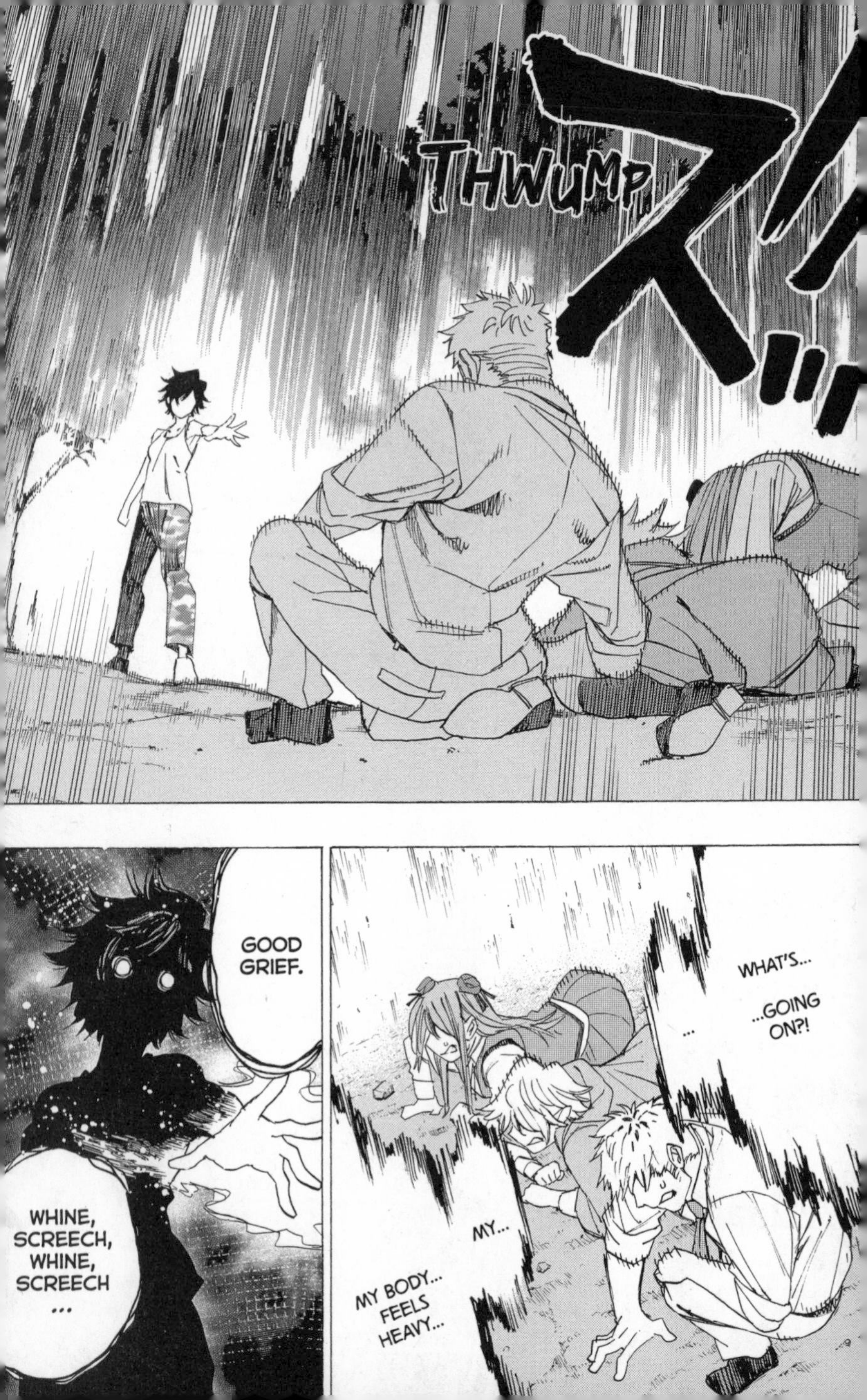
THWUMP
WHAT'S...
...GOING ON?!
...
MY...
MY BODY... FEELS HEAVY...
GOOD GRIEF.
WHINE, SCREECH, WHINE, SCREECH ...

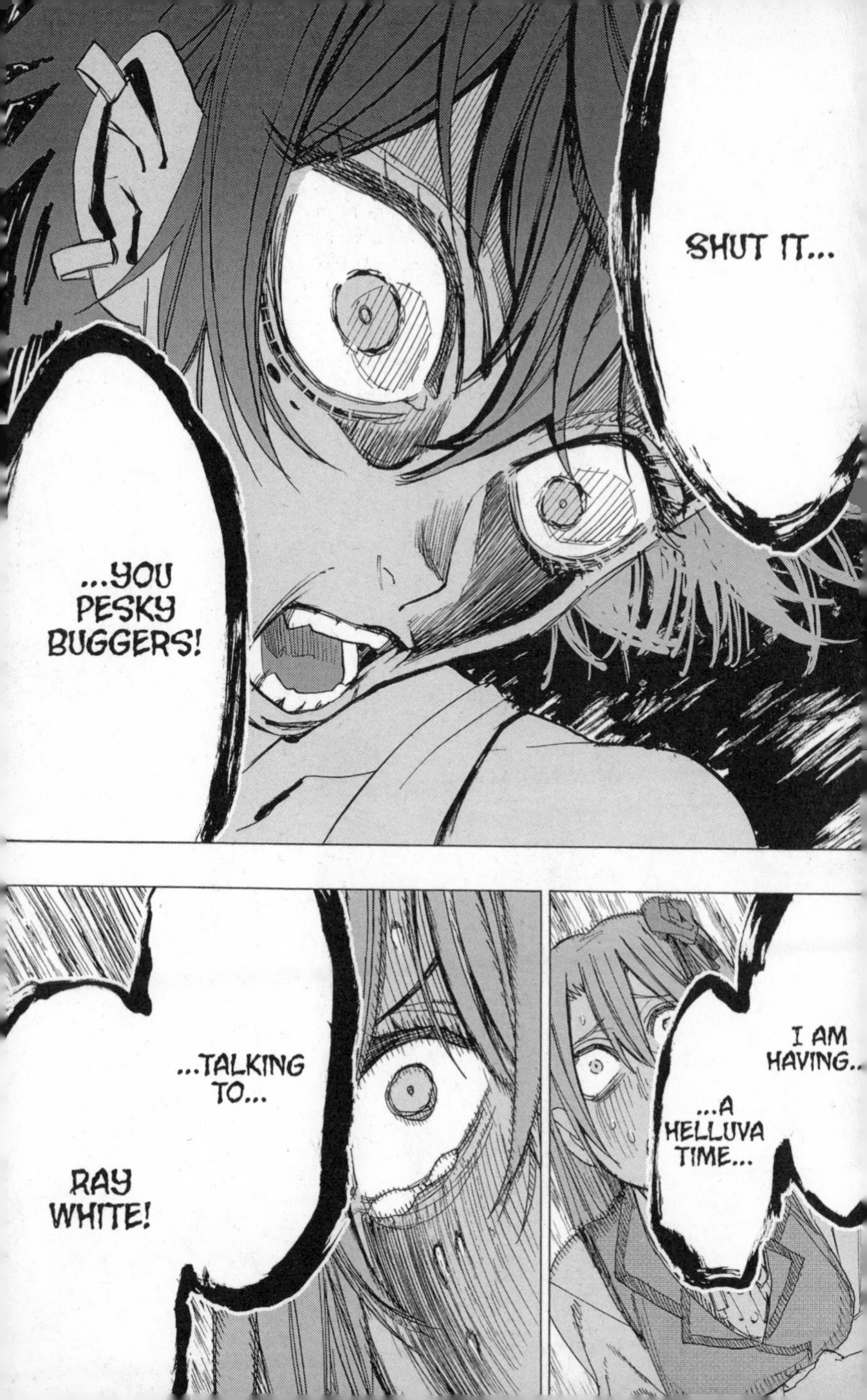
SHUT IT...
...YOU PESKY BUGGERS!
I AM HAVING..
...A HELLUVA TIME...
...TALKING TO...
RAY WHITE!

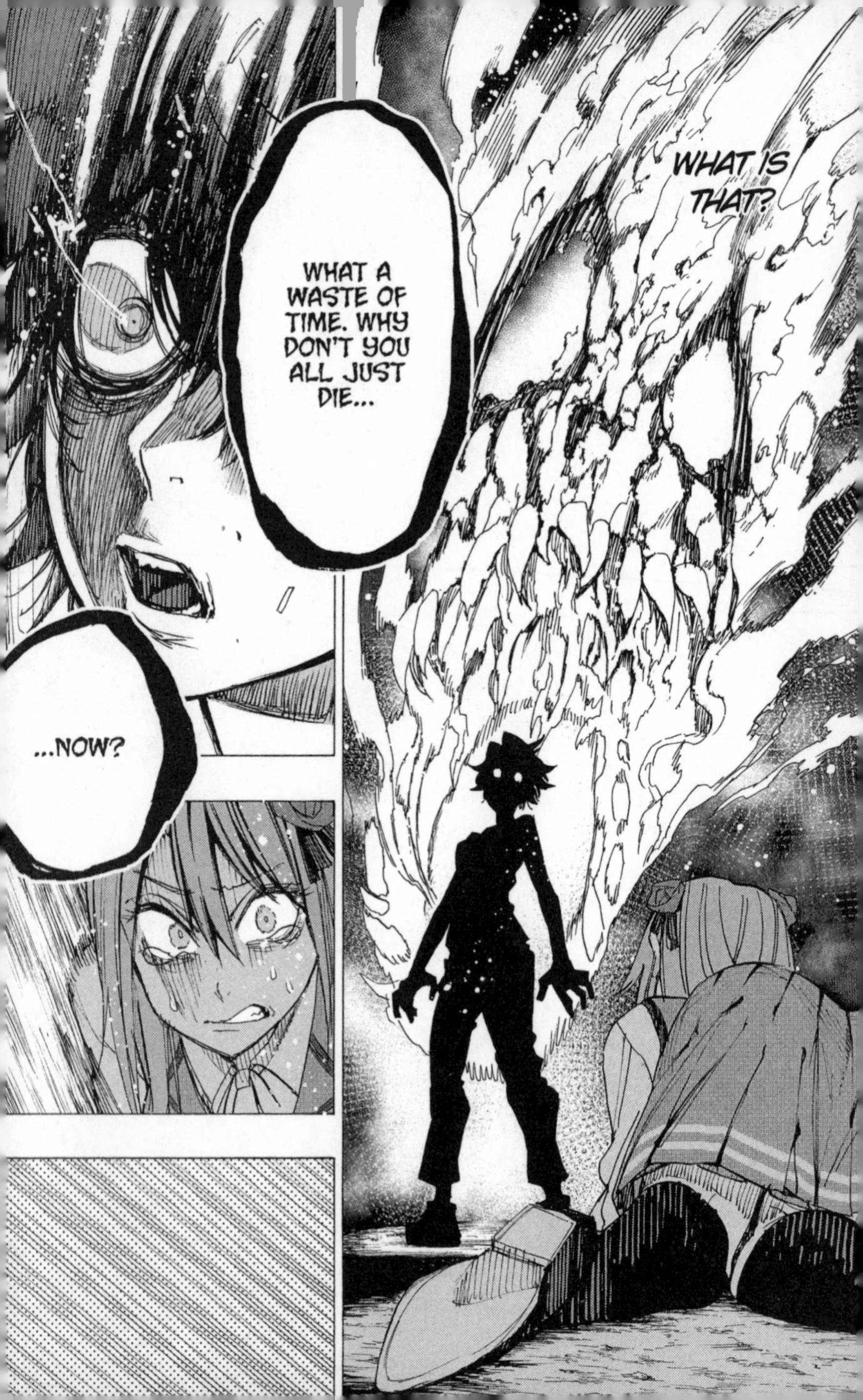
WHAT IS THAT?
WHAT A WASTE OF TIME. WHY DON'T YOU ALL JUST DIE...
...NOW?

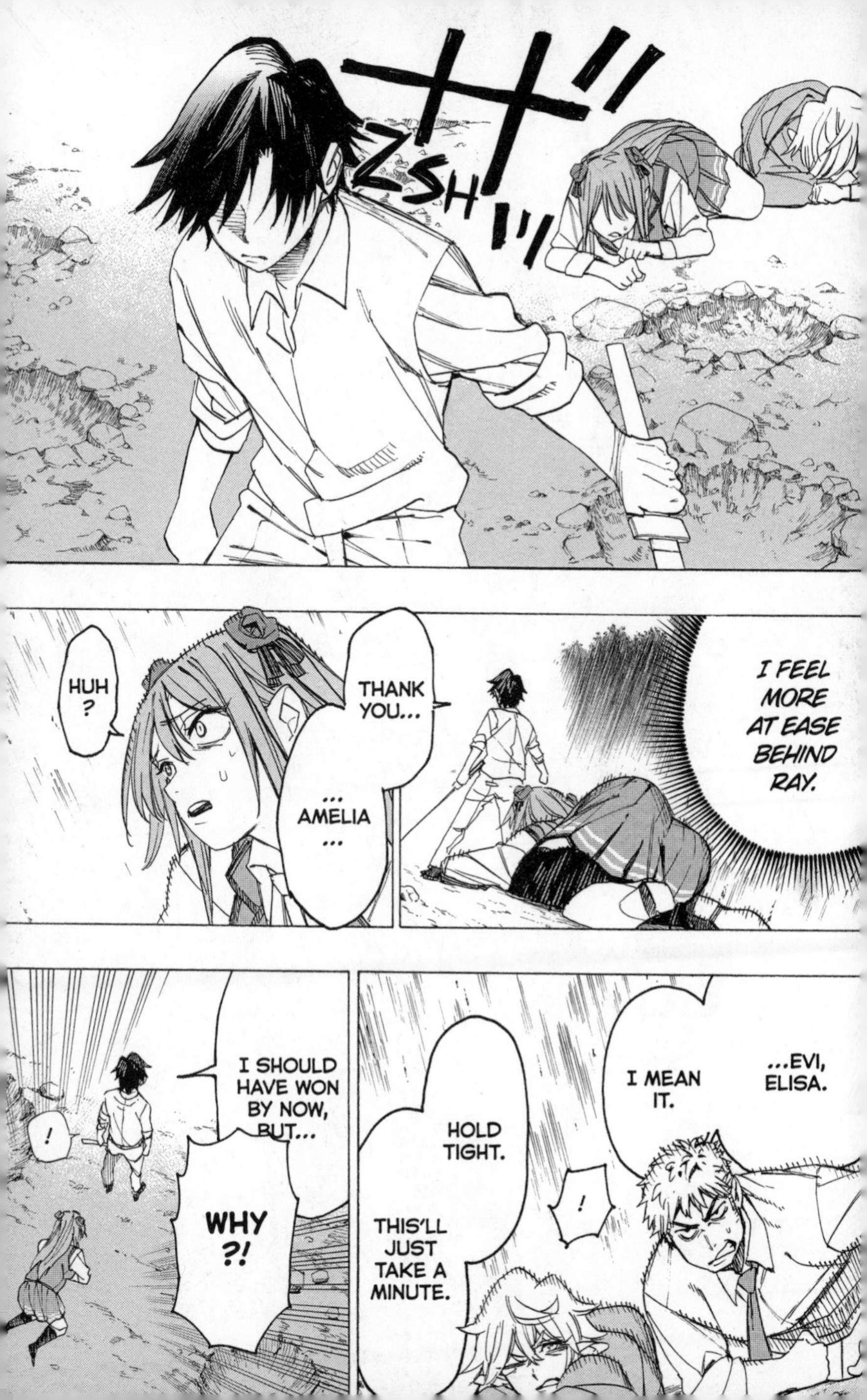
ZSH
I FEEL MORE AT EASE BEHIND RAY.
THANK YOU...
...AMELIA...
HUH?
...EVI, ELISA.
I MEAN IT.
HOLD TIGHT.
!
THIS'LL JUST TAKE A MINUTE.
I SHOULD HAVE WON BY NOW, BUT...
!
WHY?!

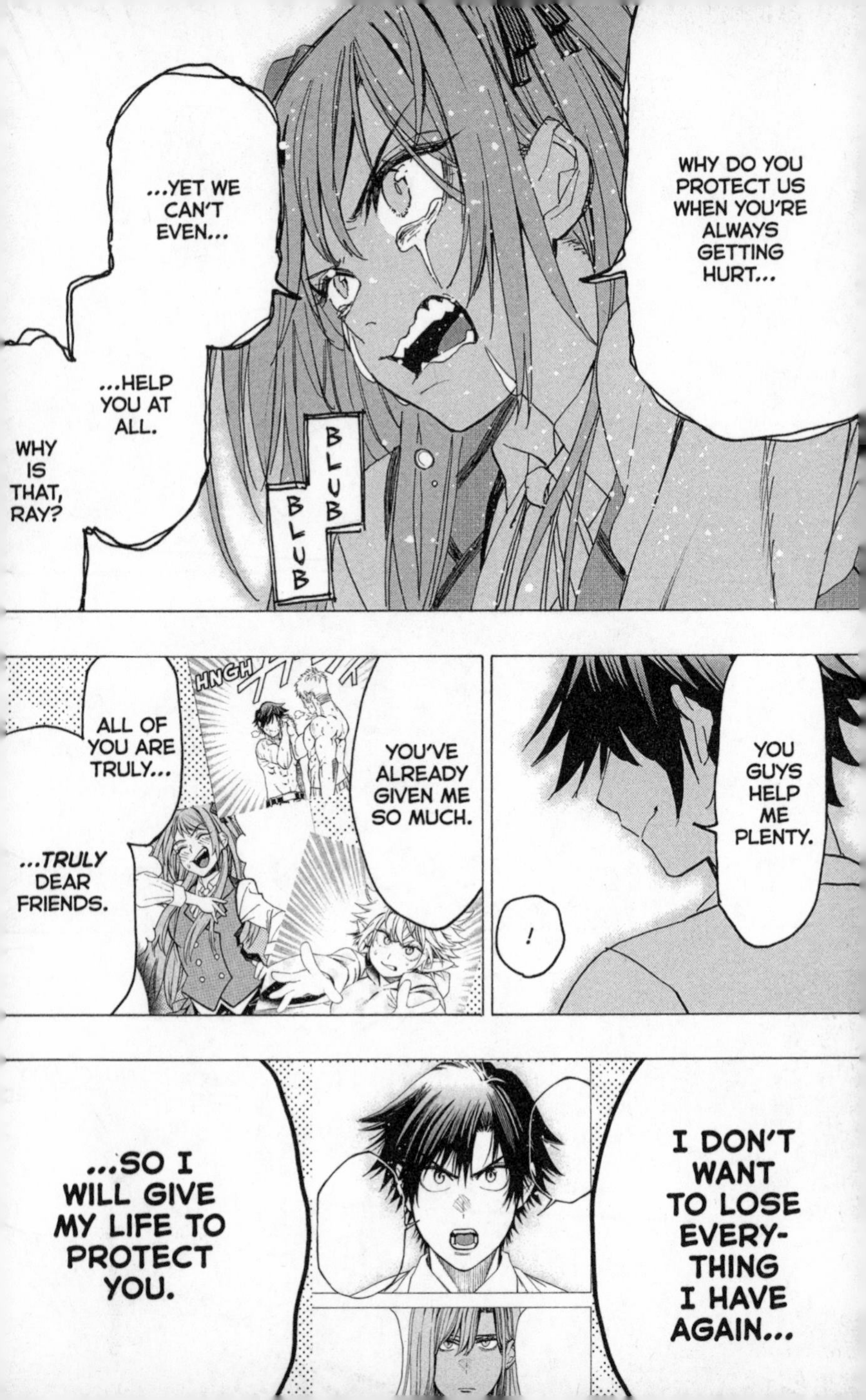
WHY DO YOU PROTECT US WHEN YOU'RE ALWAYS GETTING HURT...
...YET WE CAN'T EVEN...
...HELP YOU AT ALL.
BLUB BLUB
WHY IS THAT, RAY?
YOU GUYS HELP ME PLENTY.
!
YOU'VE ALREADY GIVEN ME SO MUCH.
HNGH
ALL OF YOU ARE TRULY...
...*TRULY* DEAR FRIENDS.
I DON'T WANT TO LOSE EVERY-THING I HAVE AGAIN...
...SO I WILL GIVE MY LIFE TO PROTECT YOU.

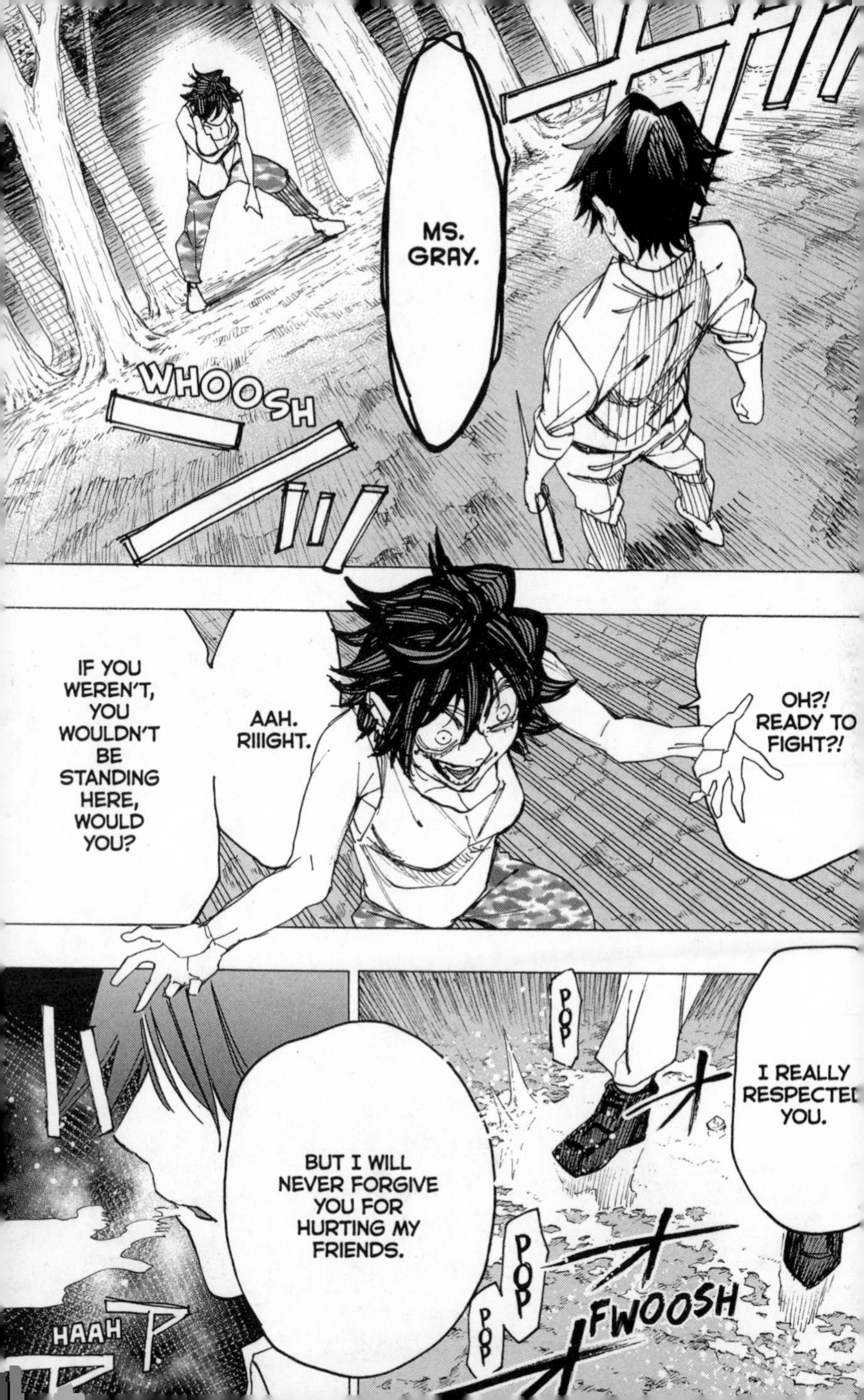
MS. GRAY.
WHOOSH
OH?! READY TO FIGHT?!
AAH. RIIIGHT.
IF YOU WEREN'T, YOU WOULDN'T BE STANDING HERE, WOULD YOU?
I REALLY RESPECTED YOU.
POP
POP
FWOOSH
BUT I WILL NEVER FORGIVE YOU FOR HURTING MY FRIENDS.
POP
HAAH

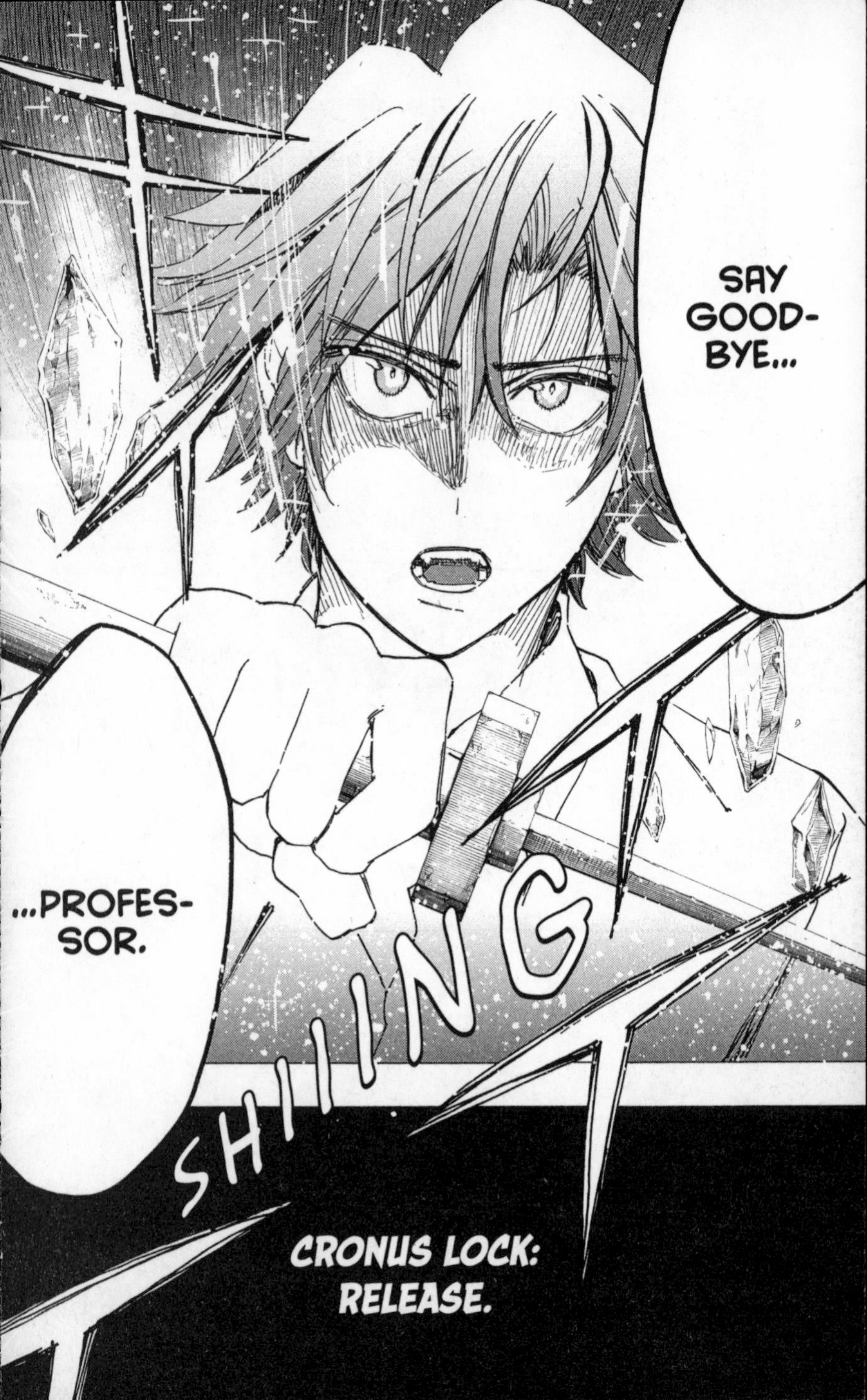
SAY GOOD-BYE...
...PROFES-SOR.
SHIIING
CRONUS LOCK: RELEASE.

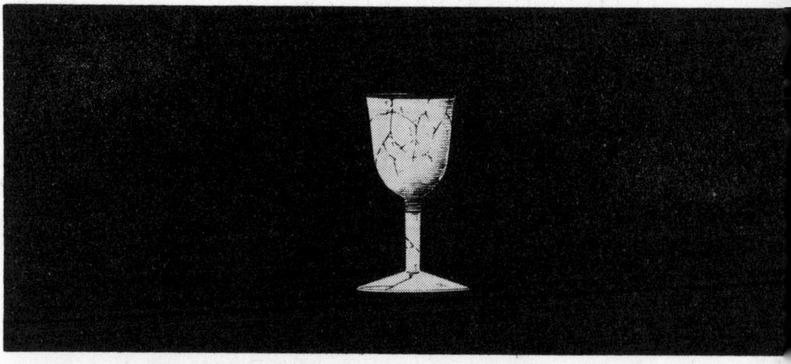

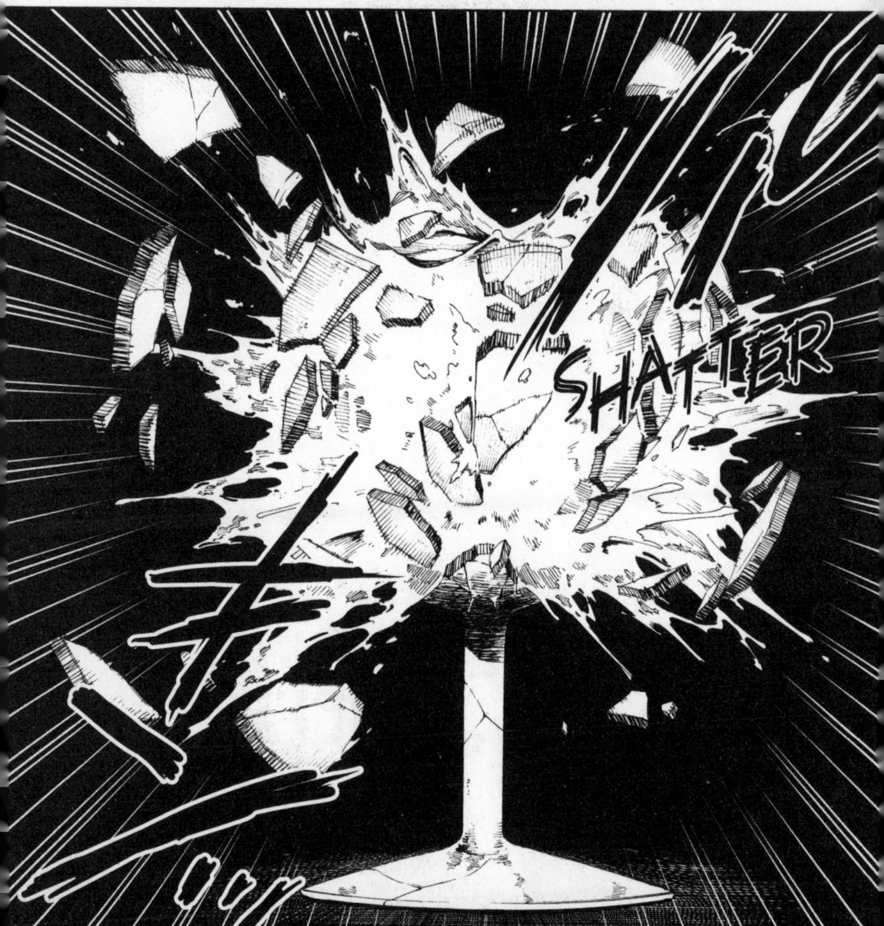
SHATTER

The Iceblade Sorcerer Shall Rule the World

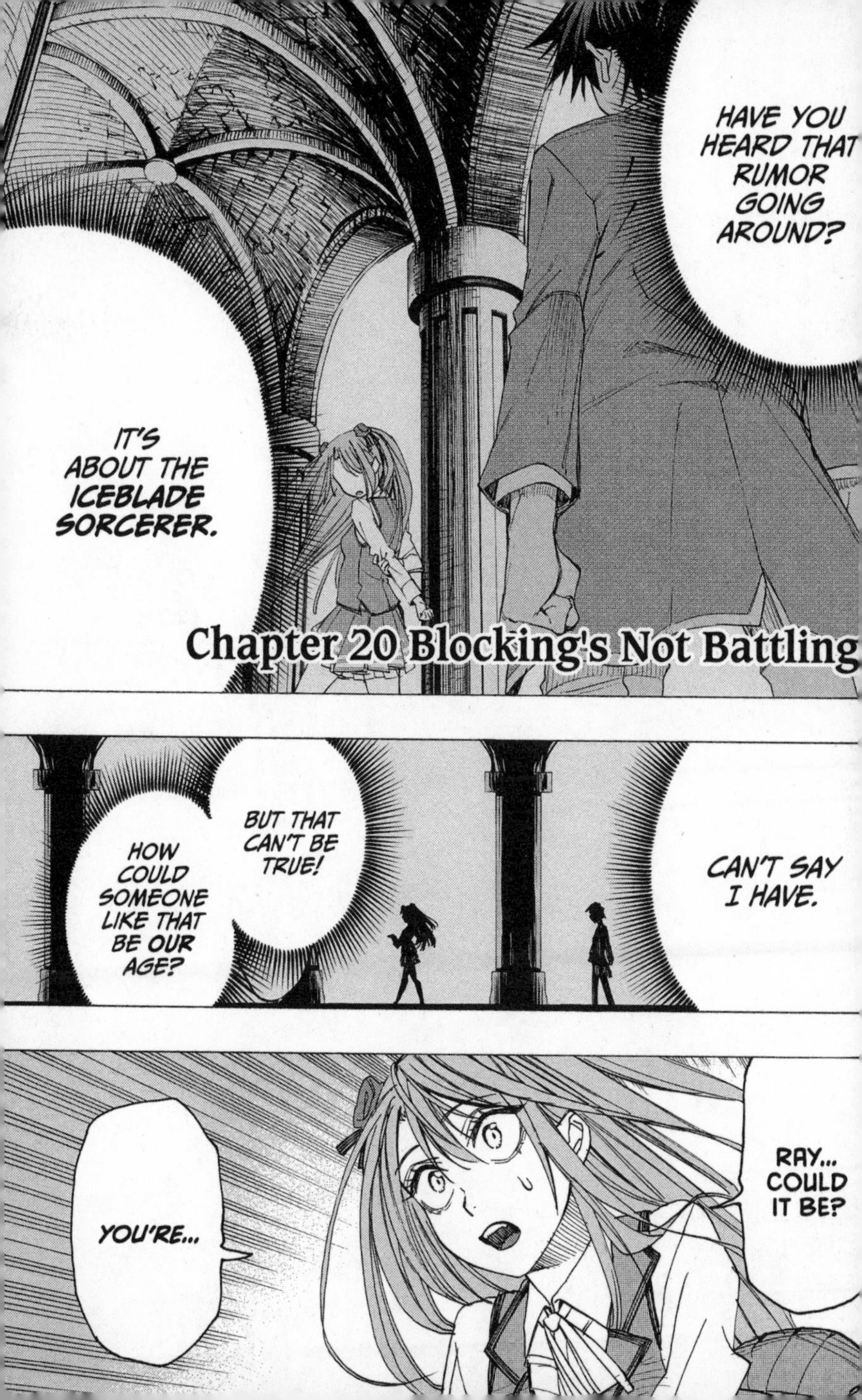
HAVE YOU HEARD THAT RUMOR GOING AROUND?
IT'S ABOUT THE ICEBLADE SORCERER.
Chapter 20 Blocking's Not Battling
CAN'T SAY I HAVE.
BUT THAT CAN'T BE TRUE!
HOW COULD SOMEONE LIKE THAT BE OUR AGE?
RAY... COULD IT BE?
YOU'RE...

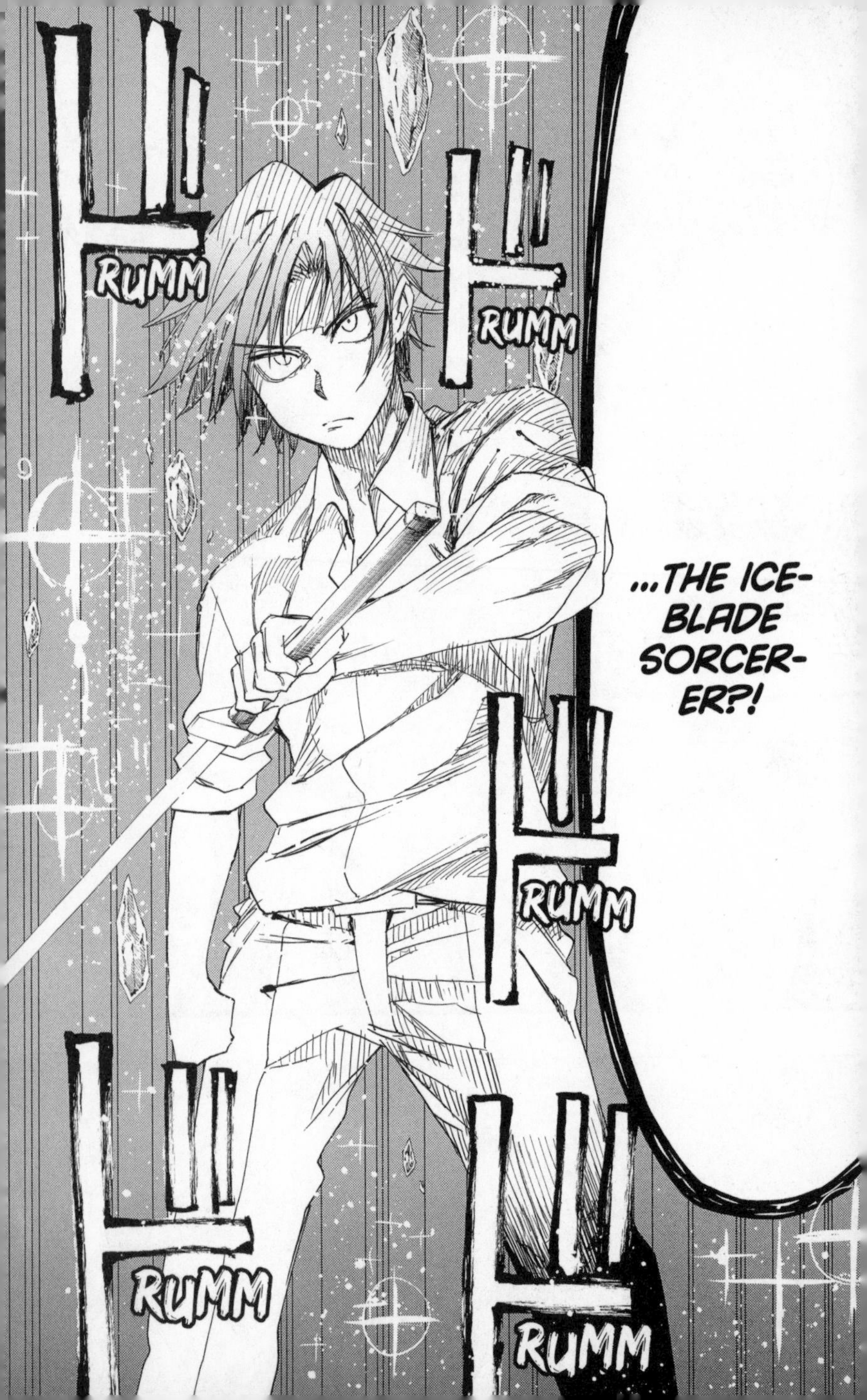
...THE ICE-BLADE SORCERER?!
RUMM
RUMM
RUMM
RUMM
RUMM

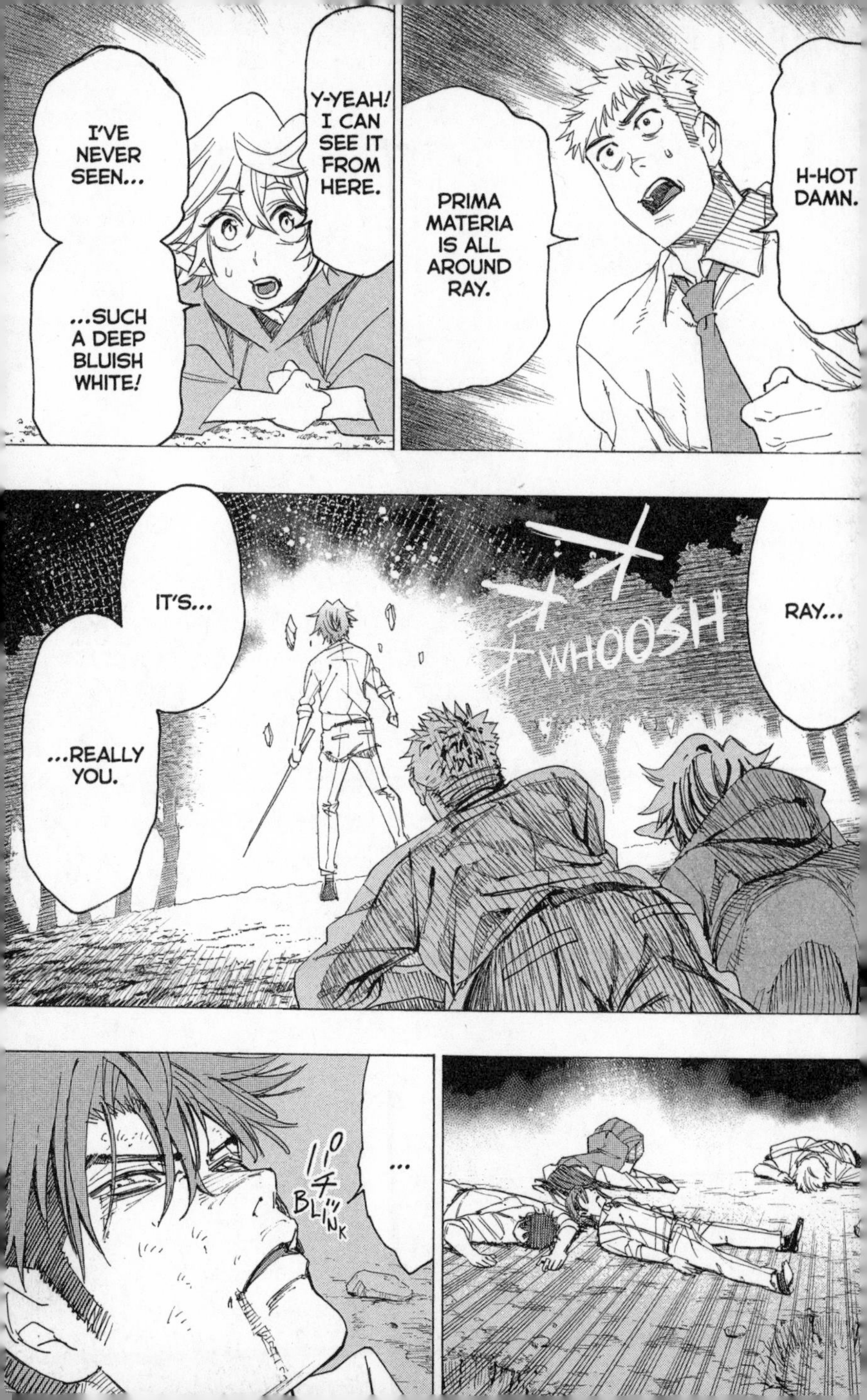
H-HOT DAMN.
PRIMA MATERIA IS ALL AROUND RAY.
Y-YEAH! I CAN SEE IT FROM HERE.
I'VE NEVER SEEN...
...SUCH A DEEP BLUISH WHITE!
RAY...
WHOOSH
IT'S...
...REALLY YOU.
...
BLINK

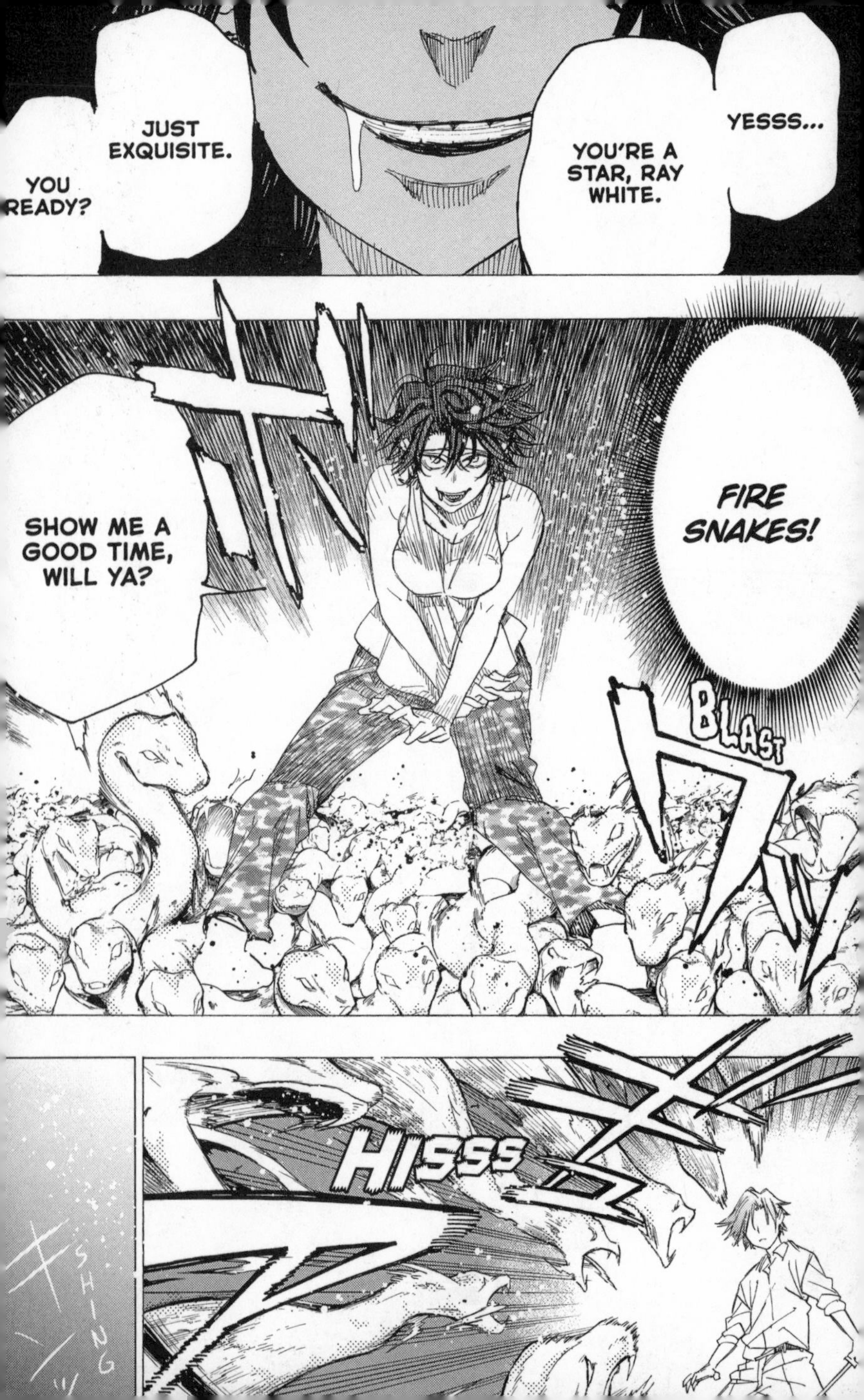
YESSS...
YOU'RE A STAR, RAY WHITE.
JUST EXQUISITE.
YOU READY?
FIRE SNAKES!
BLAST
SHOW ME A GOOD TIME, WILL YA?
HISSS
SHING

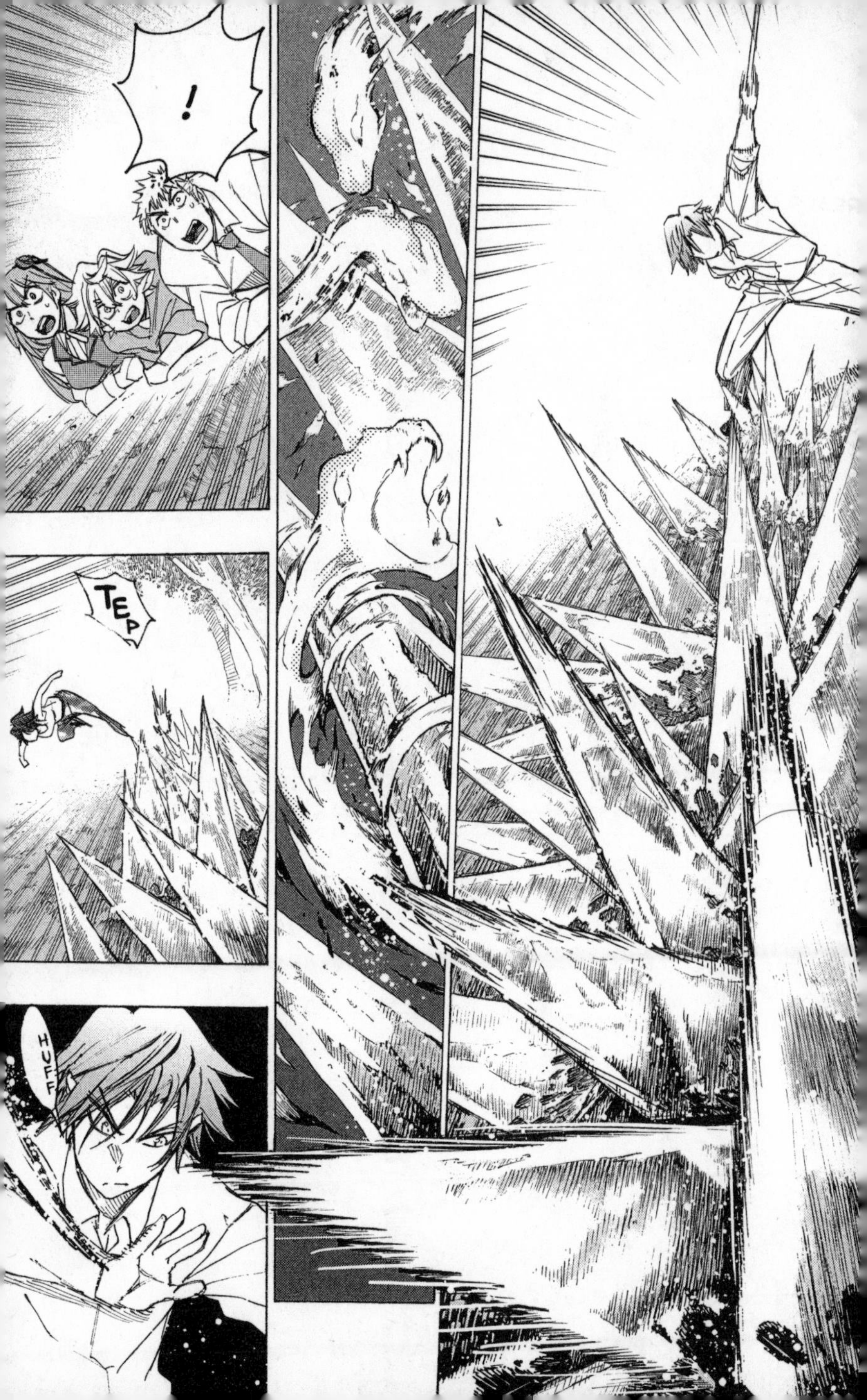
!
TEP
HUFF

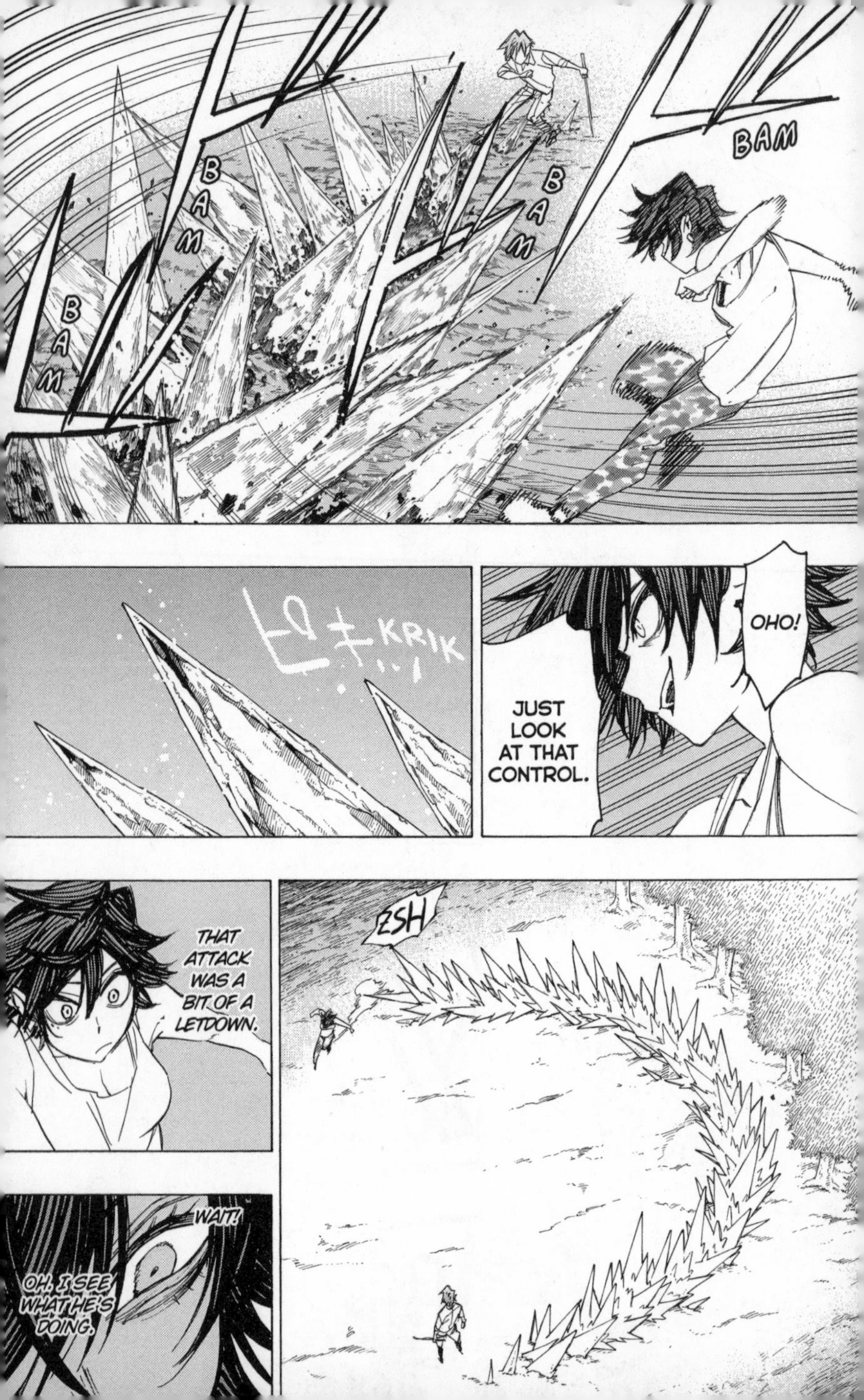
BAM
BAM
BAM
BAM
OHO!
JUST LOOK AT THAT CONTROL.
KRIK
ZSH
THAT ATTACK WAS A BIT OF A LETDOWN.
WAIT!
OH, I SEE WHAT HE'S DOING.

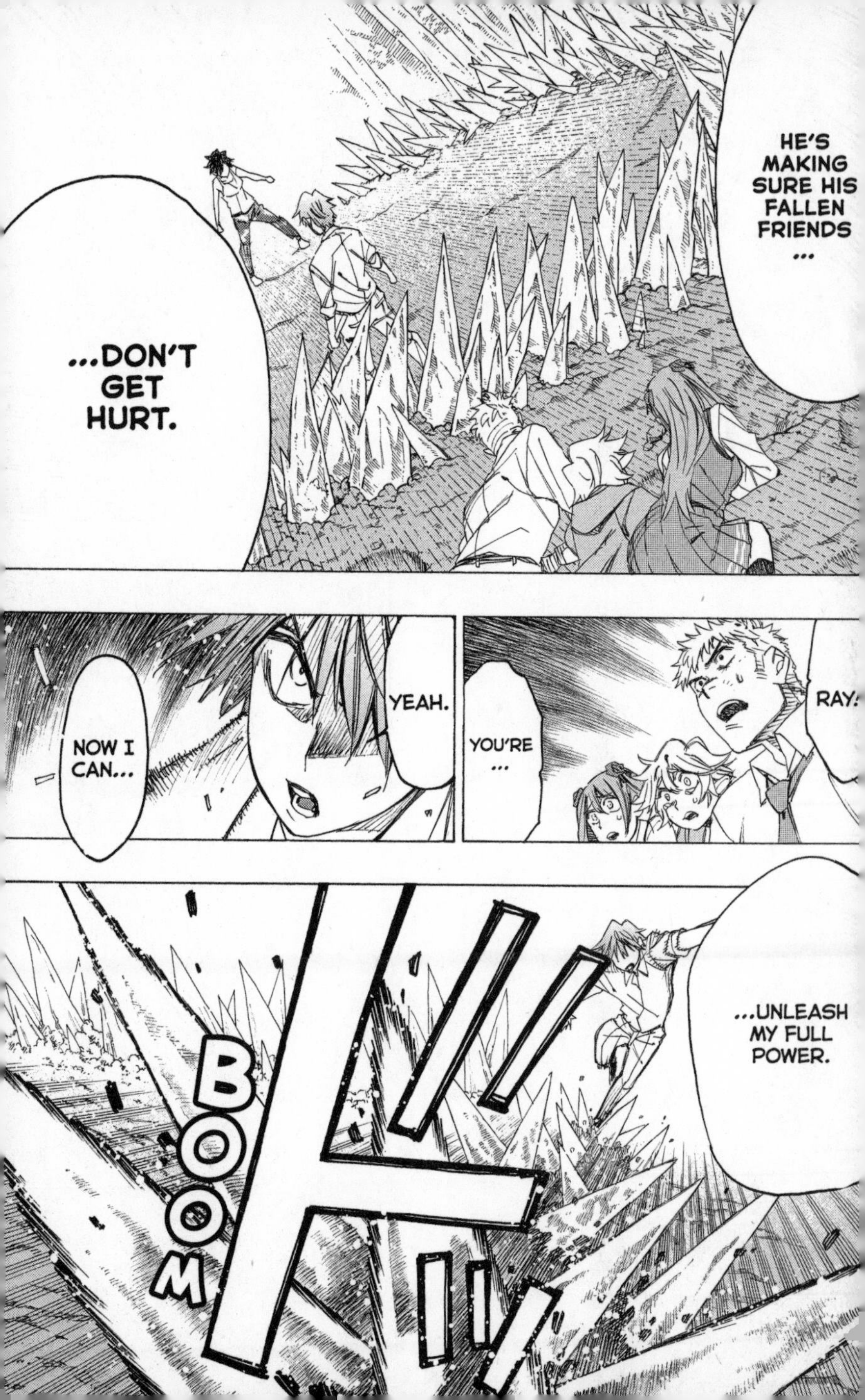
HE'S MAKING SURE HIS FALLEN FRIENDS ...
...DON'T GET HURT.
RAY!
YOU'RE ...
YEAH.
NOW I CAN...
...UNLEASH MY FULL POWER.
BOOM

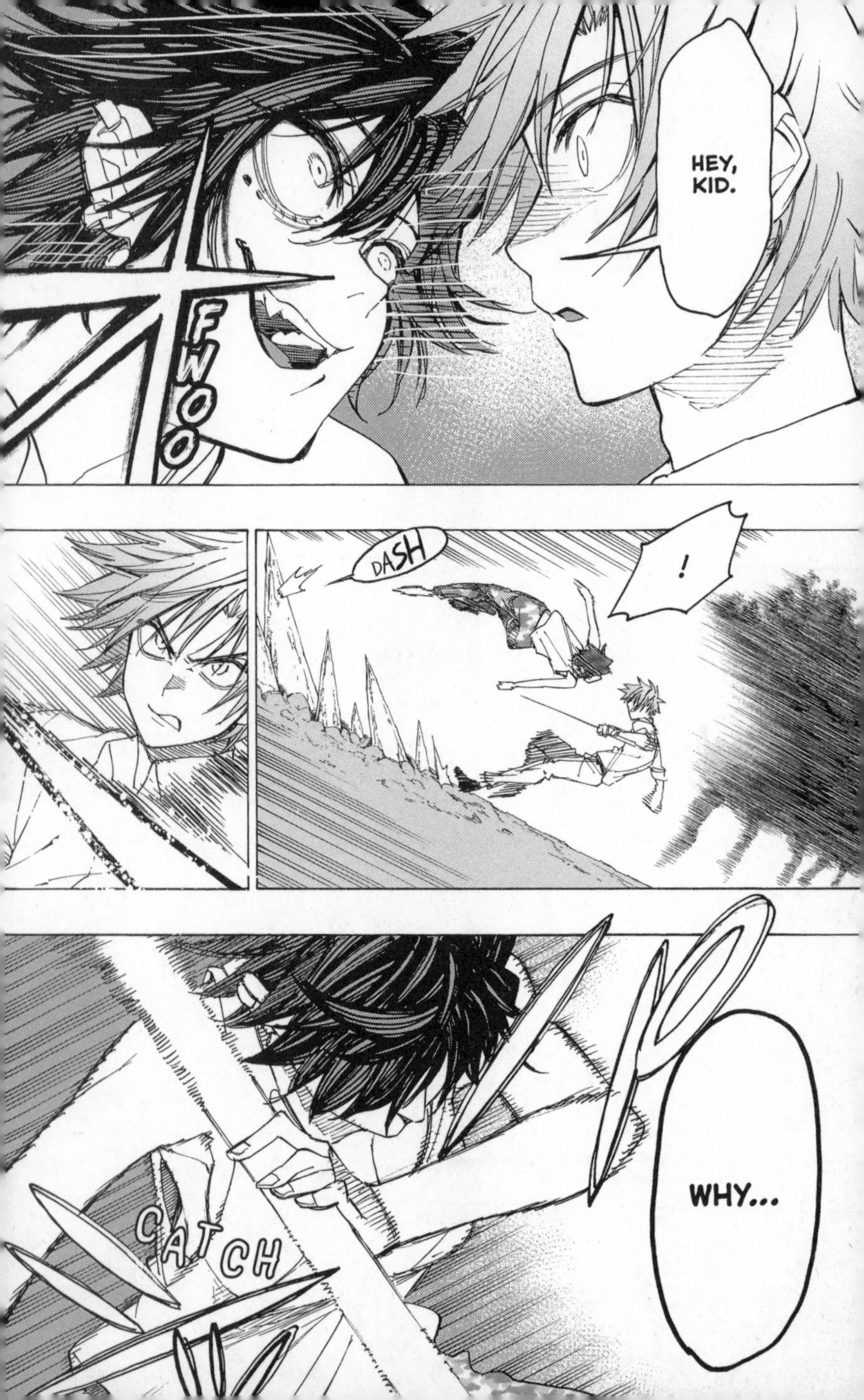
HEY, KID.
FWOO
!
DASH
WHY...
CATCH

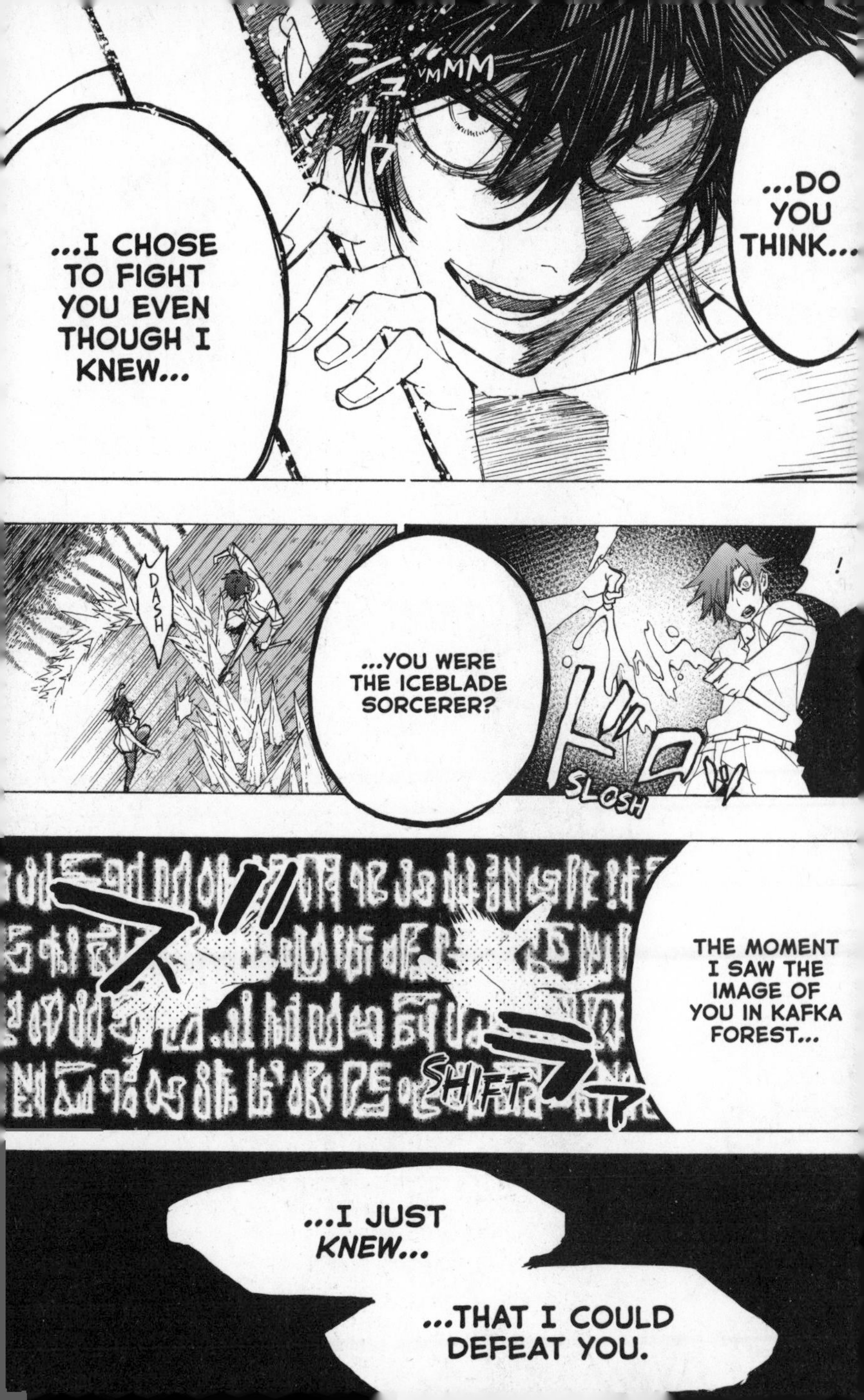
VMMM
...DO YOU THINK...
...I CHOSE TO FIGHT YOU EVEN THOUGH I KNEW...
!
SLOSH
...YOU WERE THE ICEBLADE SORCERER?
DASH
THE MOMENT I SAW THE IMAGE OF YOU IN KAFKA FOREST...
SHIFT
...I JUST KNEW...
...THAT I COULD DEFEAT YOU.

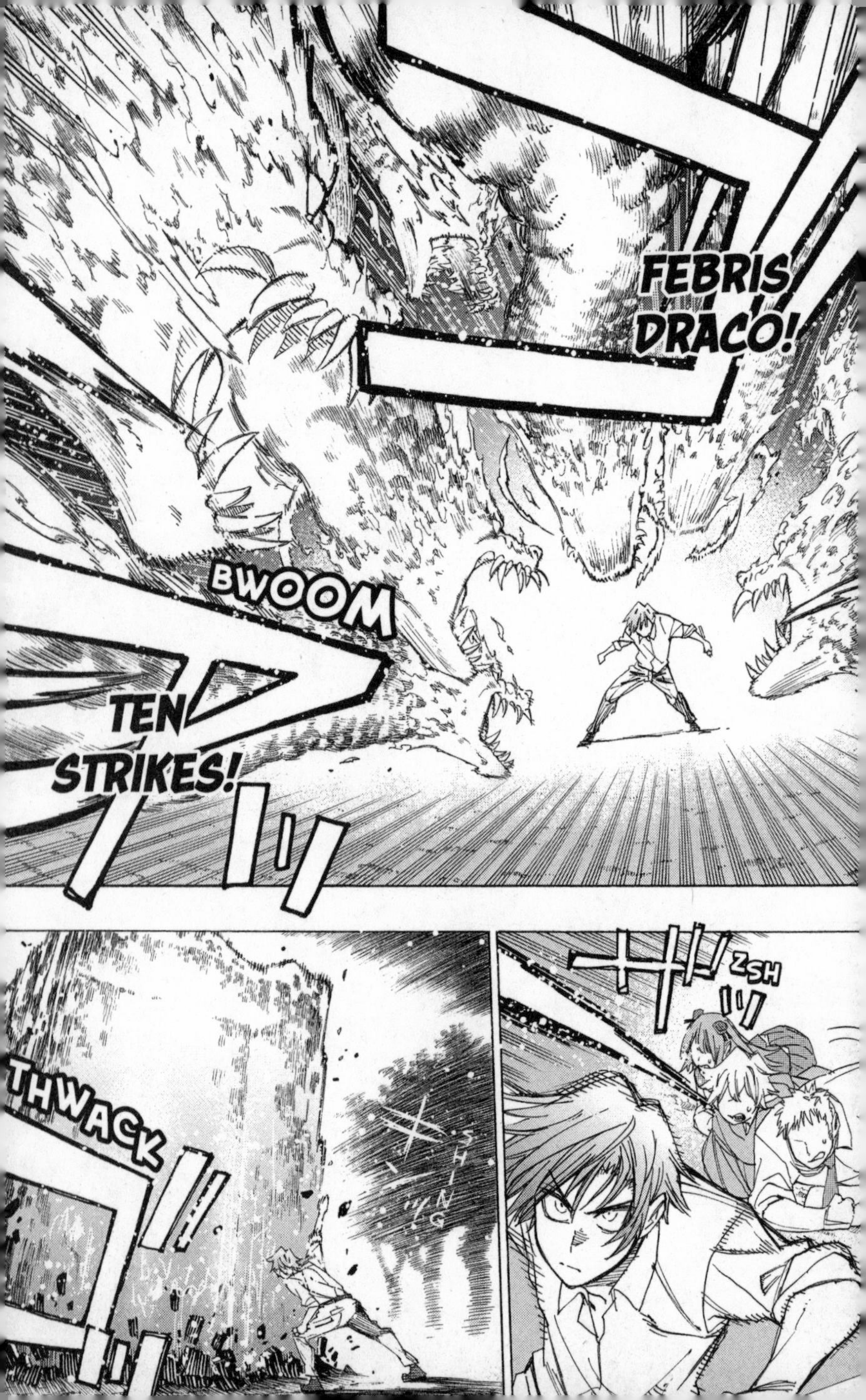
FEBRIS DRACO!
BWOOM
TEN STRIKES!
ZSH
THWACK
SHING

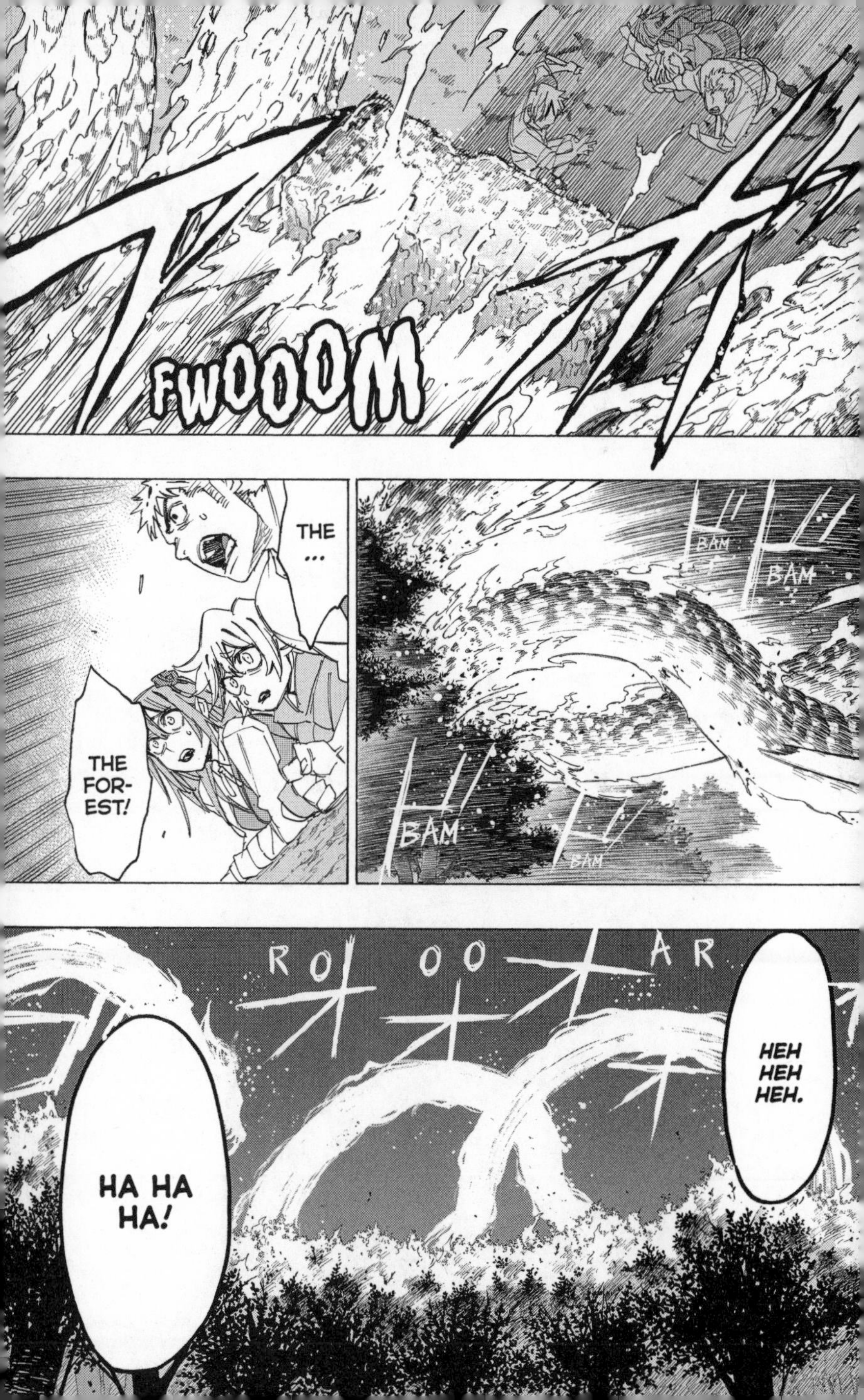
FWOOOM
BAM
BAM
BAM
BAM
THE ...
THE FOR-EST!
RO OO AR
HEH HEH HEH.
HA HA HA!

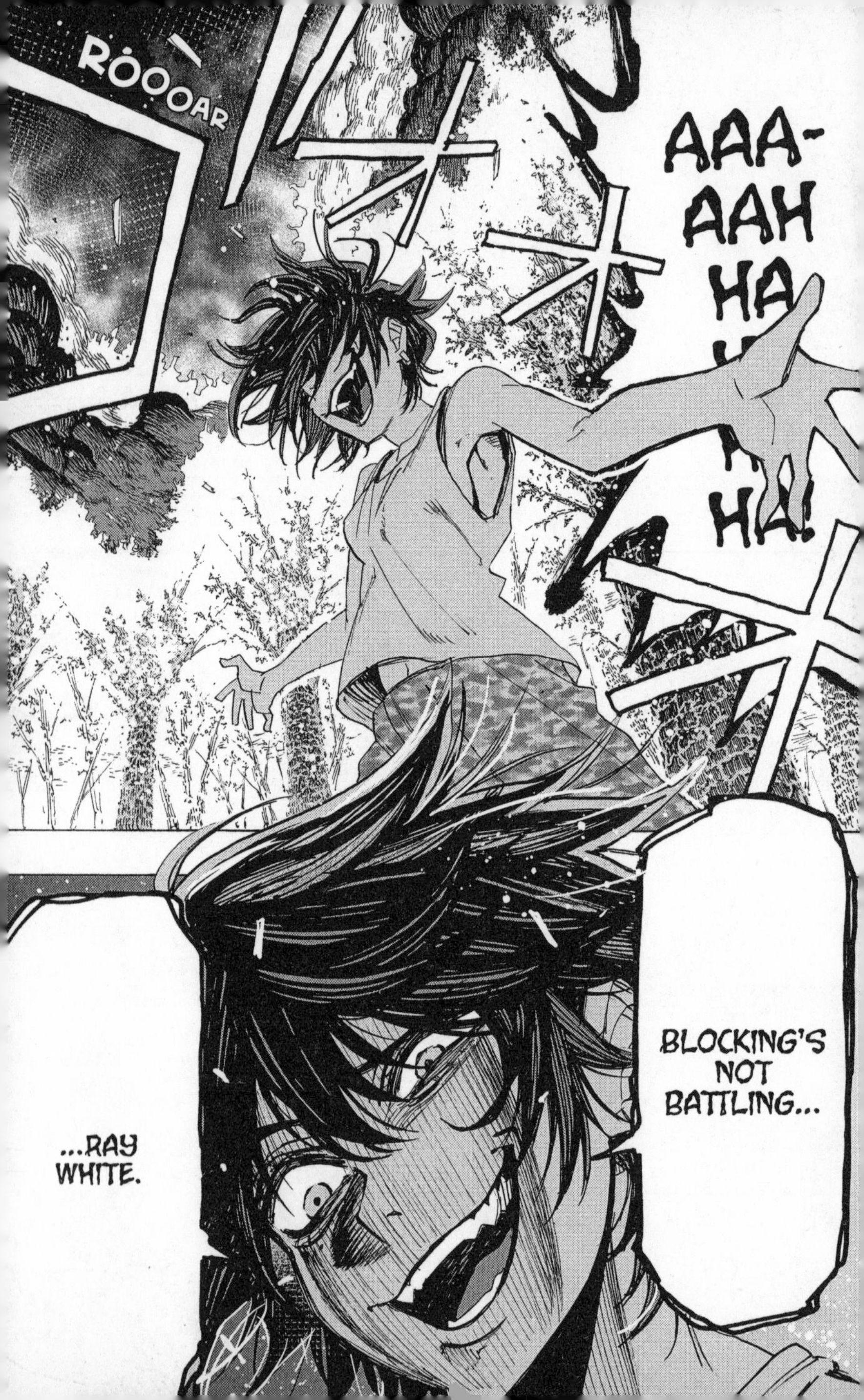
AAA-AAH HA HA!
RÖOOAR
BLOCKING'S NOT BATTLING...
...RAY WHITE.

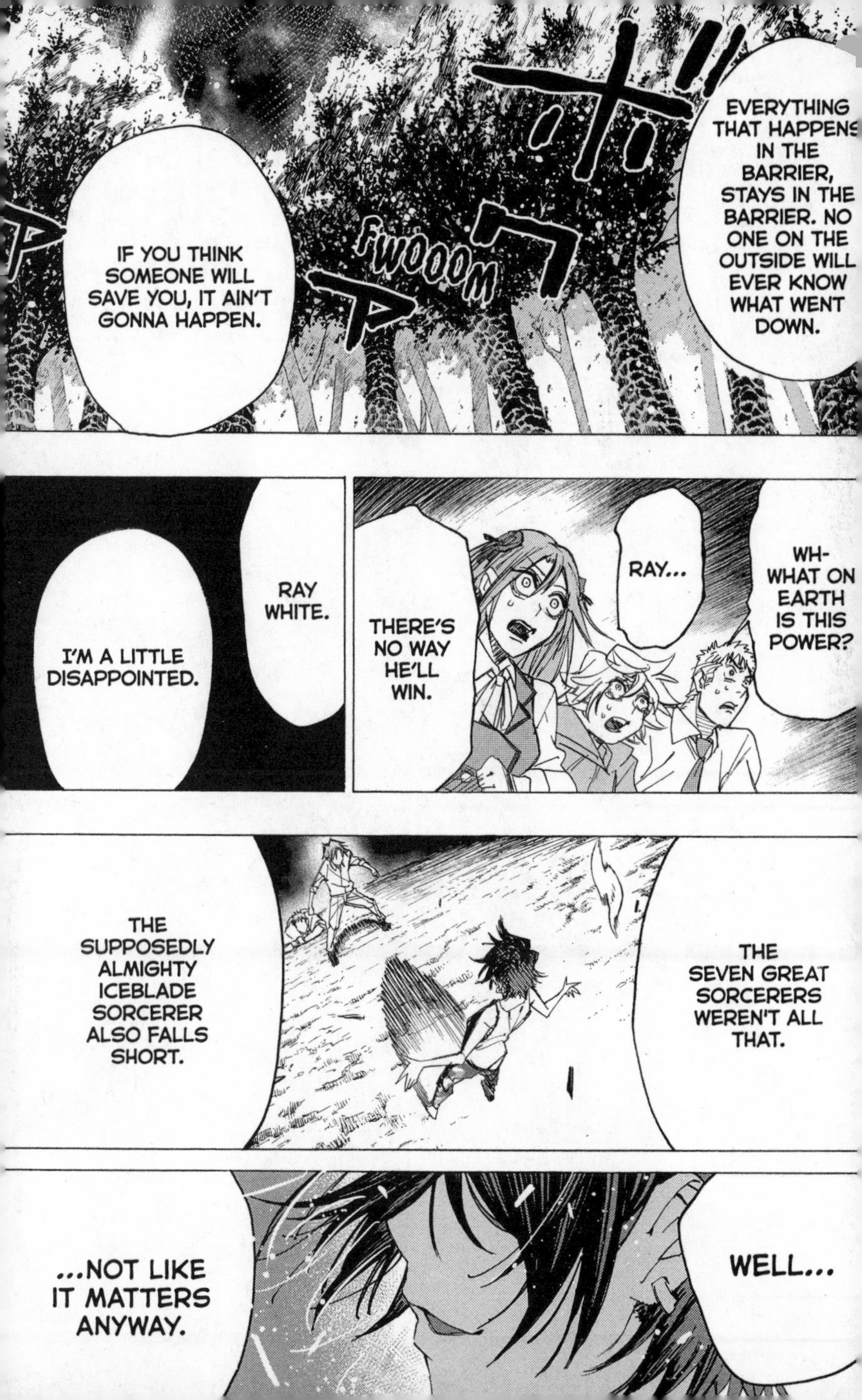
EVERYTHING THAT HAPPENS IN THE BARRIER, STAYS IN THE BARRIER. NO ONE ON THE OUTSIDE WILL EVER KNOW WHAT WENT DOWN.
FWOOOM
IF YOU THINK SOMEONE WILL SAVE YOU, IT AIN'T GONNA HAPPEN.
WH- WHAT ON EARTH IS THIS POWER?
RAY...
THERE'S NO WAY HE'LL WIN.
RAY WHITE.
I'M A LITTLE DISAPPOINTED.
THE SEVEN GREAT SORCERERS WEREN'T ALL THAT.
THE SUPPOSEDLY ALMIGHTY ICEBLADE SORCERER ALSO FALLS SHORT.
WELL...
...NOT LIKE IT MATTERS ANYWAY.

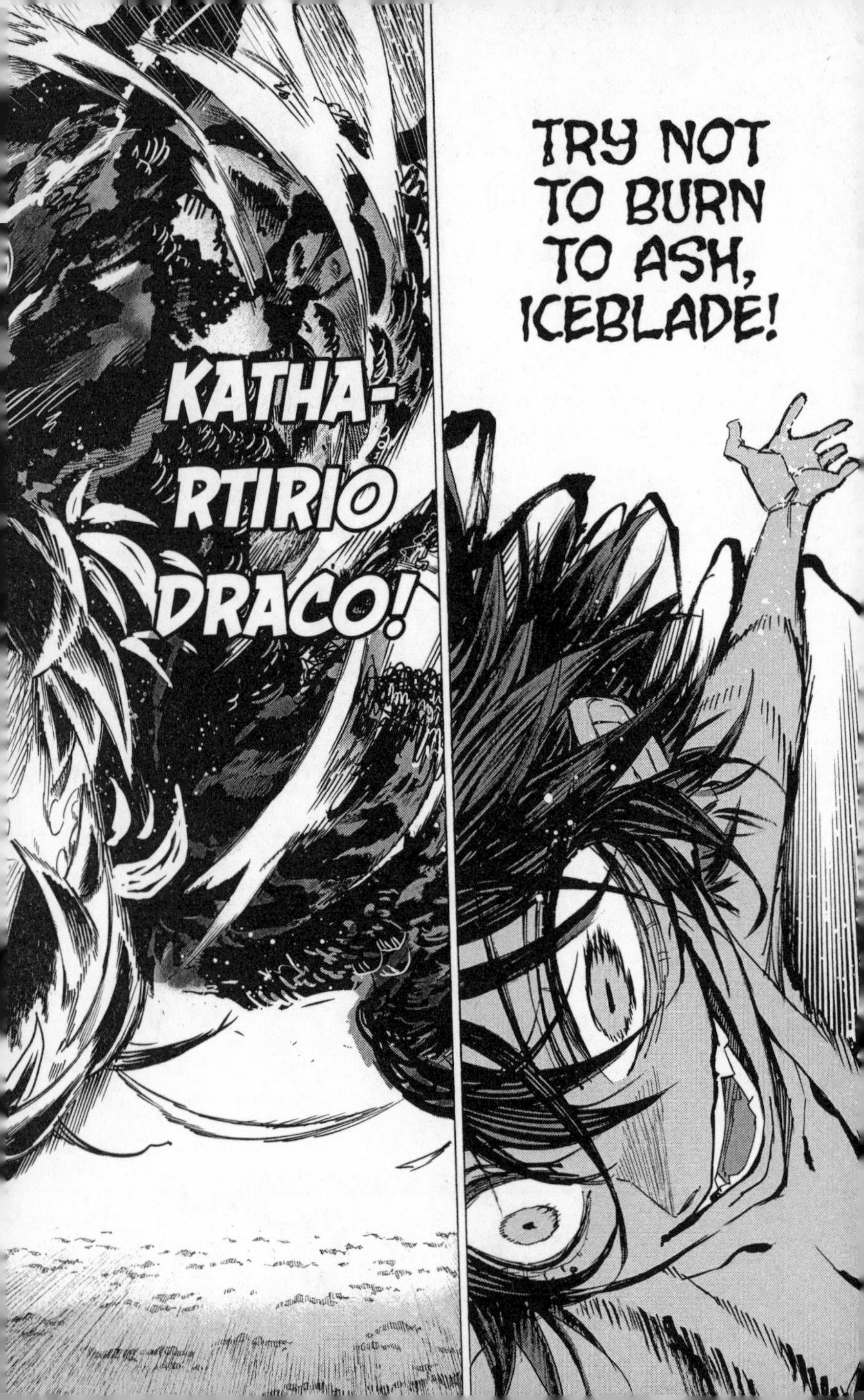
TRY NOT TO BURN TO ASH, ICEBLADE!
KATHA-RTIRIO DRACO!

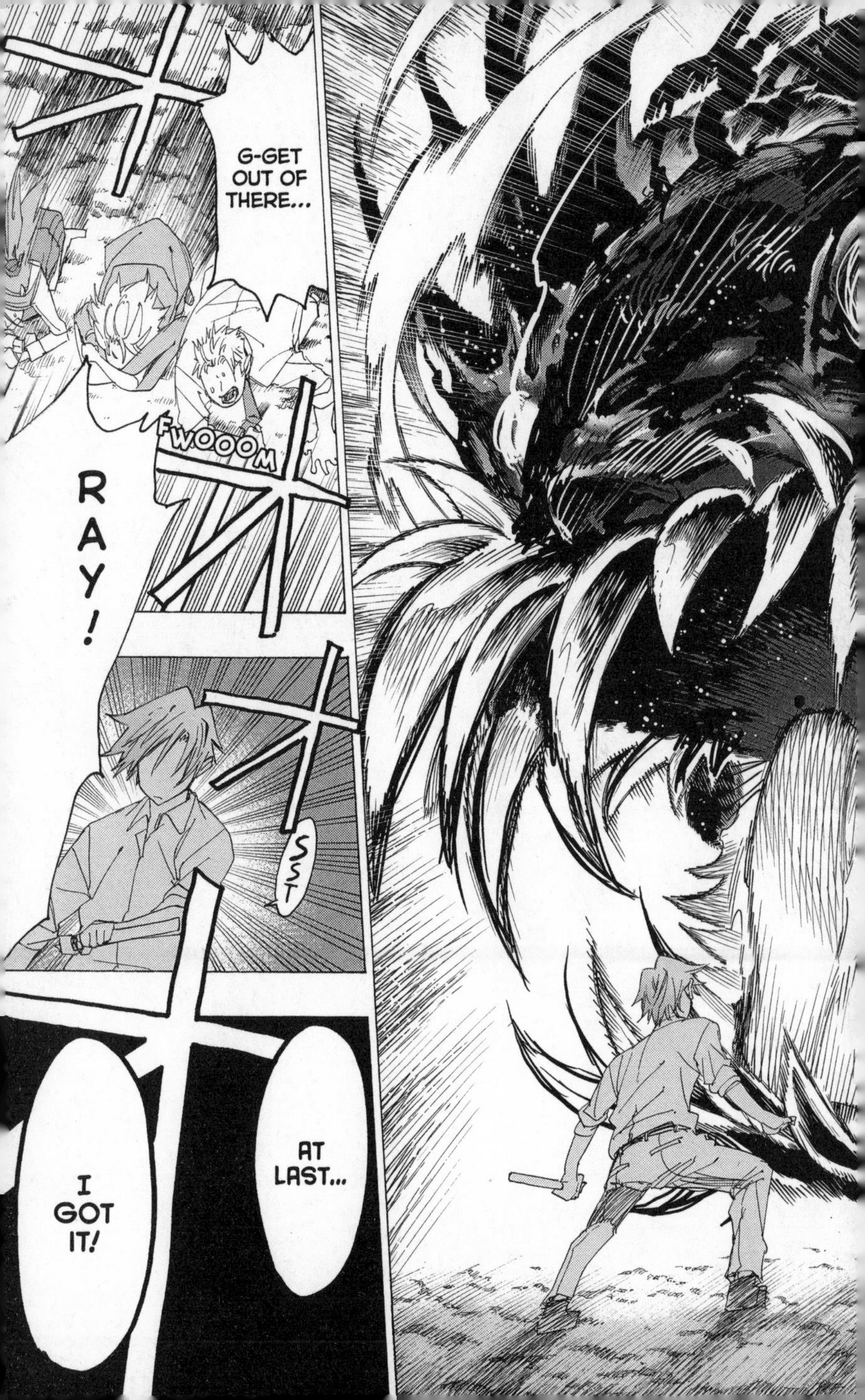
G-GET OUT OF THERE...
FWOOOM
RAY!
SST
AT LAST...
I GOT IT!

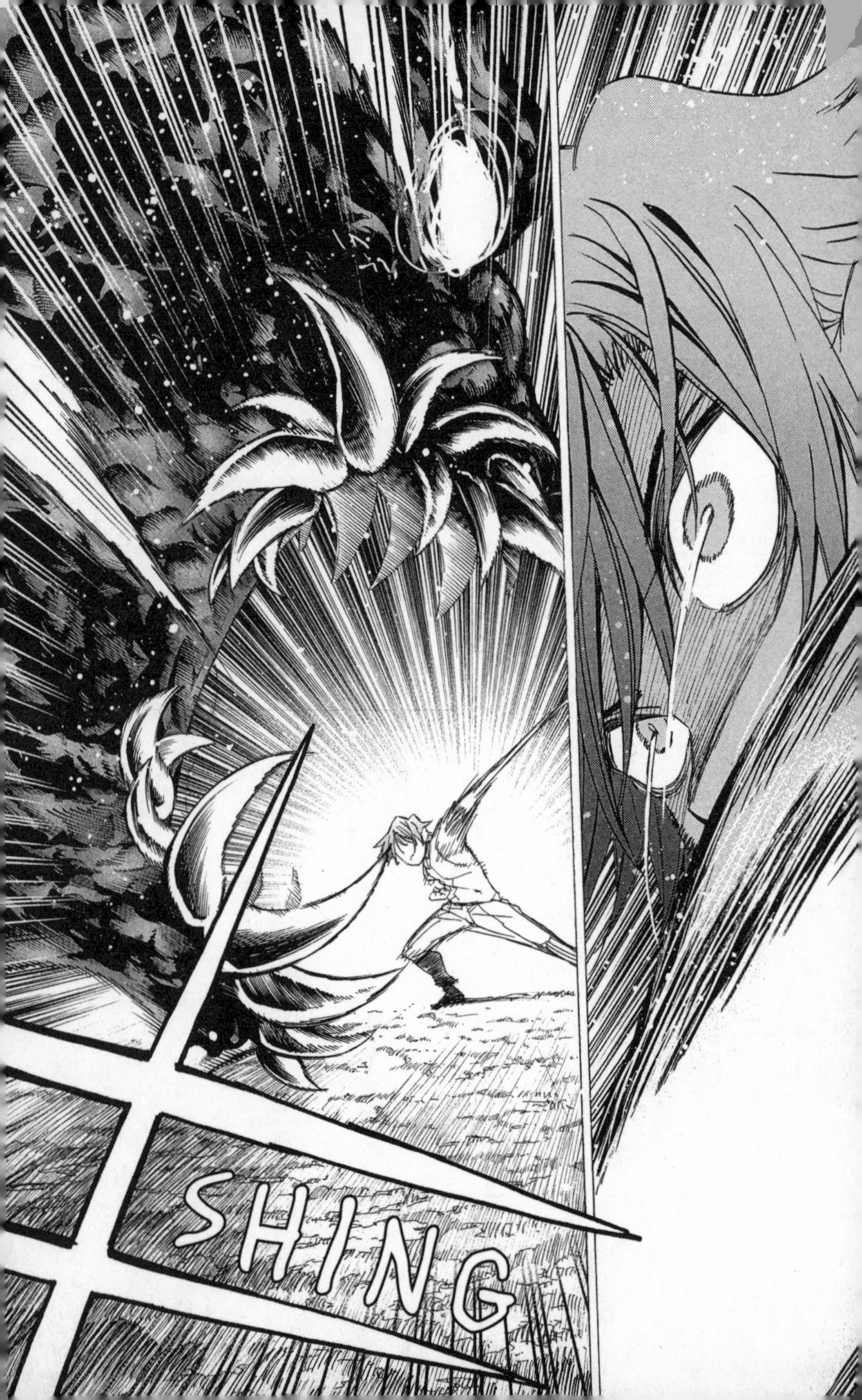
SHING

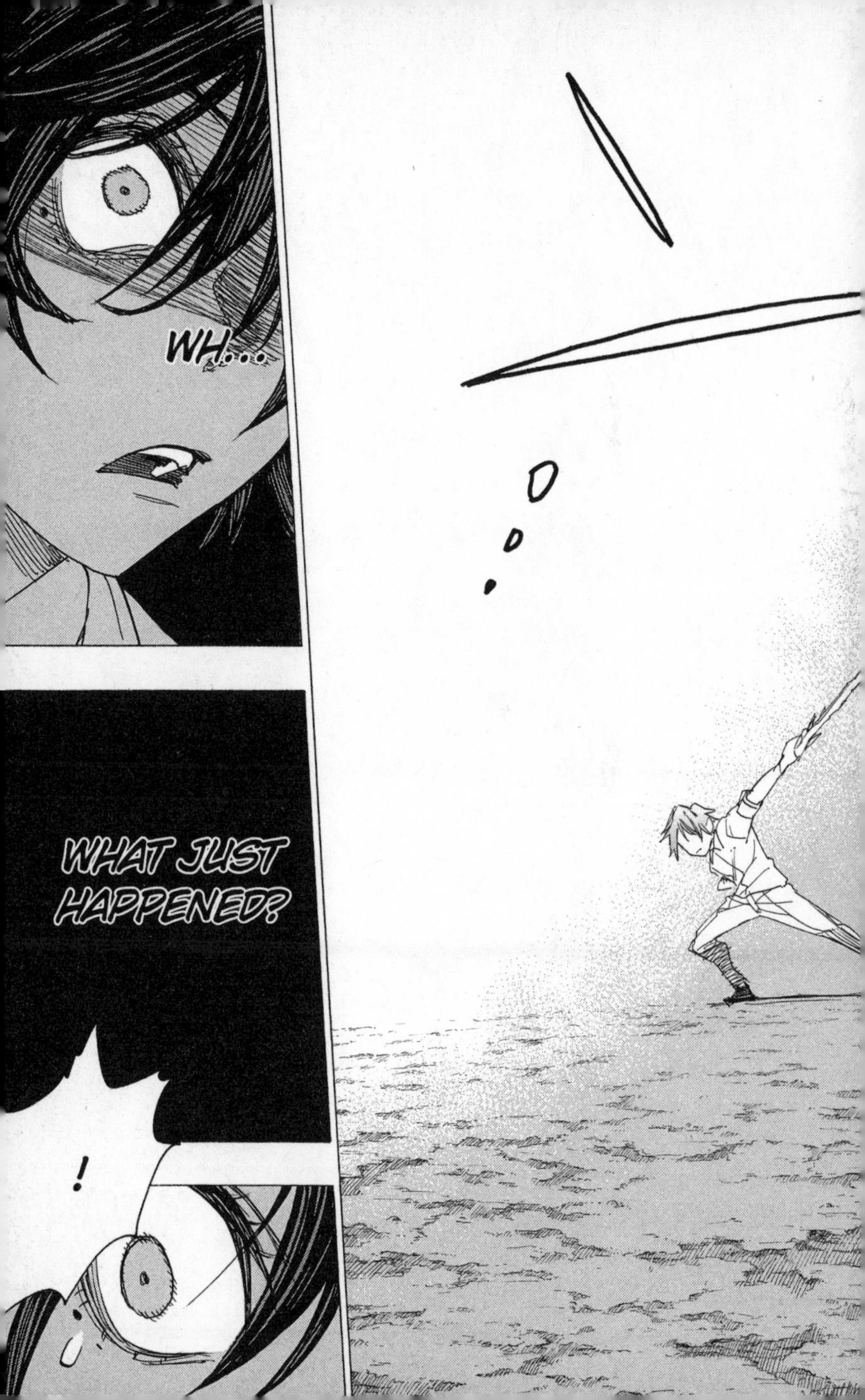
WH...
WHAT JUST HAPPENED?
!

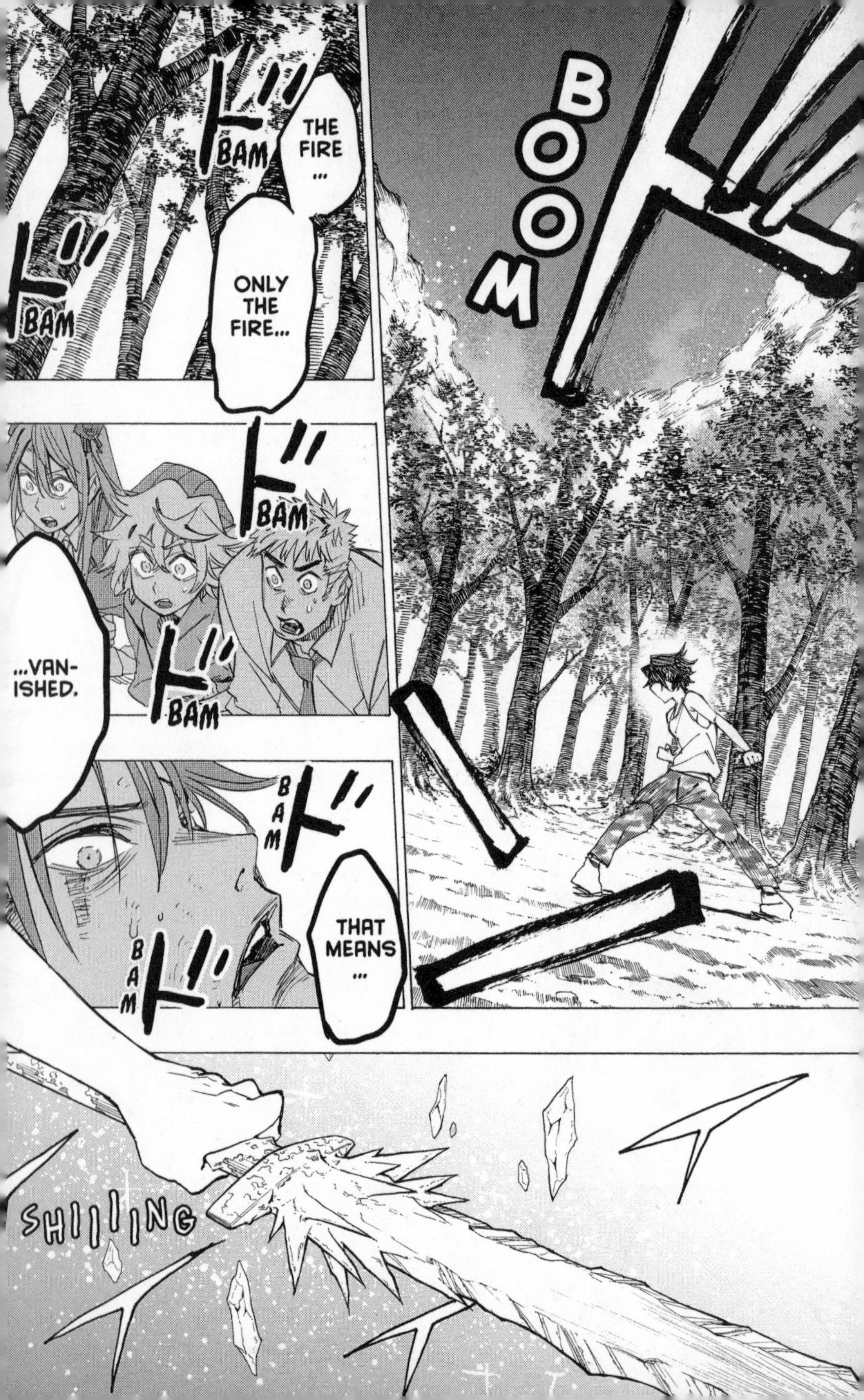
BOOM
BAM
THE FIRE...
BAM
ONLY THE FIRE...
BAM
...VAN-ISHED.
BAM
BAM
THAT MEANS...
BAM
SHIIIING

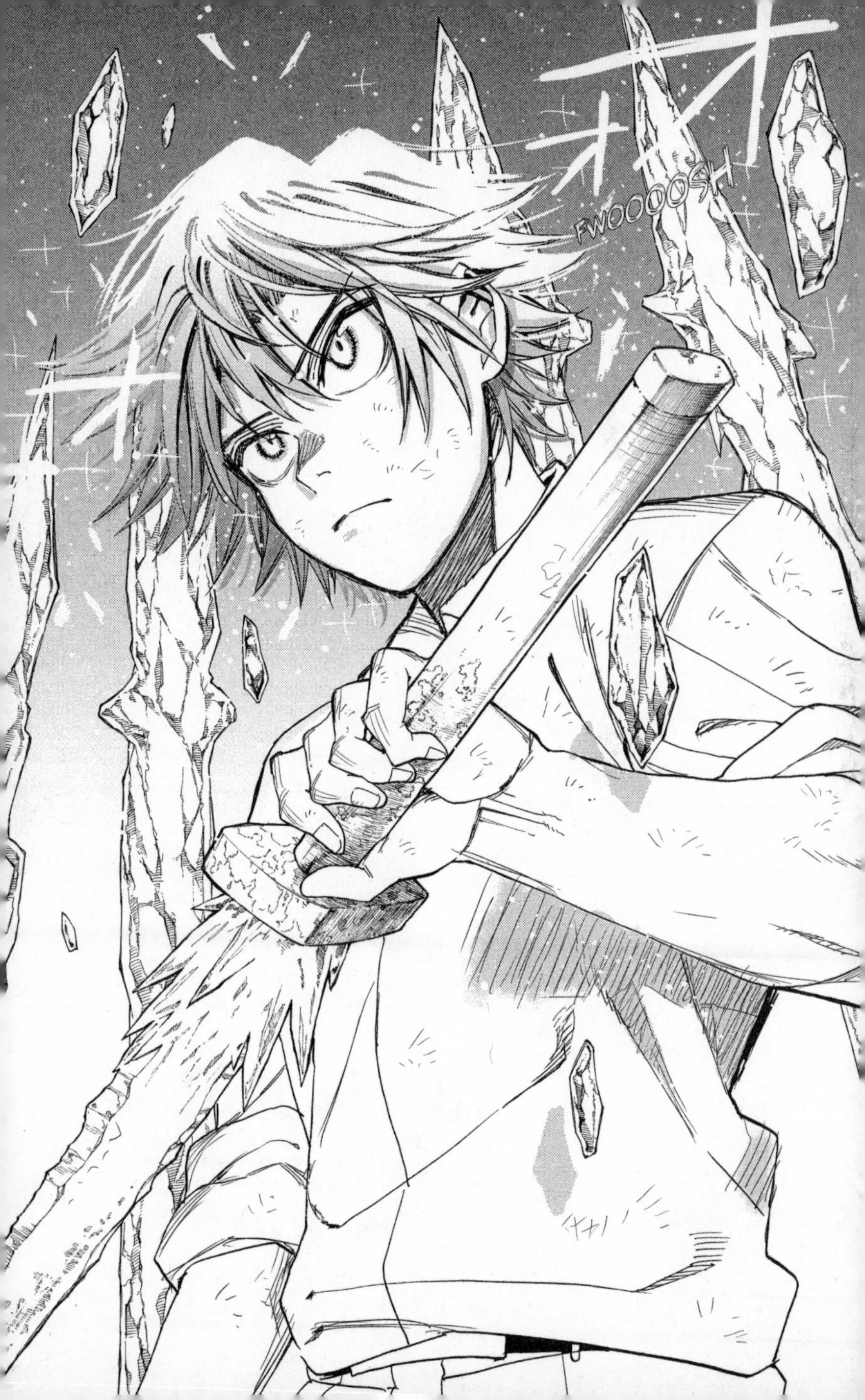
FWOOOOOSH

The ICEBLADE SORCERER Shall RULE the WORLD

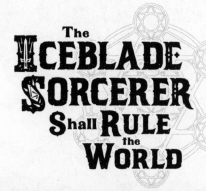

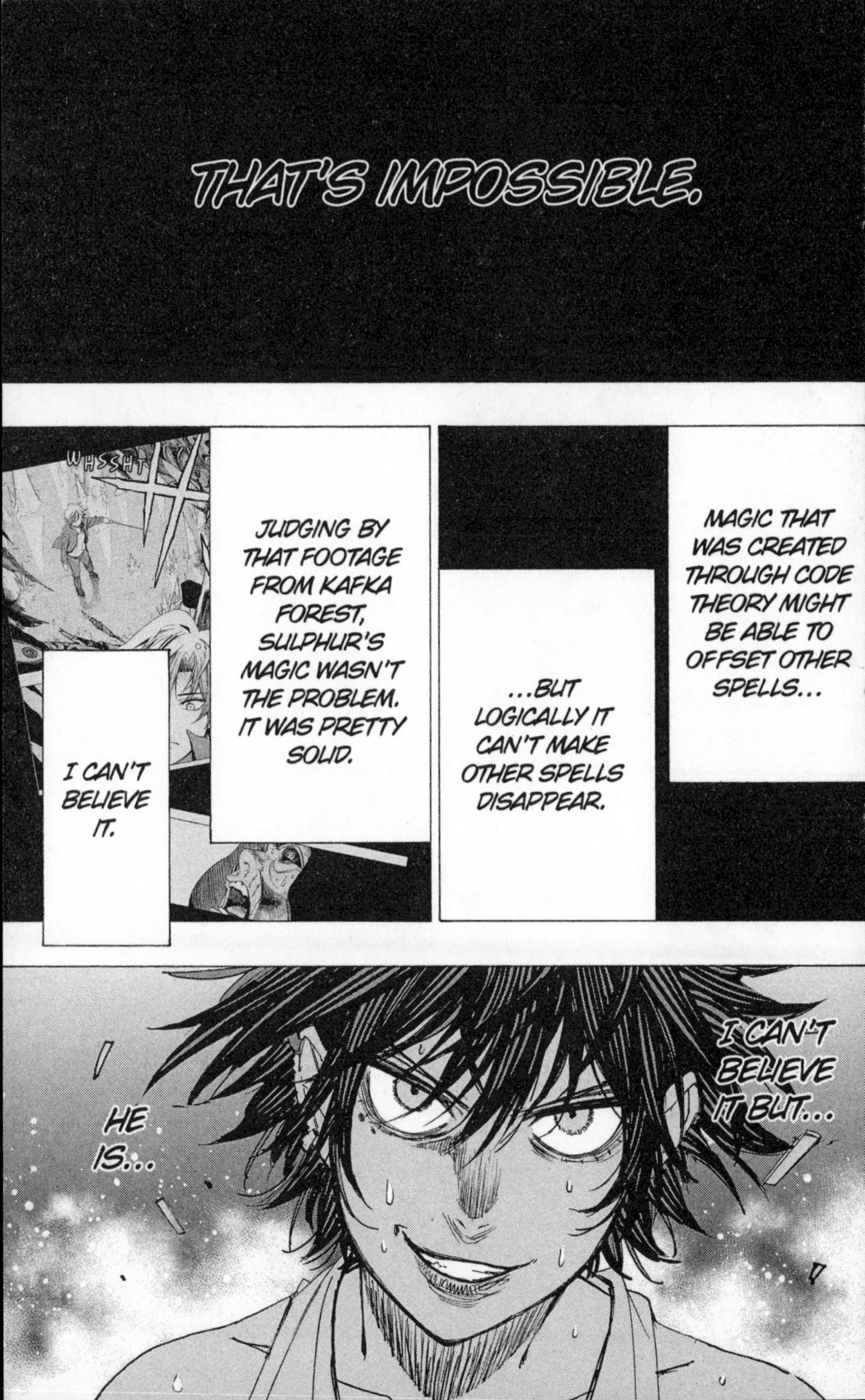
THAT'S IMPOSSIBLE.
MAGIC THAT WAS CREATED THROUGH CODE THEORY MIGHT BE ABLE TO OFFSET OTHER SPELLS...
...BUT LOGICALLY IT CAN'T MAKE OTHER SPELLS DISAPPEAR.
JUDGING BY THAT FOOTAGE FROM KAFKA FOREST, SULPHUR'S MAGIC WASN'T THE PROBLEM. IT WAS PRETTY SOLID.
WHSSHT
I CAN'T BELIEVE IT.
I CAN'T BELIEVE IT BUT...
HE IS...

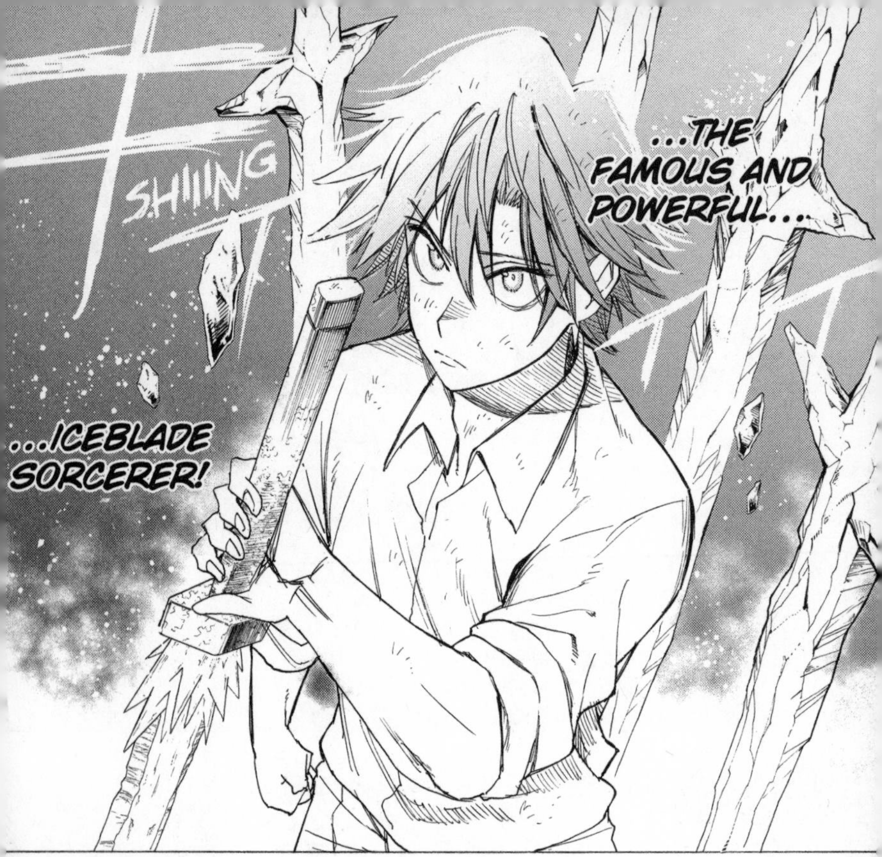
...THE FAMOUS AND POWERFUL...
SHIIING
...ICEBLADE SORCERER!

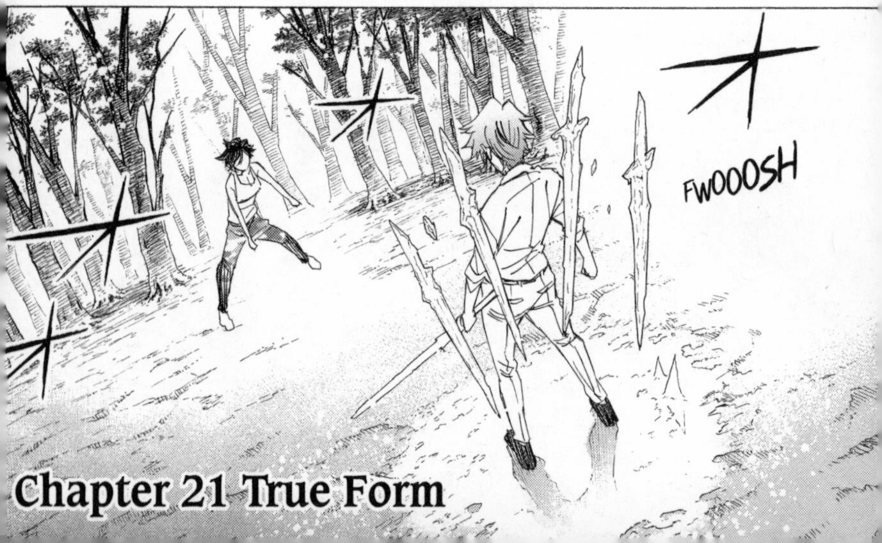
FWOOOSH

Chapter 21 True Form

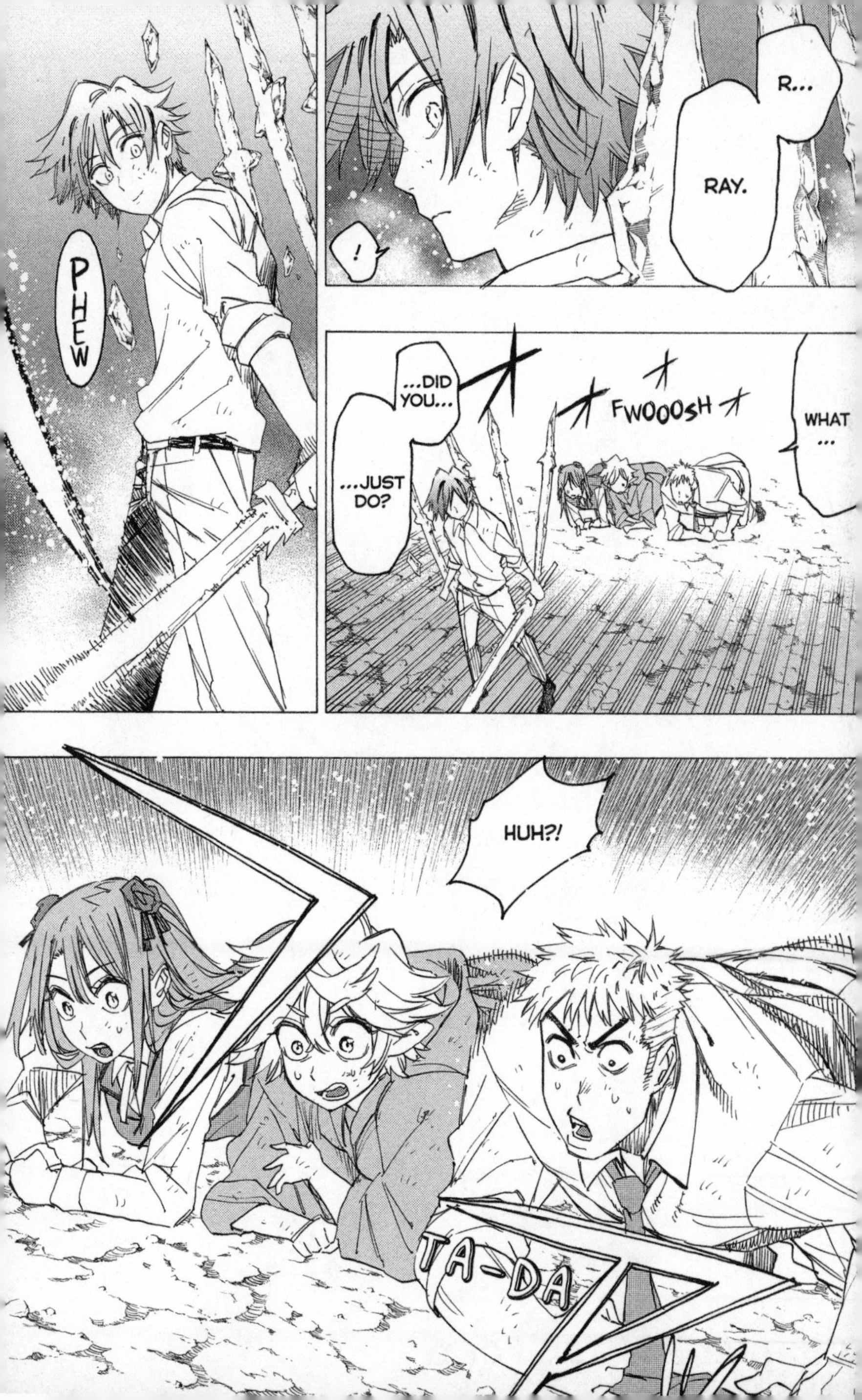
R...
RAY.
!
WHAT...
FWOOOSH
...DID YOU...
...JUST DO?
PHEW
HUH?!
TA-DA

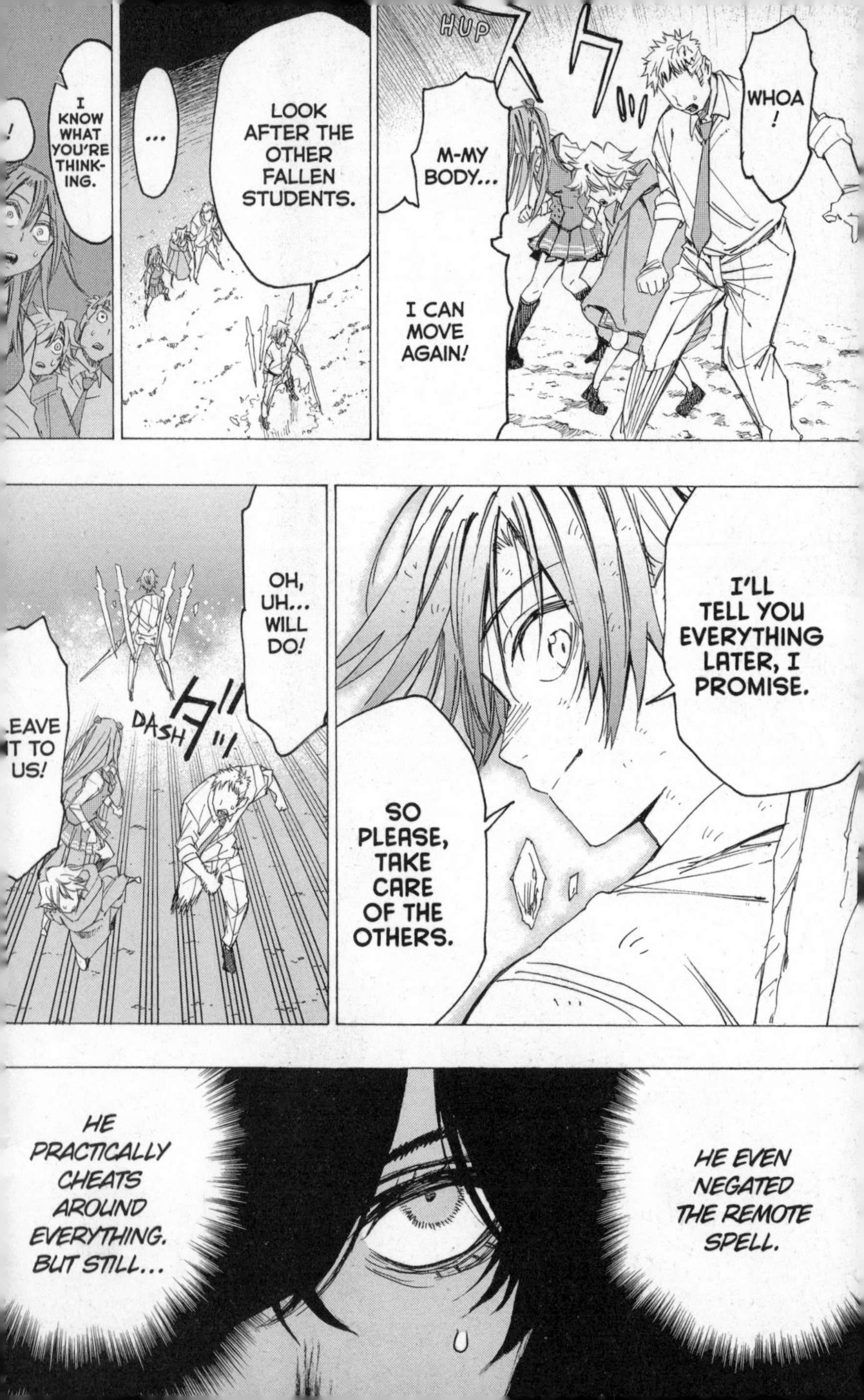
HUP
WHOA!
M-MY BODY...
I CAN MOVE AGAIN!
...
LOOK AFTER THE OTHER FALLEN STUDENTS.
I KNOW WHAT YOU'RE THINKING.
!
I'LL TELL YOU EVERYTHING LATER, I PROMISE.
SO PLEASE, TAKE CARE OF THE OTHERS.
OH, UH... WILL DO!
DASH
LEAVE IT TO US!
HE EVEN NEGATED THE REMOTE SPELL.
HE PRACTICALLY CHEATS AROUND EVERYTHING. BUT STILL...

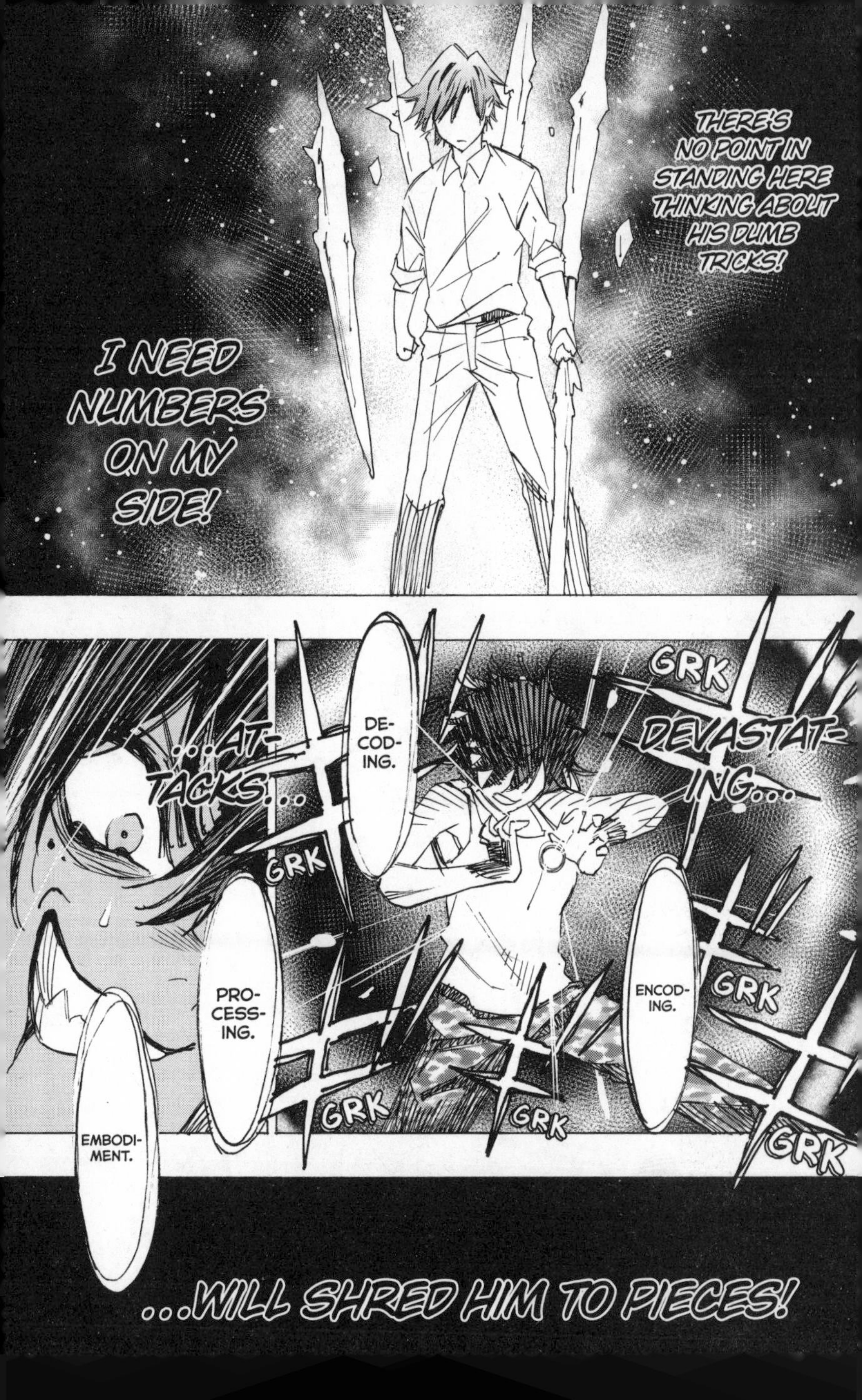
THERE'S NO POINT IN STANDING HERE THINKING ABOUT HIS DUMB TRICKS!
I NEED NUMBERS ON MY SIDE!
GRK
DEVASTAT-ING...
DE-COD-ING.
ENCOD-ING.
GRK
GRK
GRK
GRK
...AT-TACKS...
GRK
PRO-CESS-ING.
EMBODI-MENT.
...WILL SHRED HIM TO PIECES!

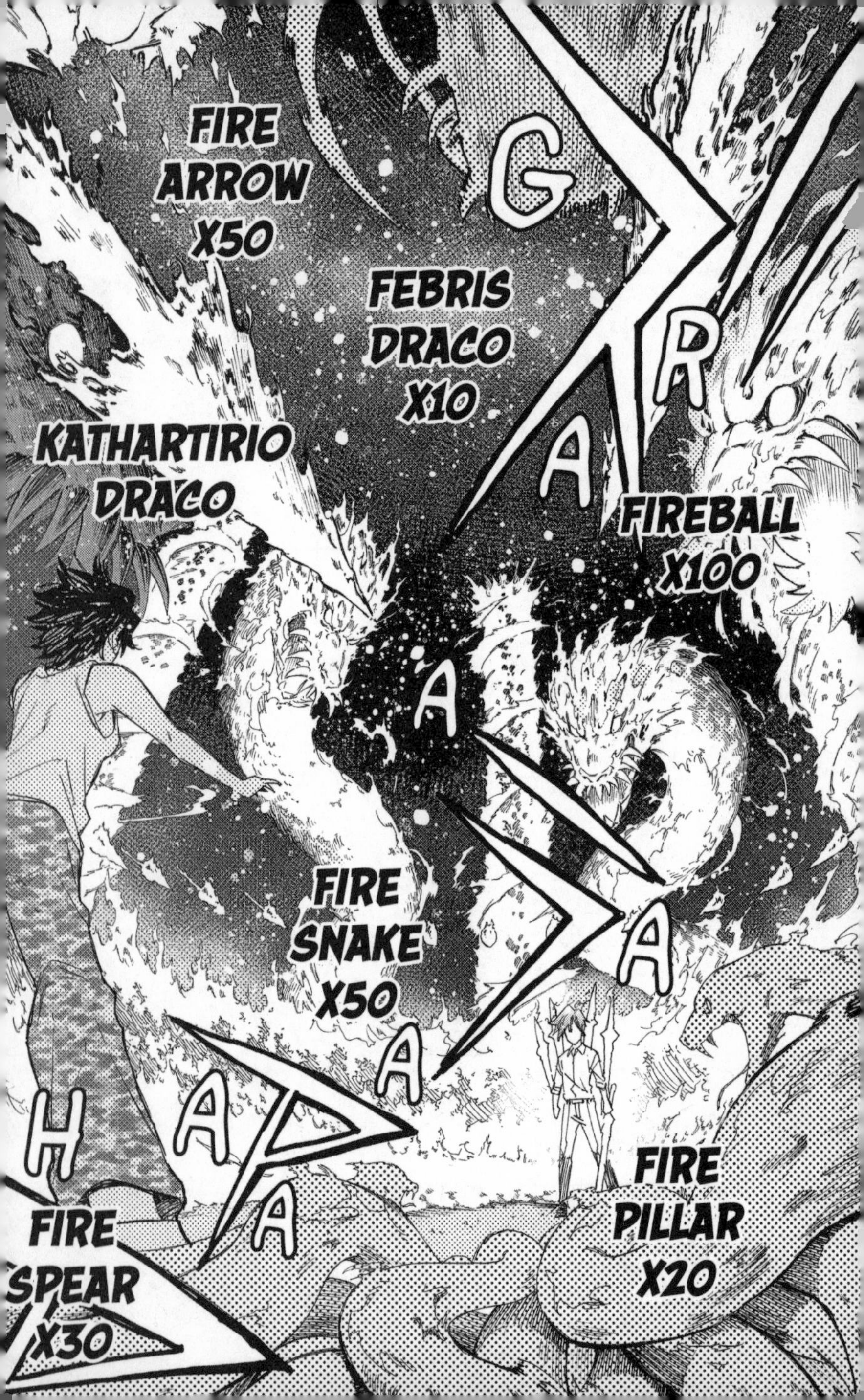
GRAAAA
FEBRIS DRACO X10
FIRE ARROW X50
FIREBALL X100
KATHARTIRIO DRACO
FIRE SNAKE X50
FIRE PILLAR X20
HAA
FIRE SPEAR X30

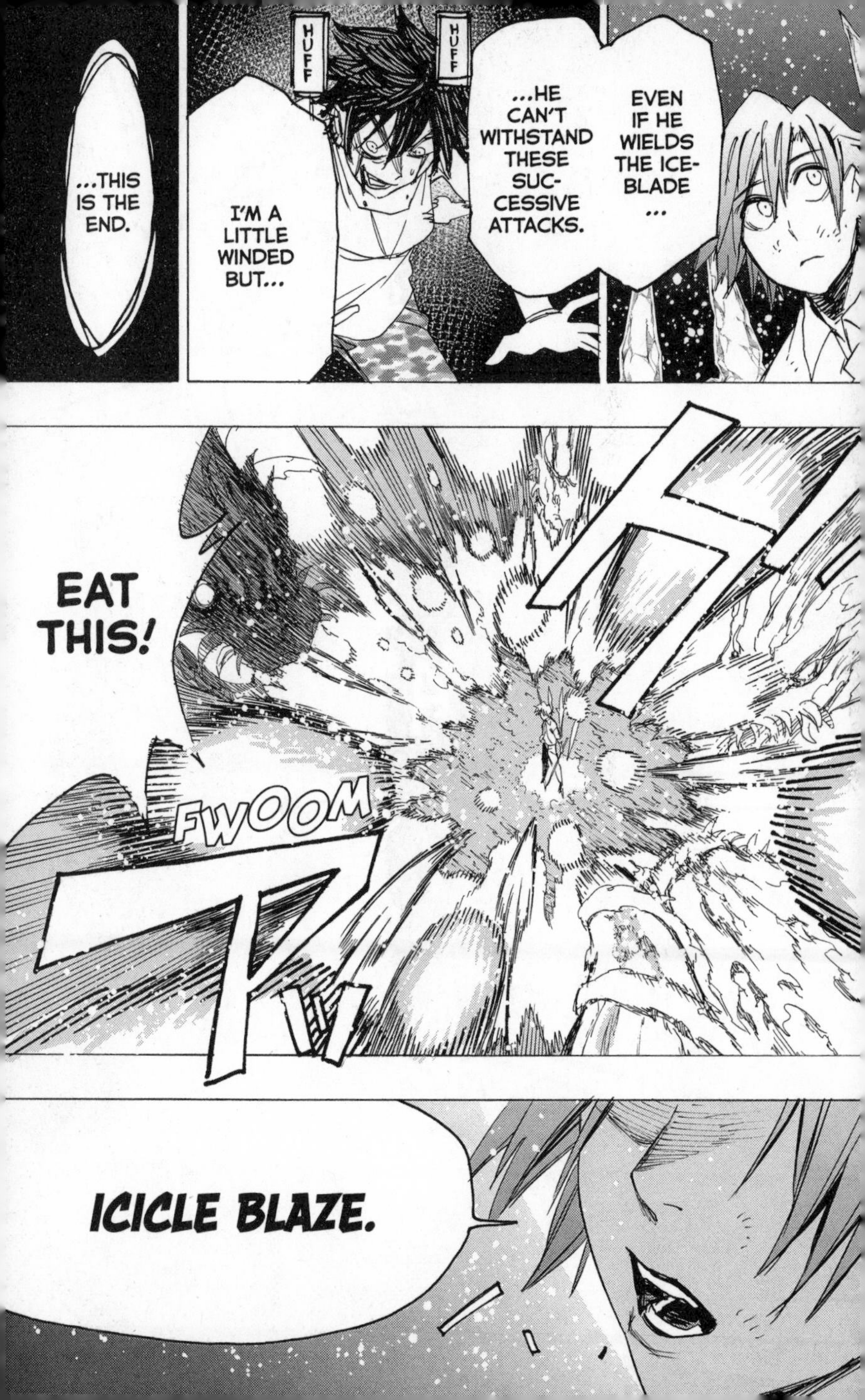
EVEN IF HE WIELDS THE ICE-BLADE...
...HE CAN'T WITHSTAND THESE SUC-CESSIVE ATTACKS.
HUFF
HUFF
I'M A LITTLE WINDED BUT...
...THIS IS THE END.
EAT THIS!
FWOOM
ICICLE BLAZE.

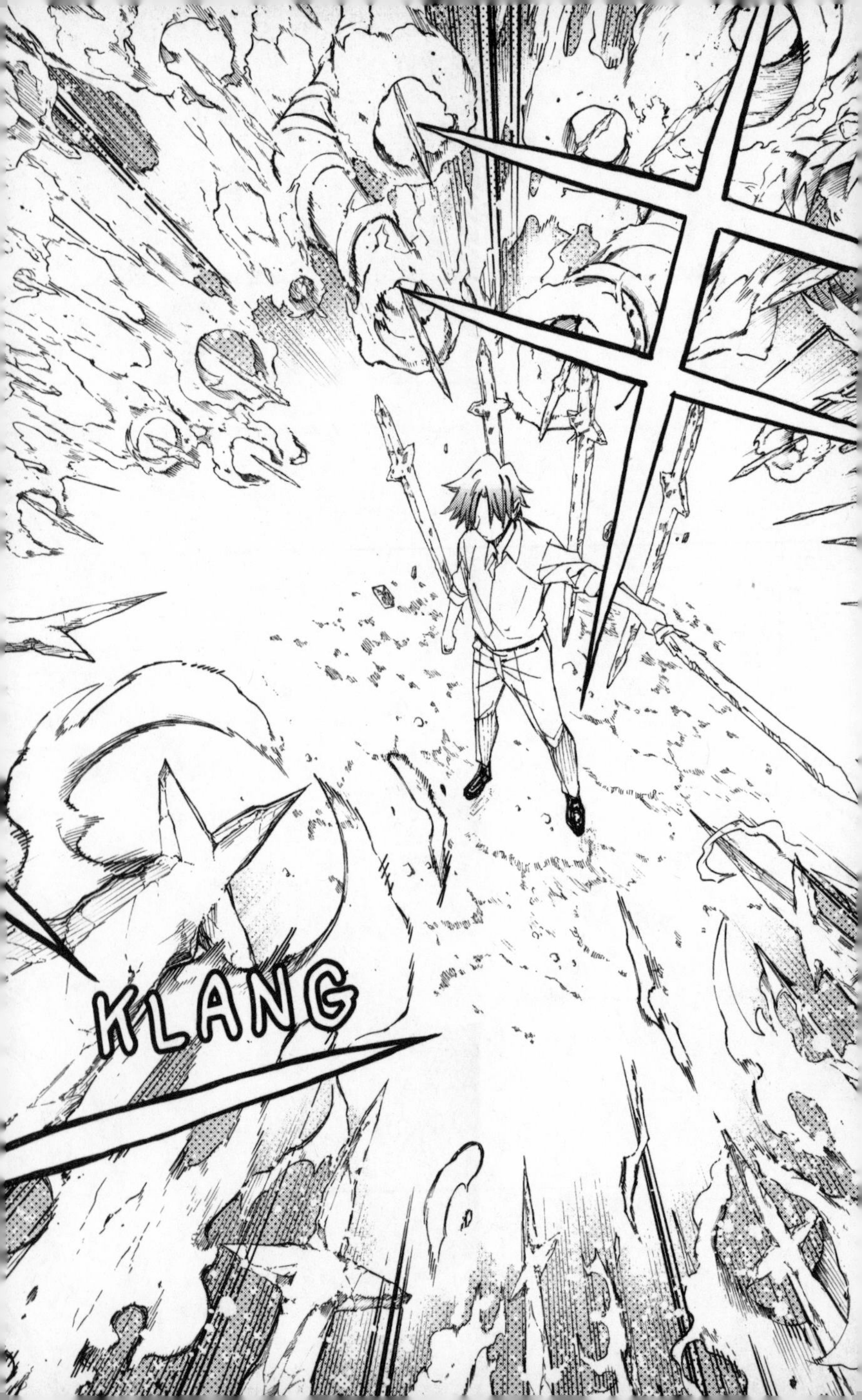
KLANG

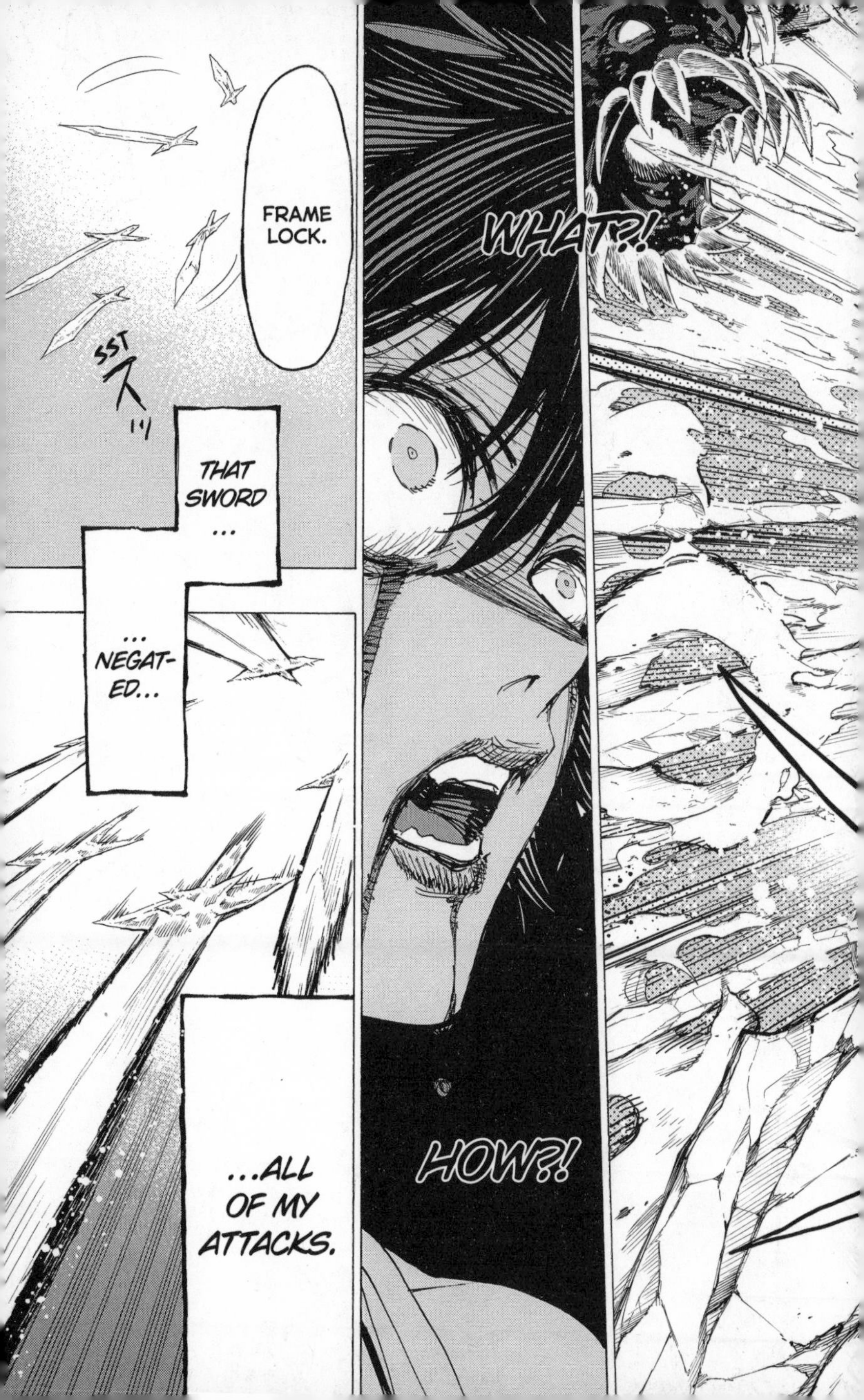
WHAT?!
FRAME LOCK.
SST
THAT SWORD...
...NEGATED...
HOW?!
...ALL OF MY ATTACKS.

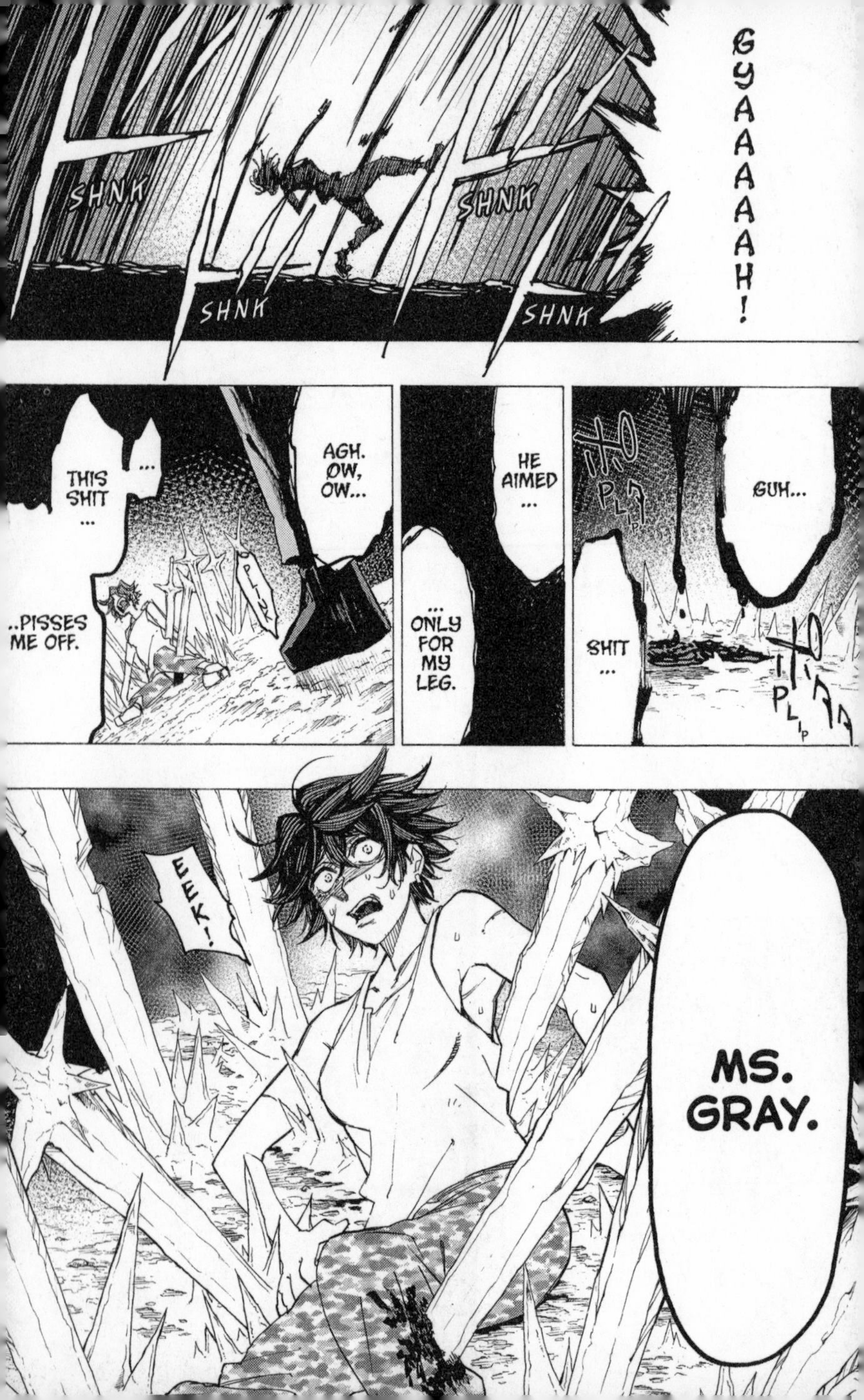
GYAAAAAAH!
SHNK
SHNK
SHNK
SHNK
GUH...
PLIP
SHIT...
PLIP
HE AIMED...
...ONLY FOR MY LEG.
AGH. OW, OW...
PLINK
...
THIS SHIT...
..PISSES ME OFF.
MS. GRAY.
EEK!

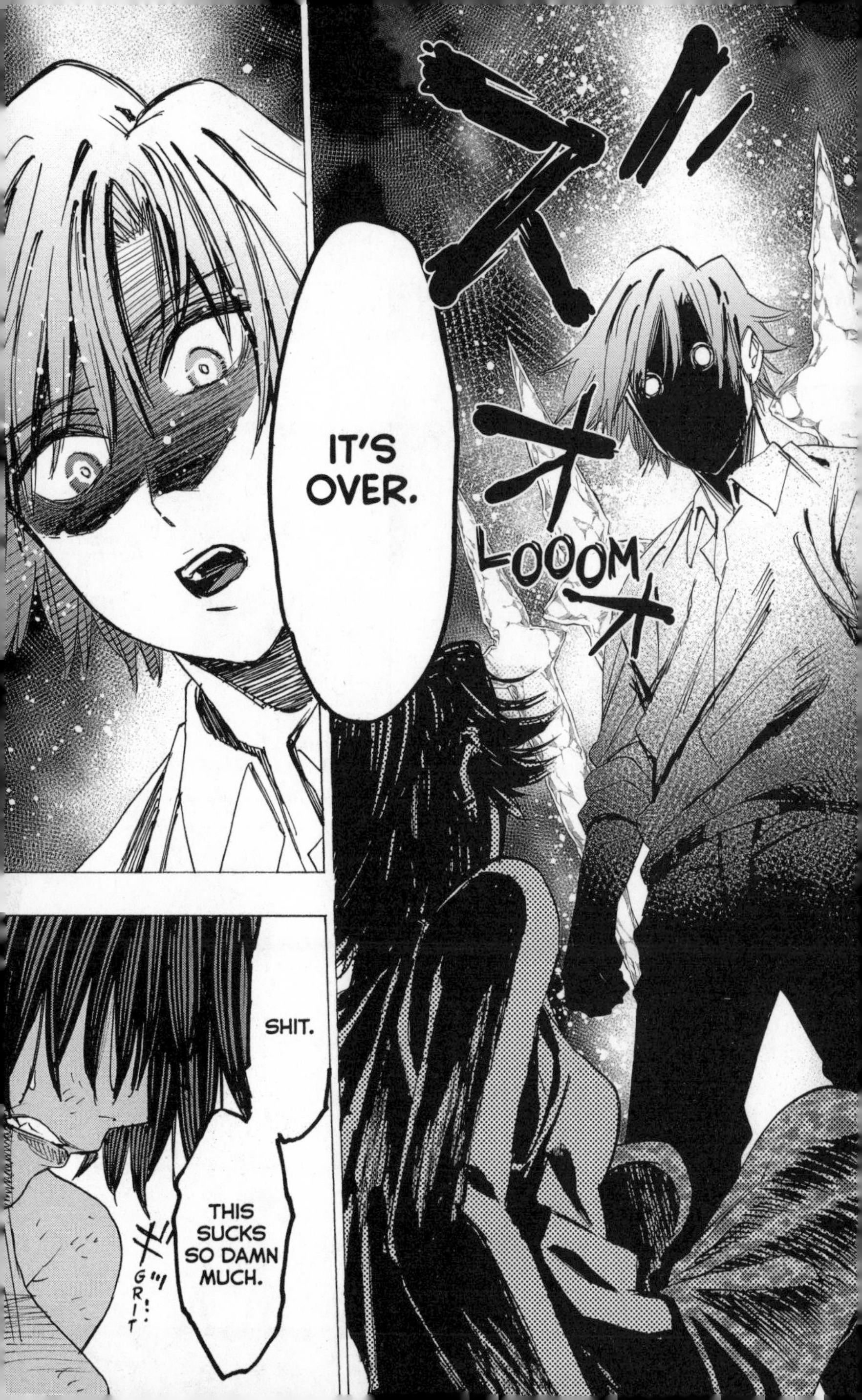
LOOOM
IT'S OVER.
SHIT.
THIS SUCKS SO DAMN MUCH.
GRIT

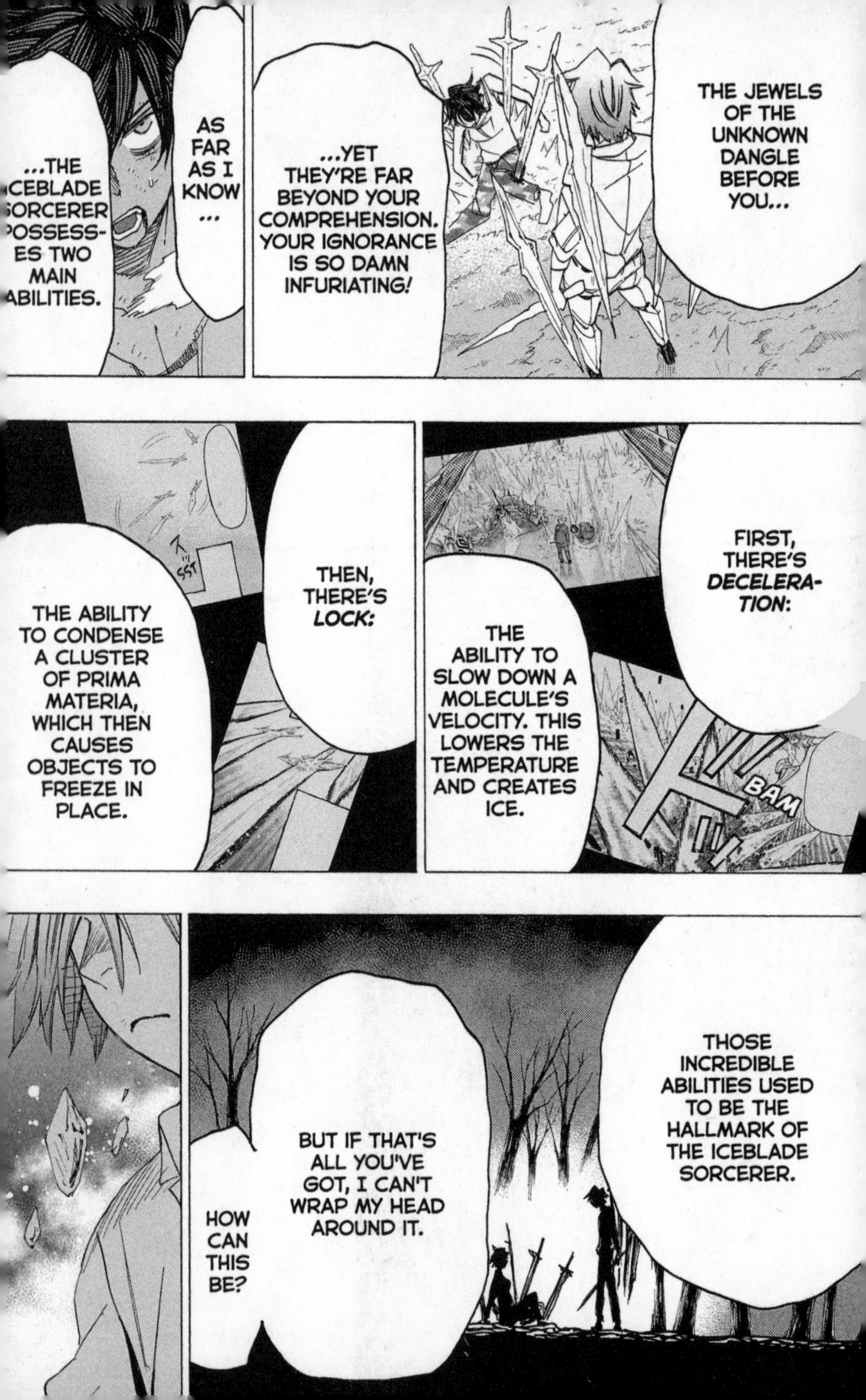
THE JEWELS OF THE UNKNOWN DANGLE BEFORE YOU...
...YET THEY'RE FAR BEYOND YOUR COMPREHENSION. YOUR IGNORANCE IS SO DAMN INFURIATING!
AS FAR AS I KNOW...
...THE ICEBLADE SORCERER POSSESSES TWO MAIN ABILITIES.
FIRST, THERE'S *DECELERATION*:
THE ABILITY TO SLOW DOWN A MOLECULE'S VELOCITY. THIS LOWERS THE TEMPERATURE AND CREATES ICE.
BAM
THEN, THERE'S *LOCK*:
THE ABILITY TO CONDENSE A CLUSTER OF PRIMA MATERIA, WHICH THEN CAUSES OBJECTS TO FREEZE IN PLACE.
SST
THOSE INCREDIBLE ABILITIES USED TO BE THE HALLMARK OF THE ICEBLADE SORCERER.
BUT IF THAT'S ALL YOU'VE GOT, I CAN'T WRAP MY HEAD AROUND IT.
HOW CAN THIS BE?

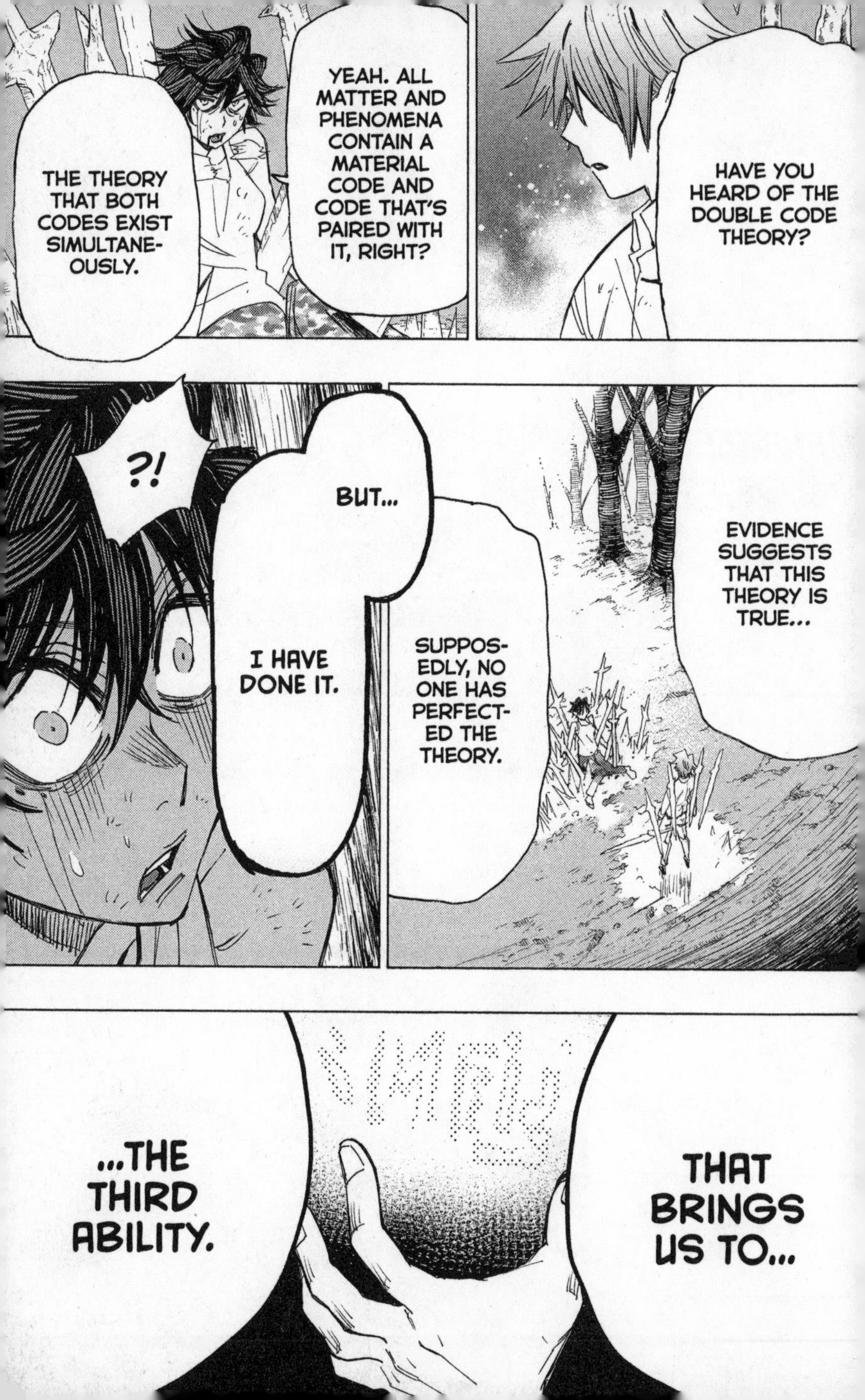
HAVE YOU HEARD OF THE DOUBLE CODE THEORY?
YEAH. ALL MATTER AND PHENOMENA CONTAIN A MATERIAL CODE AND CODE THAT'S PAIRED WITH IT, RIGHT?
THE THEORY THAT BOTH CODES EXIST SIMULTANE-OUSLY.
EVIDENCE SUGGESTS THAT THIS THEORY IS TRUE...
SUPPOS-EDLY, NO ONE HAS PERFECT-ED THE THEORY.
BUT...
I HAVE DONE IT.
?!
THAT BRINGS US TO...
...THE THIRD ABILITY.

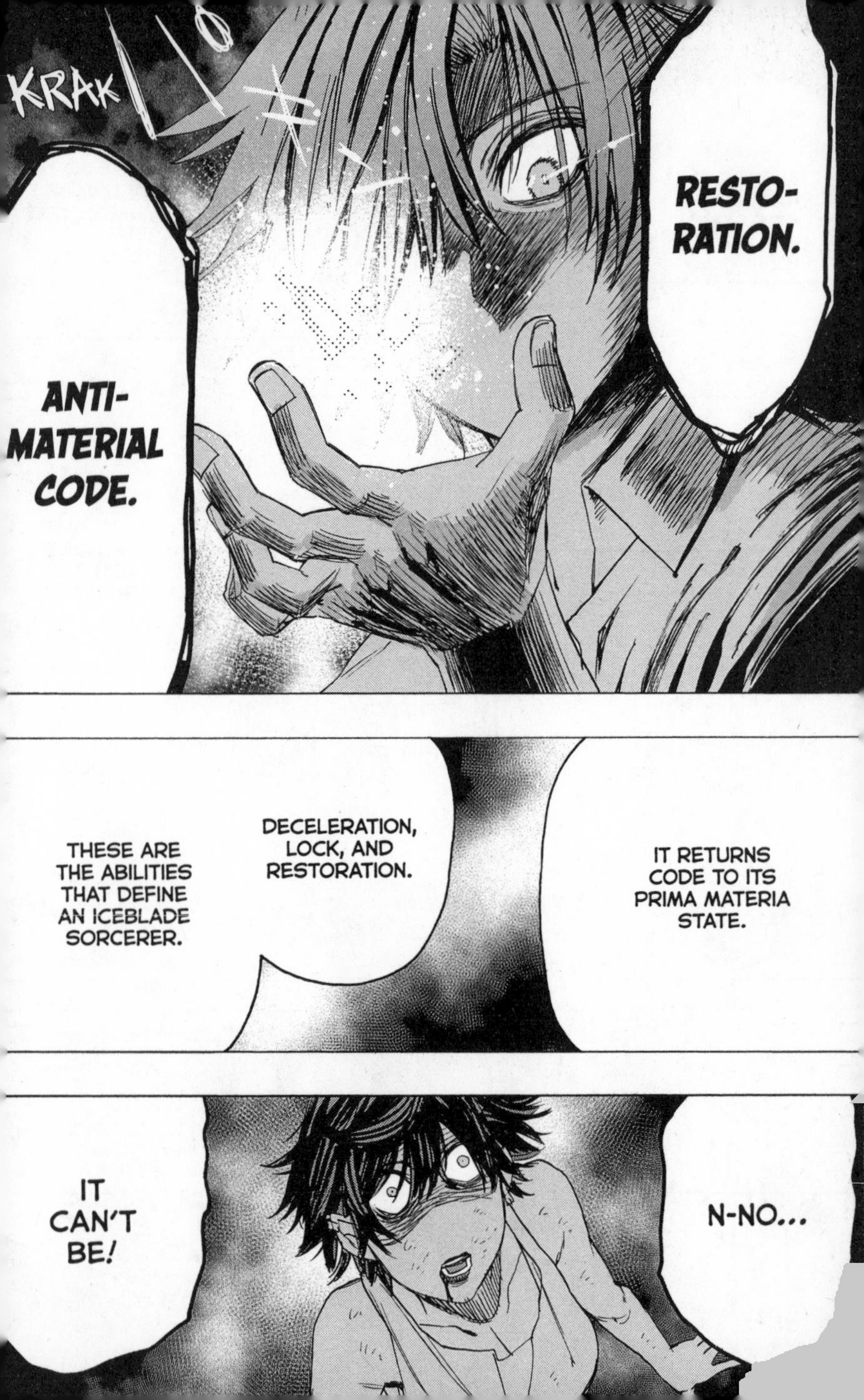
RESTO-
RATION.
KRAK
ANTI-
MATERIAL
CODE.
IT RETURNS CODE TO ITS PRIMA MATERIA STATE.
DECELERATION, LOCK, AND RESTORATION.
THESE ARE THE ABILITIES THAT DEFINE AN ICEBLADE SORCERER.
N-NO...
IT CAN'T BE!

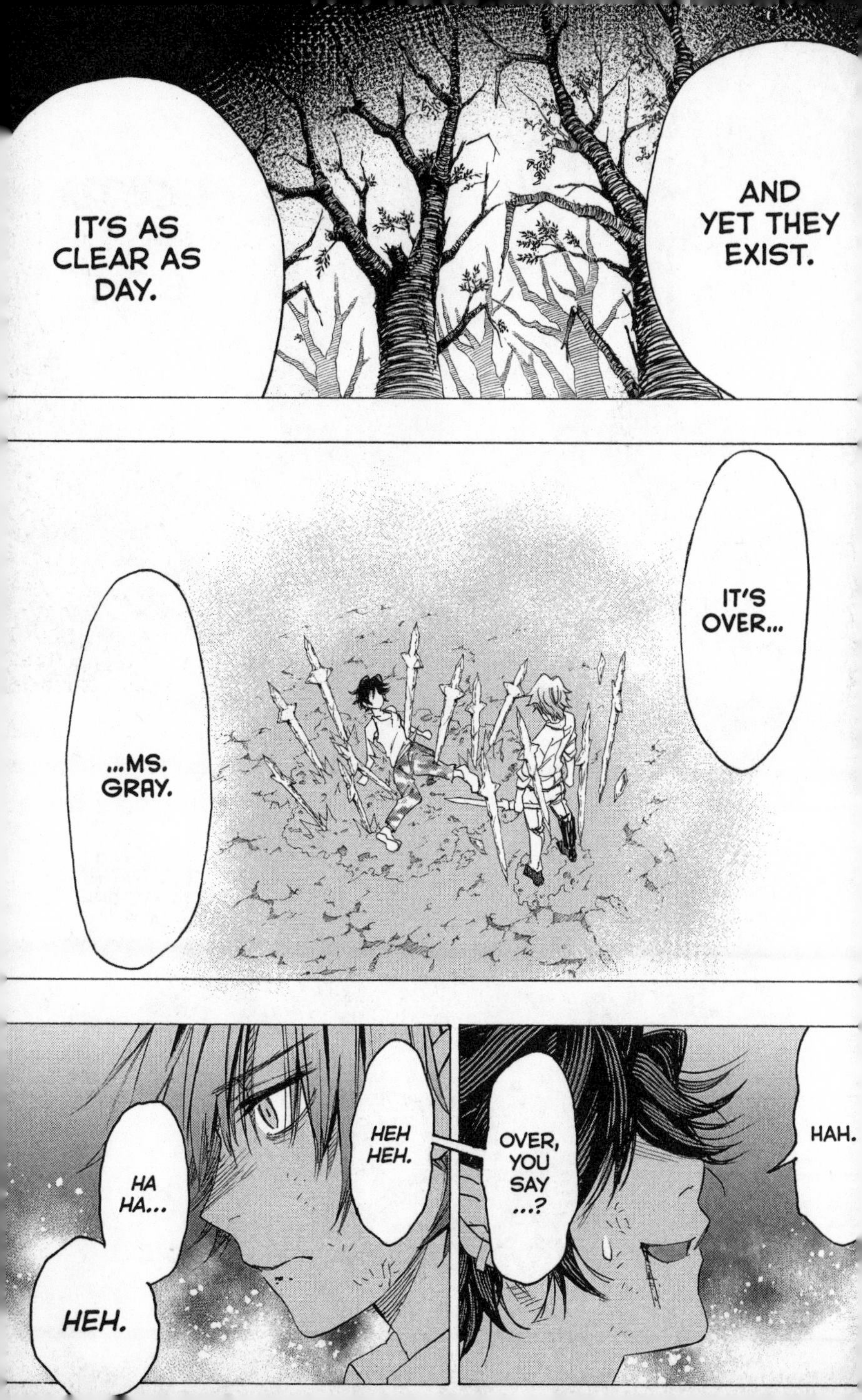
AND YET THEY EXIST.
IT'S AS CLEAR AS DAY.
IT'S OVER...
...MS. GRAY.
HAH.
OVER, YOU SAY ...?
HEH HEH.
HA HA...
HEH.

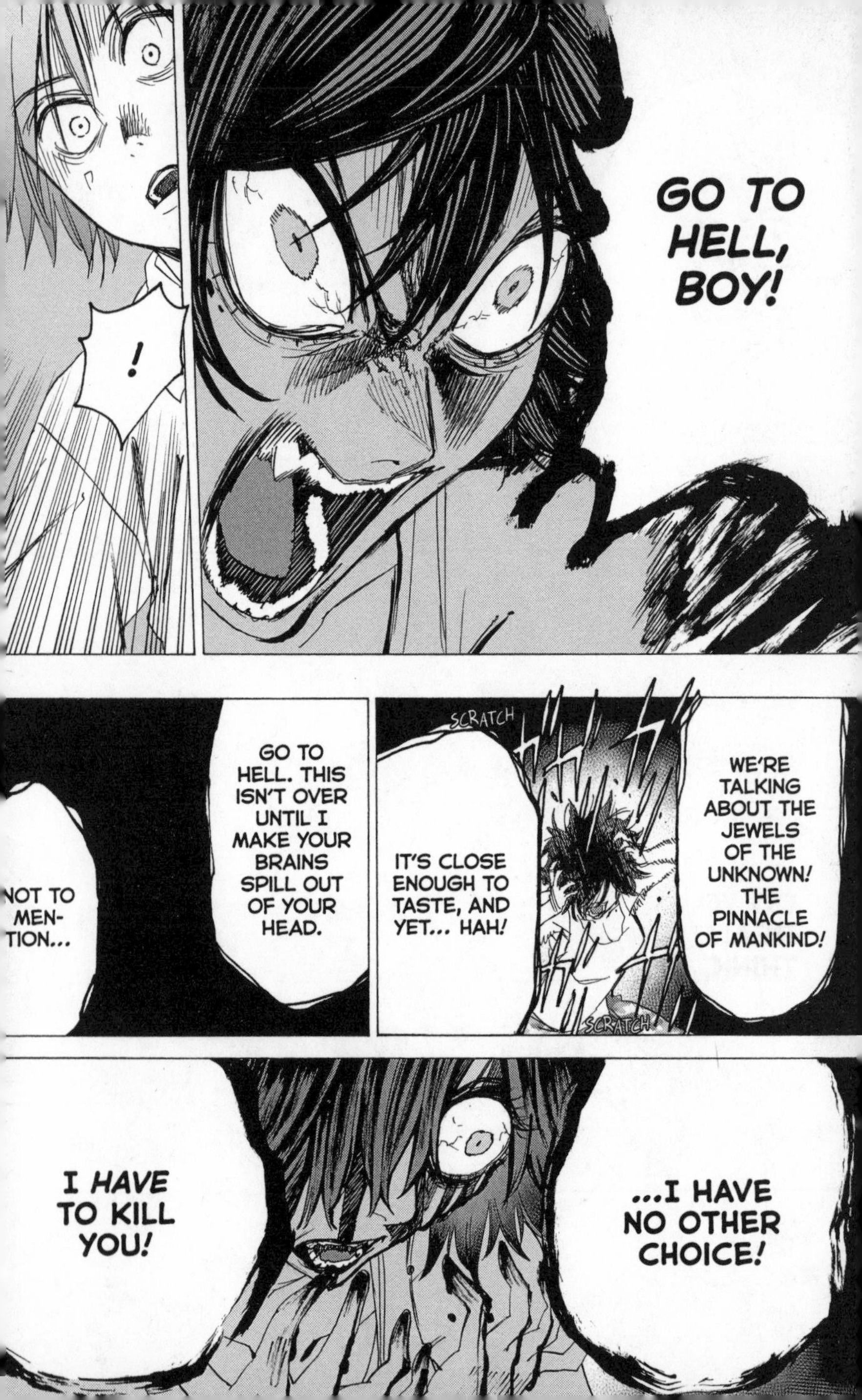
GO TO HELL, BOY!
!
SCRATCH
WE'RE TALKING ABOUT THE JEWELS OF THE UNKNOWN! THE PINNACLE OF MANKIND!
IT'S CLOSE ENOUGH TO TASTE, AND YET... HAH!
SCRATCH
GO TO HELL. THIS ISN'T OVER UNTIL I MAKE YOUR BRAINS SPILL OUT OF YOUR HEAD.
NOT TO MEN-TION...
...I HAVE NO OTHER CHOICE!
I *HAVE* TO KILL YOU!

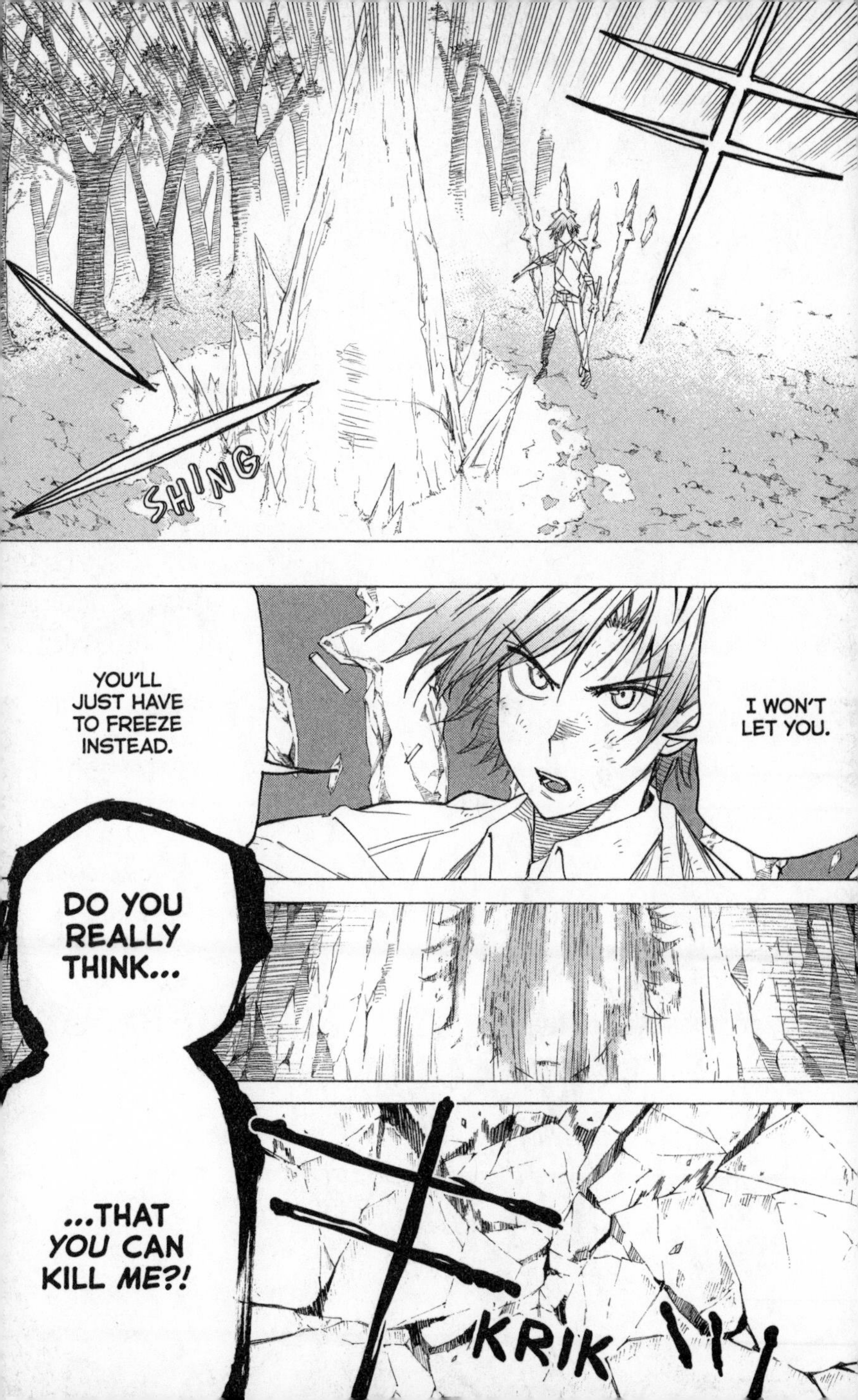
SHING
I WON'T LET YOU.
YOU'LL JUST HAVE TO FREEZE INSTEAD.
DO YOU REALLY THINK...
...THAT *YOU* CAN KILL *ME*?!
KRIK

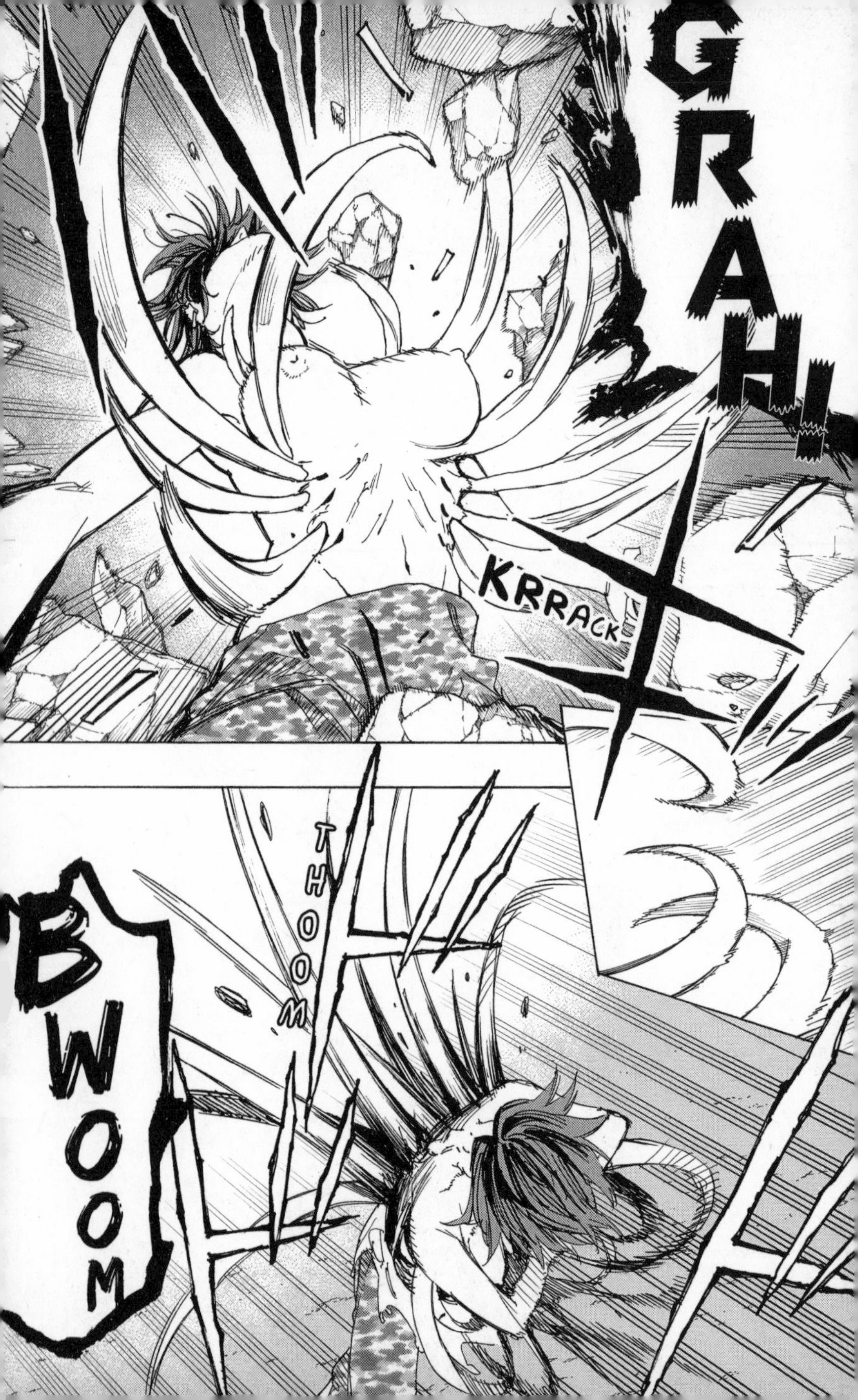
GRAH!!
KRRACK
THOOM
BWOOM

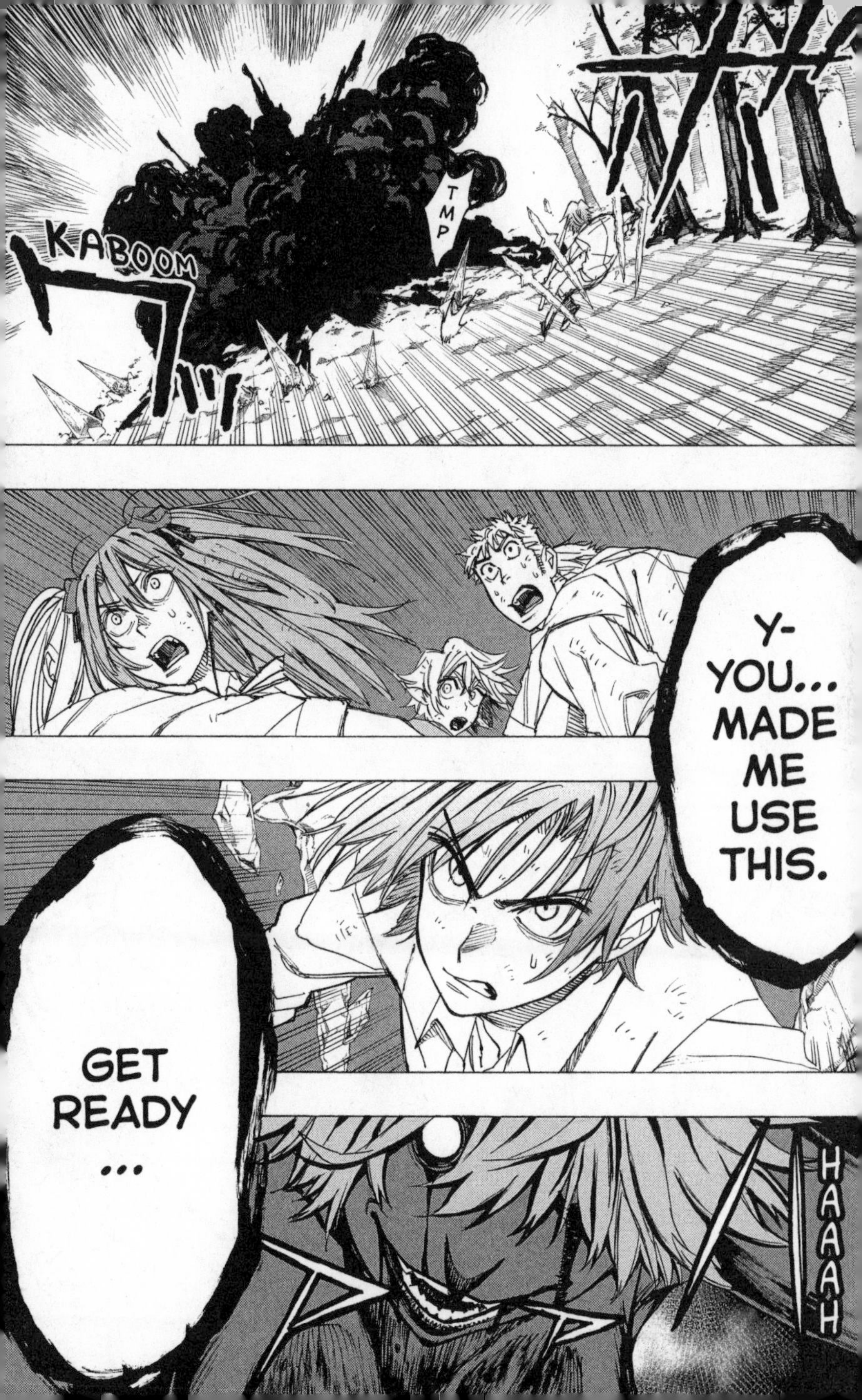
TMP
KABOOM
Y-YOU... MADE ME USE THIS.
GET READY...
HAAAAH

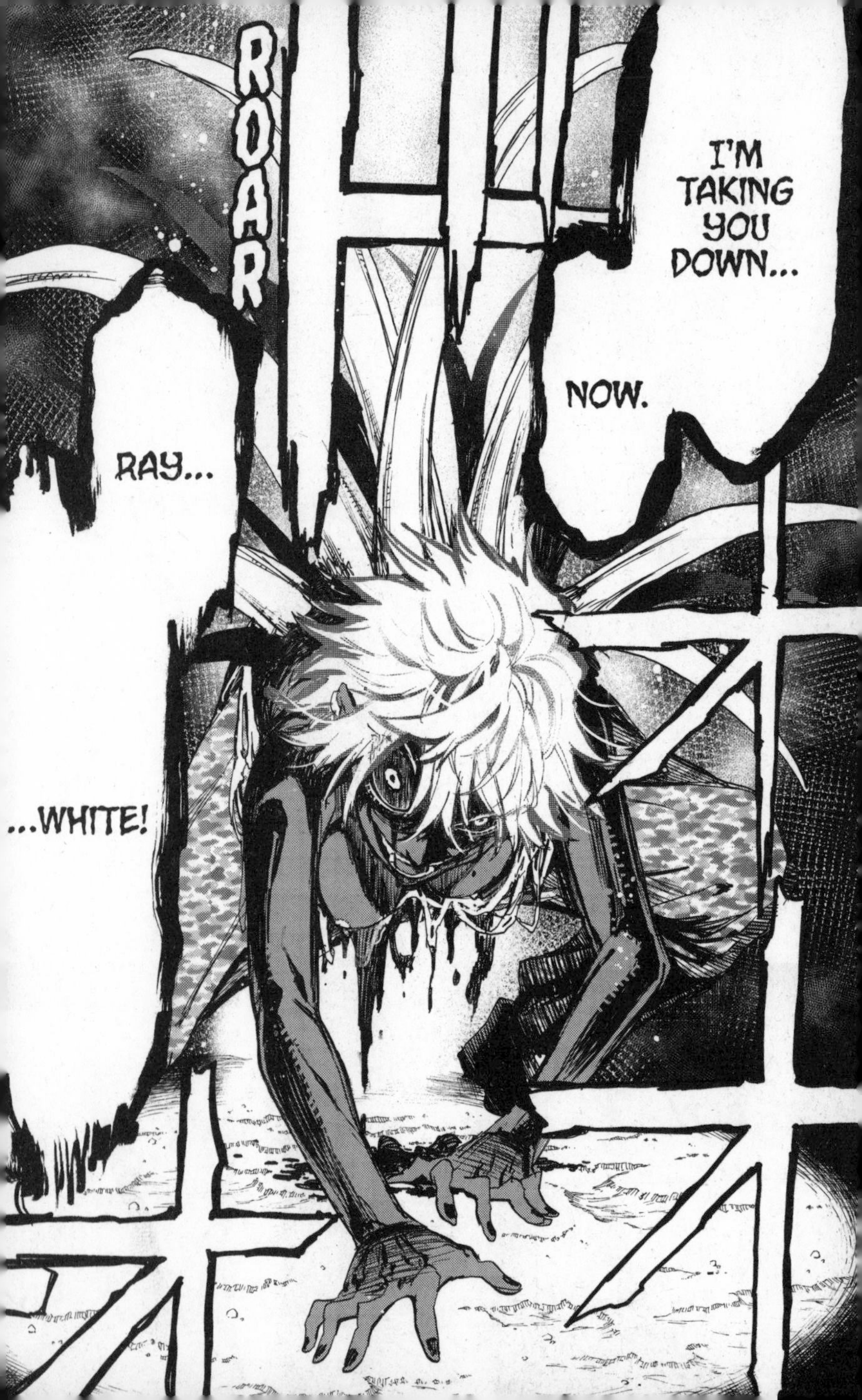
I'M TAKING YOU DOWN...
NOW.
ROAR
RAY...
...WHITE!

Chapter 22 Abyss

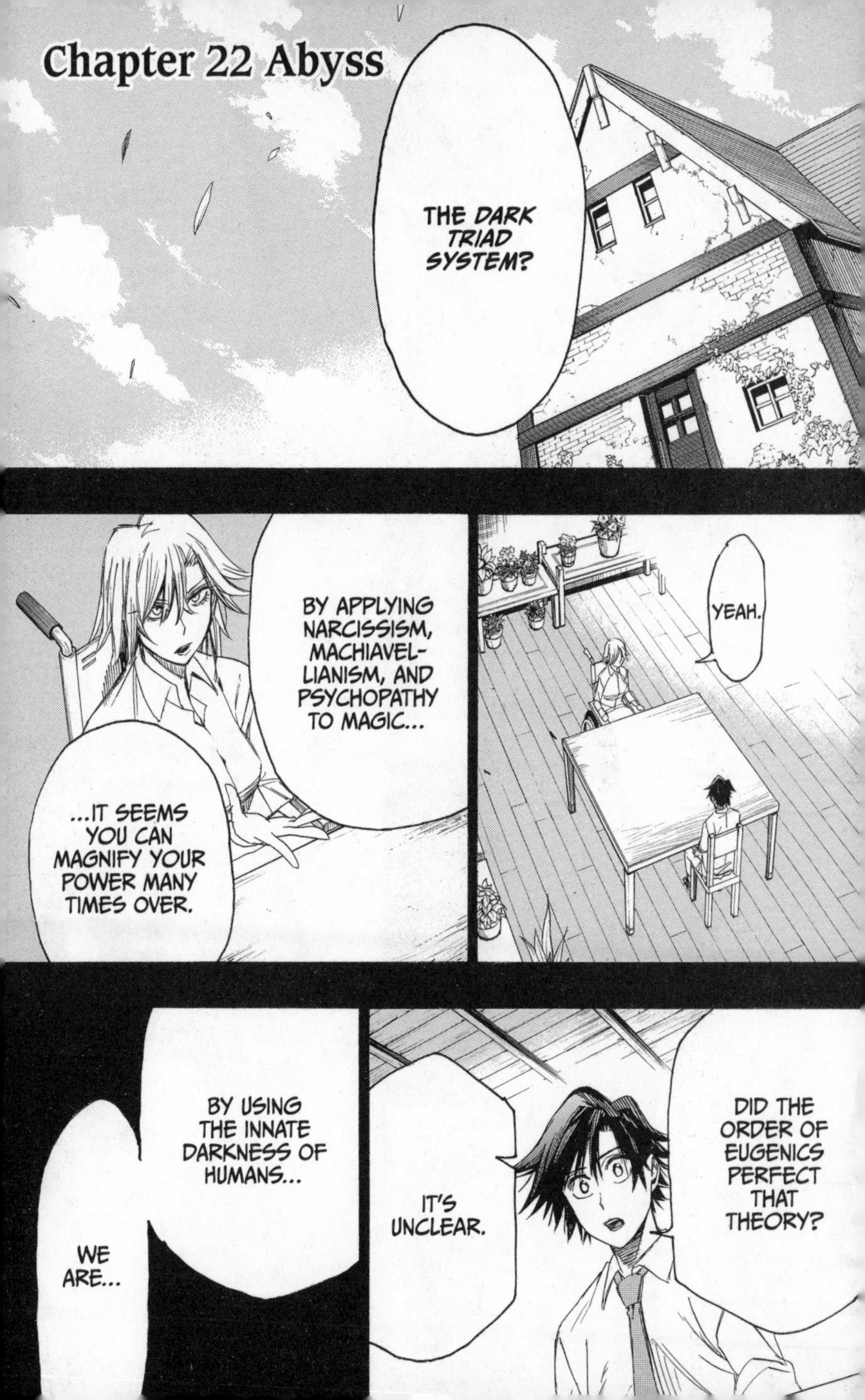

THE *DARK TRIAD SYSTEM?*
YEAH.
BY APPLYING NARCISSISM, MACHIAVEL-LIANISM, AND PSYCHOPATHY TO MAGIC...
...IT SEEMS YOU CAN MAGNIFY YOUR POWER MANY TIMES OVER.
DID THE ORDER OF EUGENICS PERFECT THAT THEORY?
IT'S UNCLEAR.
BY USING THE INNATE DARKNESS OF HUMANS...
WE ARE...

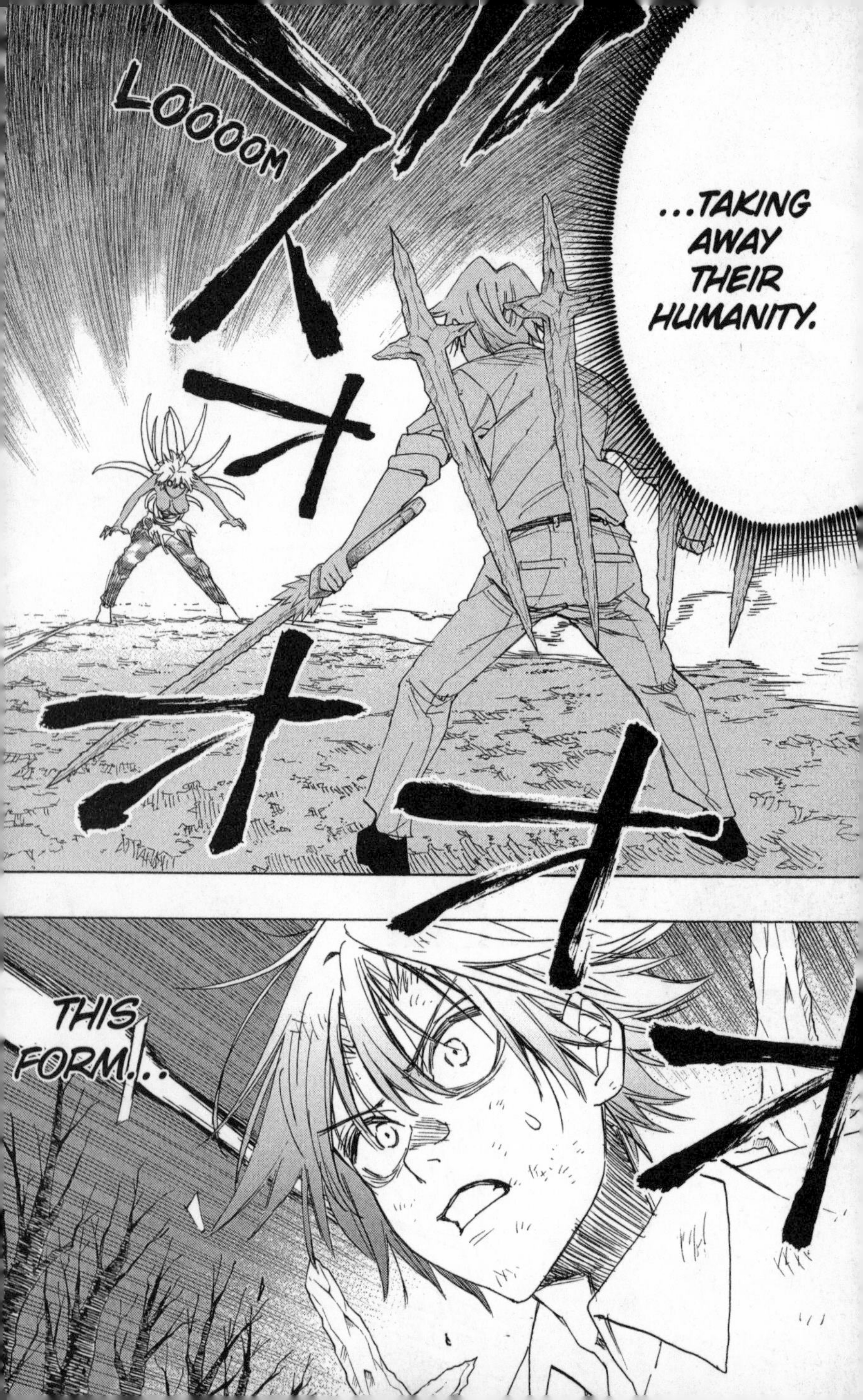
...TAKING AWAY THEIR HUMANITY.
LOOOOM
THIS FORM!...

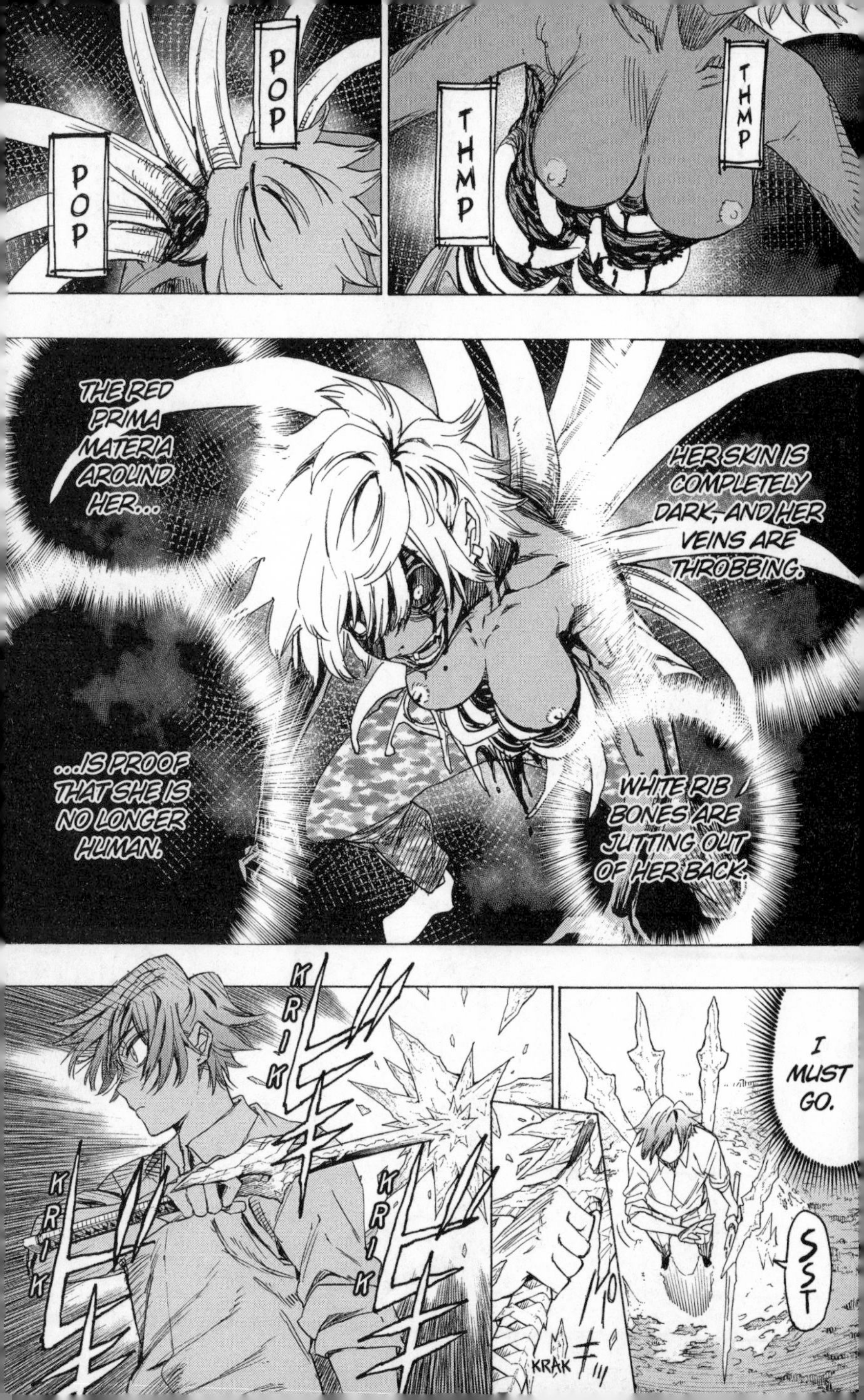
THMP
THMP
POP
POP
HER SKIN IS COMPLETELY DARK, AND HER VEINS ARE THROBBING.
THE RED PRIMA MATERIA AROUND HER...
WHITE RIB BONES ARE JUTTING OUT OF HER BACK.
...IS PROOF THAT SHE IS NO LONGER HUMAN.
I MUST GO.
SST
KRAK
KRIK
KRIK
KRIK

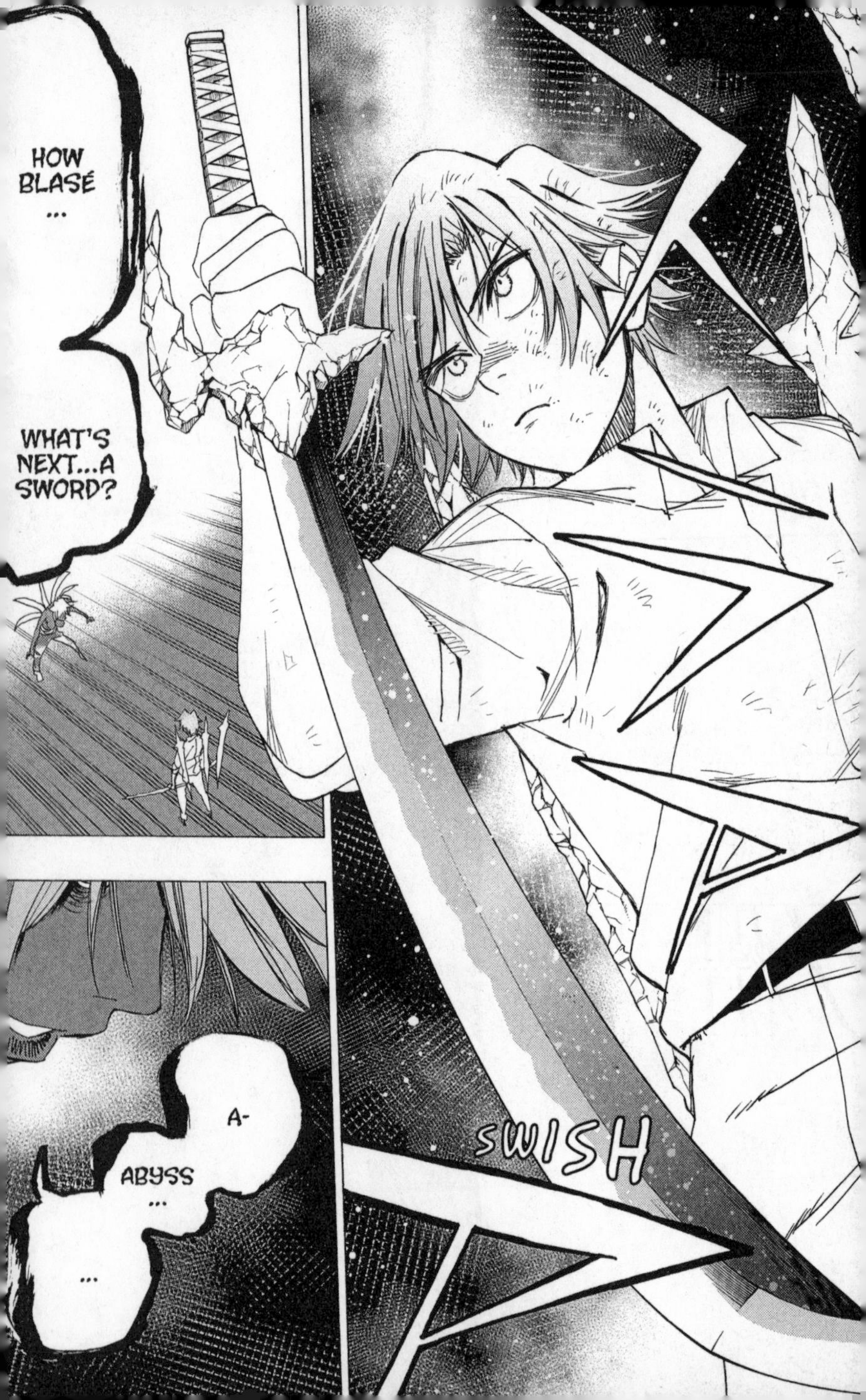
SWISH
HOW BLASÉ ...
WHAT'S NEXT...A SWORD?
A-
ABYSS ...
...

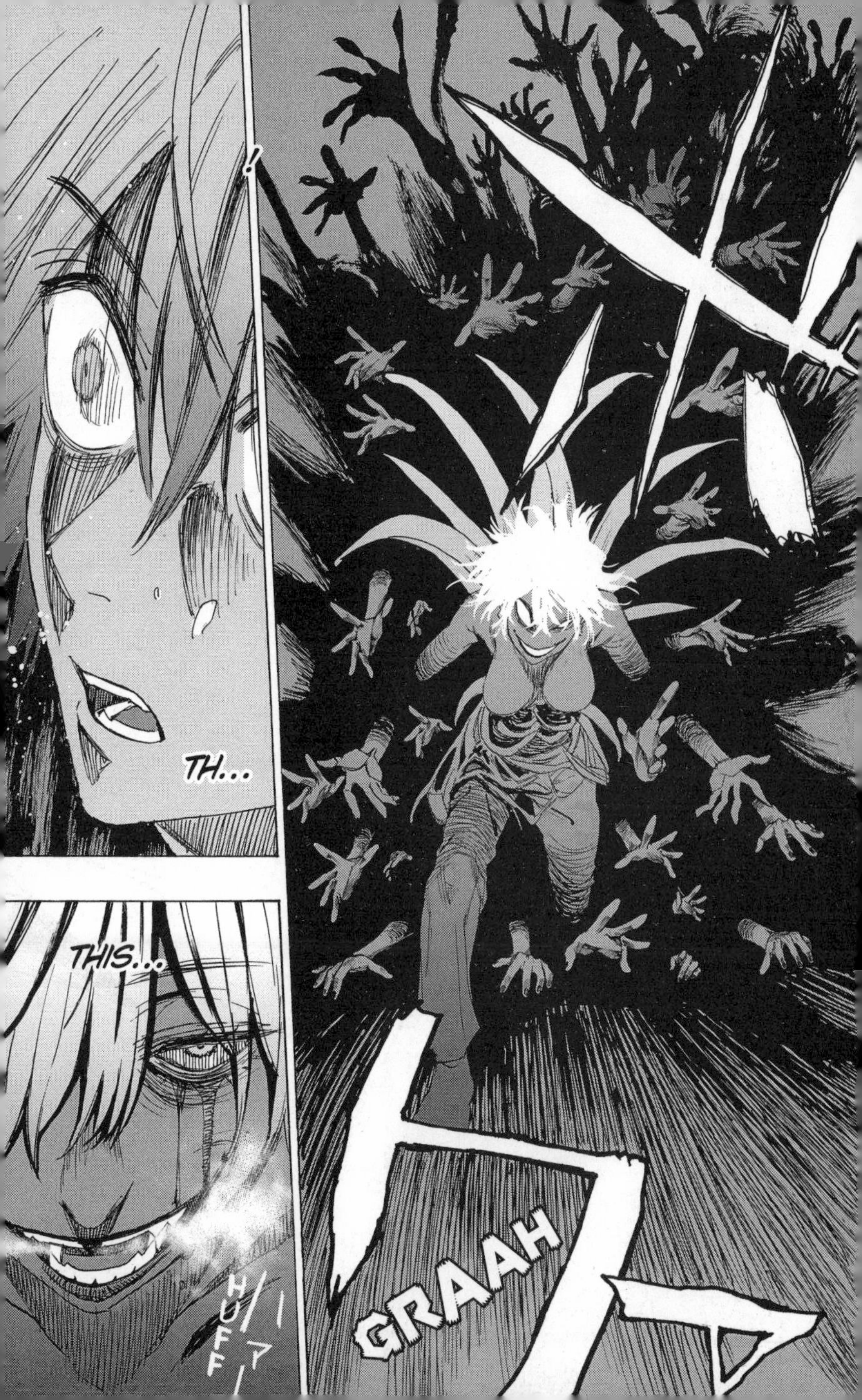
GRAAH
!
TH...
THIS...
HUFF

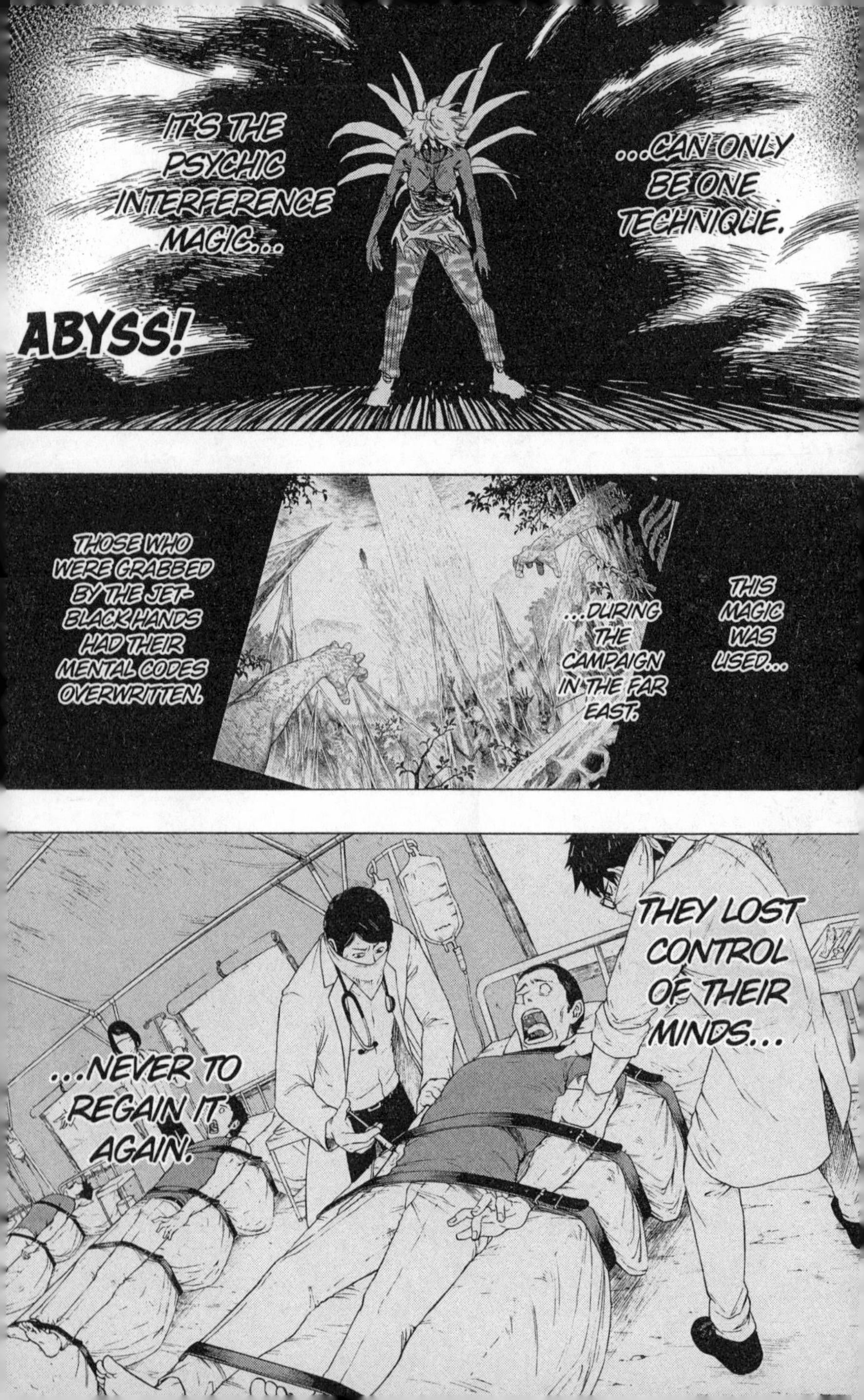
...CAN ONLY BE ONE TECHNIQUE.
IT'S THE PSYCHIC INTERFERENCE MAGIC...
ABYSS!
THIS MAGIC WAS USED...
...DURING THE CAMPAIGN IN THE FAR EAST.
THOSE WHO WERE GRABBED BY THE JET-BLACK HANDS HAD THEIR MENTAL CODES OVERWRITTEN.
THEY LOST CONTROL OF THEIR MINDS...
...NEVER TO REGAIN IT AGAIN.

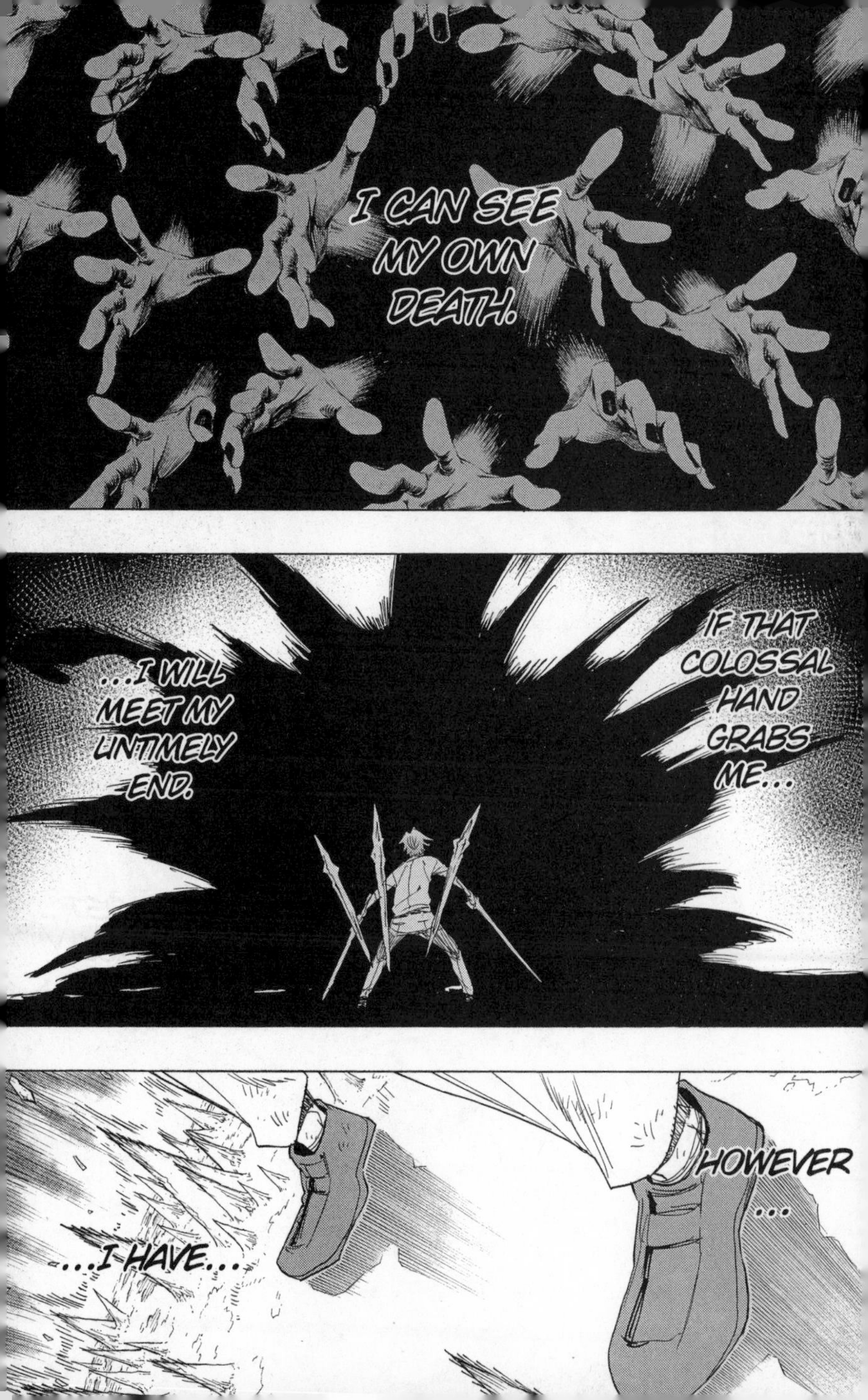
I CAN SEE MY OWN DEATH.
IF THAT COLOSSAL HAND GRABS ME...
...I WILL MEET MY UNTIMELY END.
HOWEVER...
...I HAVE...

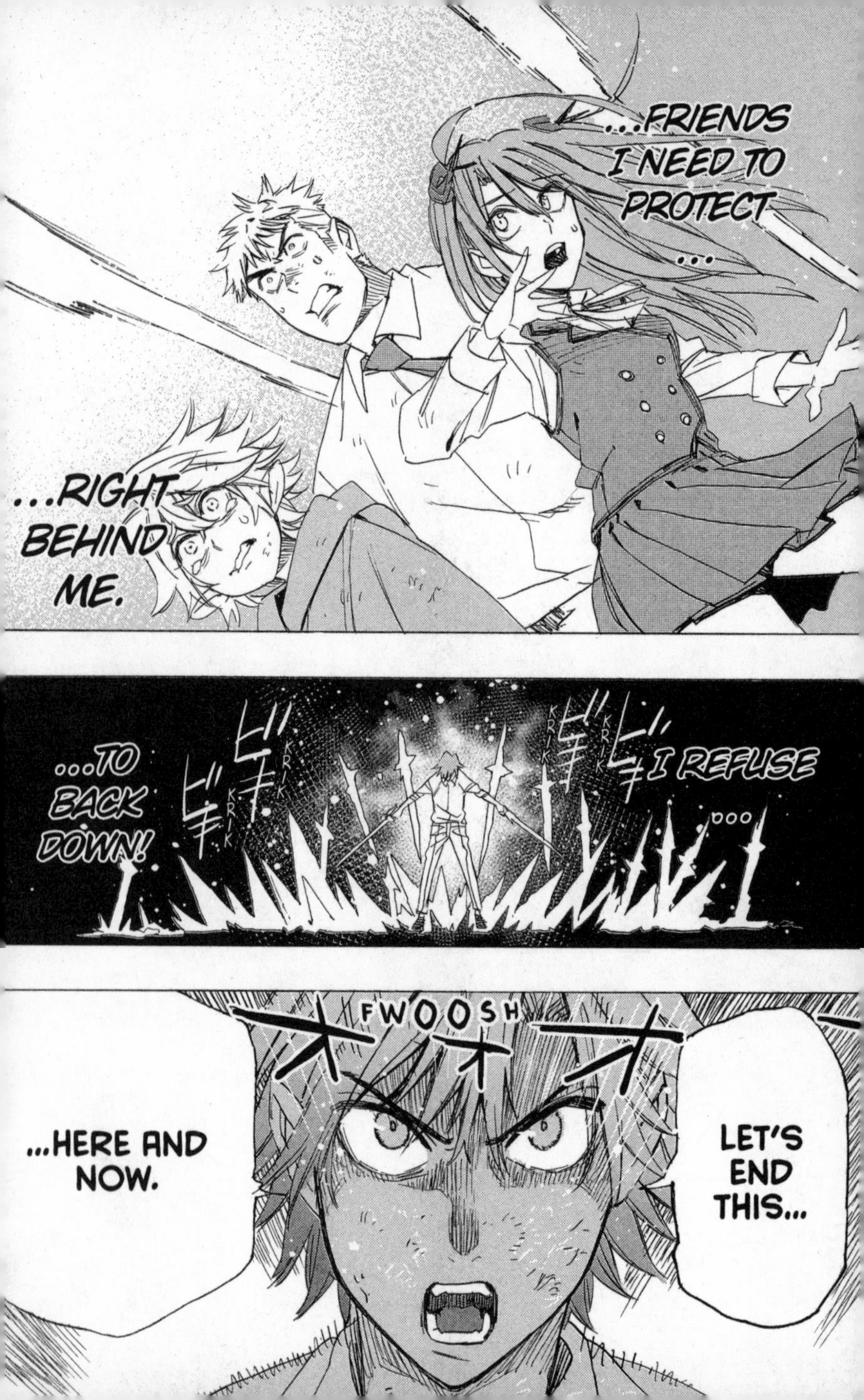
...FRIENDS I NEED TO PROTECT...
...RIGHT BEHIND ME.
I REFUSE...
KRIK
KRIK
KRIK
KRIK
...TO BACK DOWN!
FWOOSH
LET'S END THIS...
...HERE AND NOW.

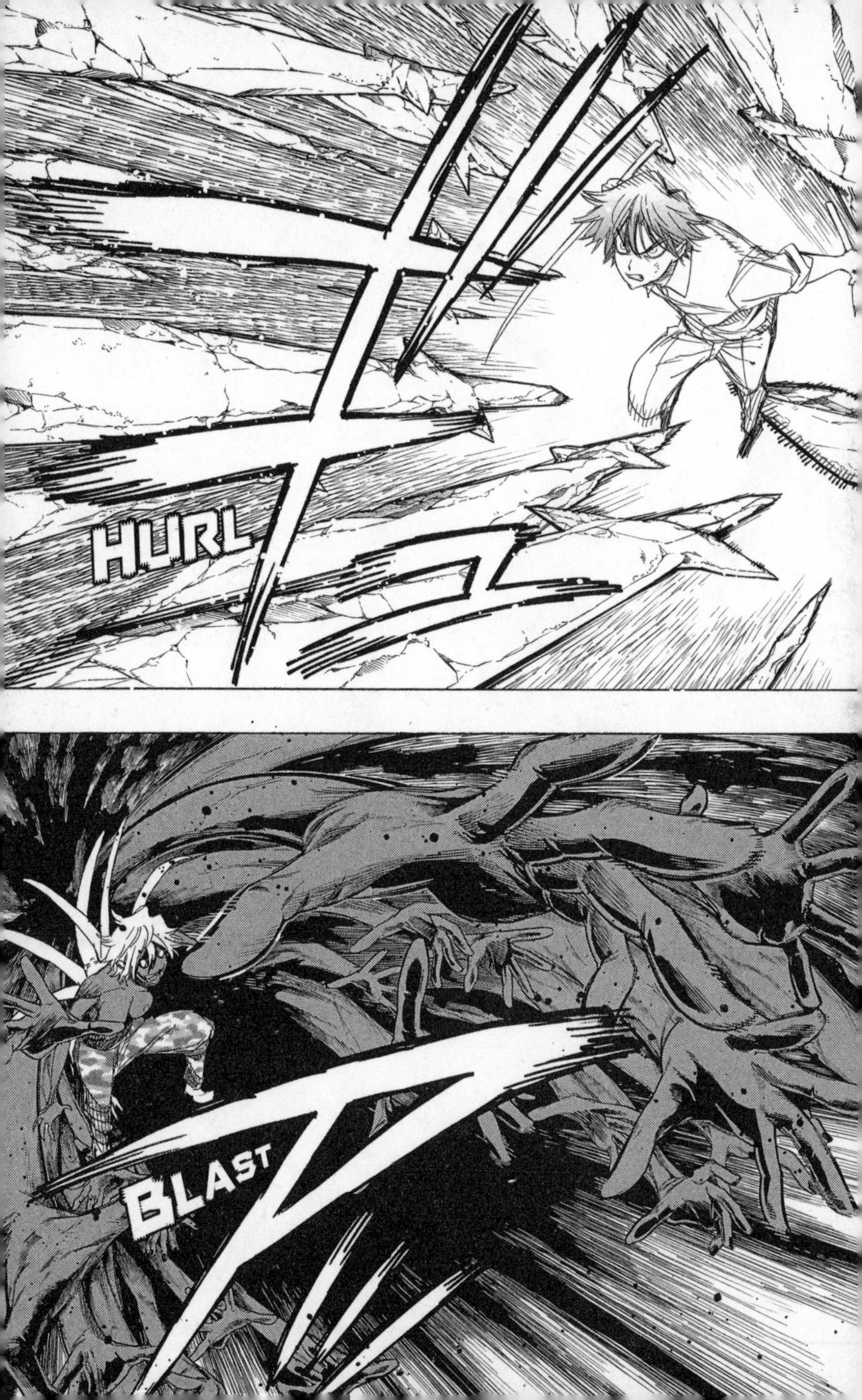
HURL
BLAST

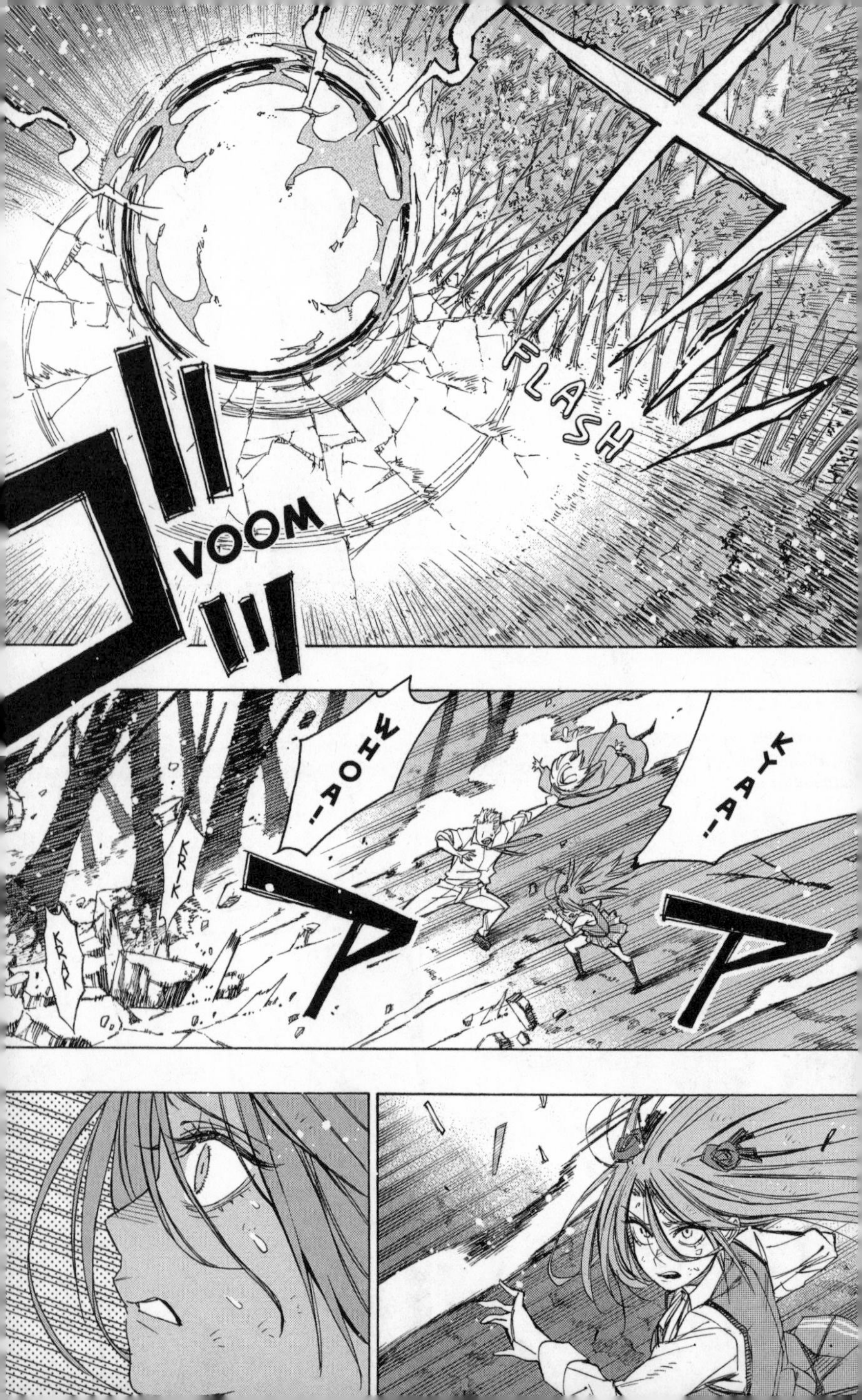
FLASH
VOOM
KYAAA!
WHOA!
KRIK
KRAK

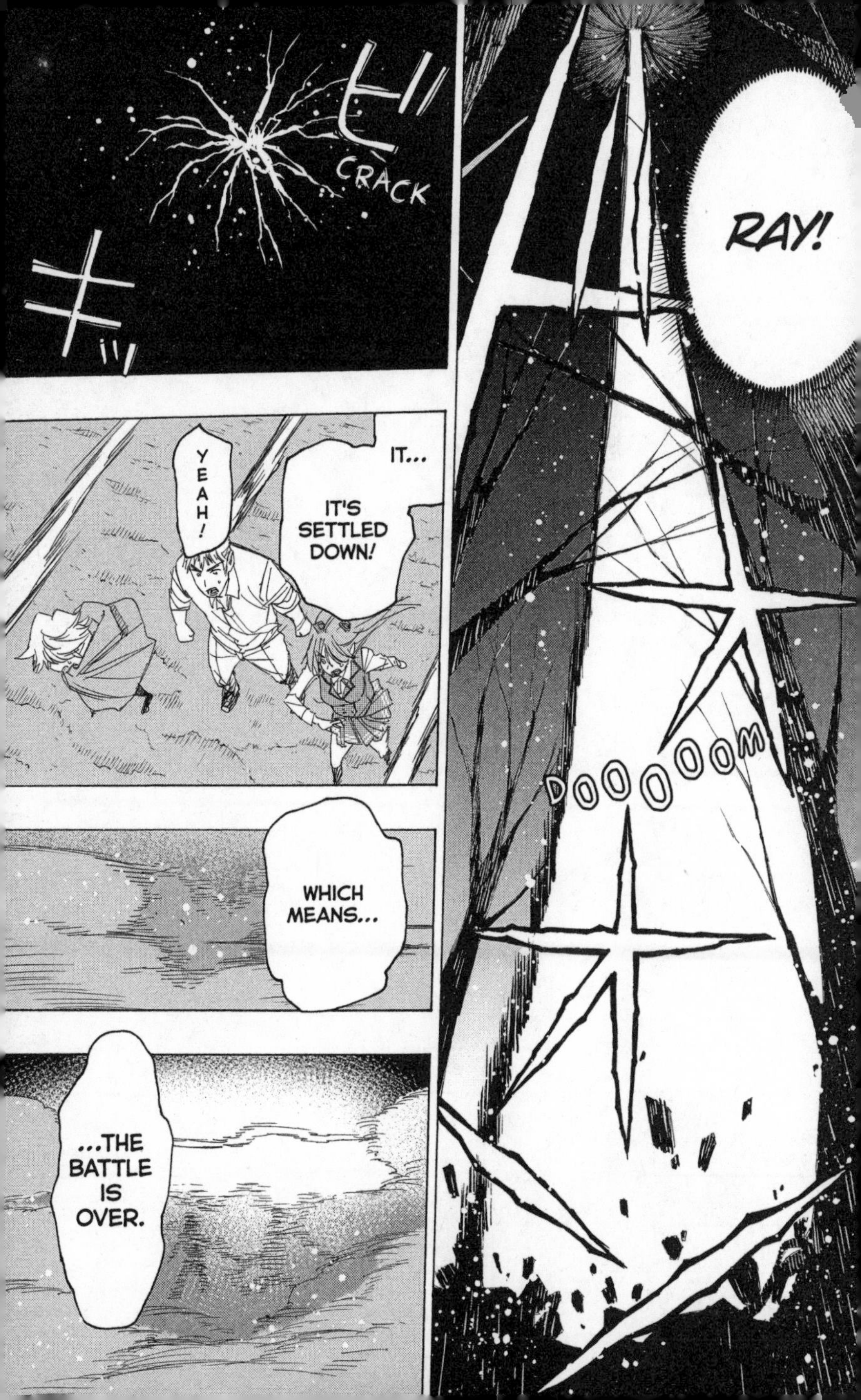

RAY!
DOOOOOOM
CRACK
IT...
IT'S SETTLED DOWN!
YEAH!
WHICH MEANS...
...THE BATTLE IS OVER.

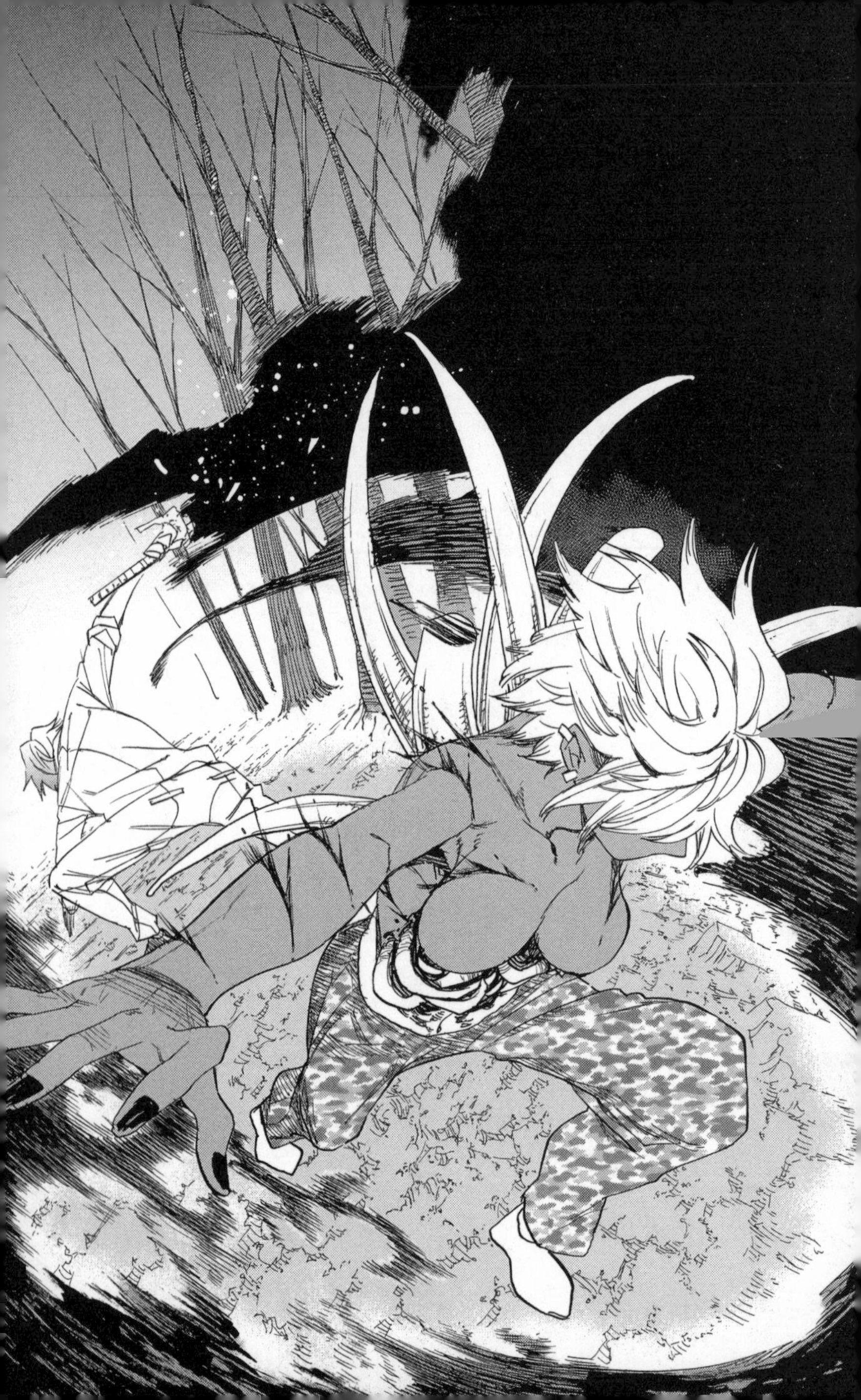

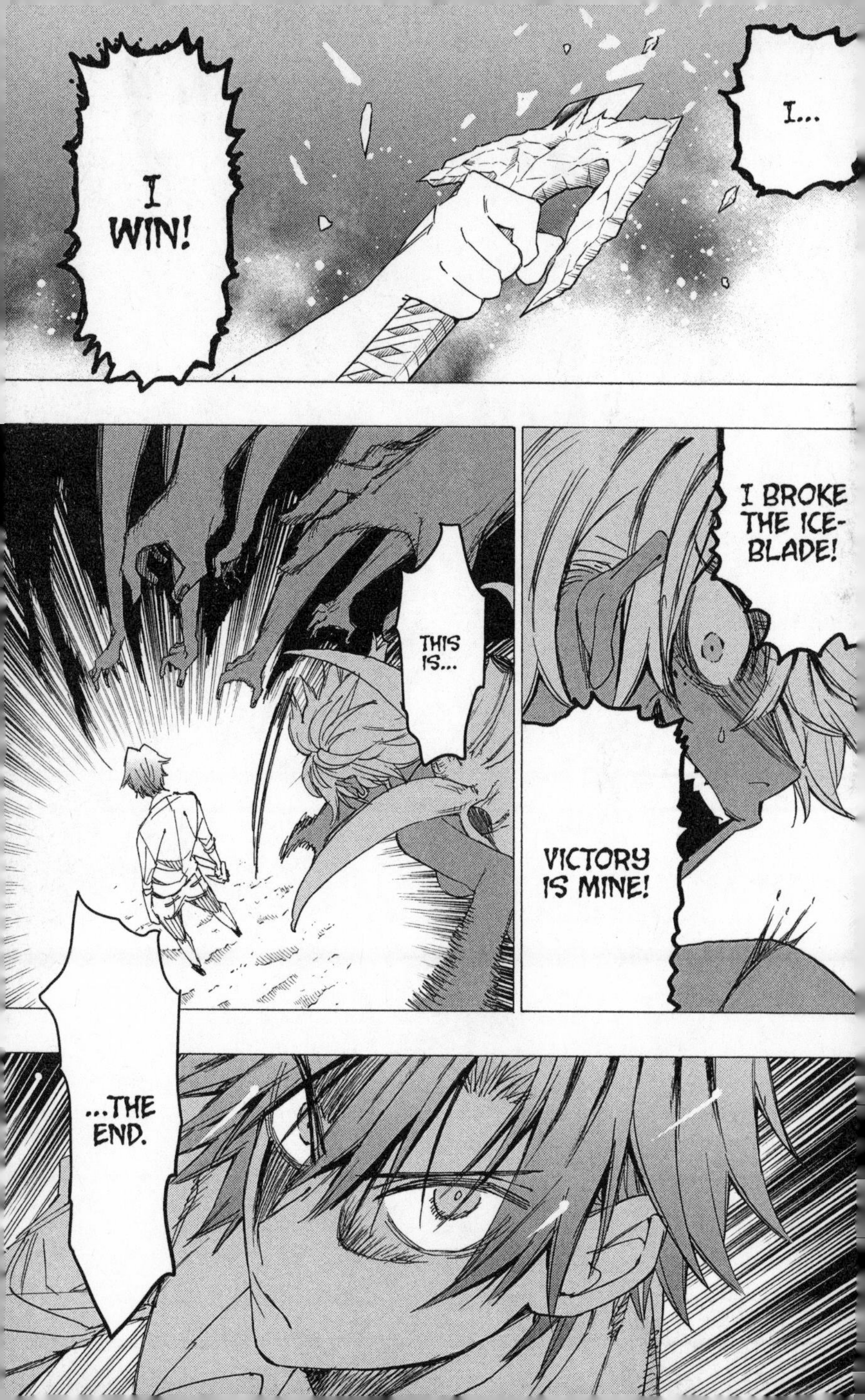
I...
I WIN!
I BROKE THE ICE-BLADE!
VICTORY IS MINE!
THIS IS...
...THE END.

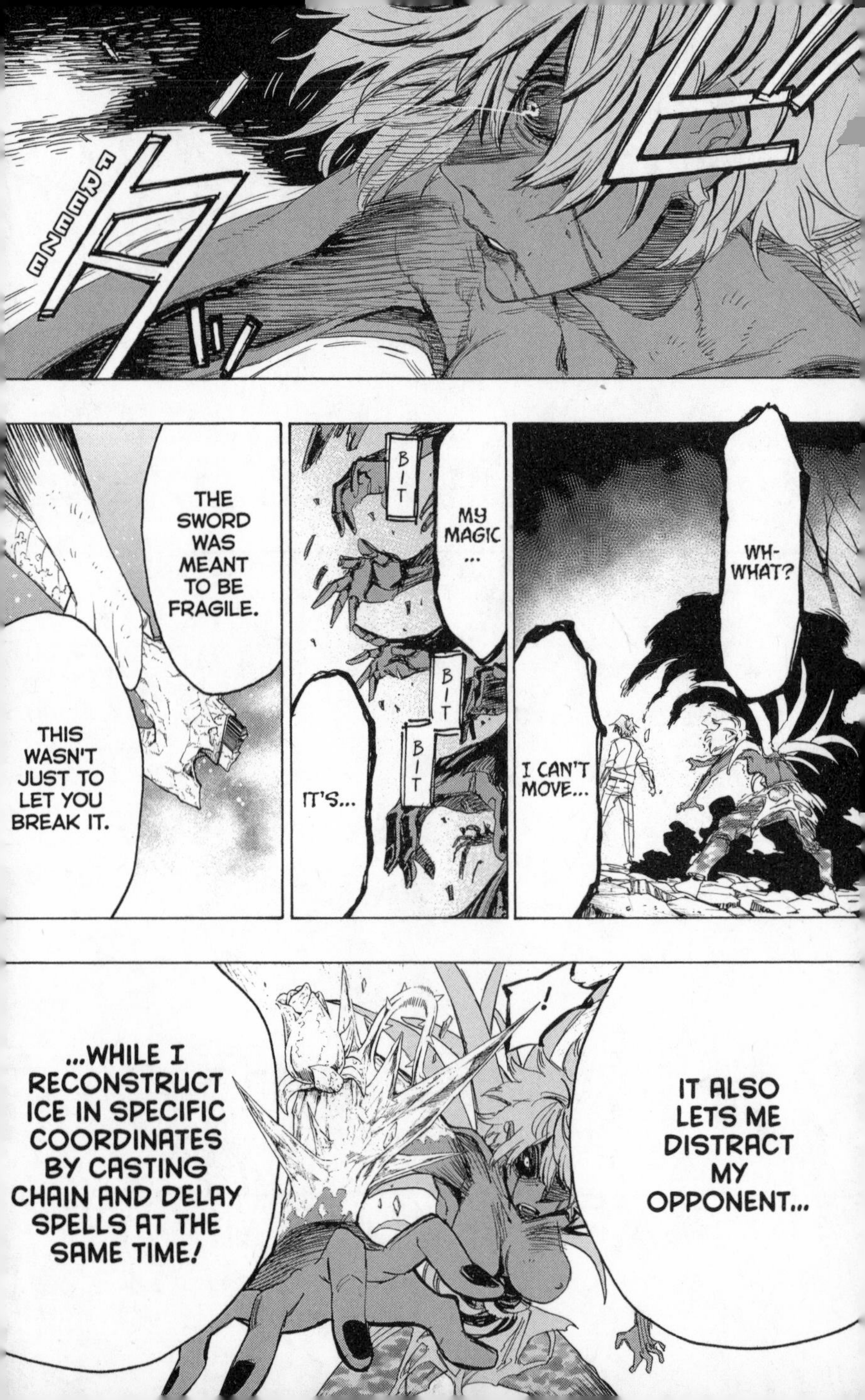
FREEZE
WH- WHAT?
I CAN'T MOVE...
MY MAGIC ...
BIT
BIT
BIT
IT'S...
THE SWORD WAS MEANT TO BE FRAGILE.
THIS WASN'T JUST TO LET YOU BREAK IT.
!
IT ALSO LETS ME DISTRACT MY OPPONENT...
...WHILE I RECONSTRUCT ICE IN SPECIFIC COORDINATES BY CASTING CHAIN AND DELAY SPELLS AT THE SAME TIME!

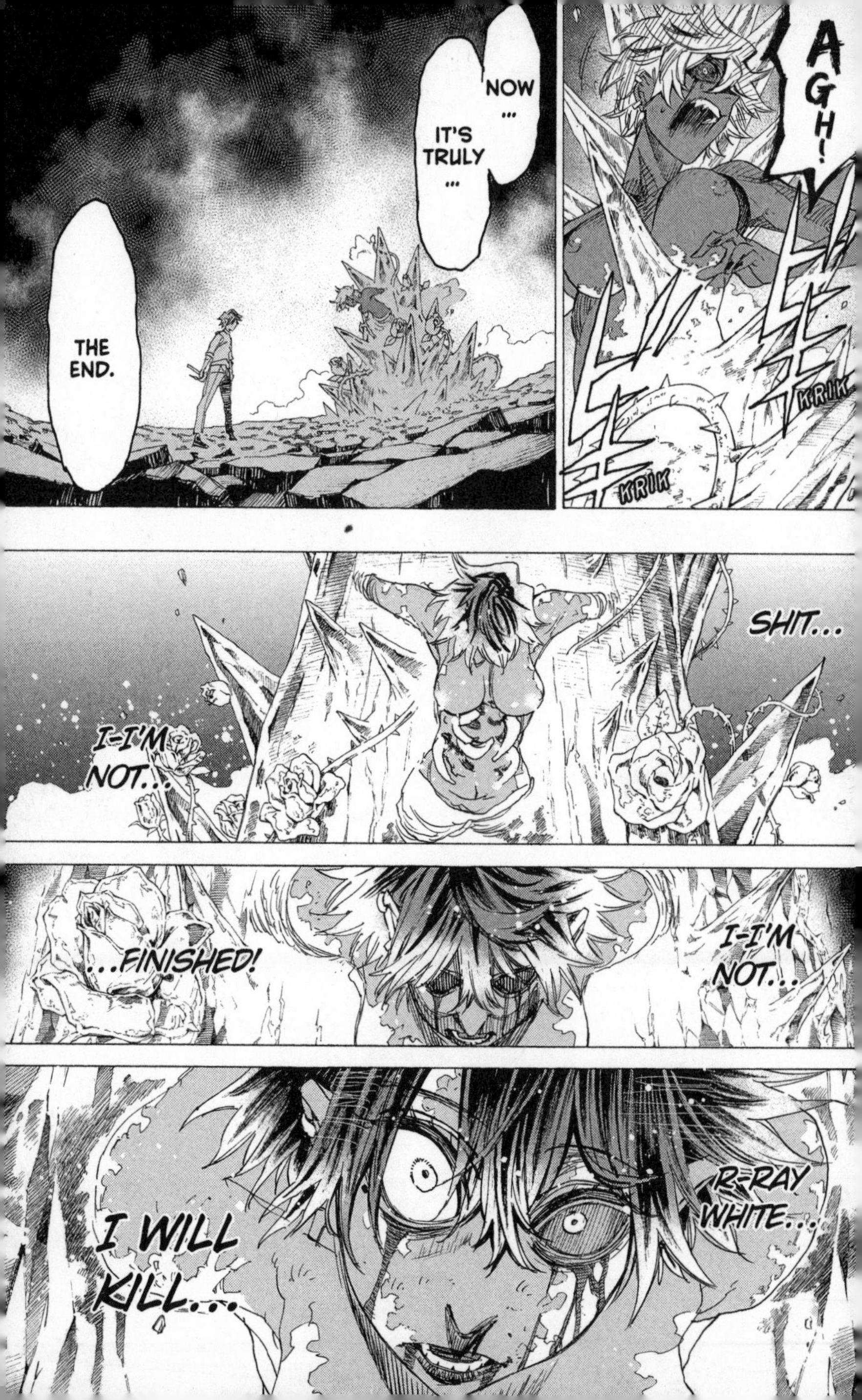
AGH!
KRIK
KRIK
NOW ... IT'S TRULY ...
THE END.
SHIT...
I-I'M NOT...
I-I'M NOT...
...FINISHED!
R-RAY WHITE...
I WILL KILL...

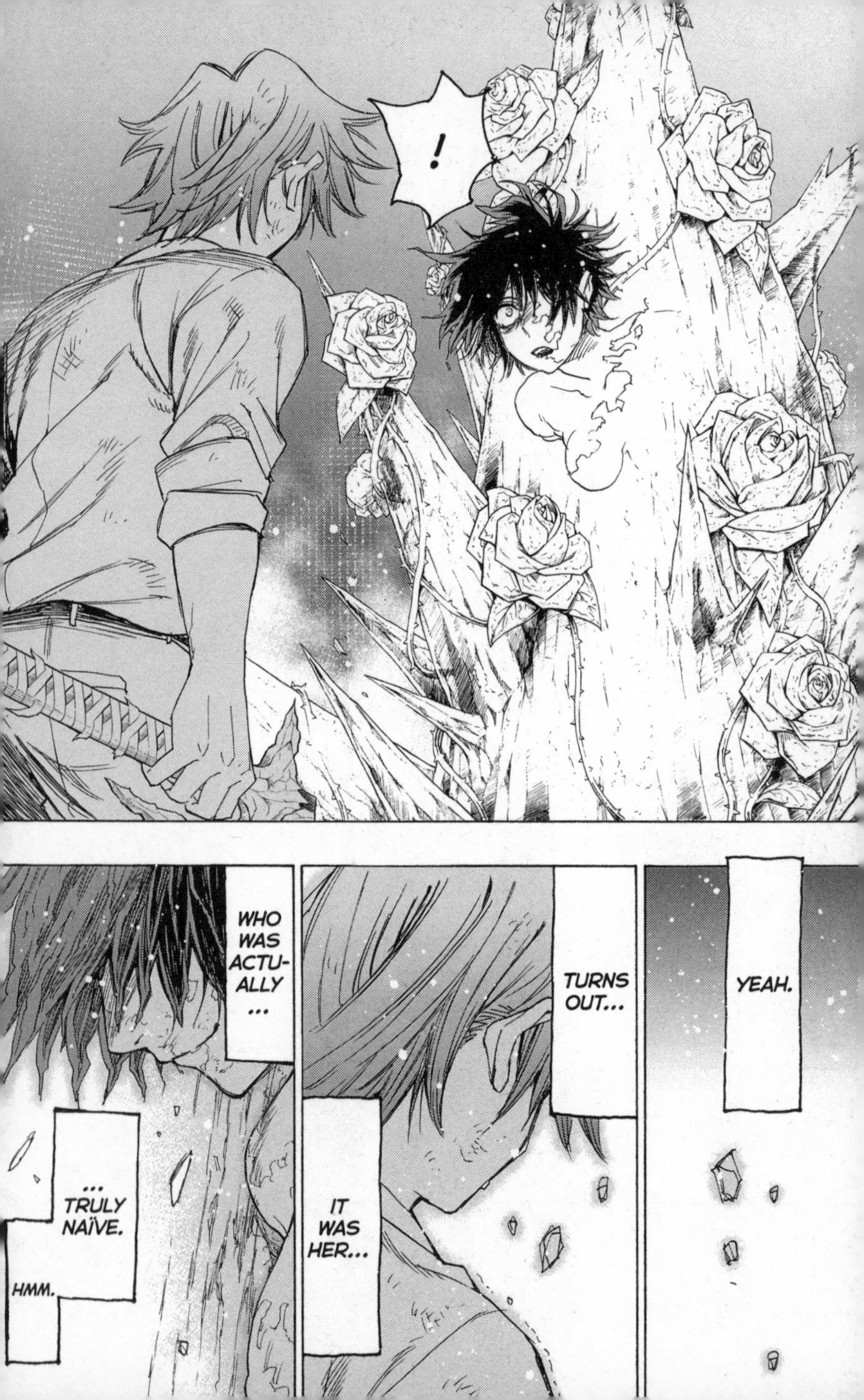
!
YEAH.
TURNS OUT...
IT WAS HER...
WHO WAS ACTUALLY...
... TRULY NAÏVE.
HMM.

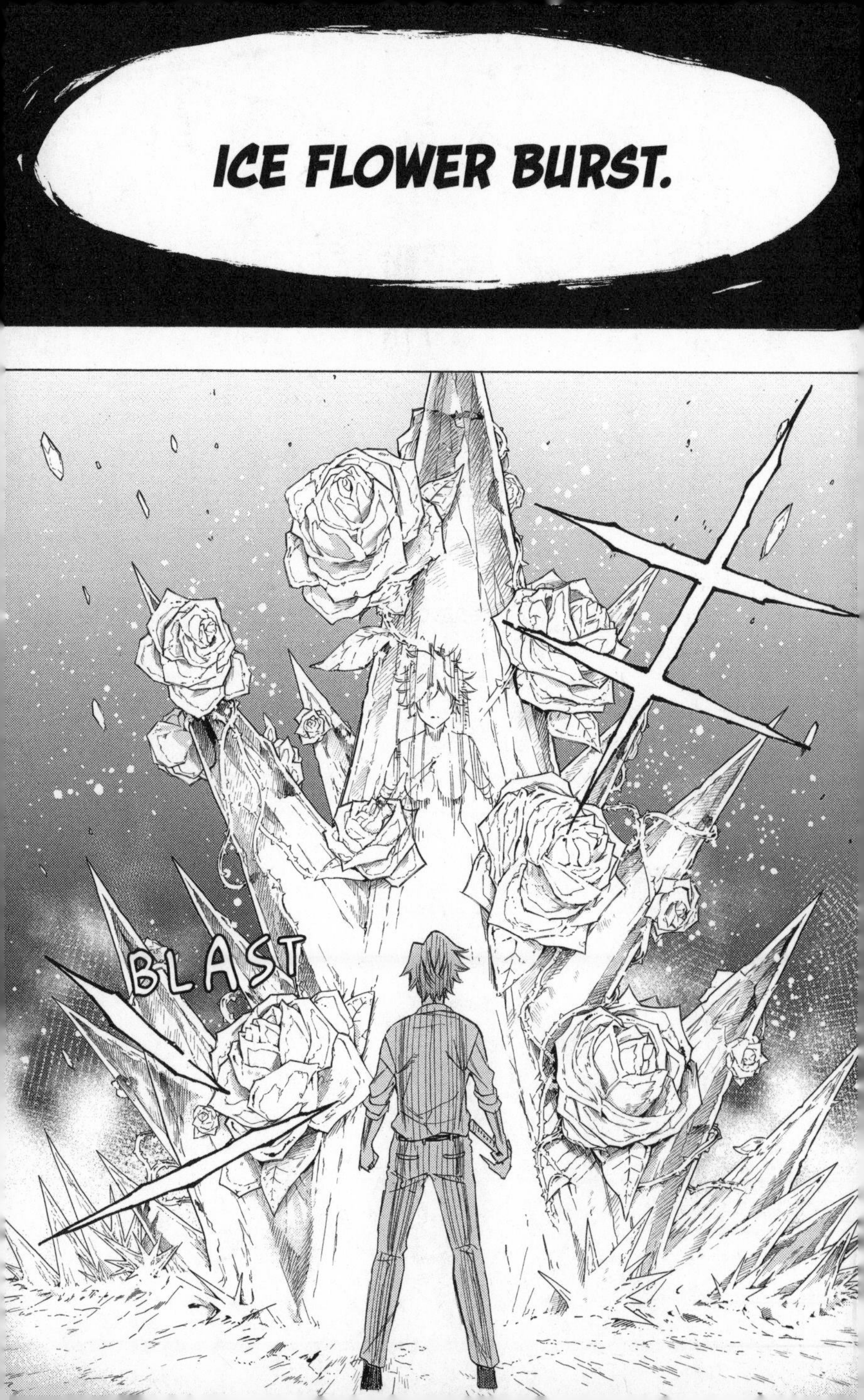
ICE FLOWER BURST.
BLAST

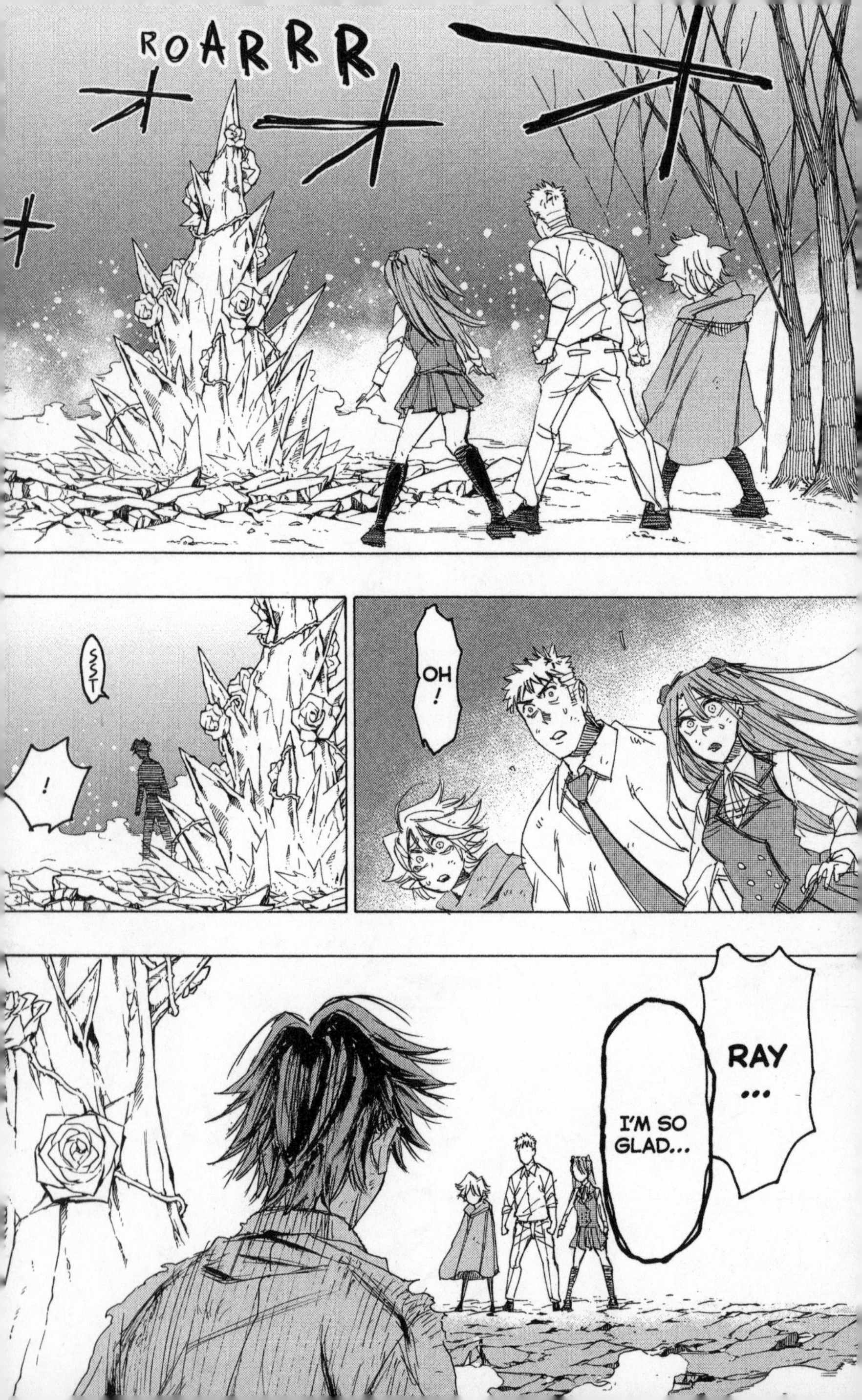
ROARRR
OH!
SST
!
RAY...
I'M SO GLAD...

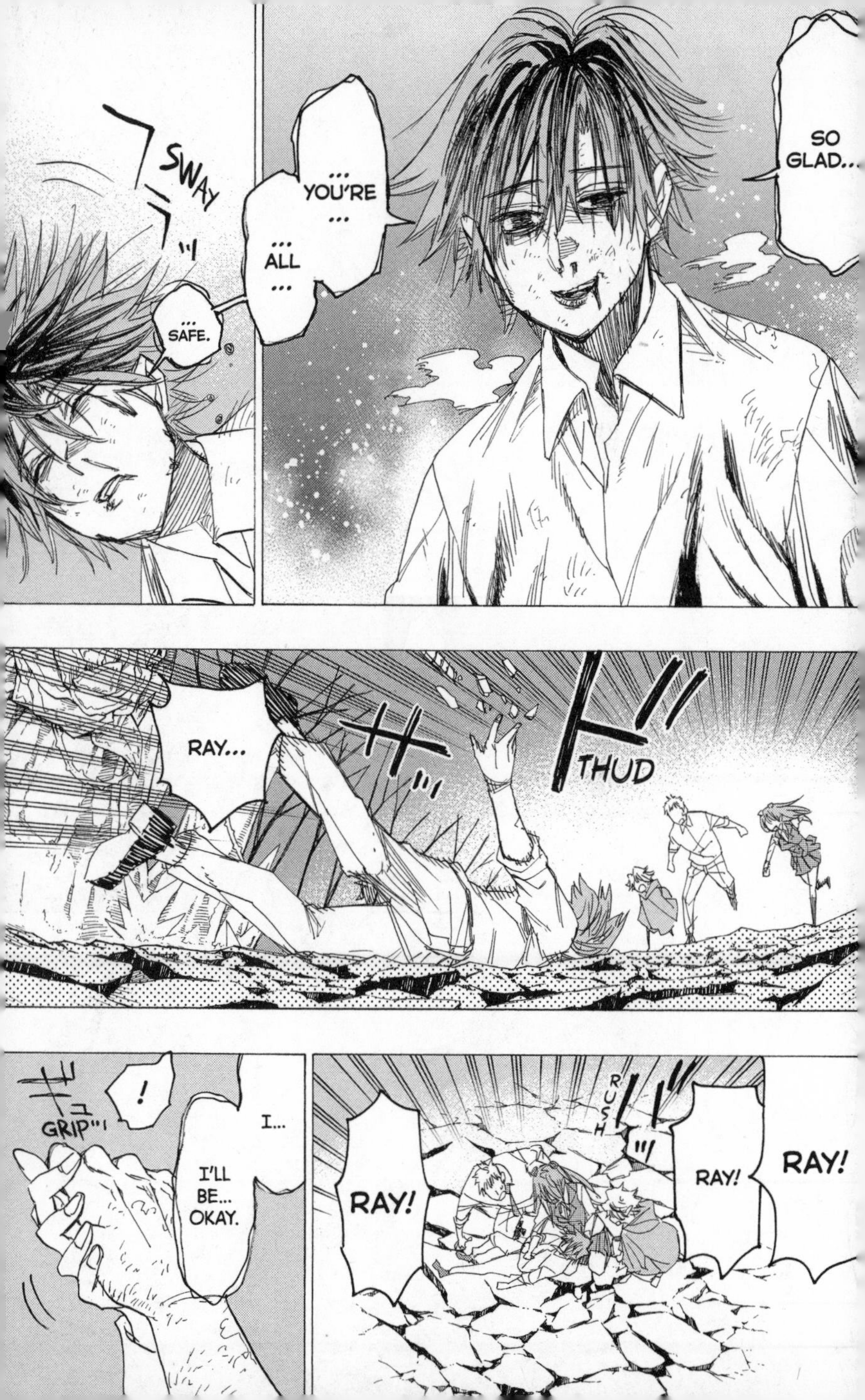
SO GLAD...
...YOU'RE ...
...ALL ...
...SAFE.
SWAY
THUD
RAY...
RUSH
RAY!
RAY!
RAY!
!
I...
I'LL BE... OKAY.
GRIP

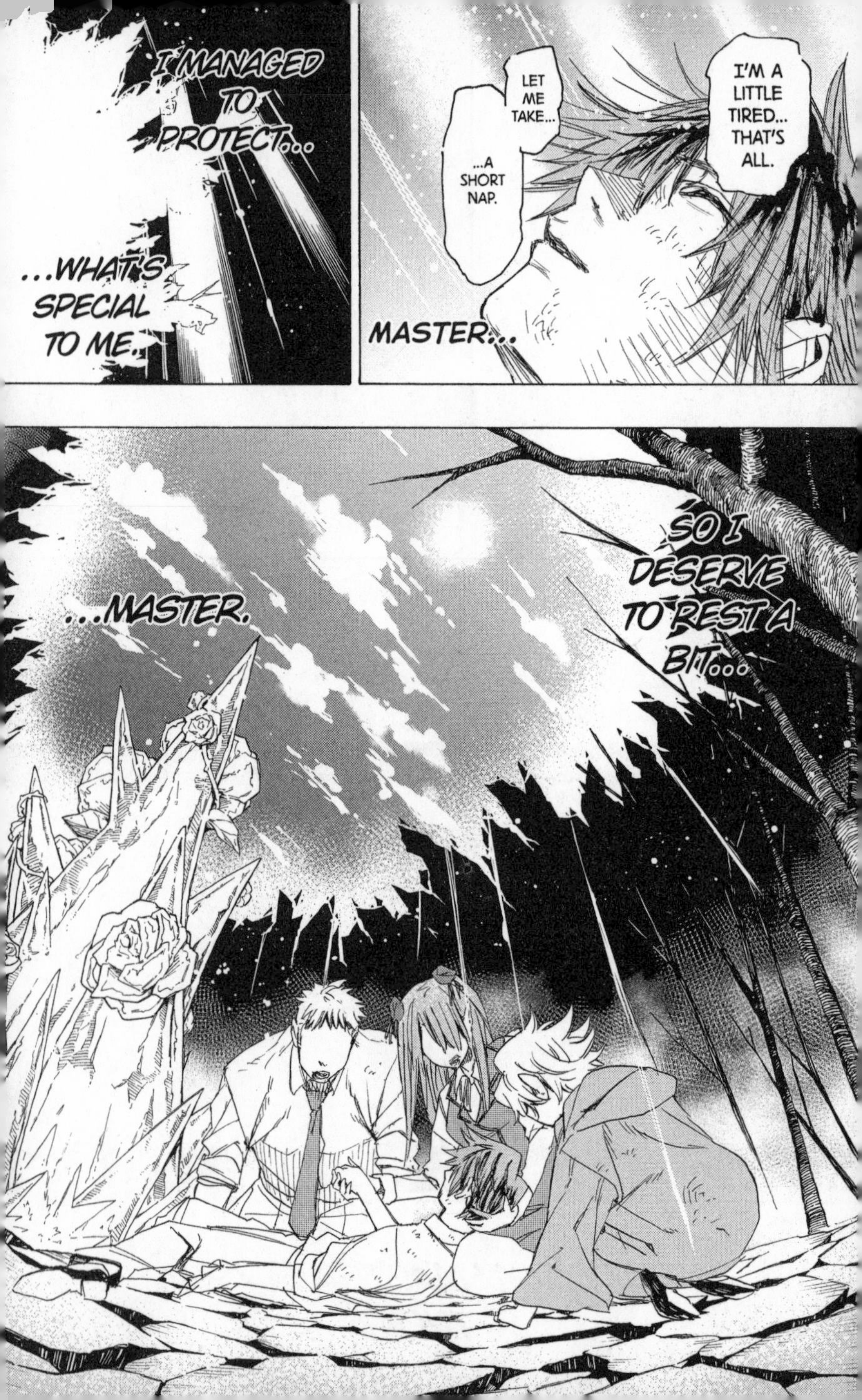
I'M A LITTLE TIRED... THAT'S ALL.
LET ME TAKE...
...A SHORT NAP.
MASTER...
I MANAGED TO PROTECT...
...WHAT'S SPECIAL TO ME.
SO I DESERVE TO REST A BIT...
...MASTER.

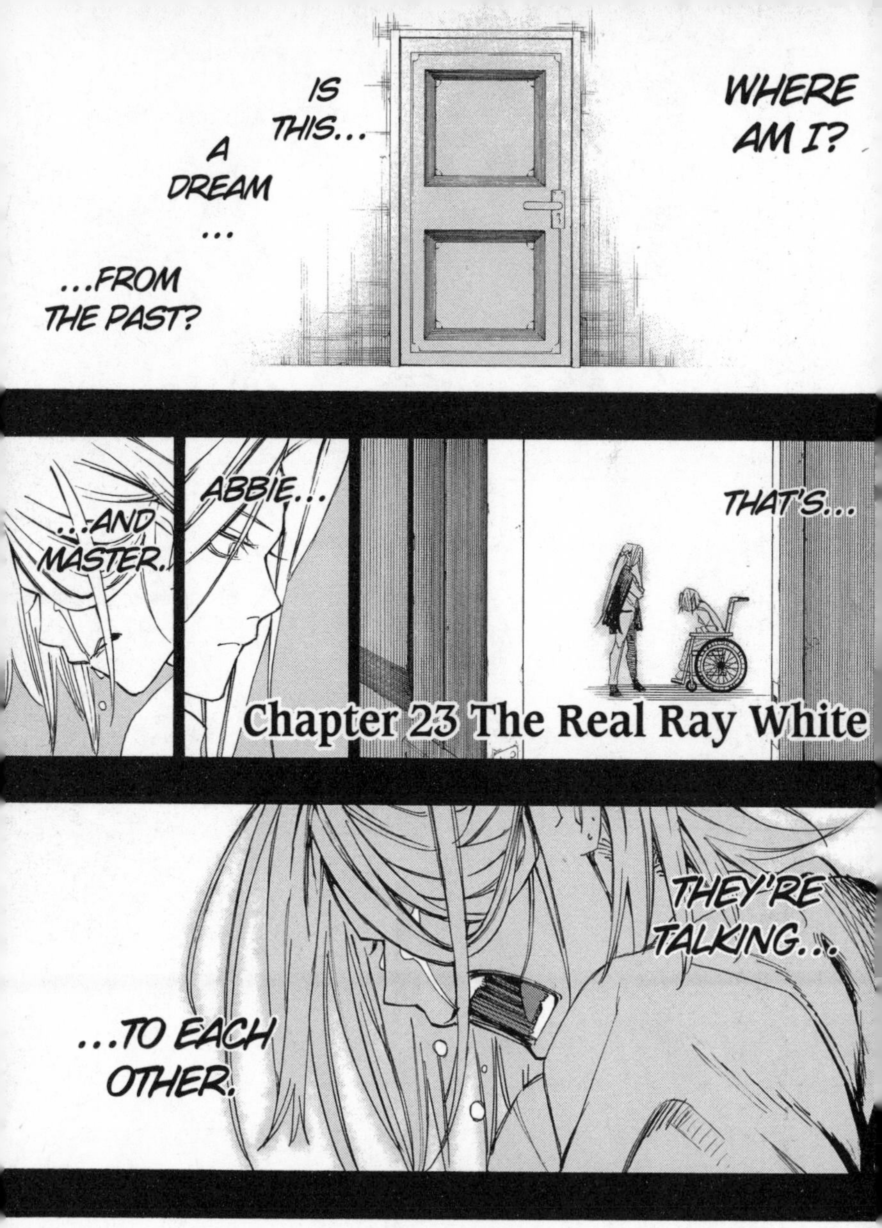
WHERE AM I?
IS THIS...
A DREAM...
...FROM THE PAST?
THAT'S...
Chapter 23 The Real Ray White
ABBIE...
...AND MASTER.
THEY'RE TALKING...
...TO EACH OTHER.

WHAT DID MY MASTER SAY BACK THEN?

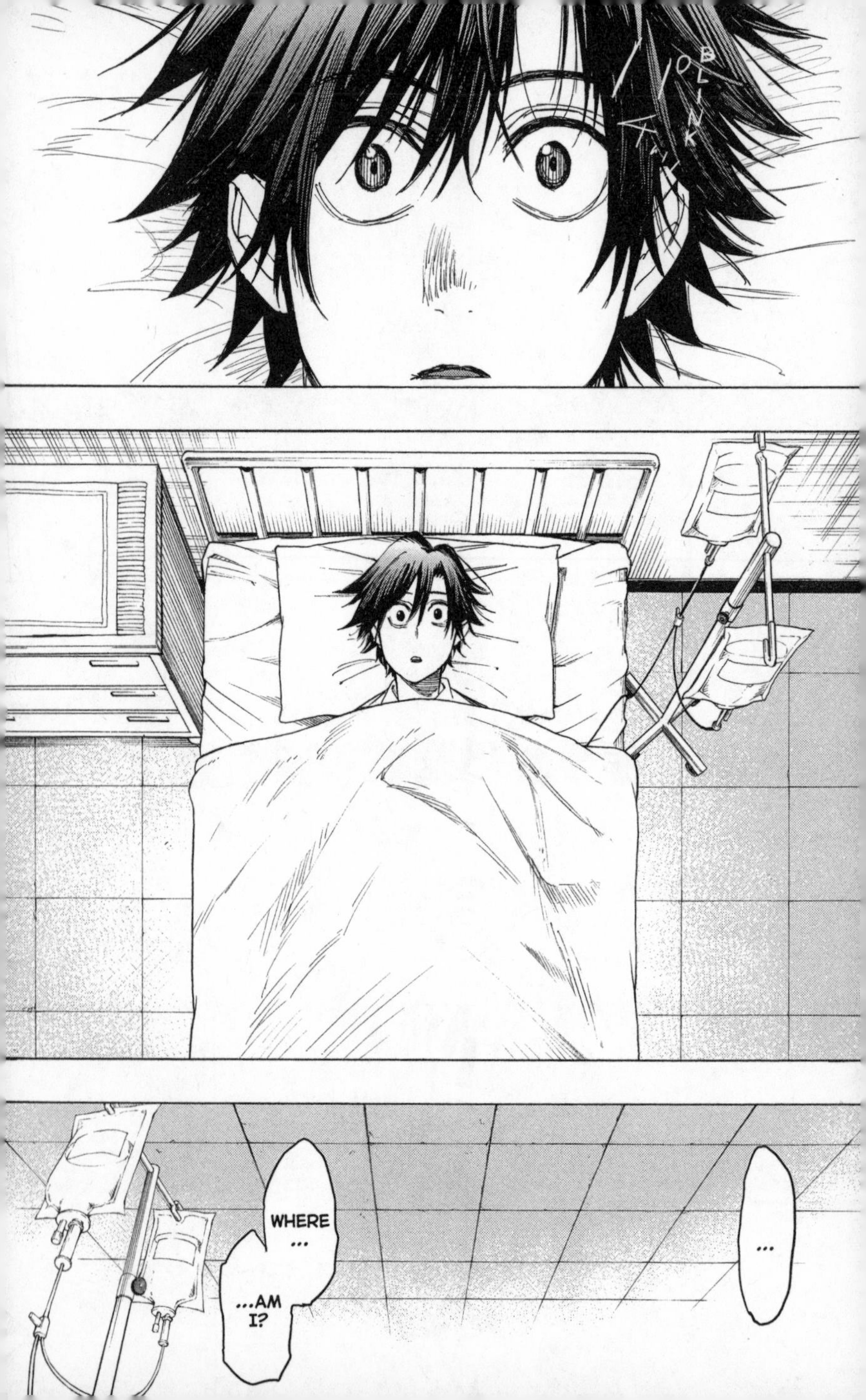
BLINK
...
WHERE ...
...AM I?

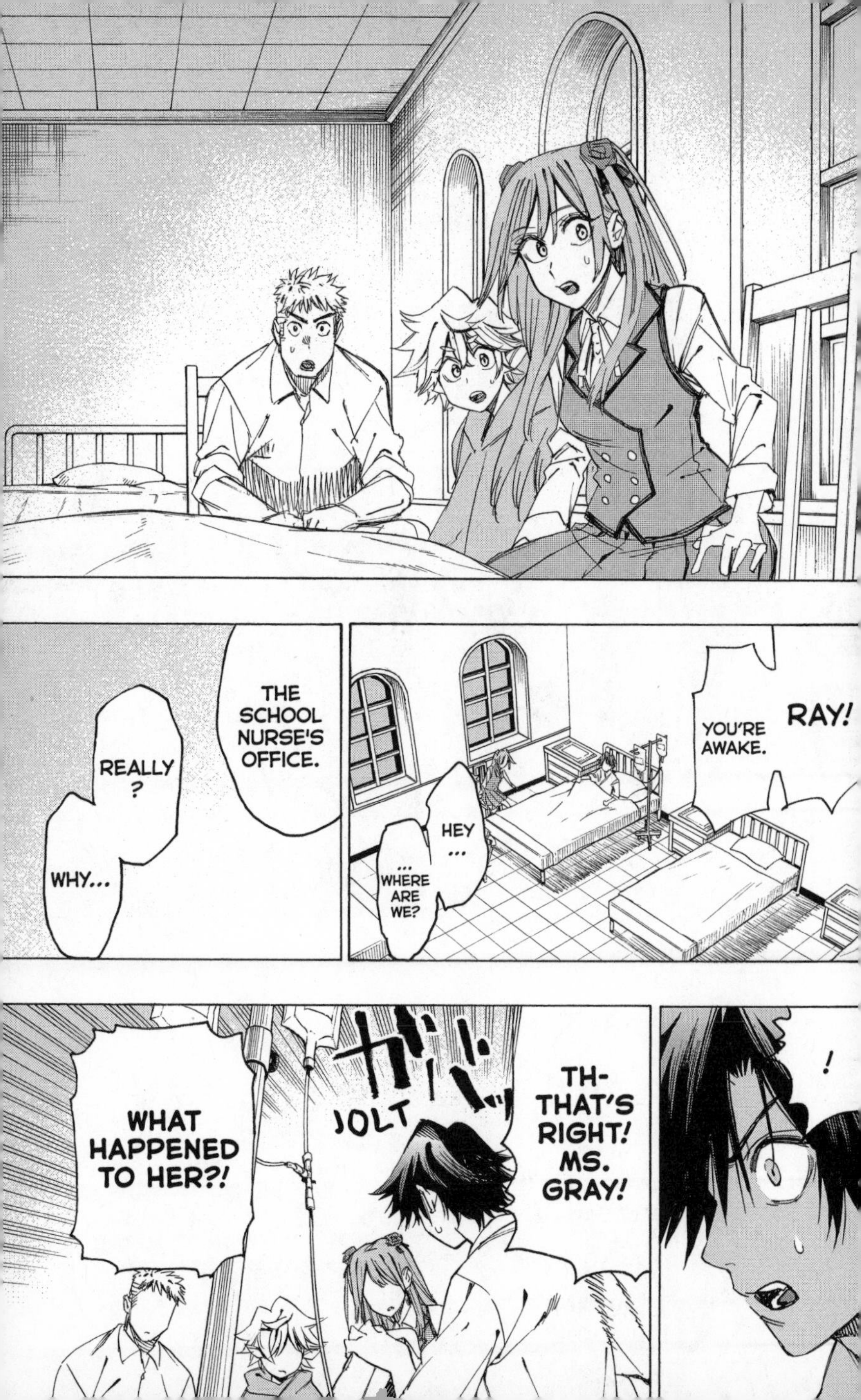
RAY!
YOU'RE AWAKE.
HEY ...
... WHERE ARE WE?
THE SCHOOL NURSE'S OFFICE.
REALLY?
WHY...
!
TH-THAT'S RIGHT! MS. GRAY!
JOLT
WHAT HAPPENED TO HER?!

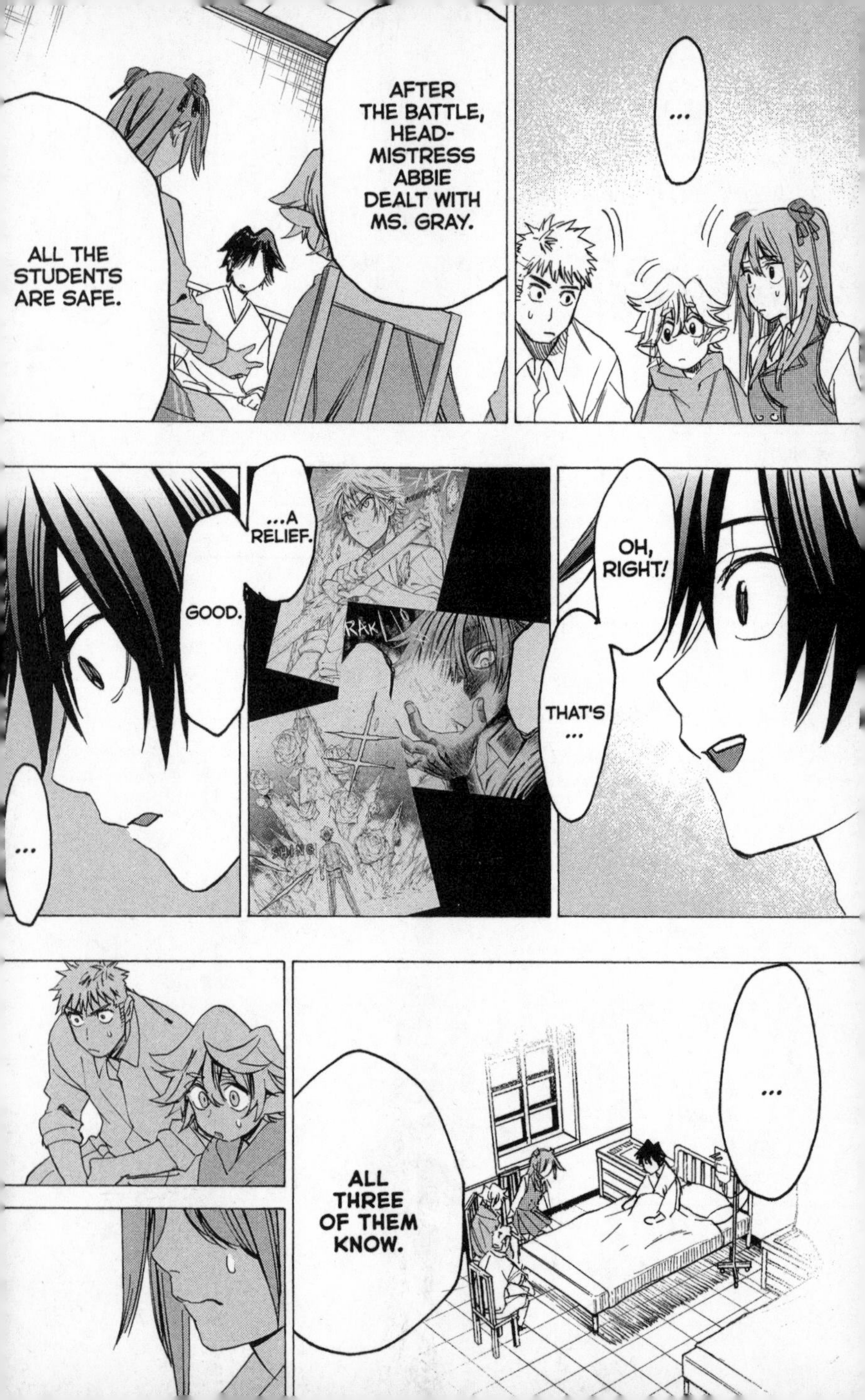
...
AFTER THE BATTLE, HEAD-MISTRESS ABBIE DEALT WITH MS. GRAY.
ALL THE STUDENTS ARE SAFE.
OH, RIGHT!
THAT'S...
...A RELIEF.
RAK
SHING
GOOD.
...
...
ALL THREE OF THEM KNOW.

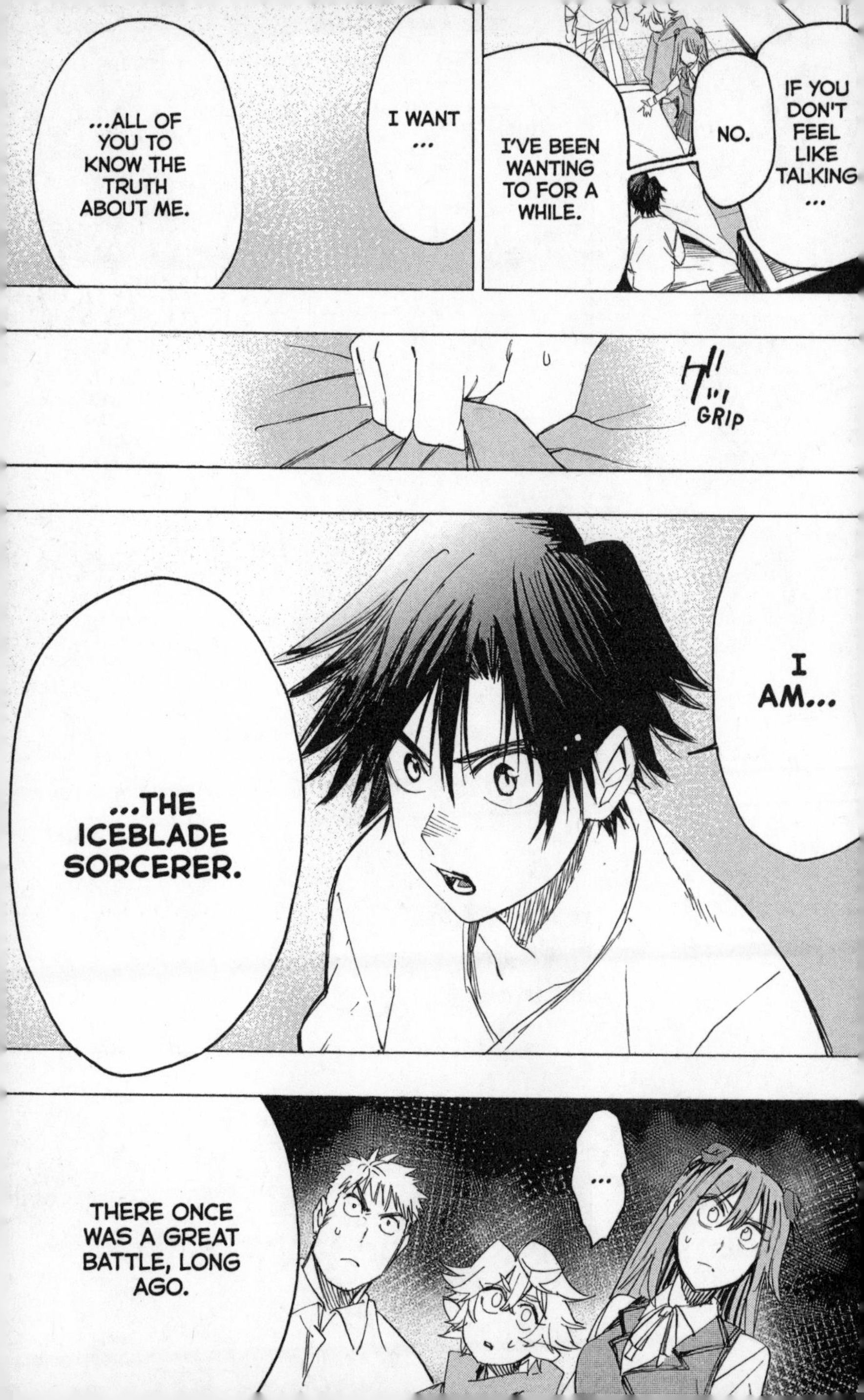
IF YOU DON'T FEEL LIKE TALKING...
NO.
I'VE BEEN WANTING TO FOR A WHILE.
I WANT...
...ALL OF YOU TO KNOW THE TRUTH ABOUT ME.
GRIP
I AM...
...THE ICEBLADE SORCERER.
...
THERE ONCE WAS A GREAT BATTLE, LONG AGO.

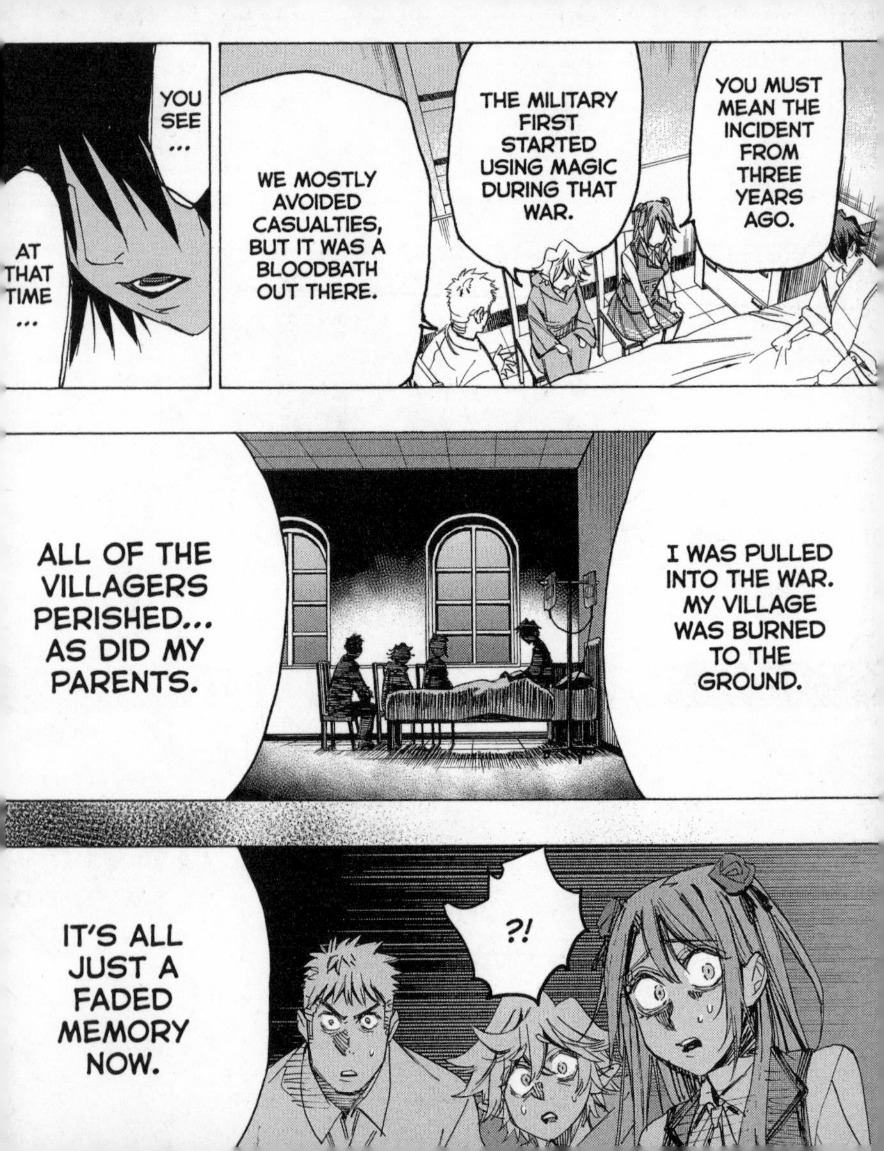
YOU MUST MEAN THE INCIDENT FROM THREE YEARS AGO.
THE MILITARY FIRST STARTED USING MAGIC DURING THAT WAR.
WE MOSTLY AVOIDED CASUALTIES, BUT IT WAS A BLOODBATH OUT THERE.
YOU SEE...
AT THAT TIME...
I WAS PULLED INTO THE WAR. MY VILLAGE WAS BURNED TO THE GROUND.
ALL OF THE VILLAGERS PERISHED... AS DID MY PARENTS.
?!
IT'S ALL JUST A FADED MEMORY NOW.

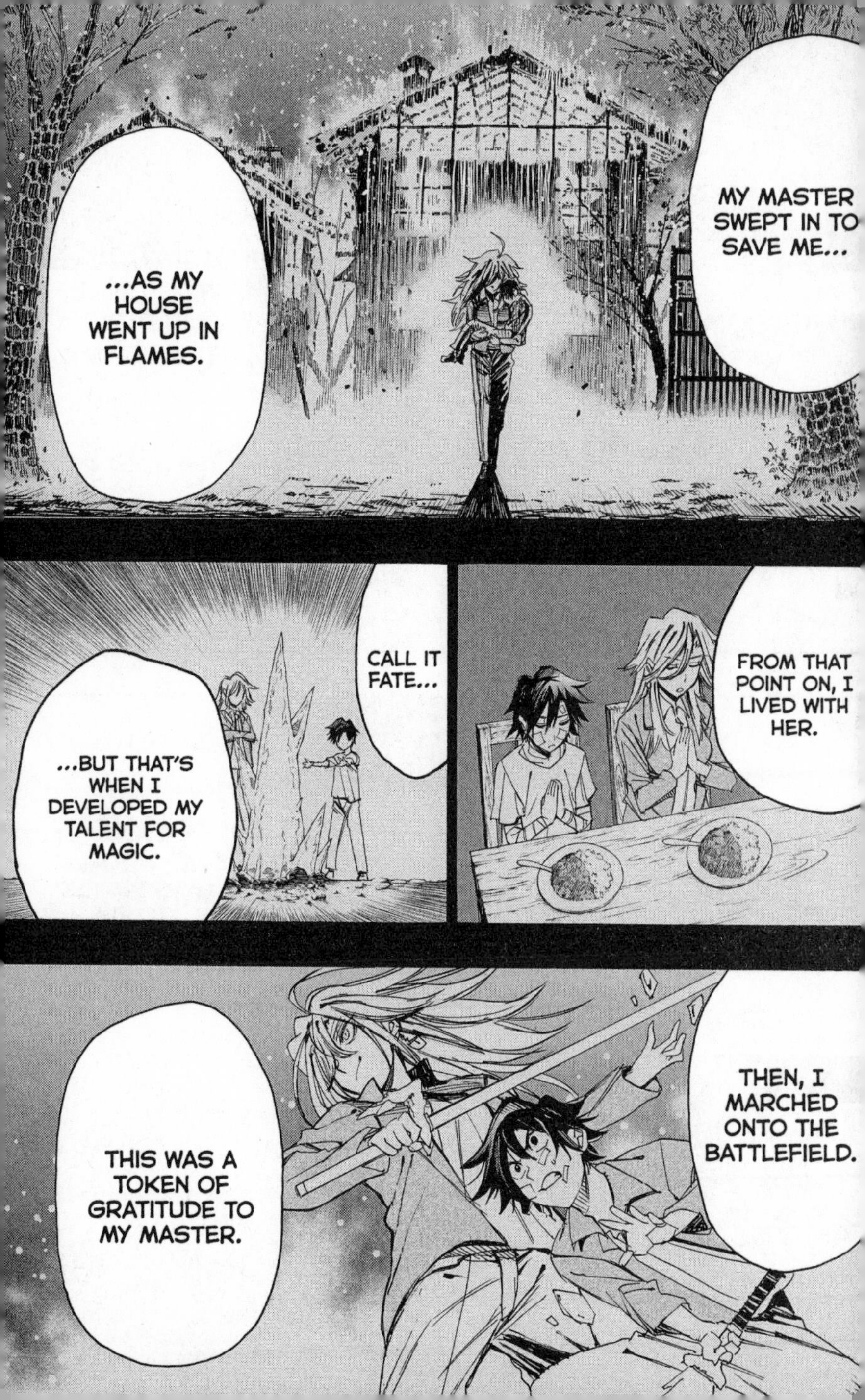
MY MASTER SWEPT IN TO SAVE ME...
...AS MY HOUSE WENT UP IN FLAMES.
FROM THAT POINT ON, I LIVED WITH HER.
CALL IT FATE...
...BUT THAT'S WHEN I DEVELOPED MY TALENT FOR MAGIC.
THEN, I MARCHED ONTO THE BATTLEFIELD.
THIS WAS A TOKEN OF GRATITUDE TO MY MASTER.

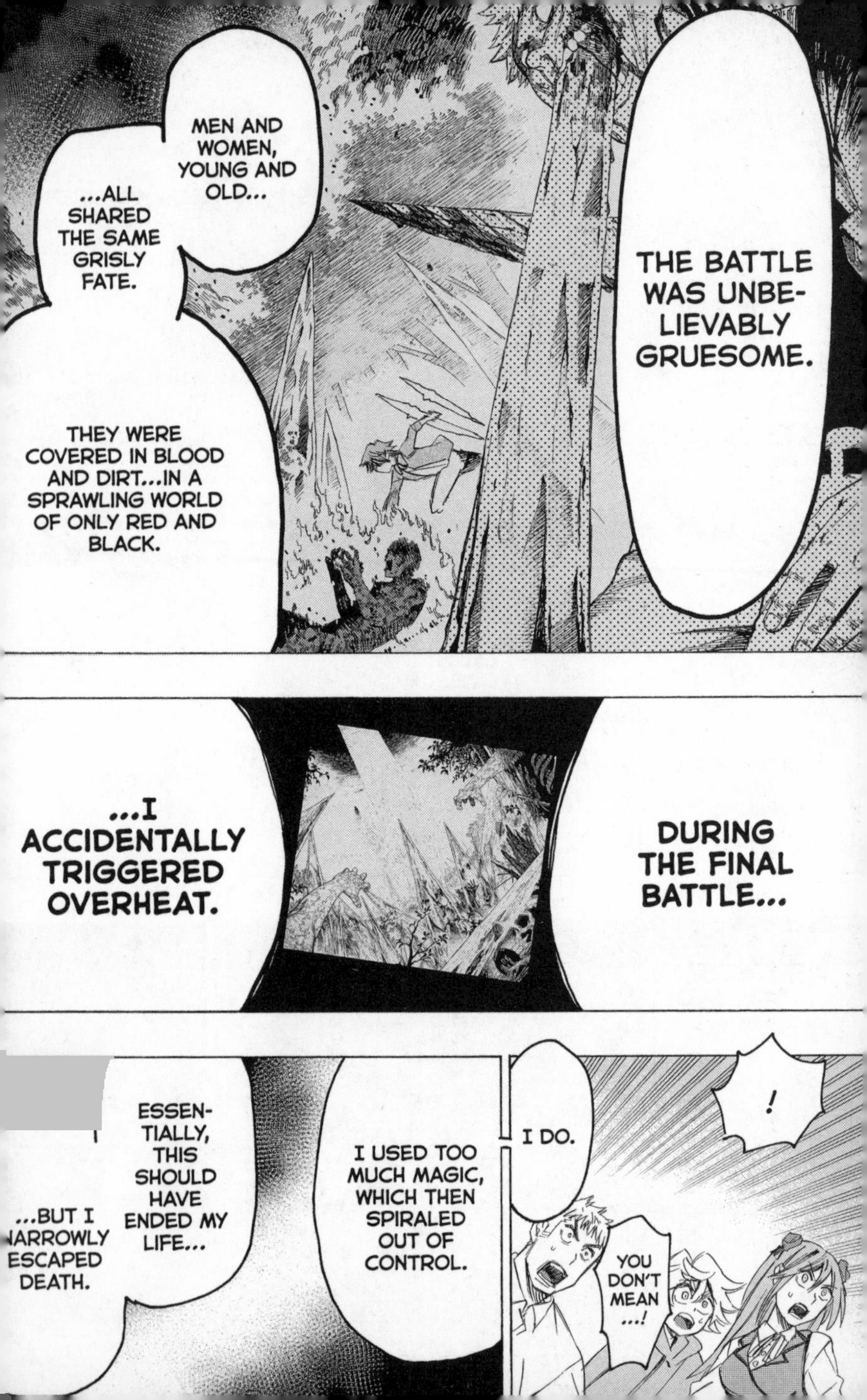
THE BATTLE WAS UNBE-LIEVABLY GRUESOME.
MEN AND WOMEN, YOUNG AND OLD...
...ALL SHARED THE SAME GRISLY FATE.
THEY WERE COVERED IN BLOOD AND DIRT...IN A SPRAWLING WORLD OF ONLY RED AND BLACK.
DURING THE FINAL BATTLE...
...I ACCIDENTALLY TRIGGERED OVERHEAT.
!
I DO.
YOU DON'T MEAN ...!
I USED TOO MUCH MAGIC, WHICH THEN SPIRALED OUT OF CONTROL.
ESSEN-TIALLY, THIS SHOULD HAVE ENDED MY LIFE...
...BUT I NARROWLY ESCAPED DEATH.

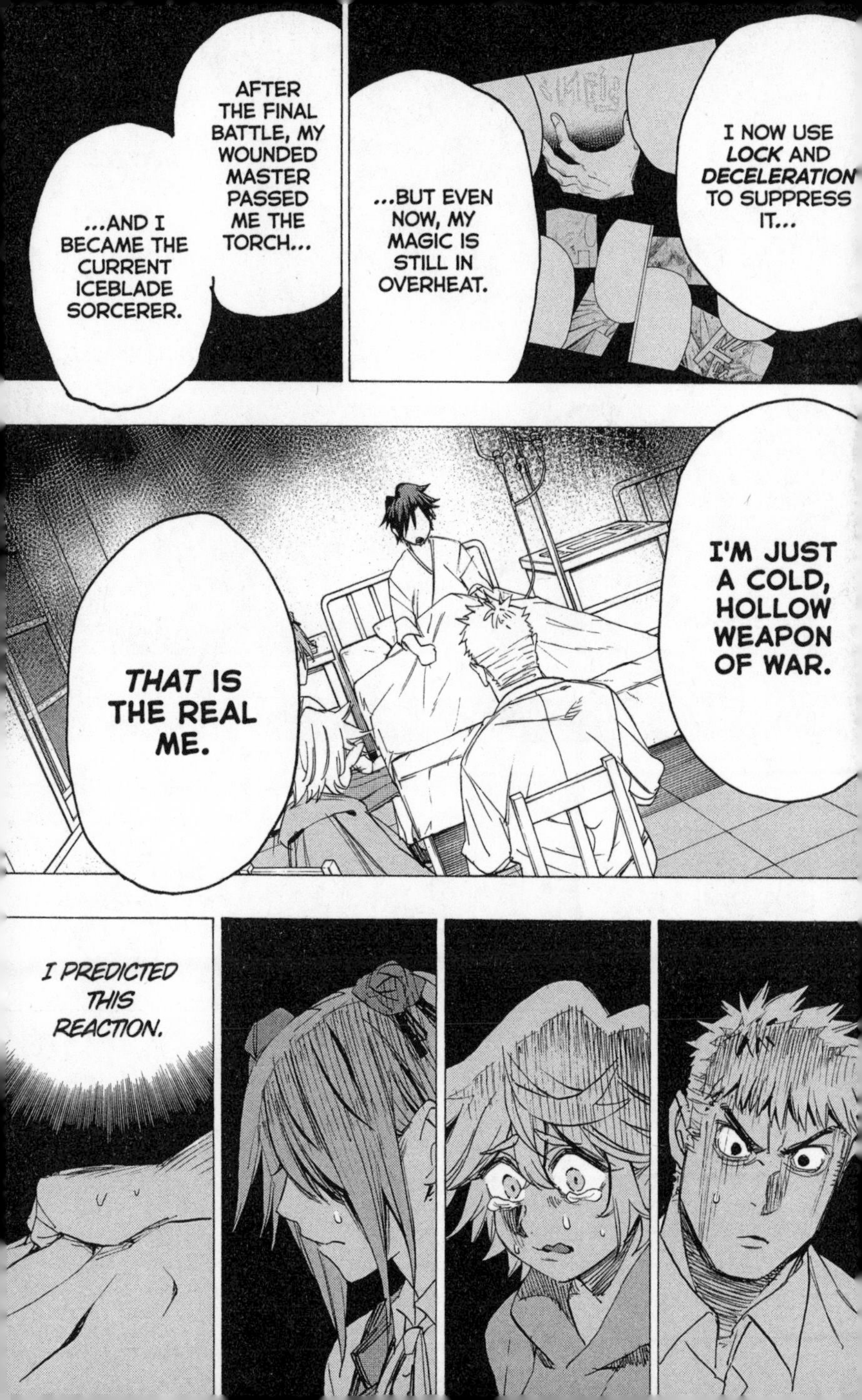
I NOW USE *LOCK* AND *DECELERATION* TO SUPPRESS IT...
...BUT EVEN NOW, MY MAGIC IS STILL IN OVERHEAT.
AFTER THE FINAL BATTLE, MY WOUNDED MASTER PASSED ME THE TORCH...
...AND I BECAME THE CURRENT ICEBLADE SORCERER.
I'M JUST A COLD, HOLLOW WEAPON OF WAR.
THAT IS THE REAL ME.
I PREDICTED THIS REACTION.

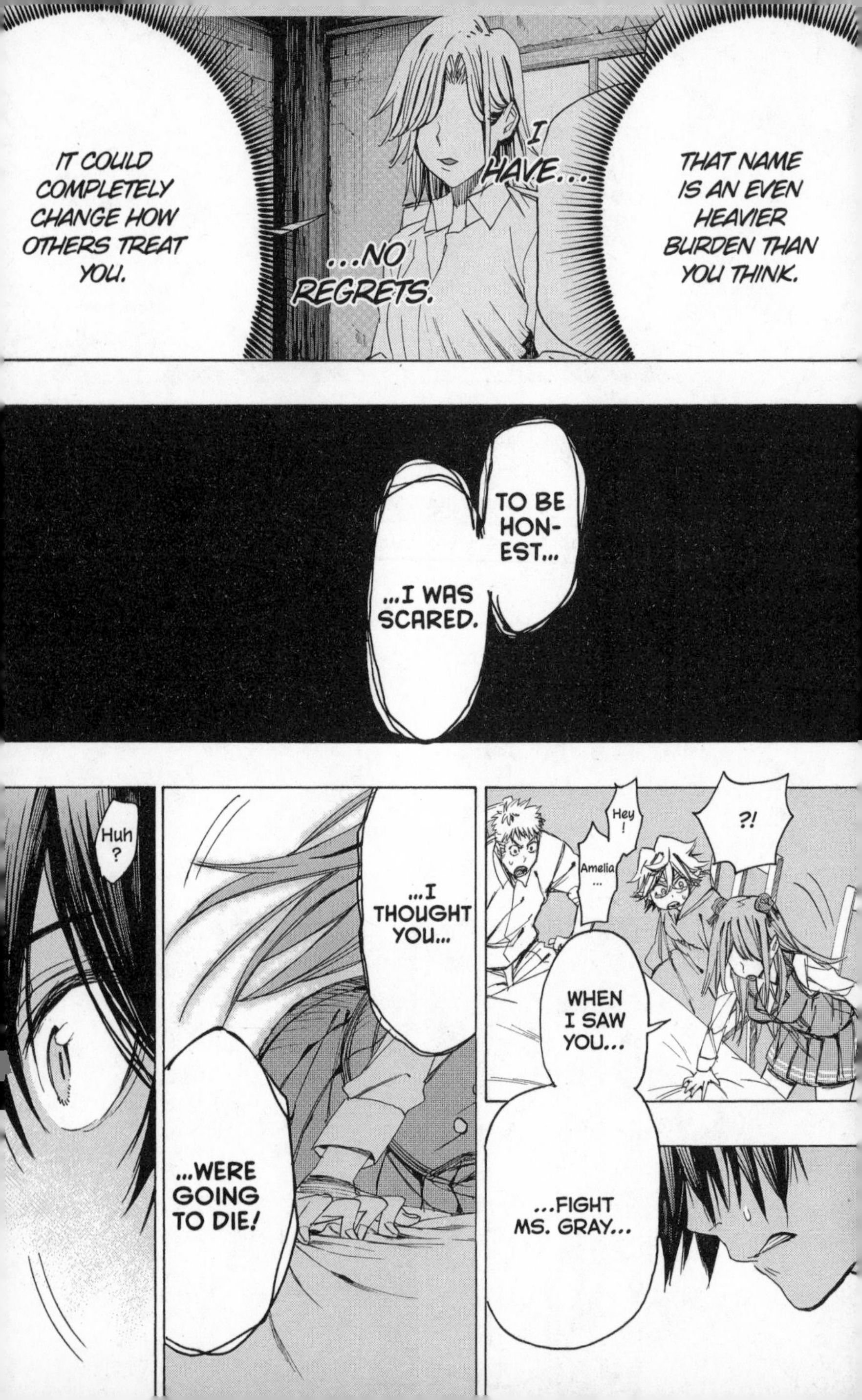
THAT NAME IS AN EVEN HEAVIER BURDEN THAN YOU THINK.
IT COULD COMPLETELY CHANGE HOW OTHERS TREAT YOU.
I HAVE...
...NO REGRETS.
TO BE HON-EST...
...I WAS SCARED.
?!
Hey!
Amelia...
WHEN I SAW YOU...
...FIGHT MS. GRAY...
...I THOUGHT YOU...
...WERE GOING TO DIE!
Huh?

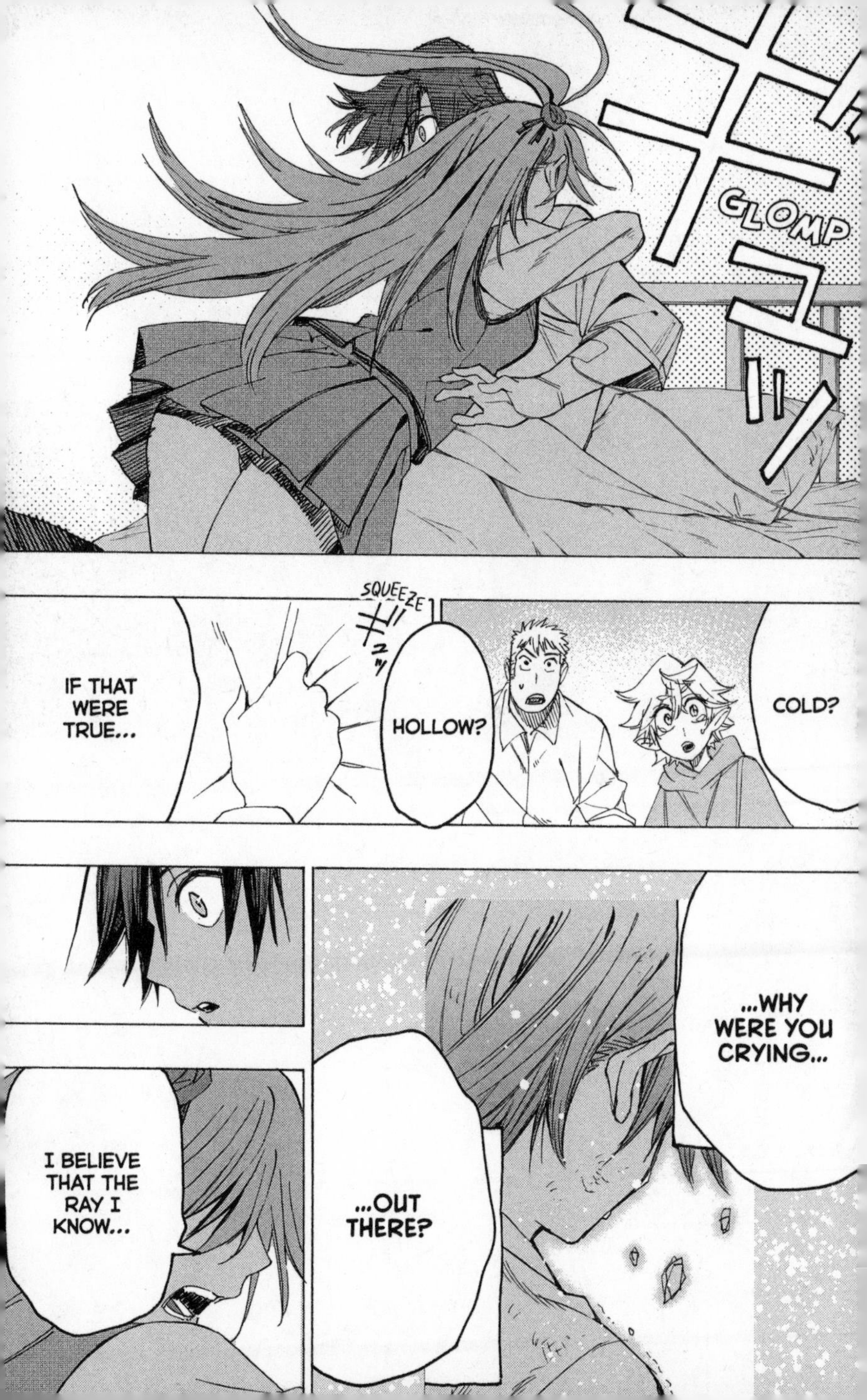
GLOMP
COLD?
HOLLOW?
SQUEEZE
IF THAT WERE TRUE...
...WHY WERE YOU CRYING...
...OUT THERE?
I BELIEVE THAT THE RAY I KNOW...

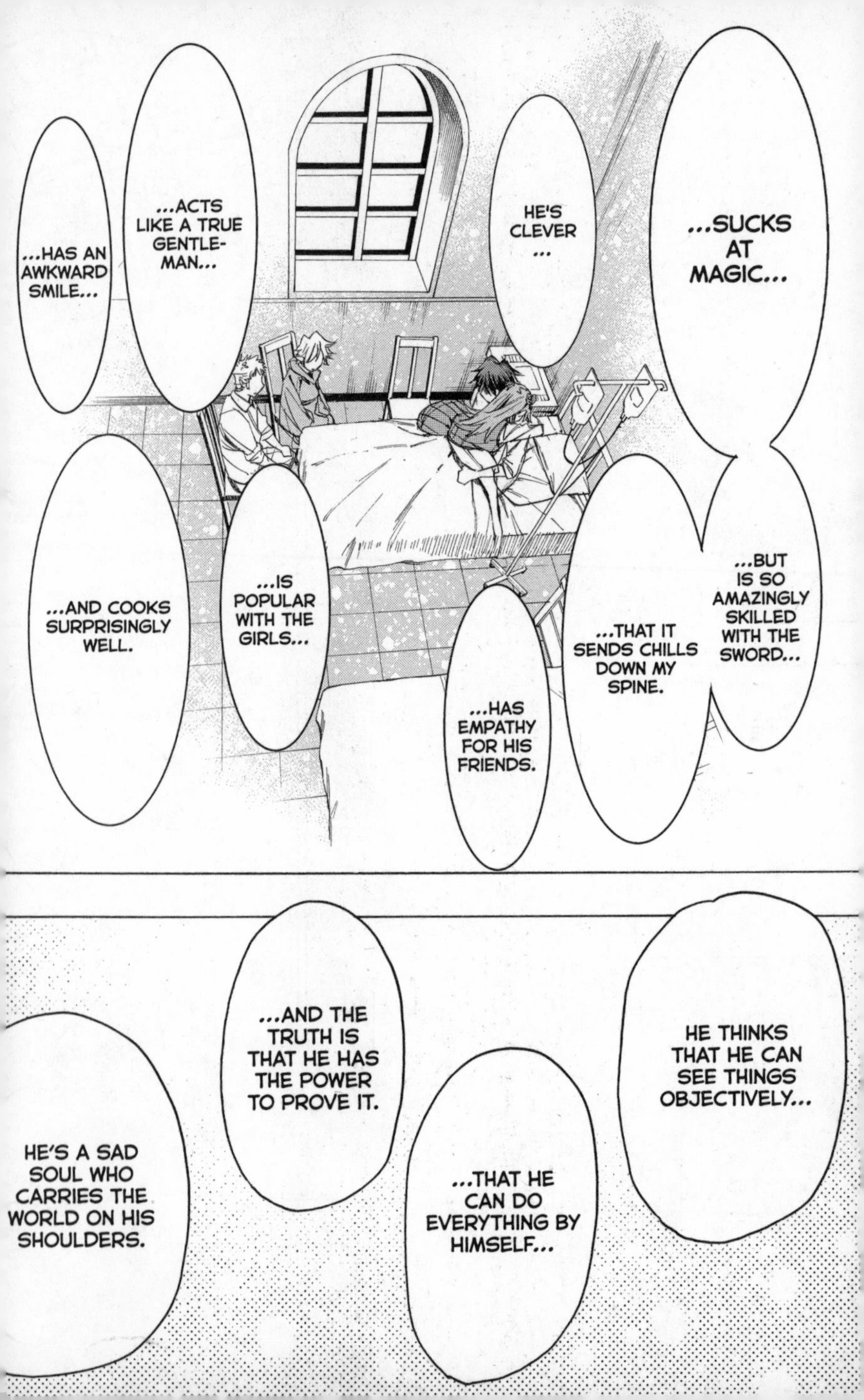
HE'S CLEVER ...
...SUCKS AT MAGIC...
...BUT IS SO AMAZINGLY SKILLED WITH THE SWORD...
...THAT IT SENDS CHILLS DOWN MY SPINE.
...HAS EMPATHY FOR HIS FRIENDS.
...ACTS LIKE A TRUE GENTLE-MAN...
...HAS AN AWKWARD SMILE...
...IS POPULAR WITH THE GIRLS...
...AND COOKS SURPRISINGLY WELL.
HE THINKS THAT HE CAN SEE THINGS OBJECTIVELY...
...THAT HE CAN DO EVERYTHING BY HIMSELF...
...AND THE TRUTH IS THAT HE HAS THE POWER TO PROVE IT.
HE'S A SAD SOUL WHO CARRIES THE WORLD ON HIS SHOULDERS.

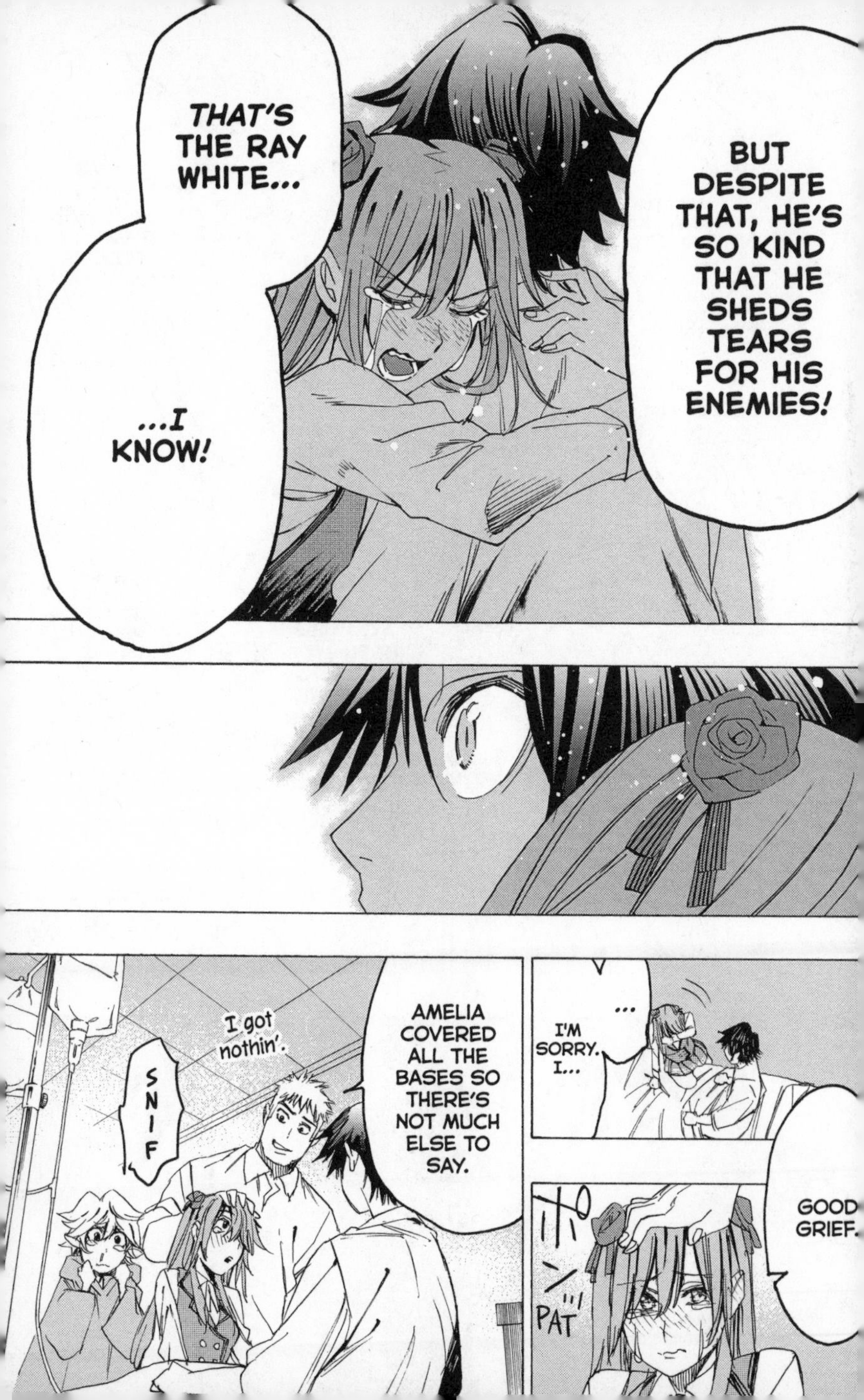
BUT DESPITE THAT, HE'S SO KIND THAT HE SHEDS TEARS FOR HIS ENEMIES!
THAT'S THE RAY WHITE...
...I KNOW!
...
I'M SORRY. I...
GOOD GRIEF.
PAT
AMELIA COVERED ALL THE BASES SO THERE'S NOT MUCH ELSE TO SAY.
I got nothin'.
SNIF

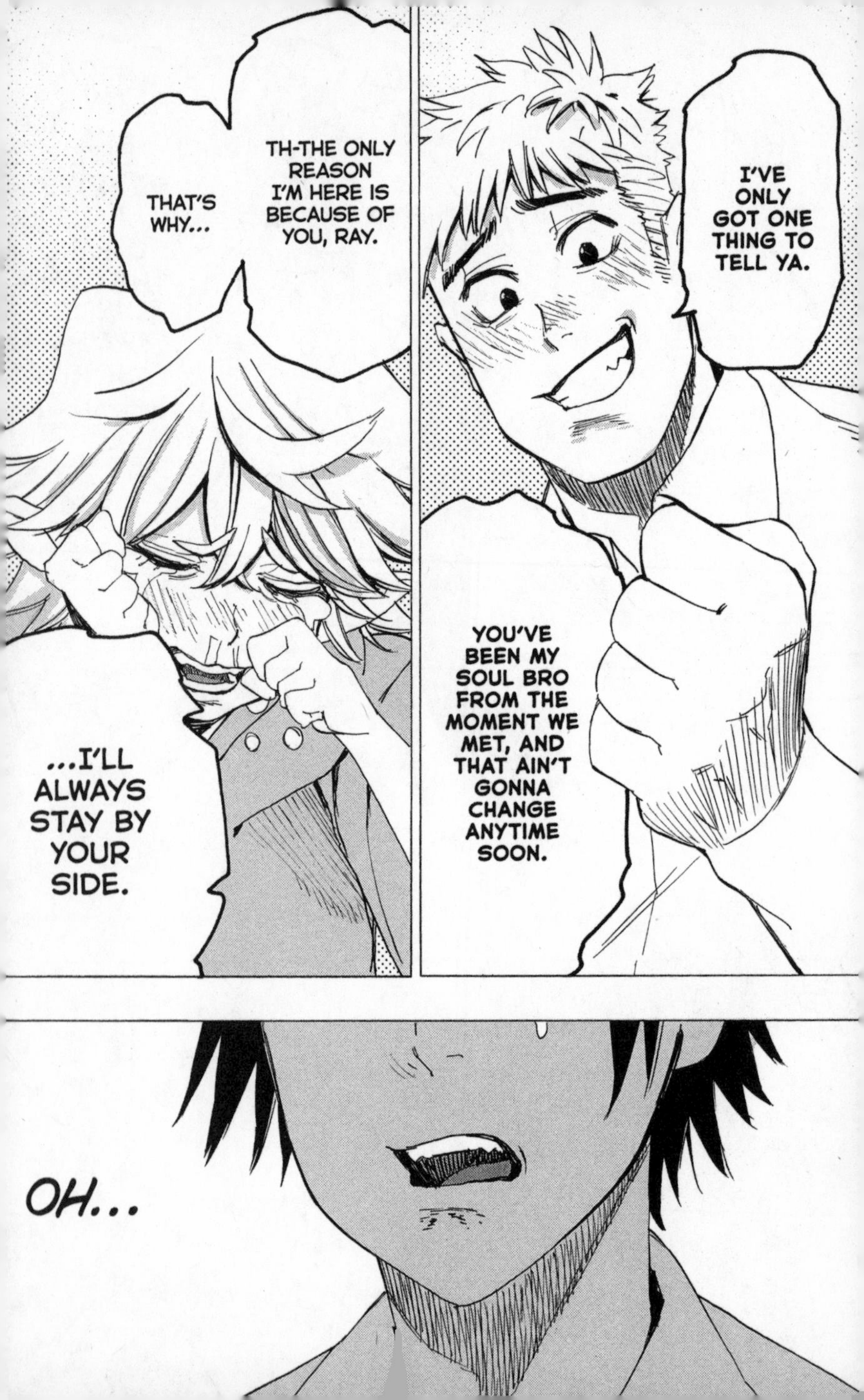
I'VE ONLY GOT ONE THING TO TELL YA.
YOU'VE BEEN MY SOUL BRO FROM THE MOMENT WE MET, AND THAT AIN'T GONNA CHANGE ANYTIME SOON.
TH-THE ONLY REASON I'M HERE IS BECAUSE OF YOU, RAY.
THAT'S WHY...
...I'LL ALWAYS STAY BY YOUR SIDE.
OH...

I SEE...

NOW I REMEMBER...

...WHAT MY MASTER SAID.

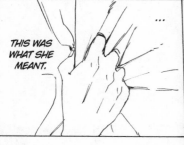

...

THIS WAS WHAT SHE MEANT.

I'M REALLY GLAD...

...THAT I CAME TO THIS SCHOOL!

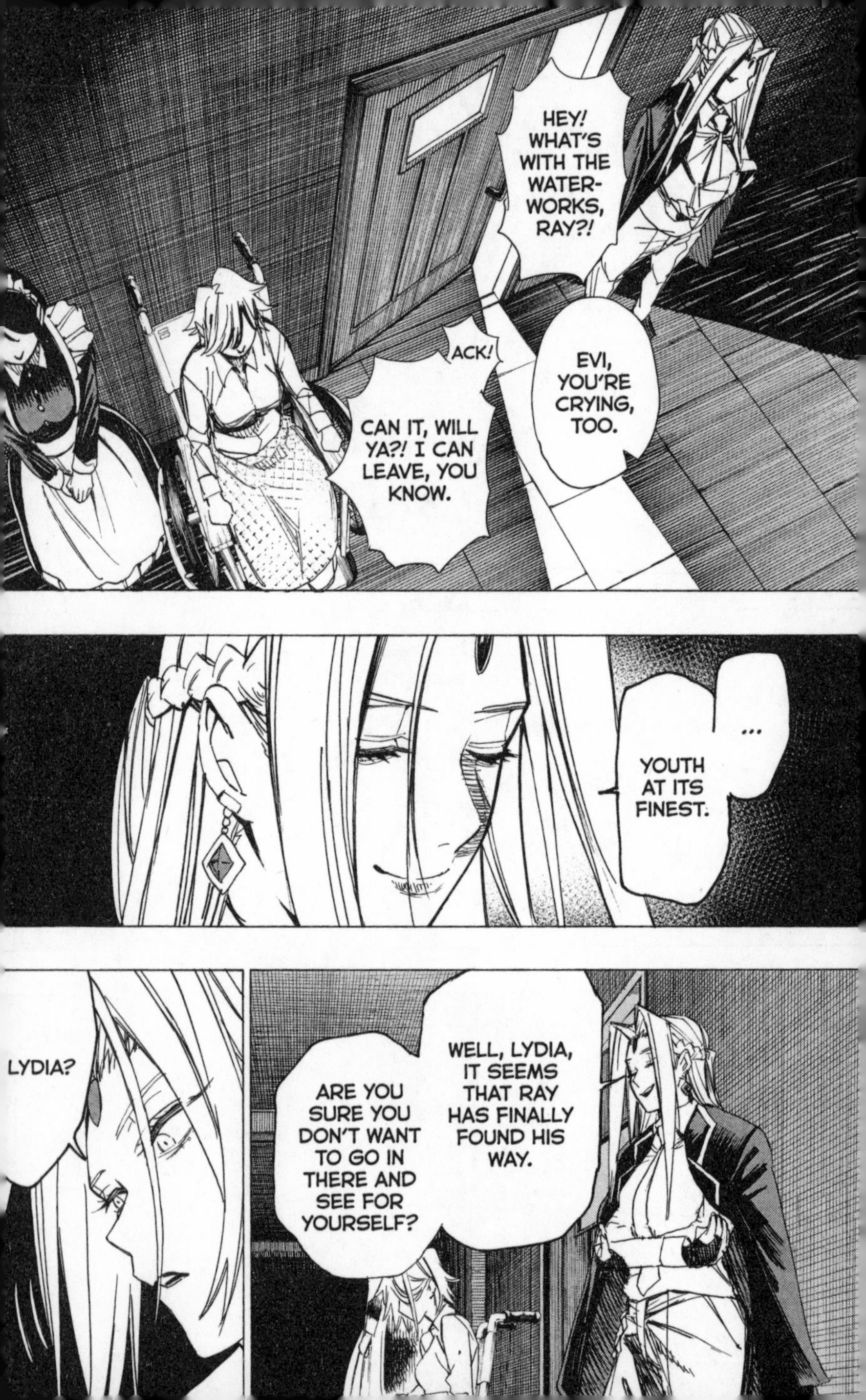
HEY! WHAT'S WITH THE WATER-WORKS, RAY?!
EVI, YOU'RE CRYING, TOO.
ACK!
CAN IT, WILL YA?! I CAN LEAVE, YOU KNOW.
...
YOUTH AT ITS FINEST.
WELL, LYDIA, IT SEEMS THAT RAY HAS FINALLY FOUND HIS WAY.
ARE YOU SURE YOU DON'T WANT TO GO IN THERE AND SEE FOR YOURSELF?
LYDIA?

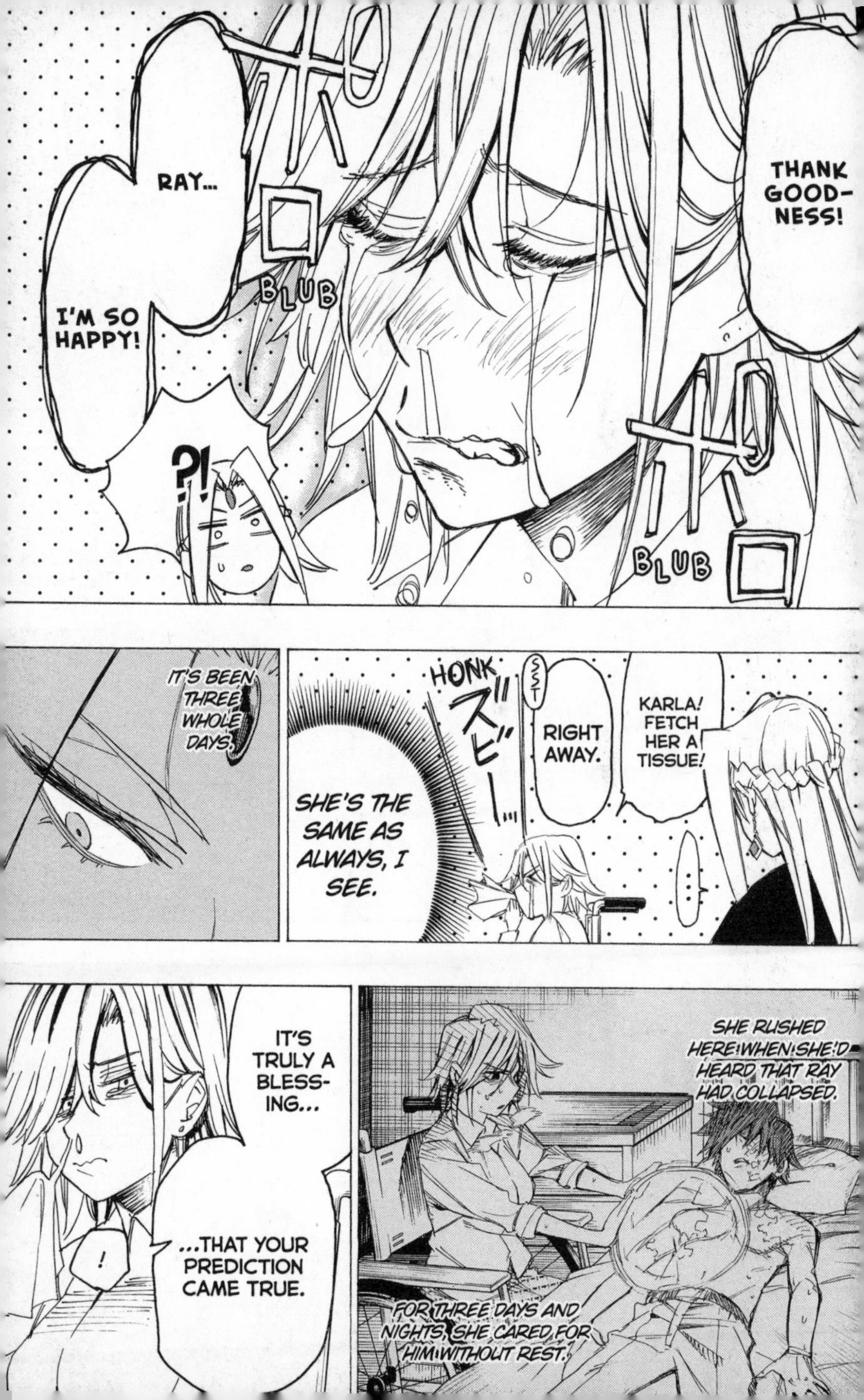
THANK GOODNESS!
RAY...
I'M SO HAPPY!
BLUB
BLUB
?!
KARLA! FETCH HER A TISSUE!
RIGHT AWAY.
SST
HONK
...
SHE'S THE SAME AS ALWAYS, I SEE.
IT'S BEEN THREE WHOLE DAYS.
SHE RUSHED HERE WHEN SHE'D HEARD THAT RAY HAD COLLAPSED.
FOR THREE DAYS AND NIGHTS, SHE CARED FOR HIM WITHOUT REST.
IT'S TRULY A BLESSING...
...THAT YOUR PREDICTION CAME TRUE.
!

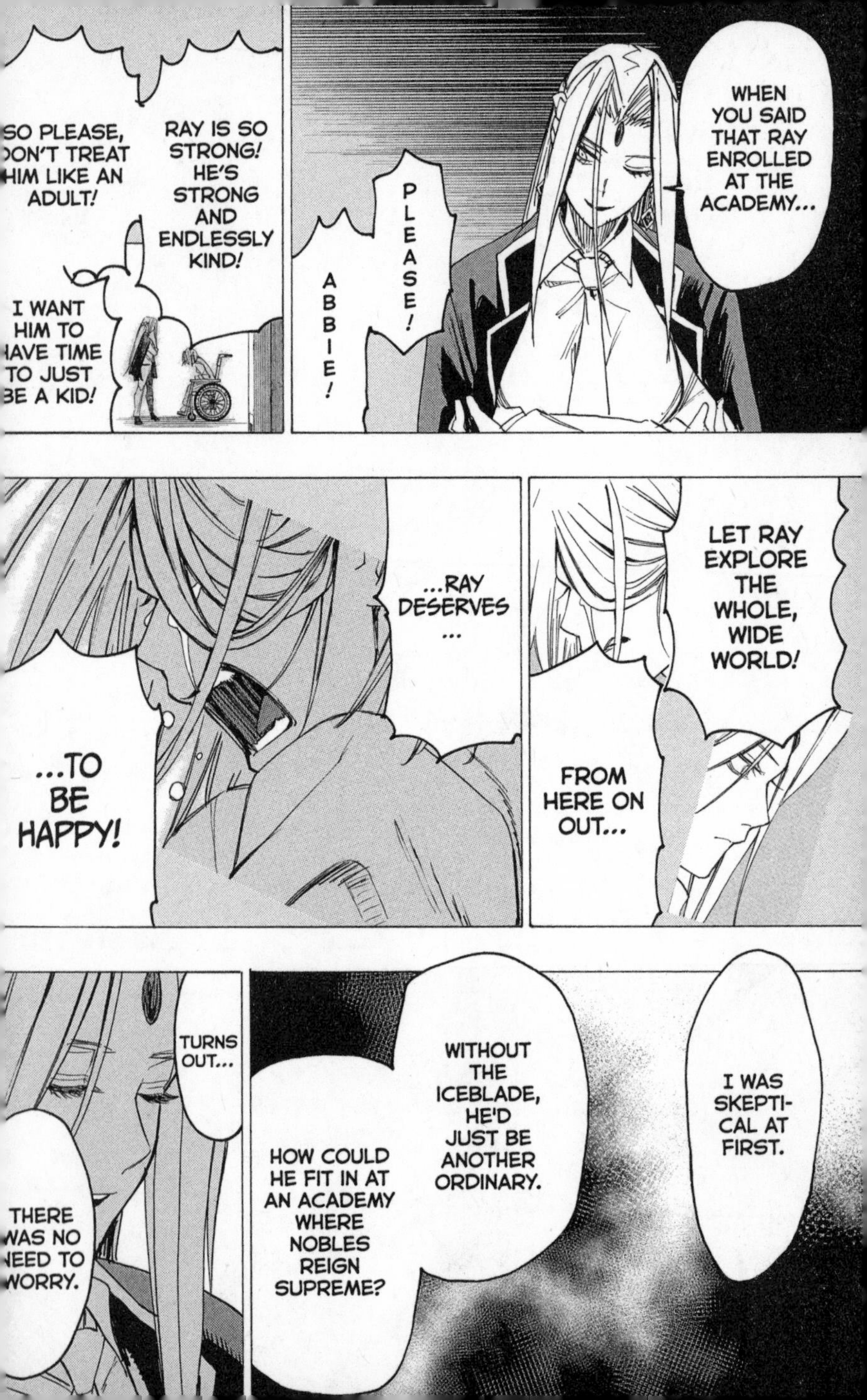
WHEN YOU SAID THAT RAY ENROLLED AT THE ACADEMY...
PLEASE!
ABBIE!
RAY IS SO STRONG! HE'S STRONG AND ENDLESSLY KIND!
SO PLEASE, DON'T TREAT HIM LIKE AN ADULT!
I WANT HIM TO HAVE TIME TO JUST BE A KID!
LET RAY EXPLORE THE WHOLE, WIDE WORLD!
FROM HERE ON OUT...
...RAY DESERVES...
...TO BE HAPPY!
I WAS SKEPTI-CAL AT FIRST.
WITHOUT THE ICEBLADE, HE'D JUST BE ANOTHER ORDINARY.
HOW COULD HE FIT IN AT AN ACADEMY WHERE NOBLES REIGN SUPREME?
TURNS OUT...
THERE WAS NO NEED TO WORRY.

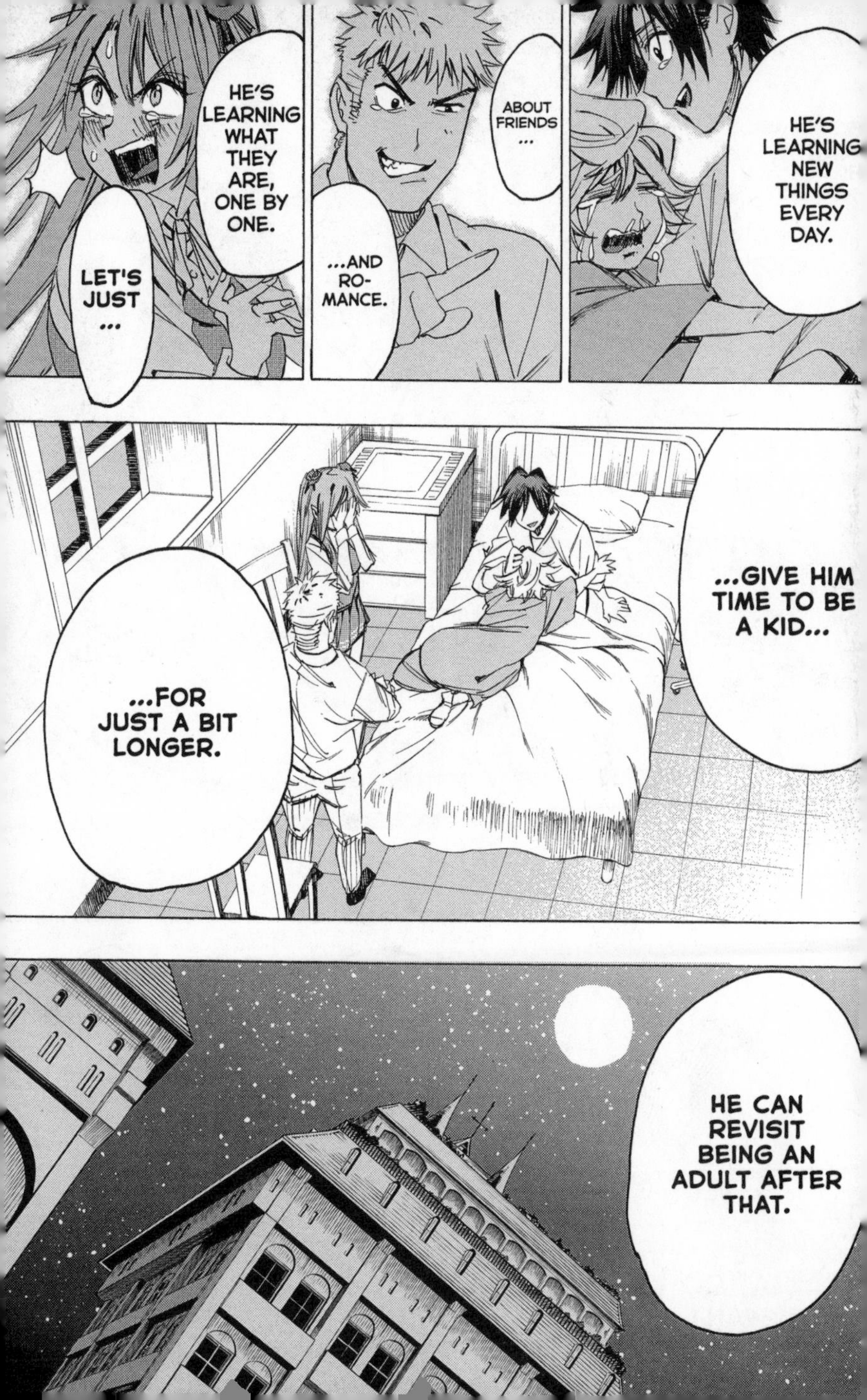
HE'S LEARNING NEW THINGS EVERY DAY.
ABOUT FRIENDS...
...AND RO-MANCE.
HE'S LEARNING WHAT THEY ARE, ONE BY ONE.
LET'S JUST...
...GIVE HIM TIME TO BE A KID...
...FOR JUST A BIT LONGER.
HE CAN REVISIT BEING AN ADULT AFTER THAT.

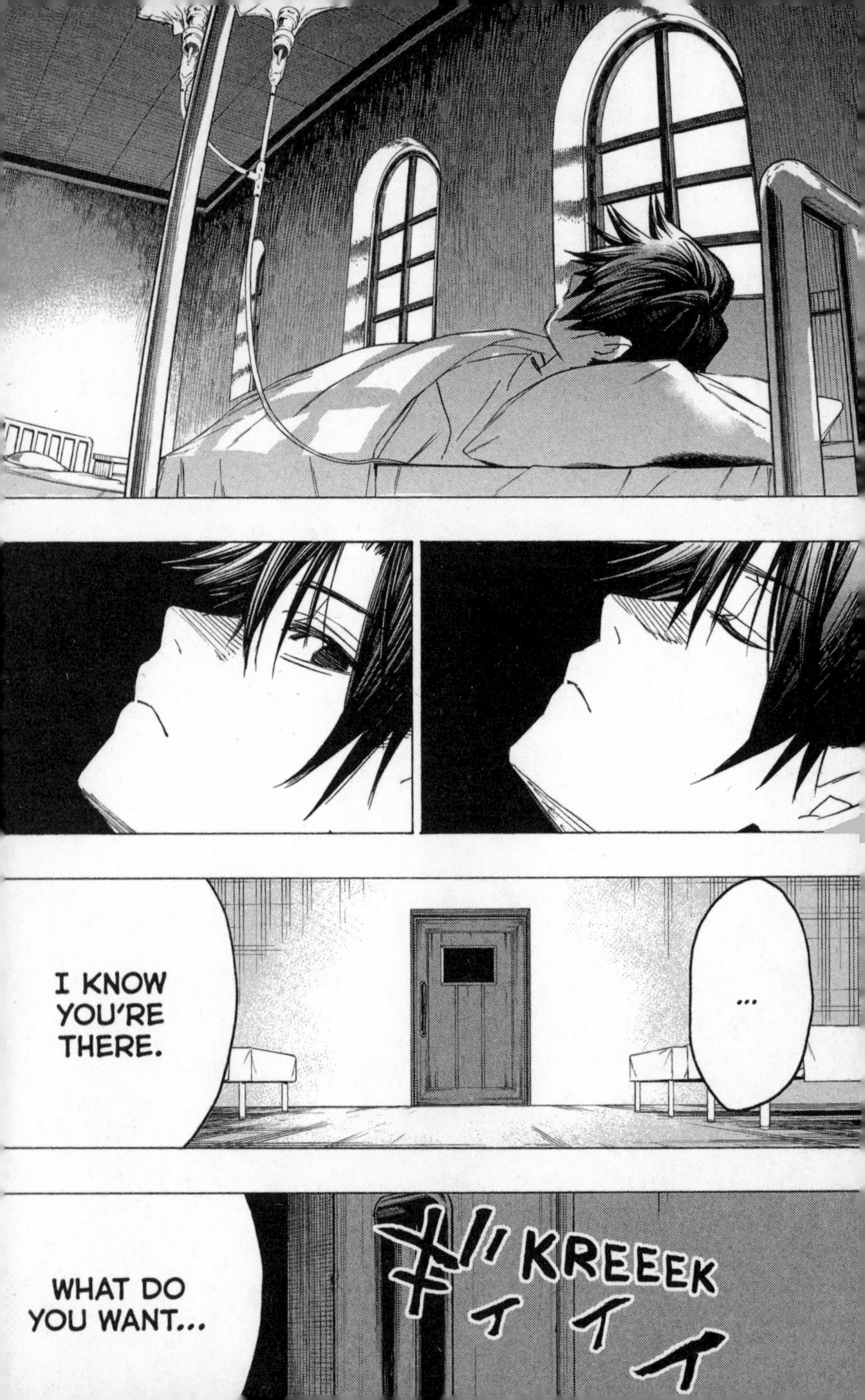
...
I KNOW YOU'RE THERE.
ギィィィ KREEEK
WHAT DO YOU WANT...

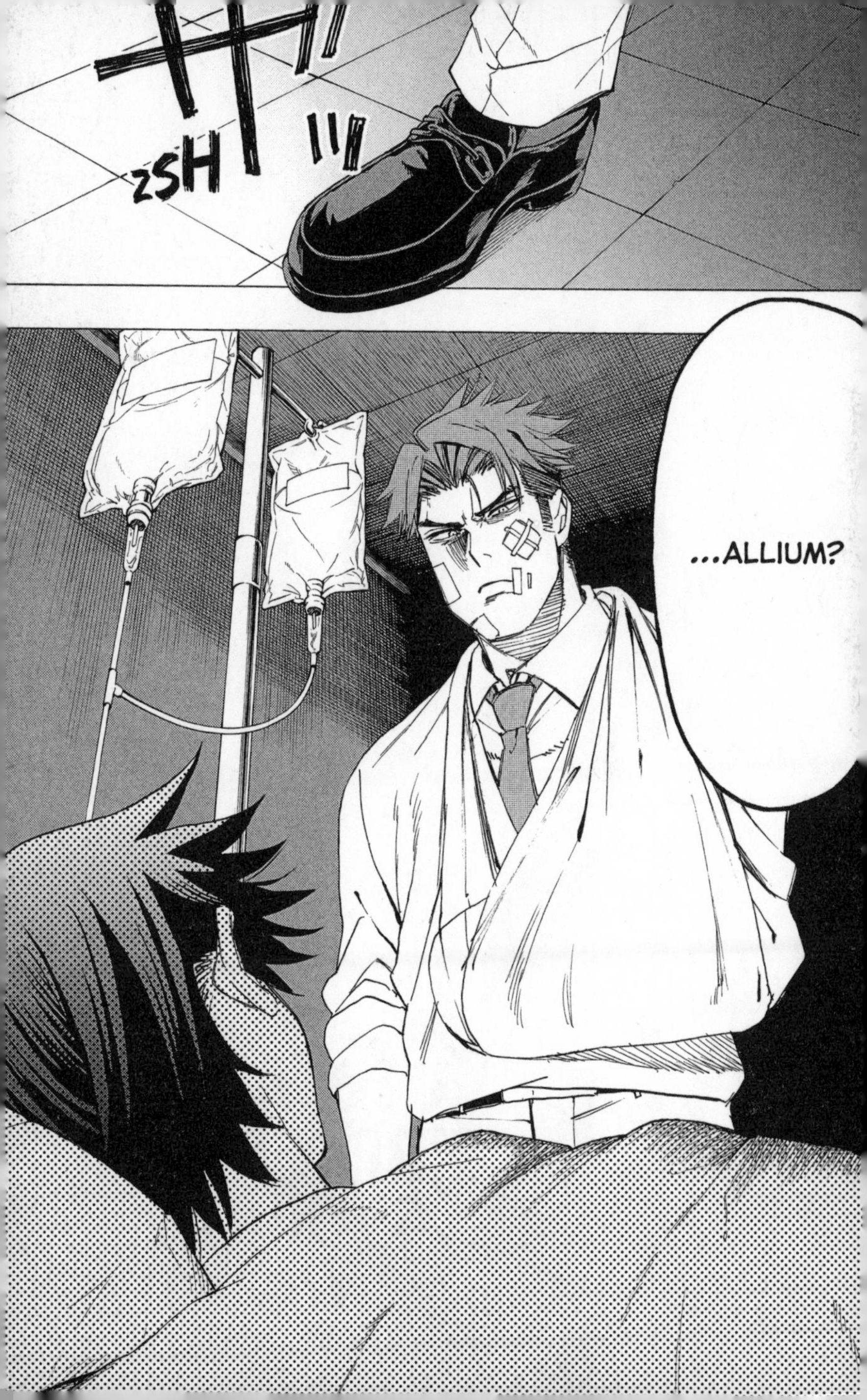
ZSH
...ALLIUM?

The ICEBLADE SORCERER Shall RULE the WORLD

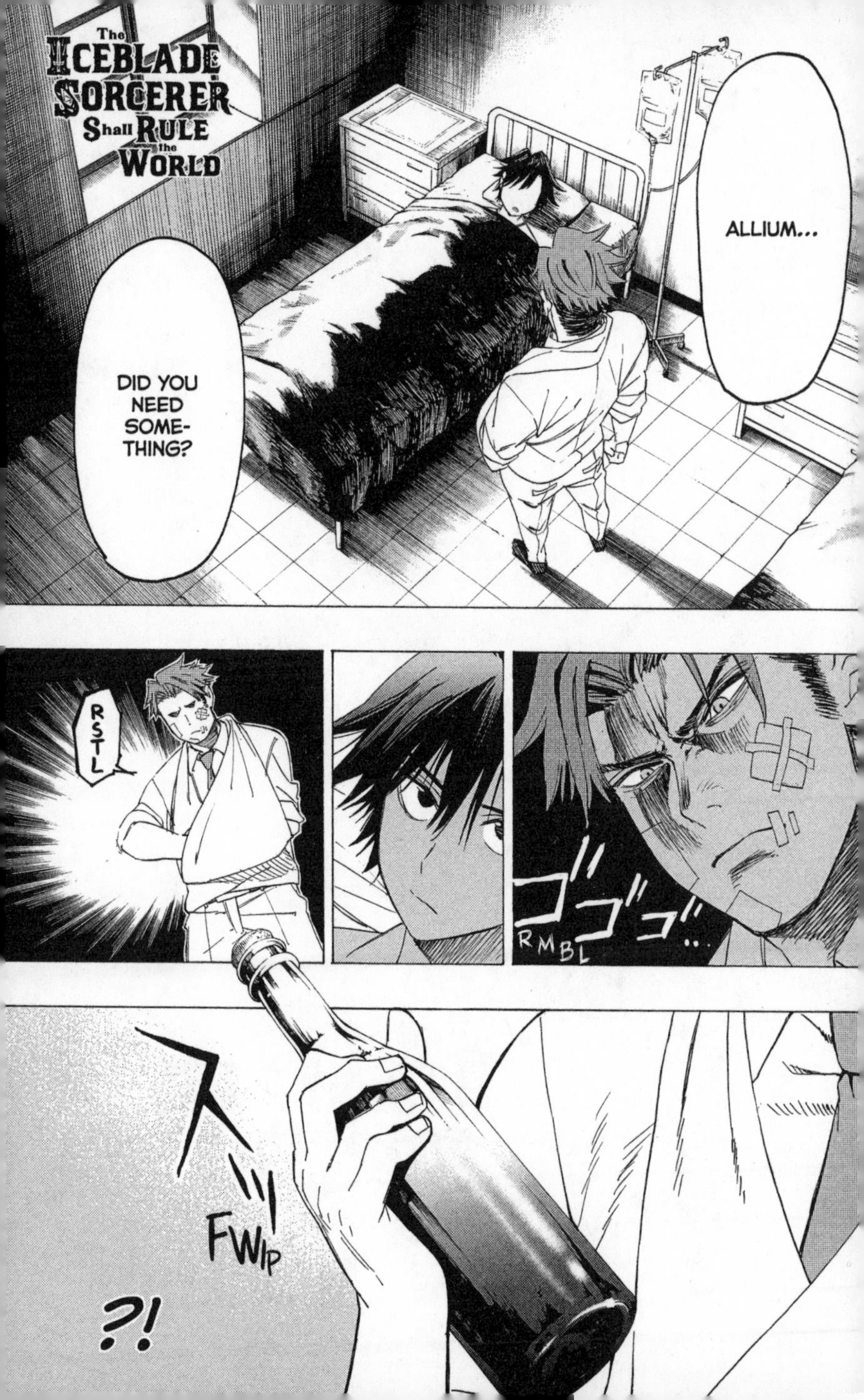
The ICEBLADE SORCERER Shall RULE the WORLD
ALLIUM...
DID YOU NEED SOME-THING?
RMBL
RSTL
FWIP
?!

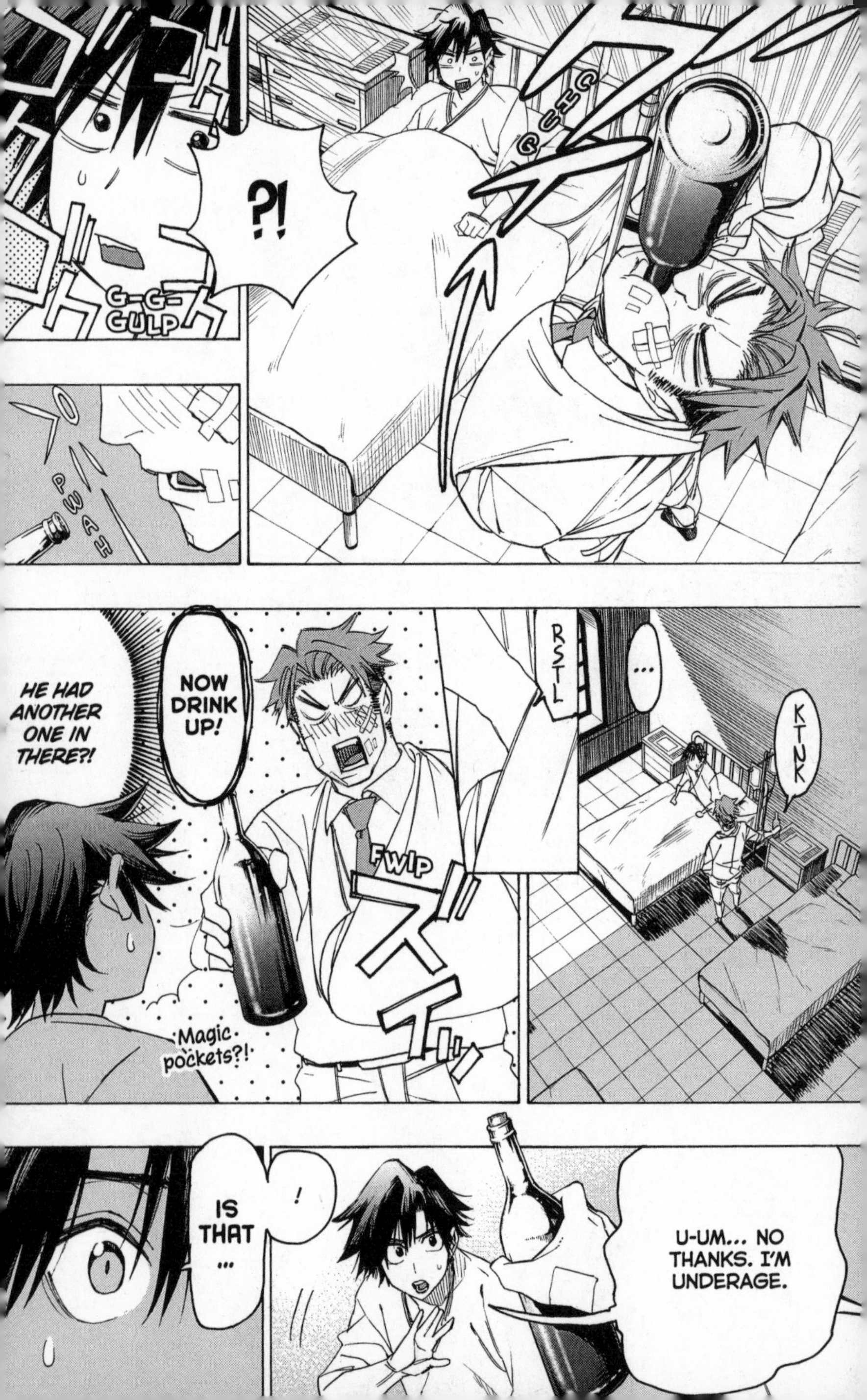
CHUG
?!
G-G-GULP
PWAH
...
KTNK
RSTL
NOW DRINK UP!
FWIP
HE HAD ANOTHER ONE IN THERE?!
Magic pockets?!
U-UM... NO THANKS. I'M UNDERAGE.
!
IS THAT ...

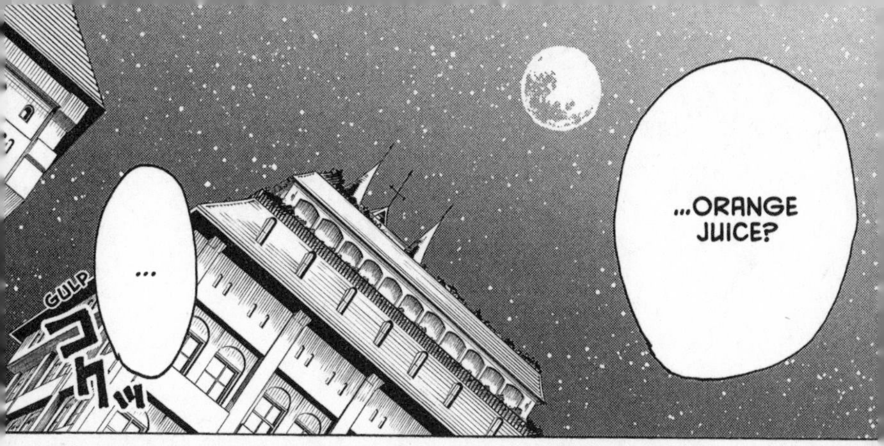
...ORANGE JUICE?
...
GULP

Chapter 24 Apology

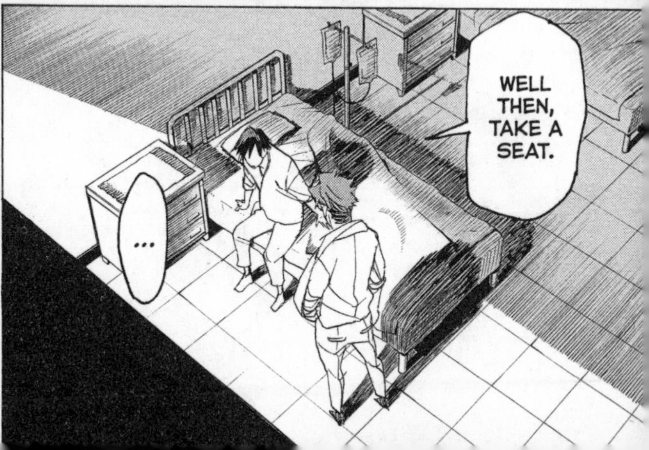
WELL THEN, TAKE A SEAT.
...

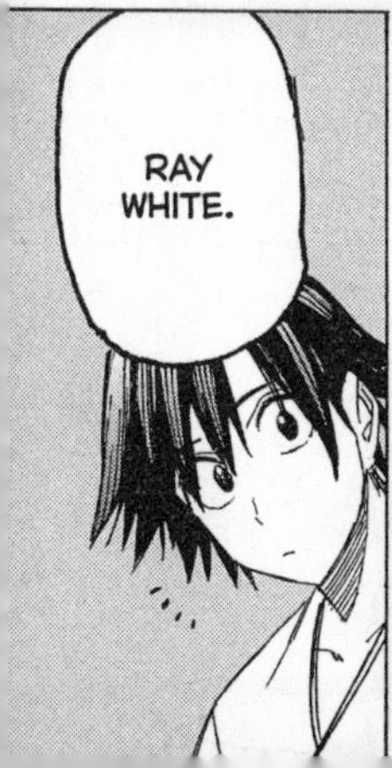
RAY WHITE.

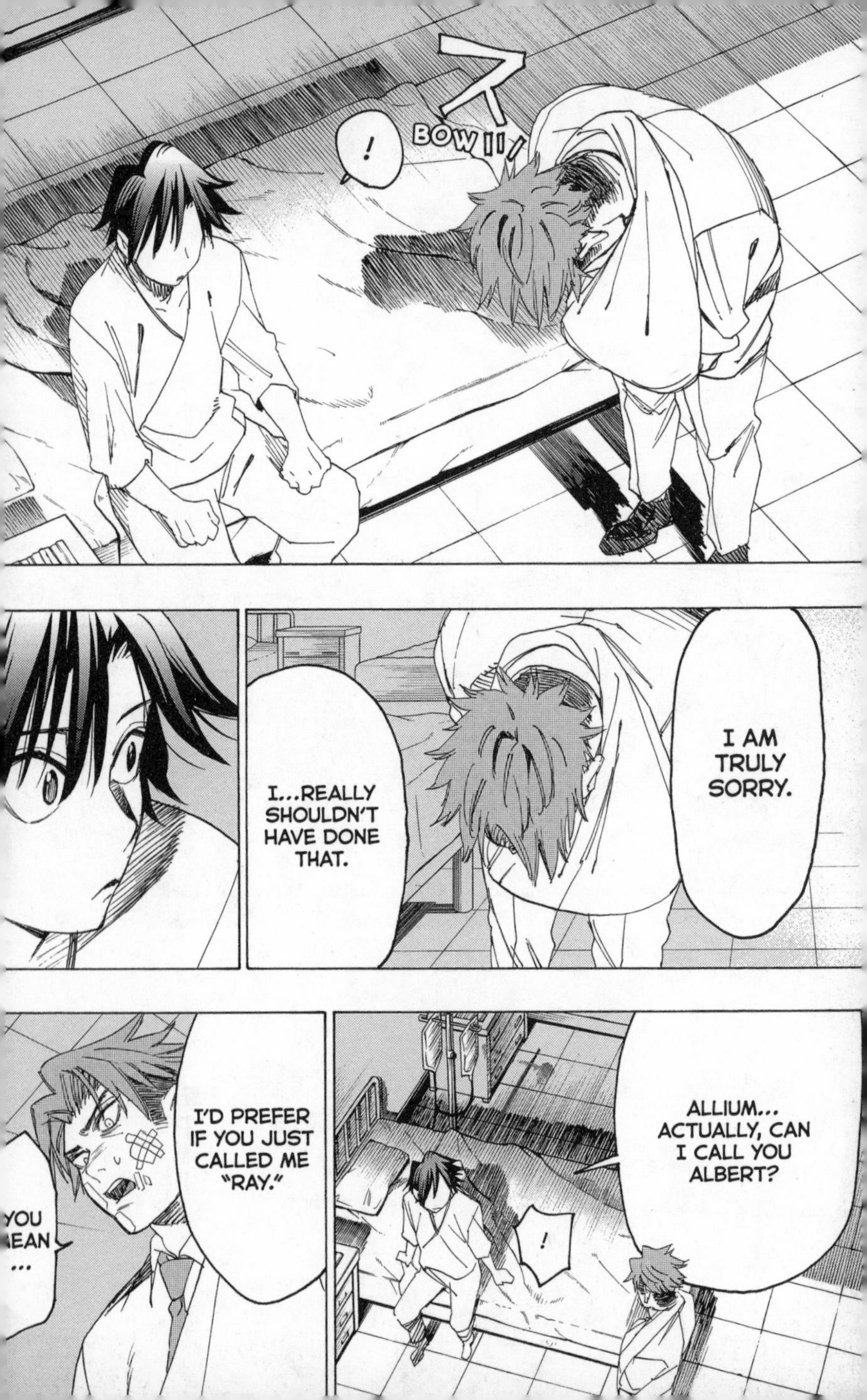
BOW!!!
!
I AM TRULY SORRY.
I...REALLY SHOULDN'T HAVE DONE THAT.
ALLIUM... ACTUALLY, CAN I CALL YOU ALBERT?
!
I'D PREFER IF YOU JUST CALLED ME "RAY."
YOU EAN ...

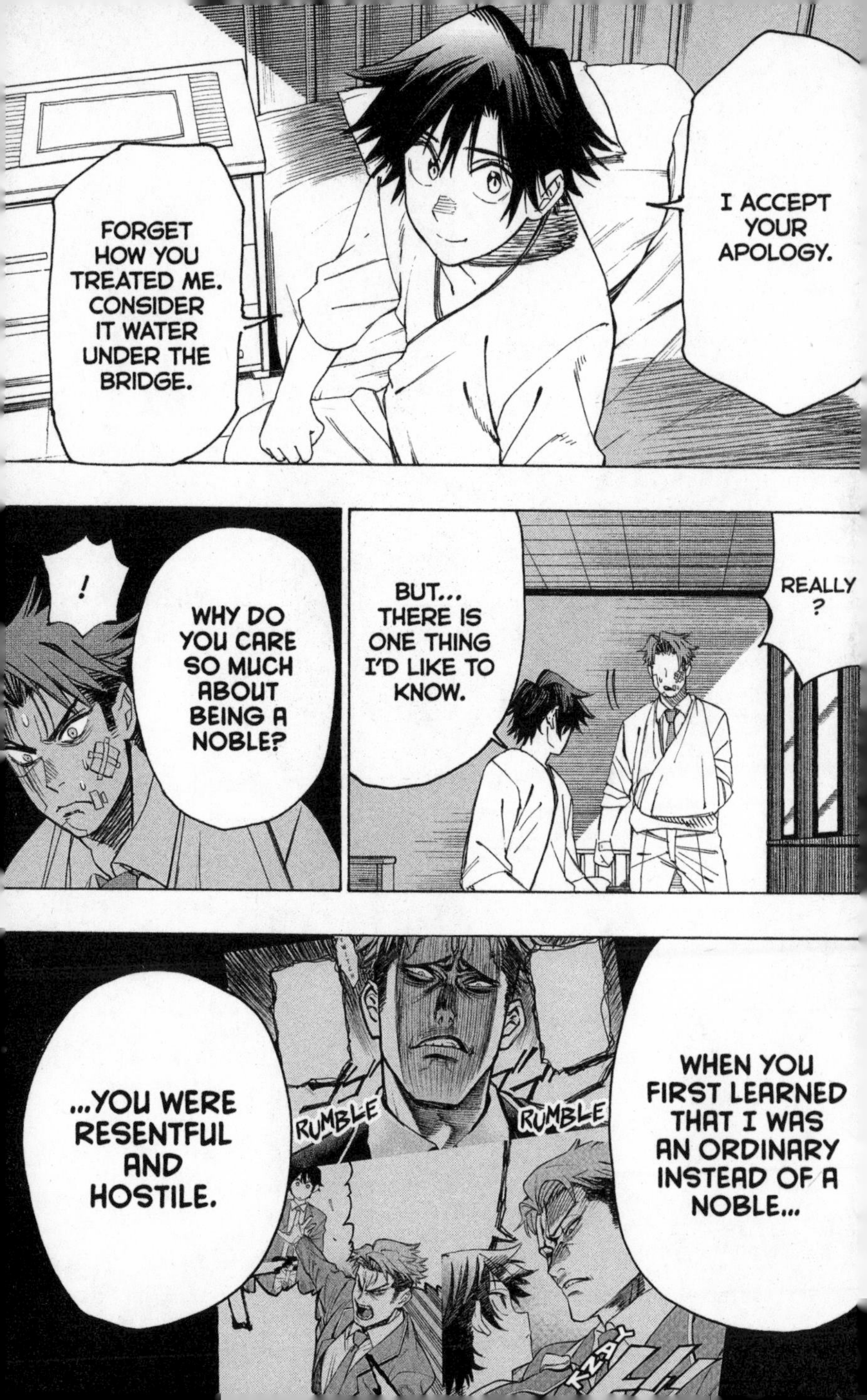
I ACCEPT YOUR APOLOGY.
FORGET HOW YOU TREATED ME. CONSIDER IT WATER UNDER THE BRIDGE.
REALLY?
BUT... THERE IS ONE THING I'D LIKE TO KNOW.
!
WHY DO YOU CARE SO MUCH ABOUT BEING A NOBLE?
WHEN YOU FIRST LEARNED THAT I WAS AN ORDINARY INSTEAD OF A NOBLE...
RUMBLE
RUMBLE
...YOU WERE RESENTFUL AND HOSTILE.

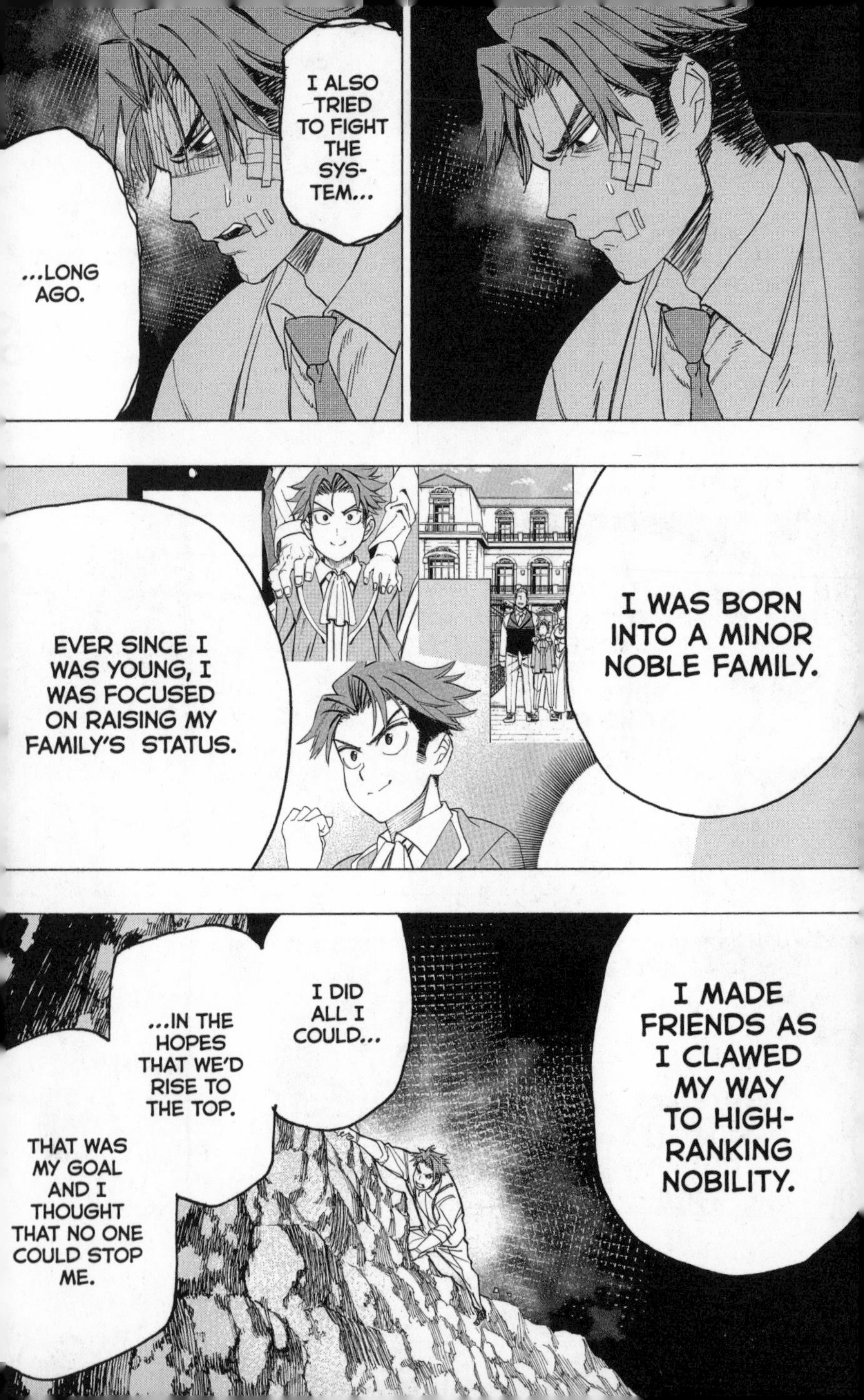
I ALSO TRIED TO FIGHT THE SYS-TEM...
...LONG AGO.
I WAS BORN INTO A MINOR NOBLE FAMILY.
EVER SINCE I WAS YOUNG, I WAS FOCUSED ON RAISING MY FAMILY'S STATUS.
I MADE FRIENDS AS I CLAWED MY WAY TO HIGH-RANKING NOBILITY.
I DID ALL I COULD...
...IN THE HOPES THAT WE'D RISE TO THE TOP.
THAT WAS MY GOAL AND I THOUGHT THAT NO ONE COULD STOP ME.

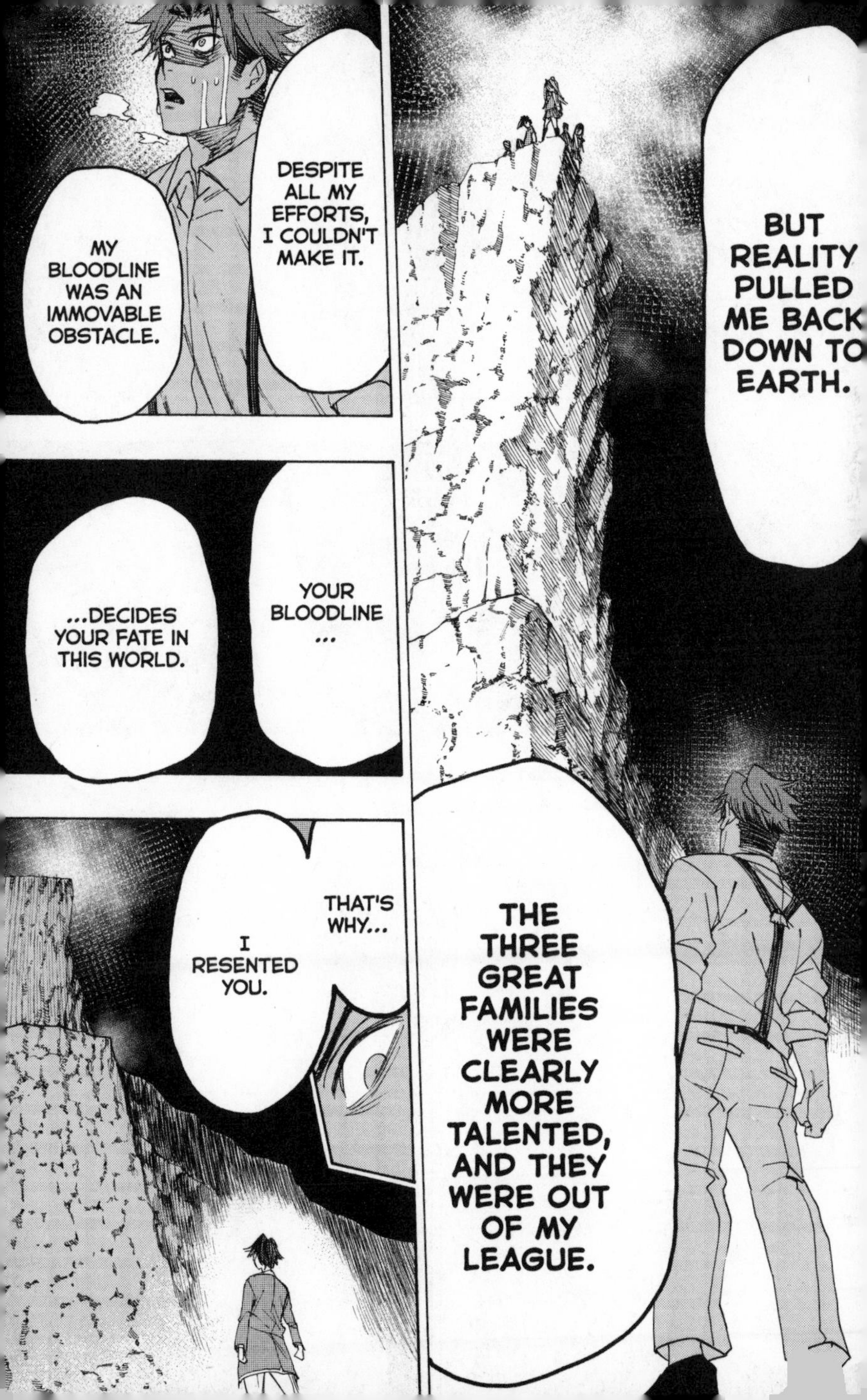
BUT REALITY PULLED ME BACK DOWN TO EARTH.
THE THREE GREAT FAMILIES WERE CLEARLY MORE TALENTED, AND THEY WERE OUT OF MY LEAGUE.
DESPITE ALL MY EFFORTS, I COULDN'T MAKE IT.
MY BLOODLINE WAS AN IMMOVABLE OBSTACLE.
YOUR BLOODLINE ...
...DECIDES YOUR FATE IN THIS WORLD.
THAT'S WHY...
I RESENTED YOU.

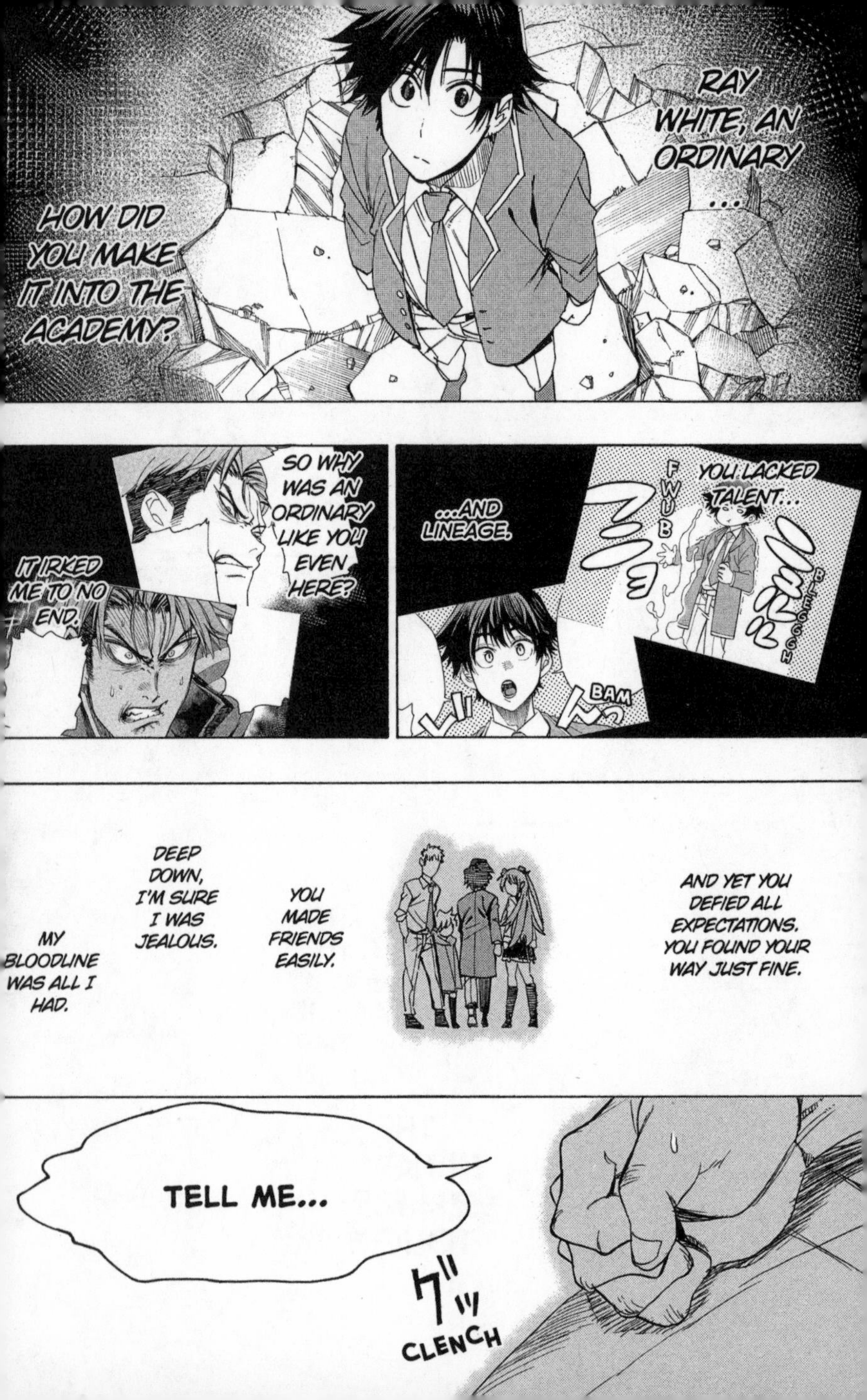
RAY WHITE, AN ORDINARY ...
HOW DID YOU MAKE IT INTO THE ACADEMY?
YOU LACKED TALENT...
FWUB
BLEGGGH
...AND LINEAGE.
BAM
SO WHY WAS AN ORDINARY LIKE YOU EVEN HERE?
IT IRKED ME TO NO END.
AND YET YOU DEFIED ALL EXPECTATIONS. YOU FOUND YOUR WAY JUST FINE.
YOU MADE FRIENDS EASILY.
DEEP DOWN, I'M SURE I WAS JEALOUS.
MY BLOODLINE WAS ALL I HAD.
TELL ME...
CLENCH

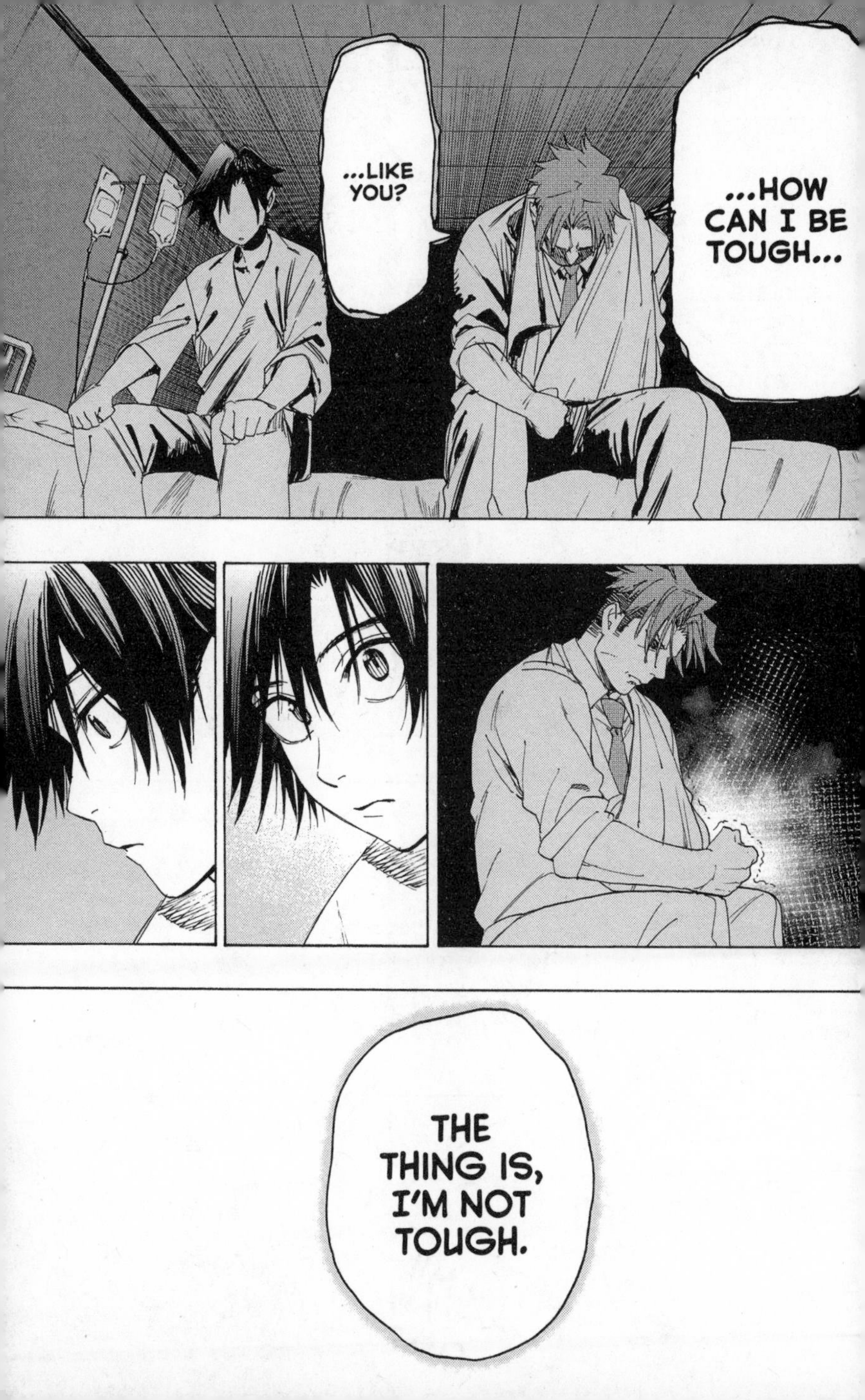
...HOW CAN I BE TOUGH...
...LIKE YOU?
THE THING IS, I'M NOT TOUGH.

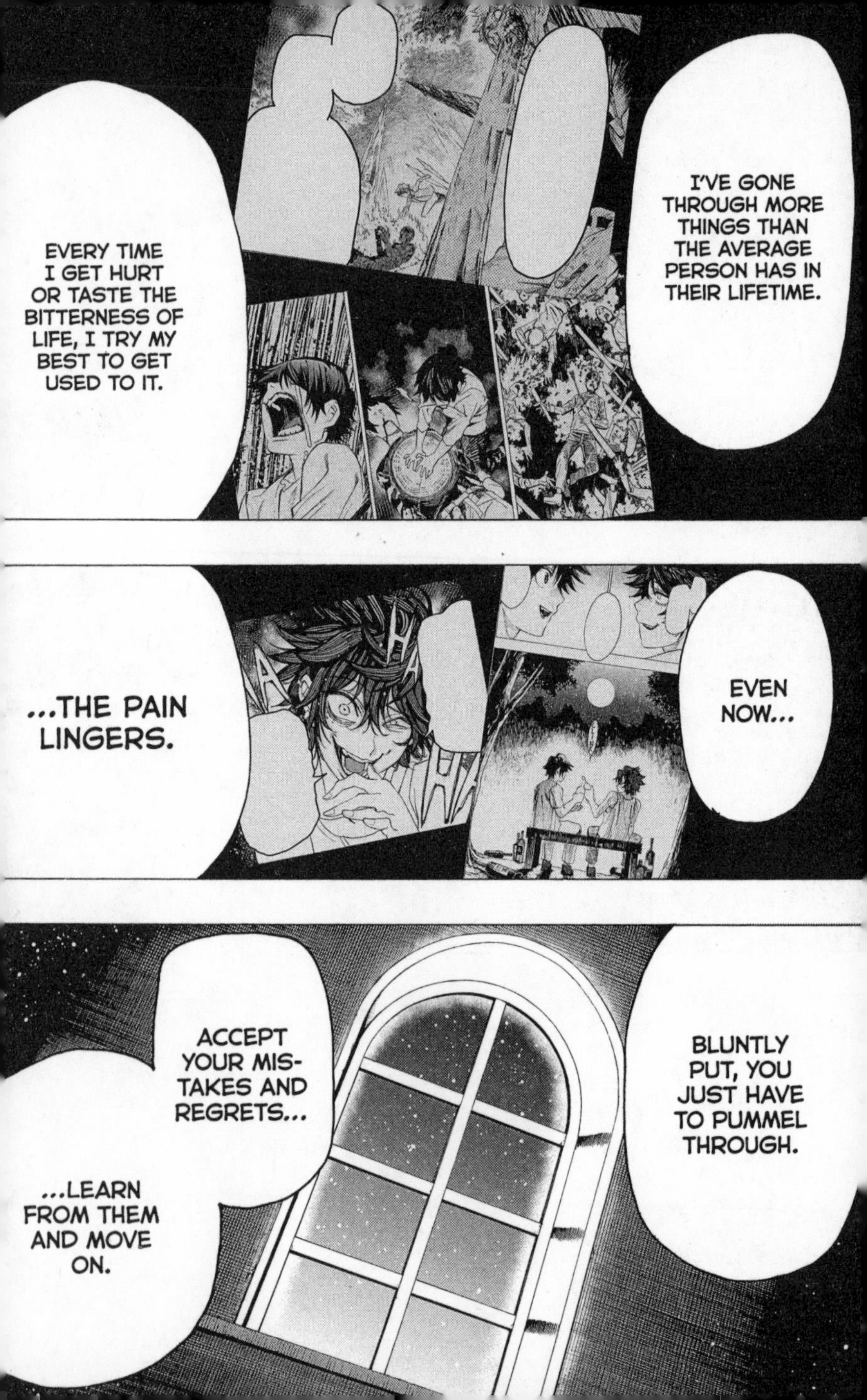
I'VE GONE THROUGH MORE THINGS THAN THE AVERAGE PERSON HAS IN THEIR LIFETIME.
EVERY TIME I GET HURT OR TASTE THE BITTERNESS OF LIFE, I TRY MY BEST TO GET USED TO IT.
EVEN NOW...
...THE PAIN LINGERS.
BLUNTLY PUT, YOU JUST HAVE TO PUMMEL THROUGH.
ACCEPT YOUR MIS-TAKES AND REGRETS...
...LEARN FROM THEM AND MOVE ON.

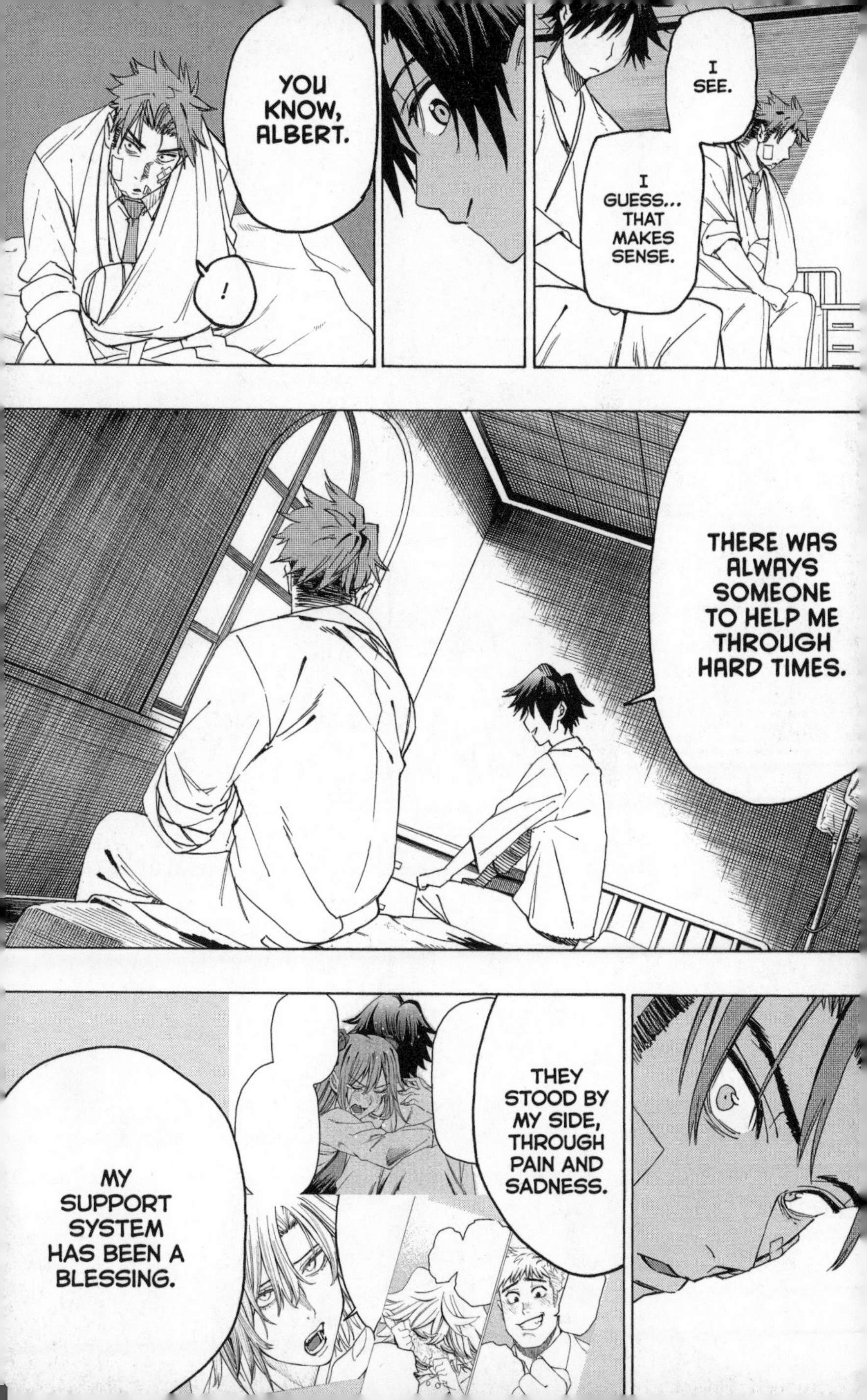
I SEE.
I GUESS... THAT MAKES SENSE.
YOU KNOW, ALBERT.
!
THERE WAS ALWAYS SOMEONE TO HELP ME THROUGH HARD TIMES.
THEY STOOD BY MY SIDE, THROUGH PAIN AND SADNESS.
MY SUPPORT SYSTEM HAS BEEN A BLESSING.

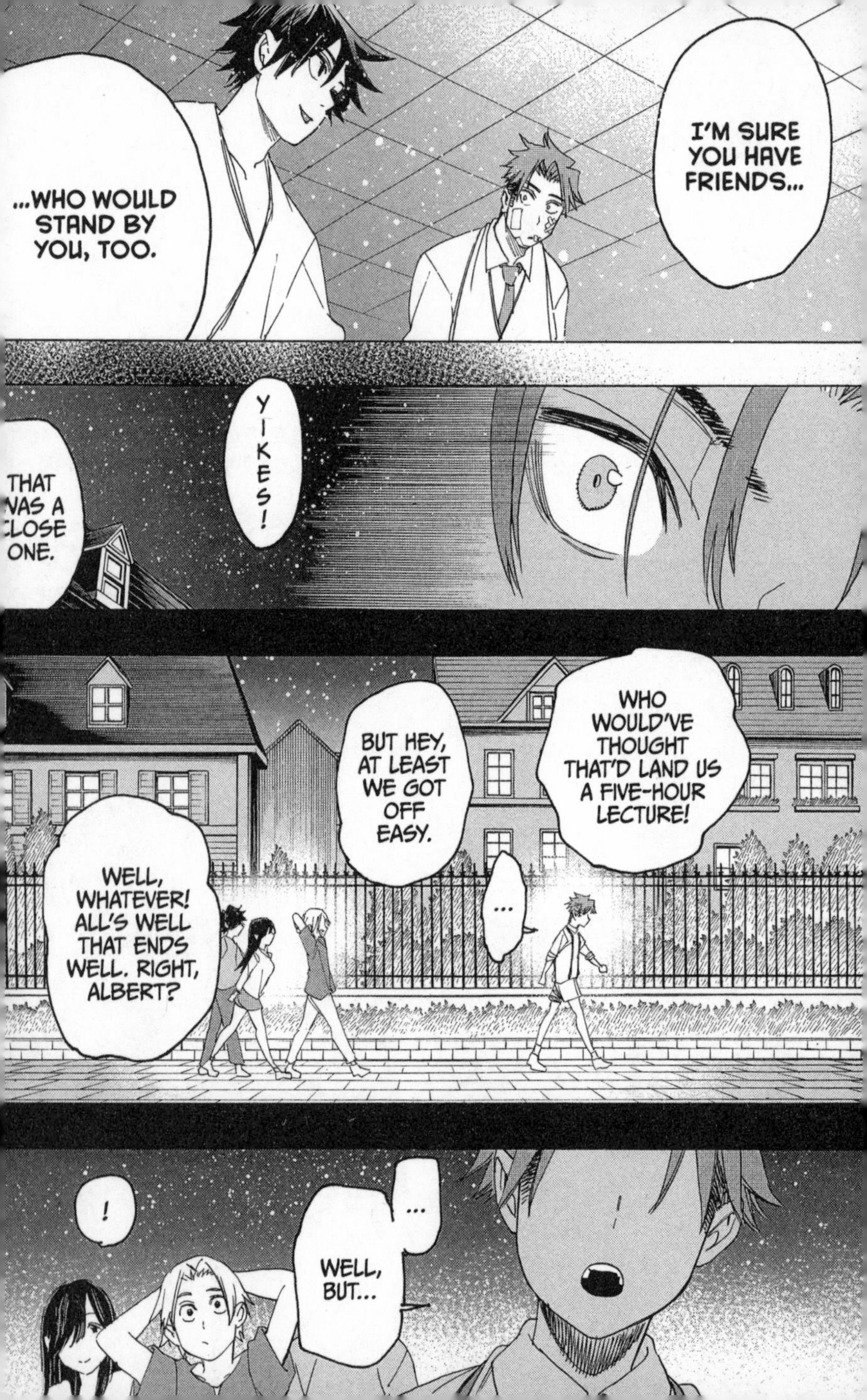
I'M SURE YOU HAVE FRIENDS...
...WHO WOULD STAND BY YOU, TOO.
YIKES!
THAT WAS A CLOSE ONE.
WHO WOULD'VE THOUGHT THAT'D LAND US A FIVE-HOUR LECTURE!
BUT HEY, AT LEAST WE GOT OFF EASY.
...
WELL, WHATEVER! ALL'S WELL THAT ENDS WELL. RIGHT, ALBERT?
...
WELL, BUT...
!

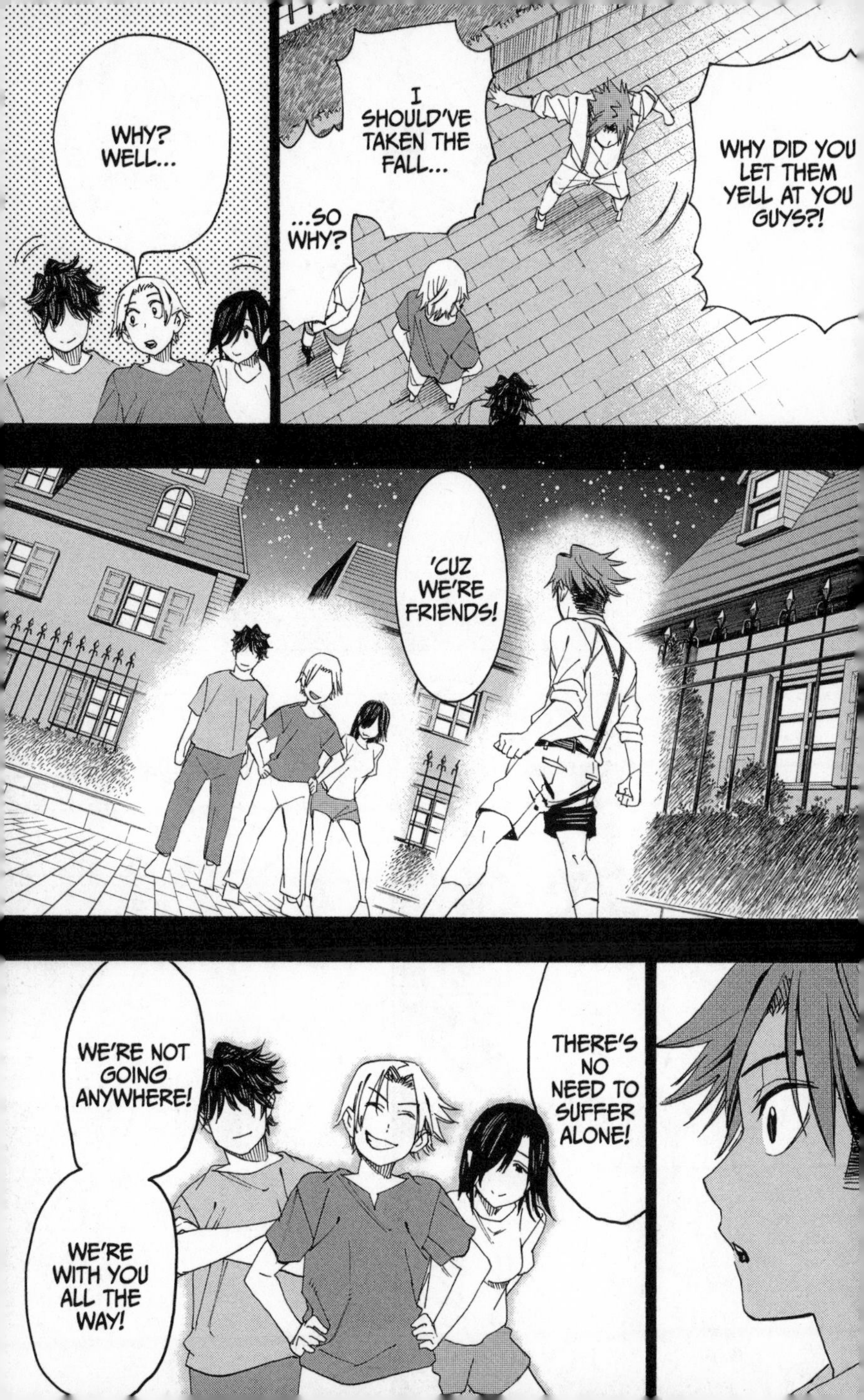
WHY DID YOU LET THEM YELL AT YOU GUYS?!
I SHOULD'VE TAKEN THE FALL...
...SO WHY?
WHY? WELL...
'CUZ WE'RE FRIENDS!
THERE'S NO NEED TO SUFFER ALONE!
WE'RE NOT GOING ANYWHERE!
WE'RE WITH YOU ALL THE WAY!

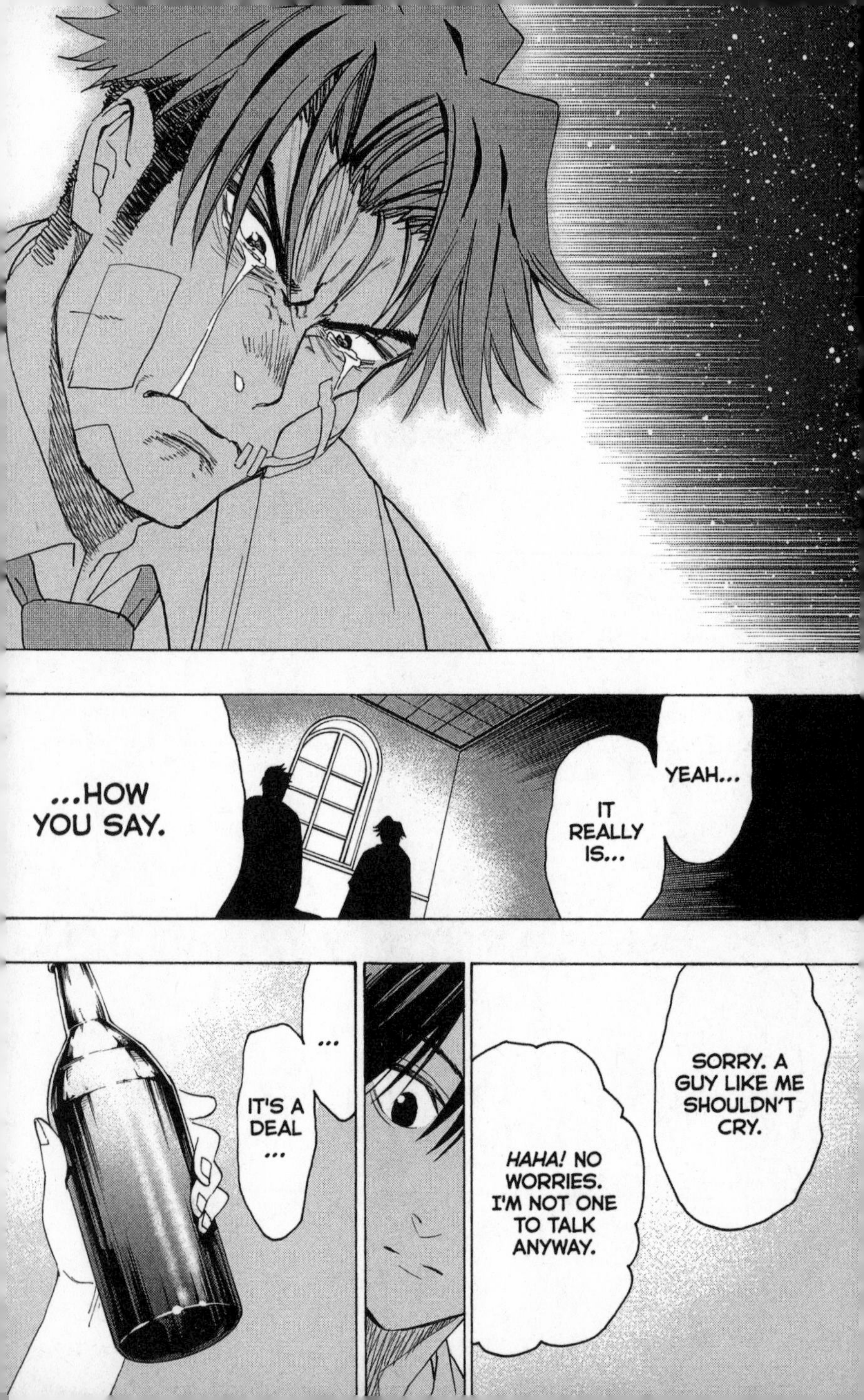
YEAH... IT REALLY IS...
...HOW YOU SAY.
SORRY. A GUY LIKE ME SHOULDN'T CRY.
HAHA! NO WORRIES. I'M NOT ONE TO TALK ANYWAY.
...
IT'S A DEAL ...

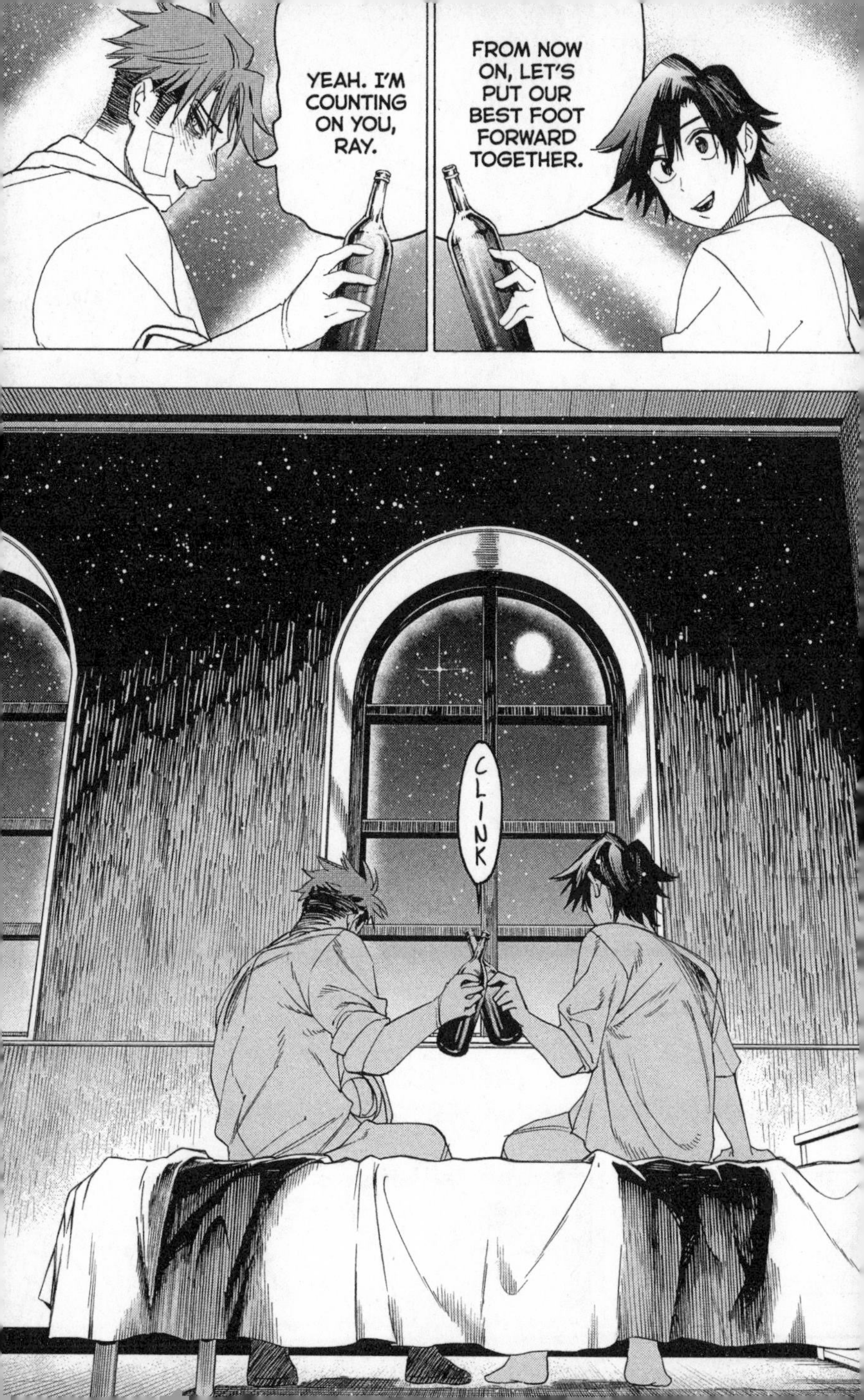
FROM NOW ON, LET'S PUT OUR BEST FOOT FORWARD TOGETHER.
YEAH. I'M COUNTING ON YOU, RAY.
CLINK

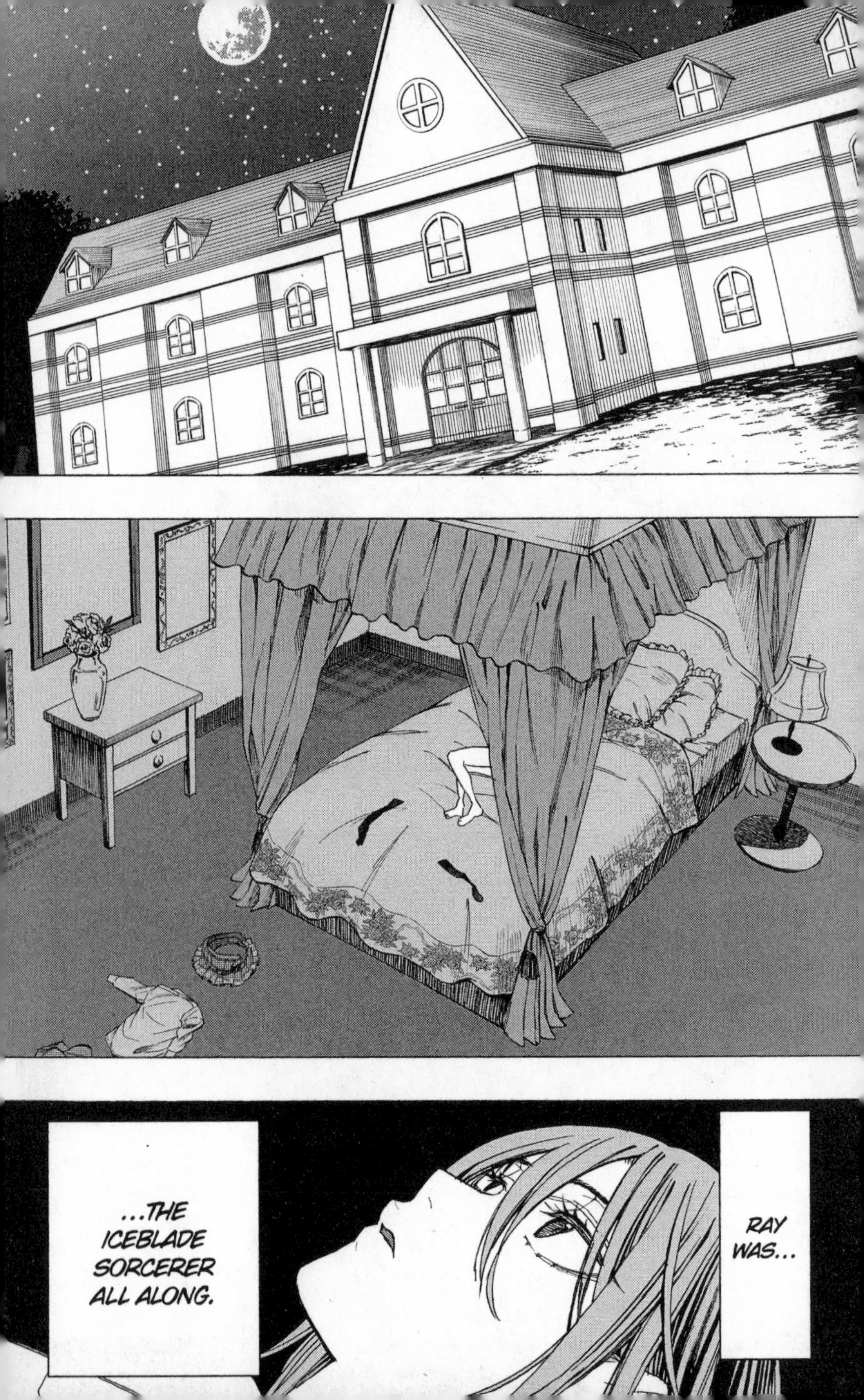
RAY WAS...
...THE ICEBLADE SORCERER ALL ALONG.

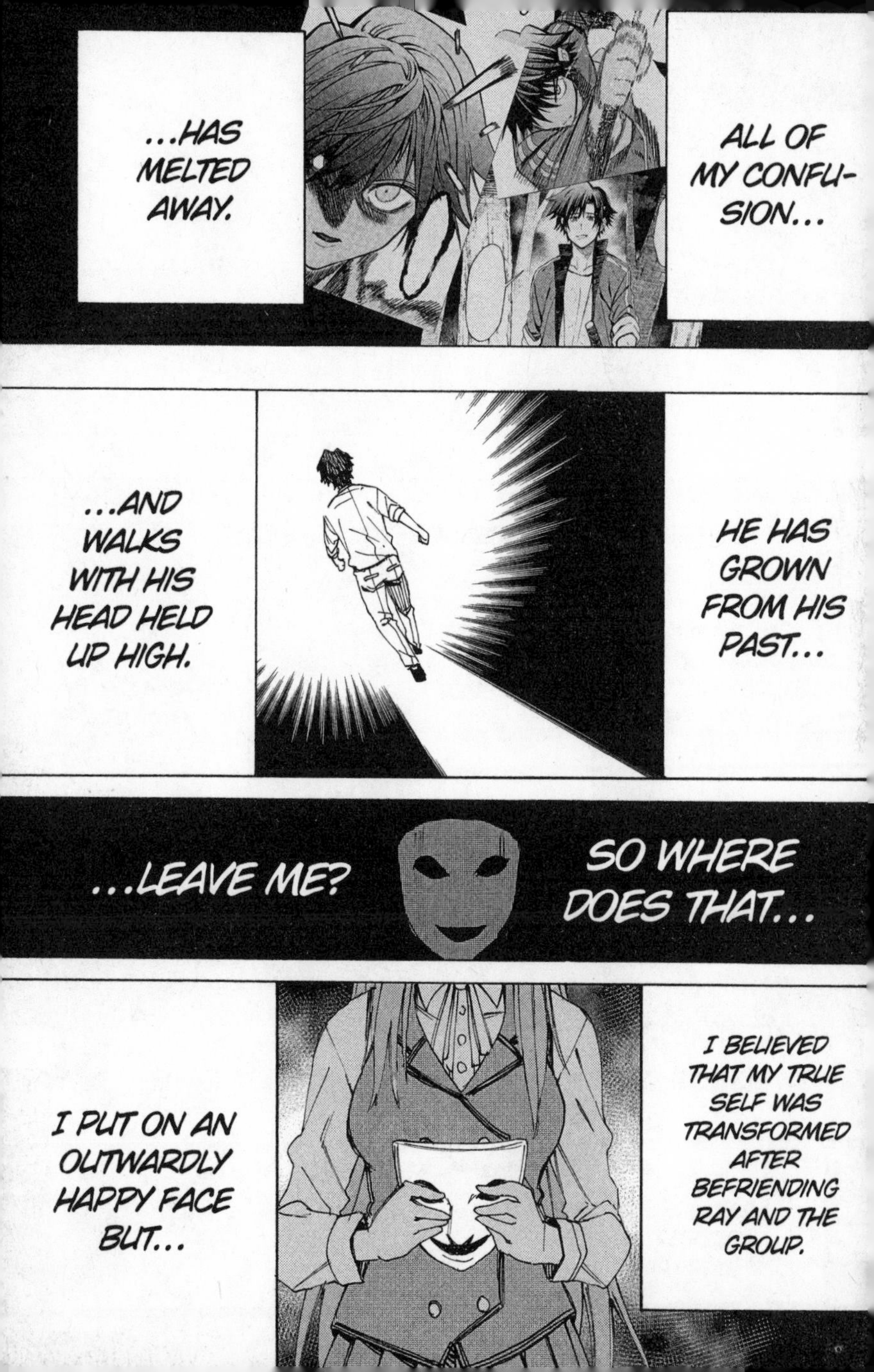
ALL OF MY CONFUSION...
...HAS MELTED AWAY.
HE HAS GROWN FROM HIS PAST...
...AND WALKS WITH HIS HEAD HELD UP HIGH.
SO WHERE DOES THAT...
...LEAVE ME?
I BELIEVED THAT MY TRUE SELF WAS TRANSFORMED AFTER BEFRIENDING RAY AND THE GROUP.
I PUT ON AN OUTWARDLY HAPPY FACE BUT...

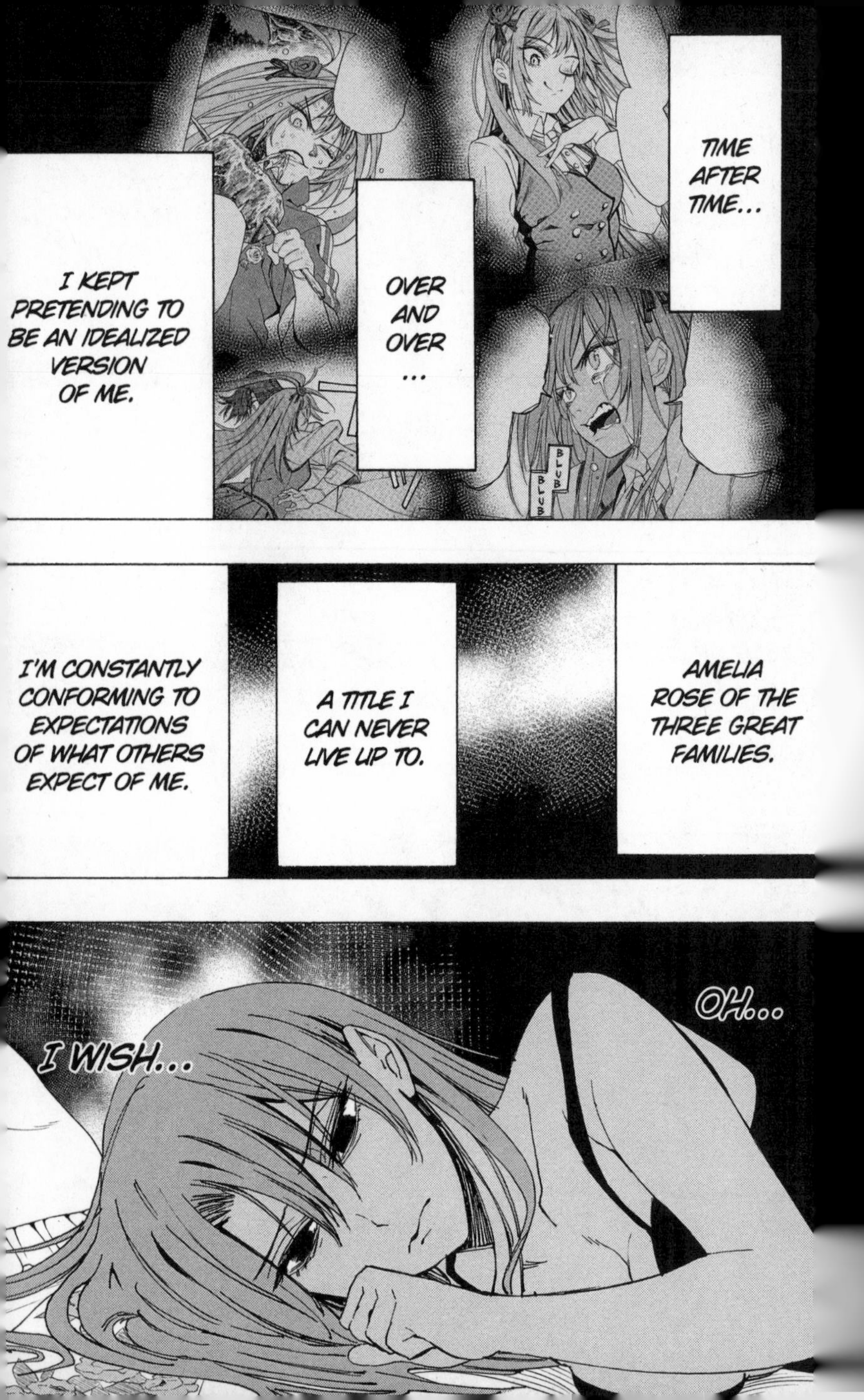
TIME AFTER TIME...
BLUB BLUB
OVER AND OVER ...
I KEPT PRETENDING TO BE AN IDEALIZED VERSION OF ME.
AMELIA ROSE OF THE THREE GREAT FAMILIES.
A TITLE I CAN NEVER LIVE UP TO.
I'M CONSTANTLY CONFORMING TO EXPECTATIONS OF WHAT OTHERS EXPECT OF ME.
OH...
I WISH...

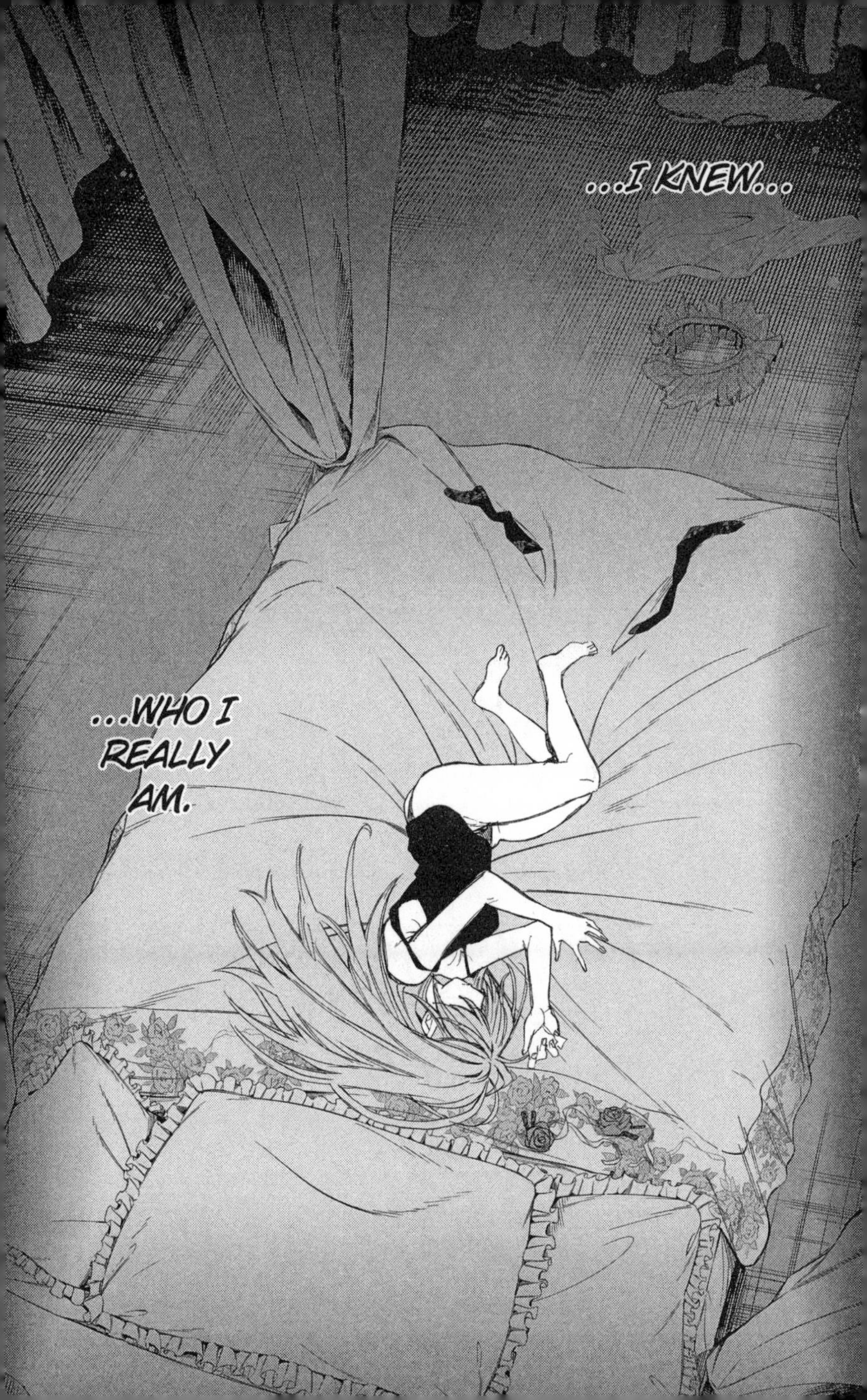
...I KNEW...
...WHO I REALLY AM.

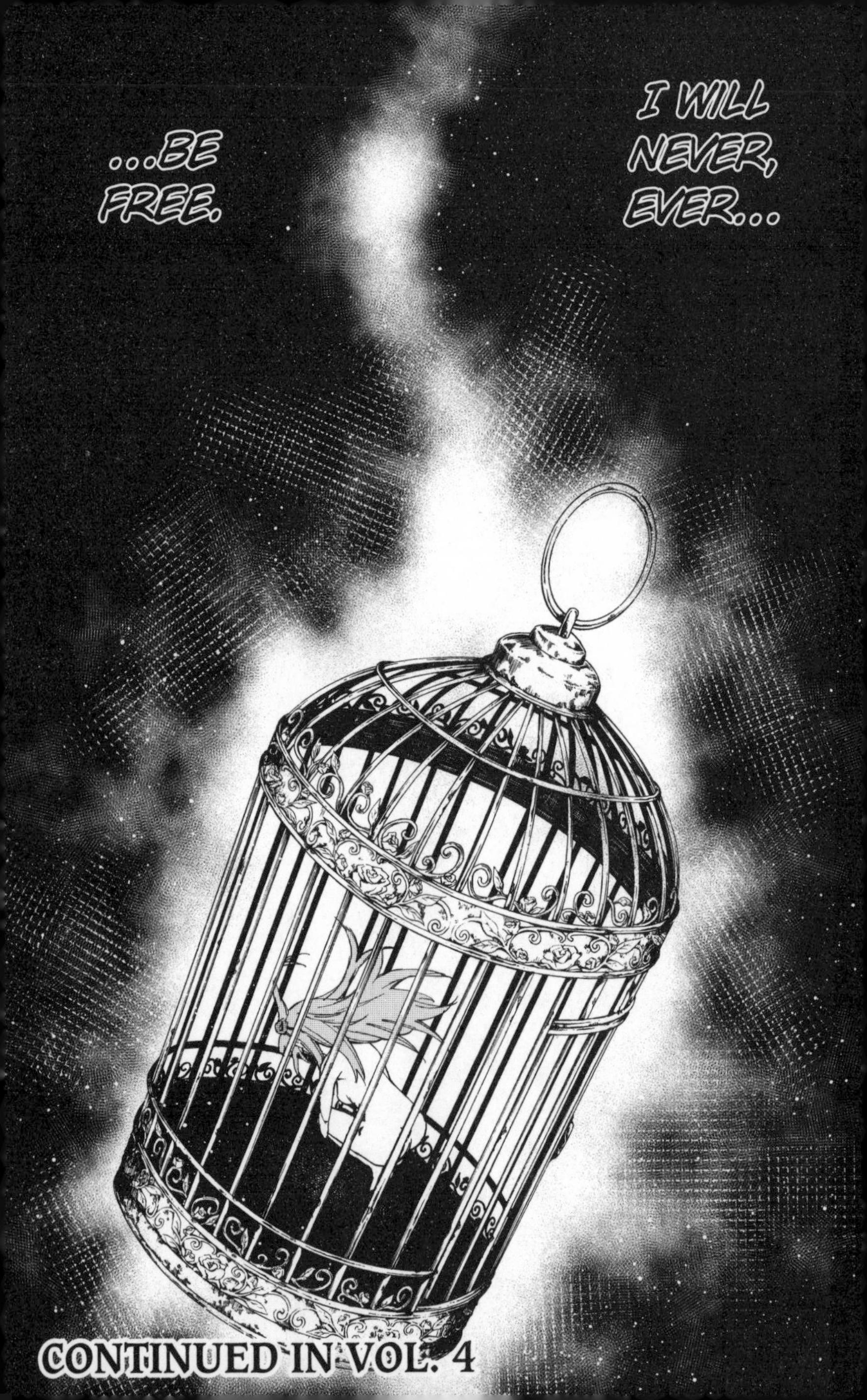
I WILL NEVER, EVER...
...BE FREE.
CONTINUED IN VOL. 4

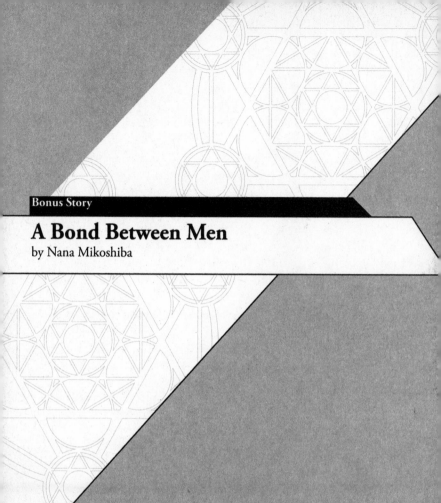

A Bond Between Men

by Nana Mikoshiba

After I battled Ms. Gray, I spent many days resting in bed at the infirmary. It took a while, but eventually I fully recovered. Ever since I triggered overheat during the campaign in the far east, I've been using every magical resource available to suppress my abilities, which had made it impossible for me to cast a proper spell.

The only magic I could use was Inner Code. However, my power was limited, and I naturally had to pay a high price to use it.

During that battle, I used what power I had to protect my friends...but I quickly reached my limit. After I was admitted to the infirmary, it became abundantly clear that it would take a while to fully recover.

I also finally understood why I came to the Arnold Academy of Magic, and it was all because I'd spent quality time with my friends. Deep down, I'd always been searching for a place to belong. With the blood of the past on my hands, I never thought that the academy would be that place. And yet, despite all that, I was lucky enough to make friends who accepted me as I am.

Why did my master persuade me to go to the academy? I realized just then that she probably wanted me to make new friends...and to grow into the person that I'm meant to be.

After I left the infirmary, there was only one thing on my mind... I needed to get buff!

"Urgh...ungh! Haah...haah."

Evi and I were doing our regular sequence of exercises. Of course, my doctor first gave me the okay. I couldn't train that whole week, so I spent every waking moment I could making up for it. Exercise really reinvigorated me.

We were standing there bare chested, making casual conversation.

"How are you feeling, Ray?"

"Good! It feels great to finally work out again."

We didn't have school that day, so we'd been training in our dorm room all morning. I was going to ask him if he wanted to train more after this, but instead I made a suggestion.

"Hey, Evi. Why don't we ask Albert to train with us today?"

"Albert? Um, are you cool with that, Ray? He kind of hated your guts, you know."

Albert and I were the only people who knew we made up. Of course I didn't go into detail, but I told Evi that everything was cool between Albert and me.

"Oh, really? Let's invite him then."

"Yeah. Sounds good."

After that, we quickly made our way to Albert's room.

I knocked on the door. Albert, as a higher noble, got a dorm room to himself. It was just past eight in the morning, so I was pretty sure he was awake...but then again, we didn't have class. Some students might be just like my master, who would sleep until noon on a day off, but I wasn't sure if Albert was the same way.

"Oh... Wasn't expecting you, Ray, Armstrong."

Albert, who was lightly covered in sweat, opened the door. There was a towel around his neck that made it seem like he was in the middle of training.

"Call me Evi."

"All right. You can call me Albert. What brings you two to my dorm?"

Since Albert had asked, I figured I'd give him an honest answer.

"Me and Evi are training today. You want in?"

"You're inviting me? Are you sure? I..." said Albert as he lowered his eyes.

He had a sorry look on his face, probably because of how he'd treated me in the past. In fact, it wasn't just me he'd been cruel to—he'd been unkind to Evi, too. Albert must have been thinking about that as he stood there. Evi immediately spoke up.

"Listen. If I'm being honest, how you treated Ray wasn't right. But as long as you apologized for what you did, and he's cool with it, then I think it's best to move on. Maybe it's different for you nobles so perhaps that's got something to do with it," snickered Evi, flashing his pearly whites.

Albert looked surprised. "Yeah... I'll say it again, but I'm really sorry. You're right," he explained with a bow to show his sincerity.

"All right! Now that that's out of the way, it's all good! Ain't that right, Ray?"

"Yeah, of course."

When Albert raised his head, Evi and I jumped right into the topic at hand.

"So what kind of training are we doing today?"

"Ray seems to have something in mind."

"I got you both covered."

With that, the three of us headed to the training grounds. Summer was just around the corner, so the sunlight was pretty intense. We changed into t-shirts and shorts that were easy to move around in and then reconvened at the grounds.

"Today I'd like to tackle some high-intensity interval training."

"The hell's that?" Evi asked, looking confused.

I then explained what the training would entail.

"It involves short bursts of high-intensity exercises to increase strength. Basically, we'll run for thirty seconds, then rest thirty more."

"For real?" Evi scoffed. "Sounds pretty easy."

"I'm not too sure. I guess we'll have to see for ourselves," remarked Albert.

"You've got a lot of muscle, Evi, but you lack endurance. This training should help."

"Oh! Makes sense. Thanks for catching that, Ray!"

"All right. I'll lead the session so just follow me."

"Got it!"

"Will do."

Evi and Albert both nodded, signaling that they were ready.

"Okay. And with that… Let's go!"

I kicked off the ground and started sprinting toward the grounds. After running at full speed for about 300 meters, I walked for thirty seconds, then started running again.

"Okay, go!"

"What? I thought we had more time!"

"Nope. Not according to my timer."

"Uh-oh," Evi said, breathing heavily.

Even Albert was lightly gasping for air.

"Okay, go!" I shouted.

After that, we repeated that set ten times.

The first one to throw in the towel was Evi.

"Haaah… haaah… haaah…"

"Okay, go!"

"Ray! Wait up! I'm at my limit!"

"Hm? You sure?"

"Y-Yeah… I'm beat. This is a lot worse than running long distance."

"Okay. You can rest, Evi. How are you feeling, Albert?"

"Haah… I-I've still got some fight in me!"

"Got it. Let's go!"

I could tell that Albert was pushing himself past his limit. Even though he ran as far as his muscles could handle, he was gaining on me with tenacity and persistence alone.

Albert must have been trying to prove something to himself. He was clearly suffering the whole time. This was the guy who had once struggled against his own talents and lost—a guy who once defined himself by his abilities. However, if meeting me inspired him to change—even if only a little—I wanted to help him. After all, he acted a lot like I did in the past.

After five more sets, he officially gave up. "Urk… Haah… Haah… Okay. I'm done," gasped Albert. He tried to stand tall, but his legs were too shaky. "Ray, is this part of your normal regimen?" he asked.

"Yeah," Ray answered bluntly, "This isn't part of my weekday routine, but I do devote our days off for high-intensity workouts. Sunday is a rest day, though."

"Wow, you are truly extraordinary."

"Nah. I'm just thoroughly tenacious."

"Yeah. I guess that's just who you are."

It was now noon sharp, and we were making our way to Kafka Forest.

"What're we gonna do next?"

"I'd say it's time to catch lunch."

"What do you mean?"

Evi already knew that I had a hunting license. Because I learned how to hunt, I had already gotten used to surviving in the jungle and other natural settings. Today I was thinking of wrangling those huge snakes overrunning Kafka Forest.

Actually, Headmistress Abbie had asked me to hunt them before. Originally, it seemed that the wildlife in the forest was being carefully monitored...until one day, huge snakes started appearing in droves. We were now back in the forest to thin out the population.

"Hmph. There's one over there."

There was a huge snake in front of me. It was stalking a rabbit.

Someone loudly gulped behind me. This wasn't Evi's first rodeo, so it couldn't have been him. Albert must have been nervous.

"You keep watch, Albert. Evi, the usual."

"Yes, sir!"

The two of us used our Inner Code to grow stronger. Then, Evi and I sprang into action. The snake was about to secure its prey, so its defenses were down. With our opening secured, we executed a pincer attack.

"Evi! Upper cut!"

"Got it!"

The huge snake suddenly noticed us and prepared to attack. However, Evi had already slipped under its nose.

"Graaaaaah!"

Emitting a visceral roar, Evi struck the huge snake, blasting its full body into the air. His punch was backed by rippling muscles and a fist that was strengthened by Inner Code. As soon as the snake flew up, I was ready, hovering over its head. Using gravity to my advantage, I heel kicked its head, unsheathed my knife, and delivered my final blow.

"Skreeee!" The snake pierced the air with its death cry. "Skree...eesh..."

We defeated the snake and made it out without a scratch.

"Okay. Let's eat."

"W-We're gonna eat that?"

"Oh, right. You're a noble."

I didn't know what type of food nobles ate. If anything, it probably grossed him out. Evi and I always hunted like this, so even though it was too late, I felt a little bad for Albert.

"Hey, I'll try anything once. Pass it here," said Albert, accepting our offer. He wasn't forcing himself to eat it either. Instead, he seemed genuinely curious.

I took the Ainsworth mystery sauce out of my backpack. Master couldn't cook, but the sauce she made was downright delicious.

I swiftly cut up the snake, put the meat onto skewers, and coated them in the sauce. After making a good number for everyone, I cooked them over a fire until they were nice and brown.

"Smells delicious."

To be honest, I was sure that this was as good—if not better—than high-grade meat. After I finished making our kebabs, I handed them to Evi and Albert.

"Okay… Here I go," Albert said. He then put the kebab in his mouth and started chewing, being sure to savor each bite.

"Hrm?!" He was shocked at first. "Th-This is just too damn good! What the hell is this?!"

"Heh heh. The secret's in the sauce. Beh heh heh…"

"This is amazing! Nothing beats this!" exclaimed Evi, who seemed satisfied with his meal as usual.

After the three of us finished our meal, Albert started talking as he looked into the distance.

"Seriously, you guys. Thank you for everything," he said with a bow.

"You don't need to keep thanking us, Albert. It's all good."

"Yeah, but…I was so blinded that I couldn't see what was around me. I was in my own little world, ignorant of everything else. Plus, I didn't make life easy for you two, either. And yet…despite all that, you invited me here. Hanging out with you guys made me realize that I haven't felt this comfortable in a while. So, thank you. I'm really glad that we met."

"I see. I'm happy to hear it," I said with a soft smile.

After enrolling at the Arnold Academy of Magic, I met so many people. There was Amelia, Elisa, Evi, and even Albert.

I had become acquainted with so many others as well. Up until now, I had spent most of my life out on the battlefield, therefore interacting only with adults. It wasn't until later that I found myself among peers, and that was a game changer.

The academy was my first real experience spending time with kids my own age. I surmised that my master wanted me to learn for myself that when you have trustworthy friends, you can raise each other up.

"Albert, I feel the same way. Since I met you, I've been able to grow in so many ways. Let's give it our all as we embark on this journey together," I said.

Evi also chimed in. "Yeah, we've bonded now! If you need advice about working out, come to us! We'll recommend the best exercises for you!"

A few tears streamed down Albert's face, which he immediately wiped away. He no longer looked gloomy.

"Right. Looking forward to it."

After we shook hands with Albert, we all started working on our afternoon training session.

Later that evening, we wrapped up our training and made our way back to the dorms. That was when we ran into Amelia and Elisa.

"Oh, my! I-Is that you, Ray?" Amelia asked.

"Ray?" Elisa asked.

"I didn't expect to see you here, Amelia, Elisa," I answered.

"Right... It certainly is a coincidence, but anyway... What are the three of you doing here?"

"Y-Yeah. I wanna know, too."

"We just finished training," I replied.

"Um... Are you guys, like, friends now or something?"

"Yeah. Albert seems to have fallen in love with the world of fitness."

In the background, Albert and Evi were talking about working out the whole time. We were sweating a lot and took our shirts off.

"Ray, those are some incredible muscles."

"You really think so?"

"I've never seen muscles like that either. They're amazing!"